Depths As Yet Unspoken

Depths As Yet Unspoken

Whiteheadian Excursions in Mysticism,
Multiplicity, and Divinity

Roland Faber

EDITED BY

Andrew M. Davis

PICKWICK *Publications* · Eugene, Oregon

DEPTHS AS YET UNSPOKEN
Whiteheadian Excursions in Mysticism, Multiplicity and Divinity

Pickwick Publications
An Imprint of Wipf and Stock Publishers
199 W. 8th Ave., Suite 3
Eugene, OR 97401

www.wipfandstock.com

PAPERBACK ISBN: 978-1-7252-5260-8
HARDCOVER ISBN: 978-1-7252-5261-5
EBOOK ISBN: 978-1-7252-5262-2

Cataloguing-in-Publication data:

Names: Faber, Roland, 1960–, author. | Davis, Andrew M., editor.

Title: Depths as yet unspoken : Whiteheadian excursions in mysticism, multiplicity, and divinity / by Roland Faber ; edited by Andrew M. Davis.

Description: Eugene, OR : Pickwick Publications, 2020 | Includes bibliographical references and index.

Identifiers: ISBN 978-1-7252-5260-8 (paperback) | ISBN 978-1-7252-5261-5 (hardcover) | ISBN 978-1-7252-5262-2 (ebook)

Subjects: LCSH: Process theology. | Whitehead, Alfred North—1861–1947.

Classification: BT83.6 .F31 2020 (print) | BT83.6 .F31 (ebook)

Manufactured in the U.S.A.   07/28/20

". . . for the next thousand years."

The use of philosophy is to maintain an active novelty of fundamental ideas illuminating the social system. It reverses the slow descent of accepted thought toward the inactive commonplace. If you like to phrase it so, philosophy is mystical. For mysticism is direct insight into depths as yet unspoken. But the purpose of philosophy is to rationalize mysticism: not by explaining it away, but by the introduction of novel verbal characterizations, rationally coordinated.

—Alfred North Whitehead

Contents

Part III: Divinity and Mystery

Copyright and Permissions

THANKS AND RECOGNITION ARE due to all editors, journals and presses for kindly granting permissions to republish, with minor edits, the select works included in this volume. Each piece has appeared elsewhere across some two decades.

The prologue was originally delivered as a lecture at the Library of Congress, February 17, 2011, to commemorate the installation of a letter from Whitehead to his student Henry Leonard in the collection of that institution. It was first published as "Three Hundred Years of Whitehead: Halfway" *Process Studies* 41/1 (Spring/Summer 2012) 5–20.

Chapter 1 was first published as the "Mystical Whitehead" in *Seeking Common Ground: Evaluation and Critique of Joseph Bracken's Comprehensive Worldview*, edited by Marc A. Pugliese and Gloria L. Schaab, 213–34. Milwaukee: Marquette University Press, 2012.

Chapter 2 was first published as "Multiplicity and Mysticism: Toward a New Mystagogy of Becoming" in *The Lure of Whitehead*, edited by Nicholas Gaskill and A. J. Nocek, 187–206. Minneapolis: University of Minnesota Press, 2014.

Chapter 3 was first published as "'Indra's Ear'–God's Absence of Listening" in *The Presence and Absence of God: Religion in Philosophy and Theology*, edited by I. U. Dalferth, 42:161–86. Tübingen: Mohr Siebeck, 2010.

Chapter 4 was first published as "Touch: A Philosophical Meditation" in *The Allure of Things: Process and Object in Contemporary Philosophy*m edited by Roland Faber and Andrew Goffey, 47–67. Lanham, MD: Bloomsbury Academic, 2014.

Chapter 5 was first published as "Bodies of the Void: Polyphilia and Theoplicity" in *Apophatic Bodies: Negative Theology, Incarnation, and Relationship*, edited by Chris Boesel and Catherine Keller, 200–223. New York: Fordham University Press, 2010.

Chapter 6 includes two pieces first published as "Intermezzo I: Polypoetic Nomoi" and "Intermezzo II: Polyphilic Pluralism" in *The Divine Manifold*, by Roland Faber, 191–97; 353–59. Lanham, MD: Lexington, 2014.

Chapter 7 was first published as "The Sense of Peace: A Para-doxology of Divine Multiplicity" in *Polydoxy: Theology of Multiplicity and Relation*, edited by Catherine Keller and Laurel Schneider, 36–56. London: Routledge, 2011.

Chapter 8 was first published as "The Crisis of Becoming: Reflections on a Whiteheadian Spirituality" *Creative Transformation* 16/2 (Spring 2007) 2–10.

Chapter 9 was first published as "§ 35. Poet of the World (Coercive Power, Creative Weakness, and the Power of Love)" in *God as Poet of the World: Exploring Process Theologies*, by Roland Faber, 201–14. Translated by Douglas W. Scott. Louisville: Westminster John Knox, 2008.

Chapter 10 was first published as "Trinity, Analogy and Coherence" in *Trinity in Process: A Relational Theology of God*, edited by Marjorie Hewitt Suchocki and Joseph A. Bracken, 147–71. New York: Continuum, 1997.

Chapter 11 was first published as "On the Unique Origin of Revelation, Religious Intuition and Theology" *Process Studies* 28/3–4 (1999) 273–89.

Chapter 12 was first published as "God in the Making: Religious Experience and Cosmology in Whitehead's *Religion in the Making* in Theological Perspective" in *L'experience de Dieu: Lectures de Religion in the Making d'Alfred N. Whitehead. Aletheia*, edited by Michael Webber and Samuel Rouvillois, 179–200. Janvier: Ecole Saint-Jean, 2005.

The epilogue was first published as "§ 40: Mystery (Life, Nondifference, and Insistence)" in *God as Poet*, by Roland Faber, 254–61. The final paragraph has been adapted and expanded from the final paragraph of this same book, Faber, *God as Poet*, 327.

Acknowledgments

WHERE DO I BEGIN to acknowledge the work of the ones I've built on, value, praise, and hold in permanent memory? How to adequately appreciate the friendships that allowed me to explore new worlds of thought in the search for truth and the meaning of the cosmos and human existence, of the relentless impermanence of its inhabitants and its encounters, and the fragile beauty of the vanishing shadows that so vividly impress themselves on us as reality? And how to appropriately recall the inclination of my students and colleagues in classrooms and beyond, peripatetically wandering and sinuating, to listen to my own transformations as we engaged in ever new avatars of approximating the meaning and future of the world we live in and want to see realized? How to convey the deep questions that arose from the common pool of traditions of process thinkers, of diverse philosophies and religions, of mysticisms and scientific insights, on the structures and functions of being and beings in this world, of material and spiritual matters and dimensions, of the impossibility of reductionisms to succeed, of the openness of maybe infinite worlds beyond this one, but in recognition of its utter relevance for such a thought to be even meaningful? And how to satisfactorily thank Andrew M. Davis, my student, friend, and companion in (the) crime (of thinking), who had engaged my work out of his own philosophical quest, and after many long walks and delightful discussions of problems related to the themes of this book, proposed it as a developmental, but integral, study of my work, delineated along the lines of some of its major threads?

I know no better than just to say "thank you!"

Let me also add a few reminiscences of appreciation regarding the others, the thinkers who impressed their insights on me. At the center of the development of thought that this book recasts in a new light, the light of interwoven threads and resonances of consistency—and, in fact, that is how I experience my own cyclical progression of thought—over more than three decades (but in fact much longer, reaching back in its origins to the seventies of the twentieth century), is my encounter with the genius of A. N. Whitehead in 1985 and, of course, the revelations that the thought of Gilles Deleuze offered to me right around his death in 1995. It was this oscillation between the French and the Anglo-American thinker, who are in a sense "unknowable," that drew my attention irrevocably to the important insight that thinking always must be escaping any attempts to pin it down to what I have called "the little machine," the alleged systems of thought a thinker is supposed to adhere to, but which only represent a shallow claim invested in security rather than truth, and which rather meanders through the wide and unfathomable universe that we cannot avoid to be at home in, but always remain in (for better or worse) as visitors only.

Equally important are the early encounters with thinkers in the energetic field between philosophy and religion, intellect and spirit, and the themes they espouse since I awoke to the consciousness of the necessity of thinking: first, there was Pierre Teilhard de Chardin; then followed the Buddha of Zen, the Yi Jing commented on by Confucius, Plotinus, Meister Eckhart, Nicolas of Cusa, Erich Fromm and Karl Rahner, among many others. They opened my understanding to the mysteries of oppositions in coincidence, like the divine-cosmic interaction and identification, the trinitarian impossibilities of divine multiplicity, the relevance of atheism and non-theism for existential authenticity, the equal shortcomings of supernaturalism and naturalism, the unavoidability of mysticism and non-dualism, and the discursive and trans-discursive nature of the more general problem of the Many and the One.

While my earlier works in German language in the decades before and after the turn of the century prepared me for the harvest of these confluences, as are appearing in this book, they also held already key insights *in nuce*: the historicity of reason and the mystical unity of intellect and modes of existence; the determination of truth by freedom, multiplicity and beauty; the importance of the diversity of tradition and thought patterns in themselves and of a multiplicity of threads of thought for truth to be real and deep and true; the motive of diversification and unification in epistemic, ontological and existential questions in the non-dual non-difference between unmanifest and manifest, apophatic and polyphilic dimensions of reality in dynamic oscillation; and the joy of the adventure of thought, of its creative branching and trials as inevitable method to accommodate the complexity of reality. In other words, as Davis summaries the efforts of the chapters: the fusion of mysticism, multiplicity, and divinity.

Finally, I want at least point to the remembrance of certain concepts that appeared to me like persons, as subjects with their own inherent activity and personality, ineffable, excitingly attractive, but difficult and resistant at times, which have accompanied my adventure in thinking ever since. All go back to my encounter with Nicolas of Cusa who facilitated my mystical, non-dualist turn in approaching process thought and Whitehead in the last years of the twentieth century: so (intellectual and experiential) mysticism was the profound catalyst of my emerging thought—a development that culminated in my conceptualization of "in/difference" (as the apophatic coincidence of difference and non-difference) in Meister Eckhart, Nicolas of Cusa, and Whitehead in the article "Gottesmeer" (2001) ("The Ocean of God" in German). Yet this was itself already a consequence of my Habilitation *Prozeßtheologie* (written in 1997, accepted in 1998 and published in 2000), for which I spent one and a half years at Claremont in 1995–1996, in which my attraction to the monistic process thought of Bernard Loomer (that Whitehead's God is "Creativity" which is coextensive with the World) transformed my reading of Whitehead into that of non-dualism mediated by Nicolas of Cusa. This book also introduced the understanding that Whitehead's "ultimate reality," which many process thinkers had variously situated in the triad of God, Creativity, and the World (and a few more), was, in fact, none of them, but rather, what Whitehead calls "mutual immanence." And this book facilitated also, as an implication, the necessity for engaging poststructuralist philosophy, not as fragmentation of thought, but as the recovery of "multiplicity," which in mutual transcendence must be understood as "ground" of Whitehead's world of processes.

At about the same time, and initiated by the fusion of these elements of thought, it was the encounter with Gilles Deleuze, forming a triad with Cusa and Whitehead, that led to inauguration of the English use of the terms "in/difference" and "in-sistence," as espoused in the article "De-Ontologizing God," which I presented in 1998 at the 8th International Whitehead Conference in Claremont, CA, and which was published in 2002 in *Process and Difference*, edited by Catherine Keller and Ann Daniell, as well as in a variant as "Insistenz" in a 2005 German text. In my 2005 lecture "In the Wake of False Unifications," for the professorship at Claremont, which I assumed in 2006, I highlighted the centrality of the concept of "multiplicity" in Whitehead's work by concurrently identifying it with poststructuralist interest in difference as the dynamic of Whitehead's "Creativity" to actually always be a process of "trans-unification" (of which any event-unity is only a passing impermanent activity). This notion was the basis for the now far more developed concept of "trans-pantheism," which I introduced in *The Divine Manifold* (2014) as an alternative reading not only of Whitehead's inclusion of God in his philosophy—over against a limited view of his understanding of the divine-mundane relationship that Charles Hartshorne had influentially labeled "panentheism," and the naturalistic readings of Whitehead which try (and still tries) to purge Whitehead's philosophy from religion and the notion of God—but also as the basis for a new kind of (religious) pluralism and an escape from the dichotomy of supernaturalism and naturalism. I have correlated all of these terms of thought and endeavored their new intertwining in a "transreligious discourse," which reaches back to the German article with the same name in 2002, but was developed in English in my more recent books: *The Becoming of God* (2017) on my current understanding of process thought, *The Garden of Reality* (2018) on the relativity of (religious) truth, and *The Ocean of God* (2019) regarding religious pluralism and the unity of religion(s) beyond reductionisms such as supernaturalism and naturalism.

And then there is the book *God as Poet of the World* (2003/4 in German; 2008 in English, but slightly developed from the German version), my understanding of Whitehead in light of the history of the process tradition, current philosophical, religious and scientific thought, and the engagement with, and offering of different solutions to virtually every theme of process thought, philosophically and religiously—that is, if one only reads Whitehead's text closely with all of its complexities and fissures, as well as living developments and contradictions, instead of fitting Whitehead into a neat little metaphysical system. Its section on "Mystery" summarizes the streams of this current book, by reflecting Whitehead's text in the apophatic and polyphilic non-dualism of Plotinus, the genius of past and future centuries. It is in the same book, the *Poet*, finally, namely in its 2008 "Postscript," that I began to explore the concept of "polyphilia" as the angle at which I see to hinge the further development of process thought as "theopoetics," a term reaching back to a lecture "Process Theology as Theopoetics," given at Claremont in 2006, and explored in the "trans-pantheism" of *The Divine Manifold*.

Of course, all of these concepts began to interact with one another until today, with ever new facets that I hope will remain surprising in the years to come.

Roland Faber

Desert Hot Springs, November 2019

Abbreviations

AI   Alfred North Whitehead. *Adventures of Ideas*. New York: Free Press, 1967.

AN   Alfred North Whitehead. "Autobiographical Notes." In *The Philosophy of Alfred North Whitehead*, edited by Paul Schilpp, 3–14. La Salle: Open Court, 1991.

CN   Alfred North Whitehead. *The Concept of Nature*. Cambridge: Cambridge University Press, 1993.

FR   Alfred North Whitehead. *The Function of Reason*. Boston: Beacon, 1958.

Imm.   Alfred North Whitehead. "Immortality." In *The Philosophy of Alfred North Whitehead*, edited by Paul Schilpp, 682–700. La Salle: Open Court, 1991.

MG   Alfred North Whitehead. "Mathematics and the Good." In *Essays in Science and Philosophy*, 97–113. New York: Greenwood, 1968.

MT   Alfred North Whitehead. *Modes of Thought*. New York: Free Press, 1968.

PR   Alfred North Whitehead. *Process and Reality: An Essay in Cosmology*. Edited by David Ray Griffin and Donald W. Sherburne. New York: Free Press, 1978.

"PR"   Alfred North Whitehead. "Process and Reality." In *Science and Philosophy*, 122–27. Paterson, NJ: Littliefield, Adams, 1964.

PNK   Alfred North Whitehead. *An Enquiry Concerning the Principles of Natural Knowledge*. New York: Dover, 1982.

RM   Alfred North Whitehead. *Religion in the Making.* New York: Fordham University Press, 1996.

SMW   Alfred North Whitehead. *Science and the Modern World.* New York: Free Press, 1967.

SY   Alfred North Whitehead. *Symbolism: Its Meaning and Effect.* New York: Fordham University Press, 1985.

Sparks before a Theopoetic Wildfire

Andrew M. Davis

Whitehead's imaginative metaphysics form the essential backdrop in relation to which the drama of modern process philosophy and theology continues to unfold. Indeed, his "philosophy of organism" is incredibly wide-ranging and inclusive in scope, sustaining a shocking diversity of orientations, methodologies and trajectories. This has not always been duly acknowledged. Yet, one can scarcely approach Roland Faber's ever-growing corpus (to say nothing of his courses and teaching) without laying claim to the *irreducibility* of Whitehead's thought to any one tidy philosophical or theological system, procedure or creed. One should, I suggest, rather approach Whitehead as an igniting "event" which has sparked nothing short of what Faber has aptly described as a "philosophical wildfire."[1] Consider this metaphor. Wildfires are not easily contained; their directions are often unpredictable, and their results destructive. Yet the anarchy of flames also harbors a *purifying* and *creative* element; their chaos makes way for possibilities of rebirth, growth, and novelty.

Faber has consistently articulated the ways in which the event "Whitehead" continues to set ablaze various landscapes, not only within "process philosophy" and "process theology," but also in a variety of disciplines, such that a plurality of new voices, interests, methods and creative interpretations continue to emerge. In this way, he has stressed that the philosophy *of* process must always remain *in* process. Process thought houses manifold varieties (and combinations) of philosophical and theological variants, including the empirical, rational, speculative, existential, ecological, feminist, womanist, liberationist, Christian, interreligious, transreligious, naturalist, mystical, constructive, and deconstructive postmodern and

---

1. Faber, *Becoming of God*, 100.

1

poststructuralist approaches. These are some of the key landscapes found in current applications of Whitehead's thought. Faber has rightly spoken of the ways in which process theology is an "extraordinarily complex phenomenon whose identity developed in different currents and directions" and which "cannot be understood apart from these diverse expositions and versions."[2] One should not, therefore, understand these different geographies of process thought as existing in isolation from one another, but as growing together in entangled ways out of the rich philosophical and theological soil that Whitehead's wildfire unearths.

To give one example of this, different *empirical, rational,* and *speculative* methods have long been acknowledged as the principal "schools" in process theology. These methodologies take rise from different dimensions and emphases of Whitehead's philosophy, including his radical account of human experience, his concern for rational coherence and consistency, and his appeal to the necessity of "imaginative generalization" in the play of ideas. Faber would remind us that Whitehead cannot be read honestly without grasping the necessary interrelationship—indeed, the "mutual immanence"—of these approaches often thought to be at odds with one another in the philosophical tradition.

Whitehead likens the philosophic endeavor to that of an airplane which "starts from the ground of particular observation . . . makes a flight in the thin air of imaginative generalization; and . . . again lands for renewed observation rendered acute by rational interpretation" (PR, 5). One sees in this statement that "particular observation" (the empirical), "imaginative generalization" (the speculative) and "rational interpretation" (the rational) all belong to one "method of discovery." Neither, however, can one wholly isolate the wide ranging diversity of theological and religious implications in process theology which differently emphasize these philosophical methods.

Process theologians and philosophers will naturally differ in their appropriations of Whitehead's philosophy. This is to be expected given the distinctiveness of their personal experiences, ethical inclinations, religious motivations, and philosophical commitments. Faber's penetrating interpretations of Whitehead's thought remain unique; they continue to evoke an empirical, speculative and "theopoetic" depth to his philosophy which has rarely been treated with such precision and imagination. Rather than elevating concepts, rational systematizations, order, unity, or "proofs" for the existence of divinity, Faber has prioritized the underlying welters of experience, life, process, and divine traces dimly discerned among the layered

---

2. Faber, *God as Poet*, 17. For a fuller treatment of the emergence and differentiation of process theology, see 17–43.

multiplicities of a *chaosmos* of infinite becoming. Whitehead, of course, continues to attract attention in the conceptual spaces inherent in mathematics and metaphysics, but few have recognized with Faber the deeply *mystical* dimensions of his philosophy. "If you like to phrase it so," Whitehead states, "philosophy is mystical. For mysticism is direct insight into depths as yet unspoken" (MT, 174). Where, however, do these unspoken depths *speak* in Whitehead, and what are their associated themes in his philosophy? It is this question which occasions the publication of this volume.

For decades, Faber has been one of the world's most creative interpreters of Whitehead's thought, particularly as it intersects with eastern and western mystical traditions, as well as deconstructive postmodern and poststructuralist philosophy. With these resources, Faber has not only argued that Whitehead *is* a mystical thinker, and, indeed, a mystic *himself*, but also that his work is *not silent* on mysticism. Although Whitehead's mystical inclinations may not be obvious at first, they actually constitute the apophatic backdrop to his entire philosophical corpus. What emerge in Faber's own mystical Whiteheadian hermeneutics are the mutually enhancing flames of empirical process theology, the mystical tradition, and deconstructive poststructuralism. Truly, I've come to understand Faber's own thought to be nothing short of a *theopoetic wildfire* with vast reaches into the past and deep relevance for the future.

Ideas for this volume developed out of a series of walking conversations with Faber. It will always remain a pleasure for a student to stroll with his professor. Having studied under Faber for some years, I have benefited greatly as a process thinker from his sage-like wisdom, creative expression and philosophical depth. This volume is a result both of my gratitude and admiration for Faber's work as a scholar, and also his valuable influence as a mentor and friend. My goal in the remainder of this introduction is to set the stage for this volume. For those unfamiliar with Faber and his work, I think it worthwhile to first say more about the man himself, his personal experience, central philosophical and religious influences, and burgeoning corpus. Second, I want to consider the unique contours of his own "theopoetic" rendering of process theology with its associated convictions and creative linguistic expressions. Third, I will unfold the framework and progression of the volume through its mutually immanent layers of Mysticism, Multiplicity and Divinity. Finally, to conclude, I want to name some of the valuable "conversions" Faber's own vision and excavation of Whitehead's thought initiates for a future of peace.

Faber as a "Creature of Thought":
Experience, Influences, and Corpus

Roland Faber remains a multivalent philosophical and religious thinker whose motivations are rooted both in the uniqueness of his own personal experiences and the depth of his interreligious scholarship. He has rightly described himself as a "creature of thought."[3] I speak for many of his students (themselves creaturely thinkers) who have been challenged, deepened, and expanded by his thinking. "Thinking," of course, is no ordinary endeavor; rather, it is, as Faber poetically describes, "a process of awareness; an awareness of awareness, changing with the landscape it touches; being its appreciation and its gown."[4] This thinking he likens to the "dew at dawn, fragile, always on the brink of disappearing into thin air; always only dense near the ground, always threatened by the heat of the sun."[5] Thinking can be likened to a mirror which reflects that which is beyond thought: "the invisible, too bright a sun." In this way, thought and thinking have a deeply apophatic nature; "thought" Faber insists, "is mystical – as it roams through inner reality and the unfathomable . . ." It is also prophetic as "it invites the unexpected, the not yet."[6] Indeed, the advent of the "not yet" can be sudden, intense, and existentially awakening. It was this kind of mystical awakening, in fact, that Faber recalls undergoing in his early years. This experience left him with an unceasing desire to take "thought" and "thinking" seriously.

> It is in thinking that I found myself—one day at a young age. It just happened. I remember the awakening, a sudden, intense consciousness of being-in-the-universe, in the face of its speaking to me, raising the questions of its why and whence. How can anything exist? Is it itself or empty or potentially divine? Is the All all there is? Yet, how could Reality be of and, if at all, beyond itself? And can it (and I in it) act in or on itself? I remember vividly having a metaphysical episode in which such a line of questioning led me to an intense apophatic awareness. Stripping everything away from existence, this experimental awareness left me, in the end, with—not darkness, but singing light. I wanted to become a thinker, from early age on; and I have never stopped striving, at one time, to become one.[7]

3. Faber, "My Faith in Baha'u'llah," 152.
4. Faber, "My Faith in Baha'u'llah."
5. Faber, "My Faith in Baha'u'llah."
6. Faber, "My Faith in Baha'u'llah."
7. Faber, "My Faith in Baha'u'llah," 153.

In a profound way, this apophatic episode of light did much to sustain Faber's underlying "faith in the universe" and the goodness and creative beauty of existence. It opened the way for a life of thinking, teaching and writing about philosophy, theology and the mystical depths of religious traditions. But this was not the only experience. After light, there also came fire.

> . . . I was also visited, in a mystical episode, by fire. The intuitive framework in which I could find an anchor for the interpretation of its significance was the fire on Sinai (Ex. 3). Not that I ever intended to compare myself with Moses, but I knew that this experience of fire was of a nature that in its articulation could not do less than approximate the strange language attributed to the Sinai experience: the living fire, the danger of closeness, the universal insistence, the refuge of the tent spanning the stars, the impossibility to stand (through) it, the painful joy of holiness, the inaccessible presence.[8]

For Faber, these experiences undergird the possibility of "faith" as an "awareness of being caught up with an Apophatic Beyond, beyond mind and its catches."[9] This conviction grounds his deeply interreligious roots, and in particular, his advocacy of the "relativity" and "complementarity" of religious truth as it is found in the apophatic oneness of a nameless divinity. Let me speak briefly to some of the principal influences at the heart of his vision.

Since Faber's early years, various currents of religious and philosophical thought have influenced his thinking. Daoism, Buddhism and Christianity, in particular, were of formative influence. Faber encountered "cosmic universality" in each tradition: the *dao*, the *dharma* and the cosmic Christ. The *Yi Jing* sharpened his sense for "laws of change and mutual transformation." The Buddhist *dharma* heightened his "awareness of the dialectic of emptiness and multiplicity, the cycles of becoming and decay, the connection between detachment and compassion." The deep incarnational thought of Teilhard de Chardin resonated with his "feeling of the oscillations of unity and complexity, that becoming united to Christ means a cosmic becoming of freedom from limitations of power" and "restrictions of reductionist conditioning of any kind," especially those of religious communities.[10] It was, however, the radical contours of Alfred North Whitehead's philosophy which provided an inclusive framework for considering all of these influences. Indeed, Whitehead's philosophy offered

---

8. Faber, "My Faith in Baha'u'llah," 159.

9. Faber, "My Faith in Baha'u'llah," 151.

10. Faber, "My Faith in Baha'u'llah," 155.

Faber infinite processual worlds of becoming and perishing, where "importance is a process of creativity and divine persuasion," and where "no laws are eternal or final, but invitations" that are "upheld by the visions of the community of myriads of existing events and processes . . ."[11] Whitehead's thought was founded on a relentless novelty which always "disturbs trodden paths" and a "creative transformation and salvation" which extend both from divine "perception and remembrance." What is more, these religious and philosophical currents would "fuse" in Faber's thinking with poststructuralist thought in its "intention to remind us of the powers that attach us to limited desires," those which make us "blind" to what we exclude in the creation of "simplified, smooth and controllable world-views."[12] These influences, moreover, would be enhanced for Faber, by the principles of unity, harmony, equality and justice at the heart of the Baha'i Faith and the novel revelation of Baha'u'llah as to the conviviality, mutuality and apophatic oneness of religion beyond violence, divisiveness, and hatred. Faber's excavations of Baha'u'llah's mystical writings only ignited and entangled his longstanding endeavors to develop the mystical dimensions of Whitehead's cosmogony, process theology and poststructuralism. In this way, one finds a manifold amalgam of oscillating mystical and interreligious voices in Faber's thought, from Laozi and Nagarjuna to Teilhard and Whitehead, and from Nicholas of Cusa and Meister Eckhart, to Gilles Deleuze and Jacques Derrida. These are only a precious few of the voices at the core of Faber's work as an interreligious "creature of thought."

The space-time of this volume forbids me to treat Faber's corpus in any detail, but it is, nevertheless, worthwhile to briefly mention a few of his groundbreaking English texts and their chief concerns in relation to some of the influences above.[13] Translated from the German, *God as Poet of the World: Exploring Process Theologies* (2008) remains absolutely unrivaled as an introduction to the multiverse of Whitehead's thought and the layered emergence, differentiations, concerns, and creative expressions of process theologies, including Faber's own theopoetic contributions. This text is nothing short of the *Summa* of process theology, and essential reading for anyone endeavoring to take seriously the irreducibility of Whitehead's thought and the diversity of process theology.

Faber's monumental work in the *Divine Manifold* (2014) launches into an intricate postmodern and theopoetic play on Dante's Divine Comedy,

---

11. Faber, "My Faith in Baha'u'llah."

12. Faber, "My Faith in Baha'u'llah."

13. Faber's as yet untranslated German texts include his magisterial *Prozeßtheologie* (2000); *Selbsteinsatz* (1995); and *Freiheit* (1992).

engaging fundamental questions of religion and philosophy through the aporetic dynamics of love and power, and a soteriological love of multiplicity.[14] Here, the poststructuralist approach of Deleuze and Whitehead's process philosophy meet alongside a host of other mystical and cosmological thinkers. What emerges is a processual chaosmos of irreducible multiplicity and pure love, one that uniquely addresses fundamental questions of existence, ultimate reality, religious plurality and multireligious hospitality.

In *The Becoming of God: Process Theology, Philosophy, and Multireligious Engagement* (2017), Faber furthers his fundamental concerns for theopoetic articulations of the chief contours of process theology in its wide relevance to science, philosophy, society, mysticism and religious pluralism. Of particular note, Faber reveals an "unexpected closeness" between the pluralistic potential of Whitehead's philosophy and his own Baha'i Faith. This is a largely underdeveloped kinship that only now—due to Faber's work—is reaching communities of process and Baha'i scholars.

This novel affinity between the pluralistic resources of Whiteheadian cosmology and the Baha'i Faith are masterfully treated in the *The Garden of Reality: Transreligious Relativity in a World of Becoming* (2018).[15] *The Garden* is nothing short of Faber's *magnum opus* on the relativity of religious truth, religious pluralism, transreligious discourse, postmodern cosmology and multireligious mysticism. Here, Faber navigates a shocking historical palimpsest of interlayered voices, from those of process philosophy and poststructuralism, to Sufism, Dzogchen, Babi Bahá'í traditions, philosophical Daoism, as well as Christian and Hindu conceptualizations. The book is grounded in apophatic convictions as to the universal conviviality of religions and their mutually immanent and co-creative translatability in a multiverse of radical novelty. Such novelty ever transcends (even as it includes) the gamut of their respective truth claims.

Faber's recent text, *The Ocean of God: On the Transreligious Future of Religions* (2019) expands his fundamental philosophical and religious commitments as to the multiplicity and unity of religious systems, including their ecological immersion, evolutionary situatedness and cosmological impact for the unfolding human story.[16] Here, Faber reclaims the category "transreligious" which, although he introduced it years ago, has recently come into wider parlance. Engaging a variety of minority voices in process philosophy and theology, as well as the "new axial" perspectives of the Babi Bahá'í religions, *The Ocean* situates human beings in a cosmological matrix

---

14. Faber, *Divine Manifold*.
15. Faber, *Garden of Reality*.
16. Faber, *Ocean of God*.

of becoming, relationality, and processuality over and against their apocalyptic contraries. The thesis stands for Faber: the future of religion will be *transreligious* or there will no humanity and no religion at all.

These books differently capture the depth of Faber's concerns and contributions in recent years. They have emerged from the "light" and "fire" of his personal experiences and been furnished through his unceasing scholarship. In and among these publications, of course, have been a wide variety of edited volumes, book chapters and journal articles in process philosophy, theology, metaphysics, and comparative religion. Indeed, it is the purpose of this current volume (and those that follow it) to integrate these isolated contributions of Faber's corpus into thematic narratives of their very own. Before we turn to this volume itself, however, I think readers will benefit from a brief exposition of the key outlines of Faber's own "theopoetic" approach to process theology.

Process Theology as Theopoetics

I mentioned at the outset that Faber's work has in many ways aimed to complicate discussions as to what process theology is and how it can (or should) operate, particularly by unveiling the *irreducibility* of Whitehead's universe to limited confinements, interpretations and expressions. Put simply, there is no such thing as "process theology" *as such*, but only *process theologies in particular*. Process theology is and must remain many things and not just one. Given this, how then does Faber approach the world of process theologies?

In the first place, Faber has insisted that "process theology is before all else 'theopoetics.'"[17] "Theopoetics" is a term with a diverse and winding history. A theological school influenced by Whitehead in the 1960's held this name and flourished on the east coast in the work of thinkers like Stanley Hopper, David Leroy Miller and Amos Wilder. For them, "theopoetics" was a way of articulating a *poetic alternative* to the conceptual systematics of classical theologies and their tendencies toward hermeneutical literalism in religious language and symbol. By contrast, they emphasized the poetic essence of religious language which, as Faber, describes "divulges its mystery precisely where it disrupts all categories of grasping."[18] Under the auspices of Catherine Keller, theopoetics would find further creative expression (such as in "theopolitics") at Drew University which upheld concerns for dismantling patriarchal language in theology and critiquing

17. Faber, *Becoming of God*, 177.
18. Faber, *Becoming of God*, 178.

imperialist modes of thought. Today, theopoetics continues to function as a backdrop to a variety of creative theological proposals.[19] The roots of the term, however, stretch back into antiquity. In early Christian history, "theopoetics" was closely associated with *theosis* or "making divine" (theo-*poiesis*) as the very *telos* of all creation.

Notwithstanding these historical layers, Faber has long identified the underlying theopoetic nature of Whitehead's expressions and developed them as a horizon in which process theologies variously unfold. In using the concept of "theopoetics," however, Faber has *not* insisted that all theological language is essentially *metaphoric* (in contrast to Sallie McFague and Gordon Kaufman for example) or that process theology, and with it, all theology, is *only* of a poetic nature—a "poetics of the divine."[20] For Faber, both of these approaches suffer from an aesthetic reduction of realities which, on his account, are *irreducible*. Rather, what Faber has meant is that Whitehead's theological formulations capture fundamental *intuitions* at the heart of process theology, in that God-language indicates *poiesis* as a "creative event of construction and synthesis."[21] As such, theological language will always be *more than* metaphorical in terms of its novel *poiesis*, but *less than* metaphorical in its failure to capture the *unspeakable* in language. It is with these convictions that Faber has framed process theology, particularly by pointing to Whitehead's famous theopoetic passage:

> God's role is not the combat of productive force with productive force, of destructive force with destructive force; it lies in the patient operation of the overpowering rationality of his conceptual harmonization. He does not create the world, he saves it; or, more accurately, he is the poet of the world, with tender patience leading it by his vision of truth, beauty and, goodness (PR, 346).

Faber will unfold the wider context of this statement in chapter 9. For now, however, it suffices to say that God as *Poet* is *not* the unilateral *Pantokrator* of the world, but rather the receptive *healer* of the world process. As such, God *participates* in the world not as one competitive cause among others, but as that which *gifts* the multiplicities of the world with novel possibilities of their own becoming, and which then *inhales* and *transforms* them in the divine nature. In this way, God acts through *non-violent love* and with a *patience* that seeks to *savor* the tender elements of things, even as it aims for ever-more-intense harmonies. "Theopoetics" Faber states, "is

19. See for example the various contributions in Faber and Fackenthal, *Theopoetic Folds*.

20. Faber, *God as Poet*, 322.

21. Faber, *God as Poet*.

the unfolding of an understanding of process theology that is committed to *these* elements."[22] It is these elements that he includes in his own "theopoetic definition" of process theology.

> Process theology is theopoetics, that is, a theology of perichoresis (of mutual coinherence of all things) in which the universe represents God's creative adventure and God the event of creative transformation of the world. It is within the net of interwoveness—the process itself—that God appears as the "poet of the world," as its surprising creator (the ground of its novelty), its compassionate companion (the ground of its interwoven nature), and its saving radiance (the ground of its harmony).[23]

For Faber, what such a theology demands, moreover, is nothing short of "a mystical spirituality of the unification with the world of the Poet in the flow of divine (persuasive) activity . . ."[24]

Interpreters of Whitehead have always struggled through his novel usage of language and, indeed, his creation of words, to describe a universe of infinite becoming. Faber has often highlighted this essential element of his thought. "Instead of making us kings of reality and gods of the mystery of existence in mastering fixed conceptual abstractions, the complex apparatus of Whitehead's conceptual language presents itself as a gift—a method of unknowing, if you will—forcing us always to reenter the process of thinking again."[25] So too, I claim, is Faber's creative use of language a challenge and gift, a means of apophatic *unknowing* of stagnate verbalizations of reality. Away with them! Faber's lexicon, by contrast, offers a *re-knowing* both of the world as an infinite becoming multiplicity and God as its affirmative Poet. I include below several of Faber's key terms and their associated meanings which intricately lace (and grace) the chapters that lie ahead. For new readers in particular, it may be helpful to return to this list as these terms are variously encountered throughout the movements of this volume. This list is not meant to be exhaustive, but orienting and helpful.

- **Insistence** is a philosophical term Faber uses to designate the "being-in" or "becoming-in" of ultimate reality or God in all reality and experience, and on every level of existence. The term aims to convey that ultimate reality or God is *beyond* any definition, even that of "existence" or "Being," terms which, in Whitehead's universe, are already

22. Faber, *Becoming of God*, 181.
23. Faber, *God as Poet*, 15.
24. Faber, *Becoming of God*, 183.
25. Prologue, this volume.

abstractions from processual becoming. God does not "exist," but "insists;" God does not "exist" over and against the world, but insists *in* and *on* the utter relationality and multiplicity of things.

- *Indifference* is a philosophical term Faber uses to indicate the *dialectic* of transcendence and immanence, difference and identity, detachment and compassion, especially with respect to the God-World relationship. In contrast to mere indifference, which suggests either ontological separation or emotional carelessness, Faber's indifference is used in a *non-dual* fashion as "in-difference" or "in/difference" in order to convey that in/different divine reality transcends all differentiations and "is" only "*in* the differences" of the world's multiplicity.

- *Polyphilia* is a term Faber uses for the divine "love of multiplicity" which insists in and on the multiplicity of the world in every moment. It is this divine *polyphilic* activity that loves to sustain, infuse, receive, and transform all reality. In contrast to the abstractions of other "pluralistic" positions, Faber's *polyphilic pluralism* indicates the divine insistence on, and love for, multiplicity such that religions are apophatic affirmations of Reality/Truth/God within and beyond the diversity of their experiences and organizations.

- *Polypoetics* in Faber's usage refers to the manifold of symbolic expressions which evoke *traces* of the divine among the layered multiplicities of world processes. Here, Faber speaks of the *diffusion* of the divine in multiplicity, not however in terms of divine disappearance, but as that which *symbolizes* the mysterious dignity and inexhaustibility of the infinite foldings of becoming reality.

- *Substractive affirmation* is used by Faber to express both the divine *affirmation* of multiplicity, but also the divine *subtraction* from any identification *with multiplicity*. Instead of such identifications, which have often undergirded divine power-games and coercive theologies, God's poetic *self-subtraction* is an affirmation of the worth and integrity of the world process.

- *Theoplicity* is used by Faber to designate divine apophatic activity as the *insistence on multiplicity*—both as its *initiating* Eros and *receptive* salvation.

- *Theopoetic difference* is Faber's way of speaking to the *difference* between God and Creativity and, indeed, all Ultimates at the relational heart of Whitehead's philosophy. This difference offers a *counter metaphor* to the ontotheological fantasies of divine dominion; it is the divine difference between love and power in every event.

One should notice the mutually related connotations of Faber's language as it attempts to reflect the utter relationality of his theopoetic universe. Such language is not a result of "intellectualism" with its dualistic categories of thought, but rather an expression of Whitehead's appeal for "novel verbal characterizations" (MT, 174) in our efforts to pierce the shocking depths of experience. Such language for Faber evokes "the non-duality of mysticism" and its "fresh articulation in ever-new categorizations of relationality."[26] Nevertheless, such experience will always transcend and evade the exactness of linguistic expressions. "Philosophic thought," Whitehead reminds us, "cannot be based upon . . . exact statements." Rather, "the exactness is fake" (Imm., 700). We turn now to the framework, layering, and progression of the current volume.

Insight into Depths Soon Spoken:
A Framework of Mutual Immanence

Throughout the years, Faber has continually insisted that the "ultimate of ultimates" in Whitehead's thought is not "Creativity," "God" or the "World," but rather the preeminence of *their relationship* to one another in the *togetherness* of "mutual immanence."[27] While this has not always been clearly understood by interpreters of Whitehead, it is essential for understanding much of his thought, including, Faber stresses, the entangled movements of his mystical cosmogony. In contrast to misconceived notions of "independent existence" (Imm., 696) which have haunted European philosophy and theology, Whitehead names mutual immanence as that relational vision which grasps that "each happening is a factor in the nature of every other happening" (MT, 164). In a many-sided processual world, Whitehead would put it more strongly, insisting that mutual immanence is in fact the "key to metaphysics" where each side is understood as "lending to the other a factor necessary for its reality" ("PR," 126).

As Faber has identified mutual immanence as the "key" to Whitehead's thought, so too, I suggest, is mutual immanence the proper framework for considering the relationship between the three layers of the current volume: "Mysticism and Multiplicity," "Multiplicity and Divinity," and "Divinity and Mystery." These layers are not to be understood as opaque and independent from one another, but transparent and related, such that you could (as it were) look through each of them and their associated chapters and also see into the others. While each layer does flexibly

26. Faber, "The Manifestation of God," 5.
27. Faber, *Becoming of God*, 105.

house respective and relevant themes, I have, nonetheless, tried to choreograph the movement of the volume in such a way that readers might appreciate their mutually immanent character.

In the prologue, "Whitehead's Universe: Past and Future," Faber introduces Whitehead's central themes, the different phases of his career, his relation and importance to the philosophical tradition, and promising forecasts for a "Whiteheadian future." This serves as an essential orienting discussion of the relevance and uniqueness of Whitehead, and sets the tone for the volume as a whole.

The *first layer* of the volume consists of four chapters that differently reflect the themes of "Mysticism and Multiplicity," the *experiential* and the *multitudinous*. In chapter 1, "The Mystical Whitehead," Faber delves into the various ways in which Whitehead emerges as a mystical thinker with important resonances with the mystical tradition, but also strong critiques. In dialogue with Joseph Bracken and key figures of mystical lineage, including Nicholas of Cusa, Meister Eckhart and Plotinus, Faber reveals the mystical Whitehead while also articulating the distinctiveness of his own introduction of the "divine matrix," different from that of Bracken.

In chapter 2, "A New Mystagogy of Becoming," Faber follows the "mutually attractive trace" of mystical language found in both Whitehead and Deleuze, insisting that these are in fact authentic expressions of their respective philosophies, rather than foreign contaminations by dogmatics. Here, the mystical resonances and differences of Whitehead and Deleuze are discussed in terms of wide connections to the philosophical tradition. Faber pinpoints particular concerns of Whitehead and Deleuze, including the ultimacy of becoming, the paradox of life and death, the realms of multiplicity, the mystery of novelty, and the hidden traces of God incognito.

In chapter 3, "God's Absence of Listening," Faber considers metaphysical claims as to divine "absence" and "presence" in depth and in primary dialogue with Whitehead, Jacques Derrida, and Martin Heidegger, but also a host of other thinkers including Boethius, Aristotle, Avicenna, Aquinas, and the Swedish playwright, August Strindberg. What emerges is a Whiteheadian understanding of divine "presence" or "presencing" as an *event* of un-possessive listening and un-possessing silence.

In chapter 4, "The Touch of Reality," Faber puts Whitehead and Graham Harman into dialogue as to the mystery of everyday touch, connectivity, the depth of objects, and the depth of self. In showing that both Harman and Whitehead challenge, but also mutually enhance each other, Faber locates their insights among philosophical and religious traditions, as well as identifies their respective theological allusions in Harman's secularized "allure" and Whitehead's divine "a-lure."

The *second layer* of the volume consists of four chapters which variously relate to the themes of "Multiplicity and Divinity," *polyphilia* and *theoplicity*, on a deeper level. In chapter 5, "Bodies of the Void," Faber considers the mysterious multiplicity of the body in terms of its apophatic negation and affirmation in the world process. Working with the insights of negative theology and the bodily intuitions of Whitehead, Judith Butler, Derrida, Deleuze, Julia Kristeva, and others, Faber locates "apophatic bodying" and "bodying the apophatic" at the polyphilic core of the world, particularly in its relation to the divine activity of theoplicity which *insists* upon and loves the apophatic bodying of the world.

In chapter 6, "Polypoetics," Faber considers *polyphilic polypoetics* as the love of the *poiesis* ("making") of the divine in the multiplicity of infinite "ultimates" that Whitehead's chaosmos sustains. Upholding the manifold in *subtractive affirmation*, the divine "Adventurer" is theopoetically *diffused* into the world, but always *in/different* from it. Faber then situates "religious pluralism" in this chaosmic context. In discussion with key pluralistic thinkers, from Perry Schmidt-Leukel and John Hick to S. Mark Heim, John B. Cobb Jr. and David Ray Griffin, Faber argues that his own *polyphilic pluralism* includes the strengths, but transcends the weakness, of both the "mystical monistic" and "differential pluralistic" solutions associated with these figures.

In chapter 7, "Divine Para-doxy," Faber creatively applies the counter-coercive critiques of Whitehead, Teilhard, Deleuze, Foucault, Butler and others in order to overcome the power dynamics of religious violence inherent in exclusivist and substantialist renderings of "orthodoxy." He envisions a new "sense of peace" and harmony that emerges from the *para-dox* of polyphilia in its unravelling of the idolatrous entanglement of God and Caesar. Instead of seeking "orthodoxy," para-doxy suggests *polydoxy* as a liberating vision for experiencing, theorizing, and practicing multiplicity.

In chapter 8, "Tracing the Spirit," Faber unfolds essential contours of a "Whiteheadian spirituality of Peace." In the midst of the "crisis of becoming," he maps three profound elements of "the Gift of the Spirit" in terms of "polarity," "eros" and "place." Together, these elements function as entry points into the Spirit of becoming; they ground a Whiteheadian spirituality in following divine traces into the world through the experiential praxis of Self-Transcendence.

The *third layer* of the volume consists of four key chapters in Faber's corpus that differently express themes of "Divinity and Mystery," particularly as they relate to central questions, concerns and conversations of the theological tradition, and how process theology can address and translate them. In chapter 9, "Theopoetic Creativity," Faber tackles the question of creation with respect to Whitehead's appreciation of the insights of Plato, the persuasive revelation of Jesus, and the metaphysical wisdom of the theological tradition. Against common critiques insisting that process theology has no "creator" and no doctrine of creation, Faber defends process theology's "relational alternative" of divine creation, based in the theopoetic difference between God and creativity. He then shows that process theology can and does house spaces for affirming both *creatio ex nihilo* and creation from chaos, perspectives which are not necessarily mutually exclusive.

In chapter 10, "Trinity as Event," Faber explores possible connections between the development and concerns of Trinitarian theology and the resources of process theology. Using the concepts of *analogy* and *coherence*, in particular, he uncovers how each tradition can translate the other, as well as shed light on unique problems they mutually face. What surfaces is Faber's conviction that process theology can uniquely sustain Trinitarian affirmations from within its own categories, wherein God is conceived as one actuality in everlasting self-differentiation.

In chapter 11, "The Process of Revelation," Faber inquires as to whether or not there is a genuine place for "revealed theology" in Whitehead's thought and what kind of relation it might have to metaphysics in terms of *subordination* or *mutuality*. Reflecting on the unique and non-metaphysical nature of revelation, Faber affirms the place of revealed theology in the context of process theology by advocating a more fluid interpretation of the relation between metaphysics and theology. While Whitehead's insights implicitly enable understandings of *genuine* claims of revelation, Faber insists that they cannot be justified metaphysically; rather metaphysics is *relativized* in view of a genuine revealed theology. Divine revelation, therefore, cannot be grasped either *non-historically* by metaphysical categories alone, or *non-eschatologically* by historical events that have already passed. Rather, genuine revelation is linked to the universality of singular events, as they are repeated and re-actualized in their originality through *anamnesis*.

In chapter 12, "God in the Making," Faber explores Whiteheadian resources for affirming, problematizing and creatively addressing religious experience, particularly as it relates to the *duality* of religious experience and cosmology as an ongoing discussion in Christian theology. At the heart of this discussion is the problem of a plurality of revelations, the multiplicity of cosmological interpretations, and the question as to whether these can possibly find unification into "one" Godhead. In reviewing and critiquing different solutions, including mystical temptations to withdraw into apophatic silence, Faber argues that a Whiteheadian vision of a creative *unity* of diverse decisions between God and the world, offers a way of affirming both the multiplicity of revelational experiences and their cosmological rationalizations. What is required, Faber insists, is a divine self-creative process of unification with Godself. God, therefore, is *in the making* in and through God's own creative revelations on the one hand, and from God's integration of the world's creative interpretations on the other.

In the epilogue, "(Nothing But) Mystery," Faber combats occasional charges which claim that process theology fails to recognize or allow for the "mystery of God." He argues, by contrast, that the *mysterium* is deeply infused in both Whitehead's own cosmological vision as well as in process theology itself, in terms of the mystery of life, the event, creativity, and process as the "mysticism" of the unspoken. From his own theopoetic perspective, Faber reveals the different ways in which a layered matrix of utter mystery emerges in consideration of God's *life, nondifference,* and *insistence.* The mysteries found in the epilogue function as an integrative and concluding means of drawing together the central insights of the volume with its mutually im-manent layers of mysticism, multiplicity and divinity.

Conversions for a Future of Peace

In drawing this introduction to a close, I would like to suggest some of the key ways in which Faber's mystical Whiteheadian vision offers essential re-sources for a valuable shift in orientation toward the world. It is important to stress that Faber's vision, in consonance with that of Whitehead, is deeply civilizational; it is not shortsighted, aloof or static, but imaginative, engaged and dynamic. During one of our many strolls around the "oval office" behind Claremont School of Theology, I recall Faber stating that he was writing "for the next thousand years." In the face of a deeply uncertain and precarious future, this is a bold and forward looking claim, grounded, I imagine, in his underlying "faith in the universe" and the unspoken possibilities that lie ahead. As a "creature of thought," his work is fully aware that the philosophi-cal endeavor harbors essential resources for the flourishing of civilization. Here, he fully agrees with Whitehead: "Its gifts are insight and foresight and a sense of the worth of life, in short, that sense of importance which nerves all civilised effort" (AI, 98). Indeed, Faber has emphasized the purifying and transformative nature of Whitehead's "philosophical wildfire" in its offering not simply of "theoretical analysis" but "a lens for *experiencing* the world differently."[28] It does so by sparking a renewed vision of life on a variety of interconnected disciplinary levels, from philosophy to science, theology and society. To conclude, I offer the following practical "conversions" which also burn at the heart of Faber's own "theopoetic wildfire."

28. Faber, *Becoming of God,* 220.

From Being to Becoming. In our conversion from philosophical, theological, and societal categories of being to those of becoming, we find that the world need not be imprisoned to the sameness of repetition, nor determined by patterns of the past. "In seeking novelty instead of eternity," Faber states, "we become sensitive to the liberating force of life, chaos, creativity, and difference over the forces of law, order, repetition, and sameness."[29] The ever-coming advent of divine novelty releases the world to creatively become other than what it has been. The world is never the same twice. "The essence of life," Whitehead insists, "is the teleological introduction of novelty" (AI, 207). Surrendering to a world of becoming may indeed bring anxiety, but it also brings hope.

From Independence to Mutual Immanence. In our conversion from livelihoods of independence to those of mutual immanence, the world is shown not to be a *conglomeration of independent objects*, but a *community of interdependent subjects*, wherein mutual feeling (*prehension*) is the fundamental category. The world is not made of "matter," but of *experiential compassion*, the *feeling* of fellow creatures, Faber states, "feeling their way through their life history, and feeling their feeling as spiritual and ethical responsibility . . ." This is a call—even "a mandate"—he claims, "to change the world in every event anew toward ever-greater sensibility, receptivity, prehensivity."[30] With Whitehead, there remains no such thing as "independent existence," not even for God; rather, "every entity is only to be understood in terms of the way in which it is interwoven with the rest of the universe" (Imm., 687). In Faber's language, to understand this "conversion" is to grasp the essential difference between indifference and *in/difference*.

From Force to Persuasion. In our conversion from coercive push-and-pull causalities, with their destructive religious, political and societal expressions, to those of relational persuasion and non-violence, the world emerges not simply as *externally effected*, but *internally receptive*. "The recourse to force," Whitehead insists ". . . is a disclosure of the failure of civilization . . ." (AI, 83). It is also a failure of that barbaric theology upon which civilizations have justified their triumphs. There is an inherent connection here. "The worship of glory arising from power is not only dangerous: it arises from a barbaric conception of God," Whitehead warns; "I suppose not even the world itself could contain the bones of those slaughtered because of men intoxicated by its attraction" (RM, 55). By contrast, the power of Faber's theopoetic divinity is inherently *non-violent* and counter-barbaric in its *in-sistent* persuasion. Here, civilization is called to renounce power

---

29. Chapter 2, current volume.
30. Faber, *Becoming of God*, 220.

and violence "*precisely because* such renunciation ultimately derives from the very essence of God."[31]

From Decadence to Adventure. In our conversion from frameworks of decadence and societal stasis, to those of adventure and creative advance, the world turns toward a myriad of untried possibilities. This turn, Whitehead insists, is an "adventure of thought regarding things as yet unrealized" (AI, 279). The human condition bears witness that "no static perfection is possible." This claim is "rooted in the nature of things," and, indeed, "the essence of the universe," such that "Advance or Decadence" are the only options offered to human kind (AI, 274). "Without adventure," Whitehead stresses, "civilization is in full day" (ibid., 279). So too are theology and religion in full decay without adventure; for a "learned orthodoxy suppresses adventure" (ibid., 277). In this way, Faber speaks to our abilities to spiritually discern the adventurous "traces" of the divine as it is *diffused* in *subtractive affirmation* of the world's religious multiplicity and new donnings of divine revelation.

From Dogmatism to Mysticism. In our conversion from orthodox and creedal dogmas, vertically sustained by authority and tradition, to the openness of mystical polydoxy, radiating horizontally from experience, the world's religious traditions emerge as collaborative allies, speaking anticipatory insight into "depths as yet unspoken" (MT, 174). This is not a dismissal of "tradition," but instead recognizes Whitehead's assurance that "religions commit suicide when they find their inspiration in their dogmas." Rather, "the inspiration of religion . . . is to be found in the primary expressions of the intuitions of the finest types of religious lives" which provoke intuitive responses piercing "beyond dogma" (RM, 144). In our in/difference from others and God "in a mysticism and activism of love, compassion and mutual reciprocity," Faber emphasizes the ability to intuit the reality of God "not as a supreme being . . . far above the netherworld of physicality, change and perpetual perishing, but as immanent in each of its events . . . immanent to them as their very instigation of becoming the subject of their own experiences.[32] Here, the challenge of spiritual practice is to *tune* ourselves into the marvelous gift that in every moment we are being created and re-created anew.

From Pessimism to Peace. In our conversion from pessimistic dispositions, giving rise to political, religious, and societal turmoil, to those of peace and harmony, the world becomes a place of *hospitality*, rather than *hostility*. Peace, for Whitehead, is an aesthetic reality essential to the flourishing of

---

31. Chapter 9, current volume.
32. Faber, *Becoming of God*, 220.

civilization. "It is primarily a trust in the efficacy of beauty," he states, but its "aim" always risks passing "into its bastard substitute, Anaesthesia," where the quality and value of life are subverted by destruction (AI, 285). In this way, Faber insists that "*beauty* has the same relation to *peace* as has *evil* to *tragedy*."[33] Whitehead holds that the depth, value and tragic beauty of a becoming world are derived from the immanence of God, always seeking to route discord in reach for deeper harmonies. Indeed, "peace" as Faber confirms, is this "*immanence* of the entire living nexus of God, the Spirit, in the nexic body of organisms and environments."[34] In contrast to escapist religious temperaments, hell-bent on leaving the world behind, Whitehead assures us that "religion is world-loyalty" (RM, 60). Faber thus envisions religions "breaking through the dark clouds of illusions and evil," in order to "harbor, expand and yearn" for the life of the Spirit.[35]

In the end, one cannot read Whitehead and Faber without grasping their fundamental concerns for peace. The themes of fire that have run through this introduction are relevant here too. Fire is not only "wild," blazing in *purification* and *creativity*; it also signifies *peace*, as in the lighting of a single candle. Who has not been captivated by the silence of a flickering flame? All fires begin with a spark. We are left with a gentle metaphor: the peace of a single flame, bouncing softly to the ebb and flow of a world in becoming.

---

33. Faber, *Becoming of God*, 171.
34. Faber, *Becoming of God*, 176.
35. Faber, *Becoming of God*.

Whitehead's Universe: Past and Future

How to approach the phenomenon of Whitehead? What to say, and what to conceal? How to unfold his complex work, reaching from mathematics and logics to philosophy and theology, with physics and evolutionary theory in between? And what to remember of Whitehead the human being who grounds the immense breadth of this work? Whatever I highlight will be overshadowed by a much greater cloud of oblivion. I should concede to the impossibility of the task!

While pondering this calamity, I've decided to lay out the landscape of Whitehead's universe by using a more pragmatic tool, or rather, a mnemonic device structuring the task. I call it a "binocular view." Whitehead knew of it as a "dipolar" view of things. By this, he not only indicates that it is always better to investigate more than one perspective, but, indeed, he suggests that reality is always incurably complex, while our understanding of reality tends to employ the antagonisms of opposites.

My title already hints at such a double perspective of opposite directions: It is not enough to review the *past*, the genesis of Whitehead's thought, its influence and currency, as important as this may be. We may also want to envision its *future*, the prospect of its potential. Whitehead himself was intensely concerned with the intellectual reconstruction of the thinkers of the last 300 years, their inventions and revolutions of thought and social life, while adamantly critiquing their shortcomings and downfalls, especially the newly arrived ideology of scientific materialism.

Yet Whitehead was also deeply engaged in matters of the future, possible developments of society and structures of thought that would avoid the pitfalls of the past and, instead, express the transformative processes his own thinking was meant to initiate. In 1940—Whitehead was already 80 years old—he suggested in a conversation with Charles Lindbergh that, despite the Great War under way, he believed without fear that over the "next two or three hundred years" humanity might work out the problems of civilization without undue suffering.

This hope demonstrates a deep trust in the human potential to always decide anew *for* a civilized world. And this trust is steeped in a virtually unending series of binocular perspectives that pervade Whitehead's work throughout its different levels of development: from the dipolarity of mathematics and philosophy, and the rejection of a bifurcation of nature into independent systems of matter and mind, to the co-valence of science and religion; from the *critique* of abstractions taken for the concrete, and yet the *cherishing* of abstractions as motors of the evolutionary process, to the formulation of a philosophy of organism in which both abstract ideas and concrete processes may rest reconciled; from the unending rhythms of becoming and perishing to the eventful intersection of fact and value and the meaningful oscillation between the world and God.

For Whitehead, all of these oppositions, juxtapositions, double perspectives, and bipolarities are, of course, themselves always in motion—neither sedated on abstract grounds, nor fused into a higher unity that puts their dynamism to rest. Instead, Whitehead always found ultimate refuge in this dynamics *itself* as it motivates the binary perspectives to coalesce. In forming contrasts, these differentiated, complex, moving perspectives bind together, neither by dissolving their otherness nor by remaining in mere opposition.

No wonder that Whitehead in his *magnum opus, Process and Reality*, claims that the ultimate ground of everything—that beyond which one cannot think and search for truth—is itself not anything we can arrest: neither Being or God, nor matter or mind, but the creative process itself, graciously groundless. Whitehead might well have been one of the first thinkers to reference "creativity" in such ultimate, metaphysical terms.

This indicates a mystery in Whitehead's thought: If you have ever tried to read Whitehead for the first time, and even if you have become an expert, it is almost unimaginable to understand how a philosopher with such an inclination toward "creativity" could develop the most complex system around it. One can only grasp this paradox, laid out in a whole series of books in the 1920s and 30s, if one recognizes that his very aim is to help us avoid getting caught up in our tendency to stabilize fluency again. Instead of making us kings of reality and gods of the mystery of existence in mastering fixed conceptual abstractions, the complex apparatus of Whitehead's conceptual language presents itself as a gift—a method of unknowing, if you will—forcing us always to reenter the process of thinking again. Whitehead wants us, always anew, to become creative seekers and creators of new realities and ideas in the pursuit of the art of life.

With *creativity* as ground, and with the method of contrast in mind, we can now add two further characteristics of Whitehead's binocular perspectivism: *mutuality* as the mode of togetherness and *events* as the place of its happening.

The first, *mutuality*, appears in endless variations throughout Whitehead's work, leading up to his last public lecture, "Immortality," given in 1941. Here, for the last time, Whitehead, in the strongest and most universal terms possible, summarizes his view on the ever creative, contrasting process in terms of the "essential relevance" of *every* factor of the universe *for the other*. Even the "contrast of finitude and infinity arises from the fundamental metaphysical truth that every entity involves an indefinite array of perspectives" so that no "finite perspective" can ever "shake off its essential connection with" its "infinite background" (Imm., 682).

Yet, these mutually contrasting perspectives are in need of a *creative meeting place* within the concrete flux of things. They convene in *events* of the momentary unification of differences. Created from the complex multiplicities they gather, these events add themselves to a new multiplicity of perspectives, issuing into novel expressions of the creative process that generates the universe. Yes, Whitehead was a pluralist! Yet he filtered his pluralism through concrete events in which mind and matter, past and future, facts and values, abstracts and concretes, and flux and permanence find themselves in mutual enjoyment. In such momentary suspensions of inherent conflicts, their *contrasted* opposites avoid the impasse of motionless coagulation and instead generate a creative passage into the unprecedented.

Because of the enjoyment of togetherness and the pulsation of influx and effluence, the creative contrasting of perspectives always happens as *events of experience*. Conversely, the universe exhibits a cosmic convergence of infinitely diverse perspectives, oscillating in the mutual immanence of *experiences of events*. And it is in this synthesis of universal sympathy that the universe harbors a sense of "eternal greatness" as always already "incarnate in the passage of temporal fact" (AI, 33).

Beyond all technicalities, this may explain Whitehead's trust in the future. Dispersed though its intricate modes of flux, the world-process yet exhibits a sense of an "essential rightness of things." While not a means for "preservation" (RM, 41), we may trust the world process as harbinger of the ever-renewed *potential to create a world*. And since the "creation of the world" draws on the *mutuality* of perspectives, it augurs the "victory of persuasion over force" (AI, 25). While Whitehead wants to disperse the suspicion that the "base of things" shall disclose a "mere arbitrary mystery," the eventful exchange of perspectives is its very mystery because this universe is not dominated by "harmony of logic" lying "upon the universe as an iron necessity." Instead, it is vivified by "aesthetic harmony" that "stands before it as a living ideal." Its promise is beyond our grasp; yet it stirs "the general flux in its broken progress towards finer, subtler issues" (SMW, 18).

Let me summarize this first sketch of Whitehead's thought. It reveals a polyglot thinker with a universal vision who invites us to embark on the adventures of *cosmology*. Following the multiplicity of fleeting experiences as they pervade the very texture of the universe in their rhythmic collection and release, this web of contrastive events manifests *one vast aesthetic whole*, itself infinitely moved by an adventurous harmonics of the unprecedented. As this process is patient regarding the appearance of human civilization, it refines itself through the intensities of art, ethics, and religion, while in humanity's accompanying investigations into its nature, it gives way to the discovery of mathematical, physical, and genetic patterns. As we harbor the potential to understand these realms, we are also offered the opportunity to refine our existence by practicing ever-new propositions of aesthetic satisfaction.

Phases and Evolution in Whitehead's Opus

Yet how did Whitehead's universe happen in the first place? The shortest way to circumscribe his career is to say that it began at Trinity College in Cambridge, England, and ended at Harvard University in Cambridge, New England. While his vision arose with mathematics in the tradition of Newton, he transformed himself into a metaphysician in the tradition of Plato. In fact, both mathematics and philosophy were already confluent in Plato, to whom Whitehead thought the Western philosophical tradition added itself only as a series of extended footnotes.

Whitehead was not a Platonist, however. He rather admired the depth of Plato's thought and his dialogical method, never fixating on anything, but always developing alternative views of what might have been missed in any crystallization of thought. Depth can never be systematized; it is always unspoken; its truth can only be approximated with utmost sensitivity to the vastness of the universe and humility before its never-ceasing becoming. If we are meant to find rhythms in it—mathematical, physical, and metaphysical—then it is because of the *relationality* of the cosmic ingredients rather than because of any prefabricated order simply "there" to be discovered.

We can divide Whitehead's work into three phases—roughly coinciding with the positions he held in Cambridge, London, and Harvard.

Although Whitehead was interested in many other things—history, philosophy, theology, politics, women's emancipation, and education—his professional focus at Cambridge was on mathematics, or more precisely, its interface with the physical universe in terms of topology and logics. *Universal Algebra, Mathematical Concepts of the Material World, Principia Mathematica*—to name three major works of this period—circumscribe his interest: to understand the relationship between the fundamental units of the physical world and their conceptualization. His quest has a distinctive flavor because of its sensitivity for expansive concreteness. Reality cannot be reconstructed in terms of mere abstractions, built up from dimensionless points, arrested through exact measurements, or captured by lifeless logical concepts. Instead, since physical reality is fundamentally relational, connections flow extensively over time and space, and our reasoning employs fluent symbolisms rather than fixed formulae.

With Whitehead's move to London, a reflection on the tacit philosophical presuppositions of mathematical, logical, and scientific reasoning begins to emerge that differentiates his approach from those commonly employed. Another element of Whitehead's thought appears, so prominent in his later philosophy: By conceptualizing nature on the basis of its *perception*, Whitehead defines his task against the prevailing bifurcation of matter and form, substance and relation, external and internal causality. Without yet addressing the accompanying philosophical discussion in Locke, Hume, Descartes, and Kant, he asserts that any knowledge of nature that already *includes its very perception* has already undercut the dualistic isolation of natural objects from human experience.

The works of this period—*The Principles of Natural Knowledge, The Concept of Nature,* and *The Principle of Relativity*—refine Whitehead's earlier proposal: that reality is expansive and, hence, cannot be reduced to dimensionless mathematical or pre-symbolic logical formulae; that measurement is secondary and contingent on the rules of the concrete universe, which, in turn, are also contingent. His method of "extensive abstraction" demonstrates his philosophical agenda of redefining concrete reality as a multiplicity of natural events in a unification of interactions that, by forming relatively persistent characters, generate a web of threads of spacetime. He now famously interprets the natural universe by a series of mutually interacting polarities: of events and objects, expansion and process, abstract persistence and creative passage.

This was revolutionary, indeed! If the "stuff" of the world itself consists in pulses of fleeting events to which all objects, especially scientific objects, owe their reiterative character, then *scientific* knowledge is far from *capturing* nature—as the *Tractatus* of the early Wittgenstein led us to believe—and is a far cry from its creative passage. Its abstractions are mere snapshots of a life that, if they are *substantialized* into inanimate, inert, mutually external particles of matter, only retains a funeral service, symbolically conjuring up the ghosts of disappeared souls.

Because of this inversion, Whitehead also objects to the philosophical underpinning of Einstein's General Relativity—not Relativity *per se*, to be sure, that is, the relational continuum of different, unprivileged systems of spacetime with a maximum causal velocity as the average of all of its systems in a given universe. Rather, Whitehead attacks the implication that these systems' intersecting topology be *bound* by the very particles of matter—their mass and gravity—that he viewed as mere abstractions from the continuum of events with its production of a general geometry of which matter and light are mere expressions.

The third phase of Whitehead's work coincides with his move to America. Since it is known as his *metaphysical* phase, one may wonder whether this constitutes a break with the earlier developments. All readers of Whitehead, who at that time may have mistaken him for a mere mathematician, logician, or philosopher of science, were, indeed, astounded by his metaphysical reinvention. They may have expected a different trajectory because of what they believed to be the "true" potential of Whitehead's work: namely, laying the ground for further explorations into logical positivism or the inception of analytic philosophy; or they may have simply stopped reading his later works. From today's perspective, however, we can better understand this "conversion" as a fairly *logical* extension of Whitehead's earlier thought. With his philosophical reconfigurations in place—the creative advance of nature, the perpetual passage of extended events of spacetime, the repetition of abstract characters of events as objects, and the relation between causality and perception—their philosophical synthesis as a systematic "critique of abstractions" seems almost inevitable.

The major works of this period—*Science and the Modern World, Process and Reality,* and *Adventures of Ideas*—are important not only with regard to their new metaphysical method and their inherent will to create a comprehensive cosmological system, but precisely because they were *thereby directly answering* the lingering *metaphysical* problem inherent in the rise of modern science and philosophy over the course of the previous 300 years. Now Whitehead *directly attacks and systematically deconstructs* the lingering *scientific materialism*, which was still underpinning the new physics of relativity and was only slowly loosening its grip on the revolutionary concepts of quantum physics. Since this materialism interacted with modern philosophy by isolating human subjectivity (and with it the humanities) from physical reality (and the sciences), its mechanism also led to the dismissal of values, leaving us in a meaningless, dull universe.

Whitehead's new metaphysics is a grand proposal, envisioning an *alternative* that *inverses* the hardened oppositions and oppressive abstractions that motivated the wars of the last centuries, intellectually and socially, by offering a peace-making proposition. Clothed in the construction of a universal system of creative contrasts, and contrasts of contrasts, Whitehead releases us not only into a renewed understanding of the world as a whole, but invigorates a re-envisioning of the creation of a civilized society.

Whitehead's new, *organic* paradigm establishes itself with a series of *alternatives*. Instead of invoking an onto-theological ground of being, Whitehead posits the immanence of creativity in its instantiations as the driving force of the becoming of the universe. Instead of Descartes' disconnection of extension and mind, and Spinoza's subsumption of both under a divine substance, Whitehead posits an open universe comprised of myriads of events in their organizationally diverse nexūs. Instead of adopting Leibniz's view of a pre-established order of this multiplicity in the mind of God, Whitehead delegates order to the interplay of all actualities as *their* decisions to realize their potentials, even if they were offered by the mind of God. Instead of Plato's system of ideas, flowing from an essentialized structure, Whitehead insists on grounding ideas in a trans-structural activity of becoming and poses their relative inherence in the actual becoming of the cosmos. Against Aristotle's isolated substances, Hume's digital streams of impressions, and Leibniz's hermetic holism of isolated spheres of mentality and physicality, Whitehead fuses *all* of these spheres in events of relational, physical, and creative "growing together." In this synthesis, the whole universe convenes in the moment of the activity of events and effectively releases itself again to a transcendent future beyond these events.

These *alternatives* are accompanied by an equally profound series of *reversals* of the philosophical tradition. While the substantialist scheme of the past was haunted by a division of active form and passive matter, Whitehead reverses this association: forms, structures, patterns, characters, and laws of nature are *not* the origin of activity, but sedimentations of the possible; events of becoming are *not* the mere realization of pre-given forms, but are the harmonization of actualities and their associated possibilities. Hence, Whitehead's "eternal objects" are *not* possible actual realities, as yet unrealized or realized in an alternative world, but evocations, seductions, and invitations for creative actualizations of the unprecedented.

While Kant isolated subjectivity from reality by transcendentally reconstructing empirical knowledge from projections onto the phenomenal, Whitehead *reverses* the generative relations. If subjects are *effects* of reality from which they gather themselves, they become not only all-relative to the reality they gather in their process of "concretization" or "concrescence," but also all-relative to a reality beyond themselves in which they are gathered into new syntheses of becoming.

In reversing the Western substantialist preference of being over becoming—so that now that which *is* has always had its *becoming*—Whitehead also upsets the undisputed primacy of the higher capacities of intellect and consciousness—as inherited by Descartes, Hume, Kant, Hegel, Husserl, and Heidegger. With the cosmological primordiality of *each* event *feeling* its actual past and *desiring* its relevant possibilities, intellect and consciousness are only complex modes of experiencing. This again inverts the status of humanity in the universe: while Western culture, philosophy, and religion have disconnected humanity from the evolution of nature, Whitehead articulates its ecological cradle.

A last observation on Whitehead's development: In a quartet of books accompanying the metaphysical phase—*Religion in the Making, Symbolism, The Function of Reason,* and *Modes of Thought*—Whitehead emerges as a thinker on the regeneration of civilization. While he has already made his metaphysical case for the inevitable mutuality of fact and value in all cosmic processes without any anthropocentric bias, in these works he again *reverses* the priorities, demonstrating how the factors that drive the development of human existence—aesthetics, symbolism, art, religion, reason, and social organization—emerge from cosmic forces that suggest a "civilized universe." They appear as an excess of the creative process, but must be *refined* in order to contribute to the delicate "aim" Whitehead attributes to the universal process as a whole: the appearance of Beauty through intensifications and harmonizations in processes of cosmic organizations.

Surveying the development of Whitehead's thought over these four phases could lead us to the conclusion that it was driven by a polarity of *expansion* and *inversion*: an expansive move toward the utmost universals of metaphysical magnitude *and* an inverse move towards a humble recognition of the relativity of all universal insights within the motive-force of the evolutionary process toward its aesthetic "aims": Truth, Beauty, Art, Adventure, and Peace.

The Importance of Whitehead

To estimate Whitehead's importance is an extremely delicate matter—because of three reasons. First, since the breath of his vision grounds itself in a comprehensive reversal of the intellectual sedimentations of the preceding 300 years, we cannot expect the full extent of its relevance to be grasped in such a short time, some 70 years after his passing. We may not yet have found *the* approach that fully unfolds its significance. Second, since the depth of his cosmological intuition develops considerably over a lifetime, any appraisal of his work is crucially limited by the perspective from which it starts or the phase in which it anchors itself. Third, if Whitehead's universe of thought is itself *untimely*, it will always remain in some tension with the orthodoxies it questioned and the prevalent paradigms by which it is scrutinized. While Whitehead undertook the reshaping of the conceptual conditions under which the scientific revolutions of the early twentieth century departed from past paradigms, his new philosophical prospect may well be ahead of their limitations and in tension with their currently accepted boundaries.

In a first, sharp look at the immediate impact of Whitehead's new cosmological paradigm, we find much grappling with his alternatives and inversions, mixed with a flavor of disbelief toward his polarities and contrasts. Whitehead foresaw that he might not be appreciated in a prophetic passage in *Adventures of Ideas*, when he noticed that "mental functioning introduces into realization subjective forms conformal to *relevant alternatives excluded* from the completeness of physical realization" (AI, 259). In other words: when the virus of novelty strikes, an established organism may initiate defensive counter-measures to immunize its old ways of life.

Whitehead's own development complicated things. Because of ever-widened horizons that, at the same time, overturned earlier, limited perspectives, it was only a question of time before acceptance at one level was dissolved with the arrival of a new phase. While integrating his earlier endeavors, he also contrasted its narrower conditions, in which adherence or opposition had anchored itself.

Consider only the cohabitation of mathematics and philosophy in Whitehead's work. Does Whitehead's metaphysical phase subsume the mathematical, critically resituate it, or even, at least partly, abandon its earlier preconditions? Does Whitehead's critique of the scientific, philosophic, and religious traditions isolate his alternatives outside their sphere (such that they can be ignored?) or does it instigate a new contrast with hitherto ignored alternatives? Does Whitehead's inclusion of a secularized cosmological function of God make him a dead man walking—given the magnitude of the impact of Nietzsche's declaration of the death of God on the intellectual climate of the twentieth century with its two all-encompassing wars—or does it harbor a viable alternative whose relevance we have hardly understood yet? And finally, is Whitehead's organic paradigm that finds a place for purpose in all reams of the universe a dream of lost times, to which meaningful sciences and philosophies must resist, or is it the stroke of a genius that will be part of any satisfying understanding of the eco-cosmic continuum?

Whitehead's alternatives, at the time of their inception, were met with both applause and skeptical resistance. Yet when Whitehead ventured on, they lost some friends and enemies, transformed some friends into enemies, and vice versa, and found the company of some new friends and enemies. The logical reconstruction of mathematics in the *Principia*, the alternative relativity theory, the dissolution of matter in an event-theory, the metaphysical turn, the theological turn, the turn to civilization—all of these were alternatives in themselves, hurting prevalent paradigms; but they were also *altered*, either by critique in respective fields or by an abandonment and/or sublation in Whitehead's own development. A certain air of surprise remains in all of his moves irrespective of the subtle continuity found from a later standpoint.

The harvest remains ambivalent. Was the *Principia*, arguably one of the most impressive works of 20th century mathematics and logics, dethroned by Gödel's incompleteness theorem or was its logocentrism abandoned by Whitehead's own metaphysics? Is Whitehead's alternative relativity theory, although it had some currency at the time of its inception, dead in light of the predictive power of Einstein's version, or is Whitehead's underlying mereological approach to extension still a future project? Is Whitehead's metaphysical turn the last rearing of a dinosaur, helplessly out of sync with the pulse of postmodern times, or is it a subversive spark we have yet to fully grasp? The last judgment has not yet arrived.

Whitehead's *philosophy* remains an enigma. It is steeped in paradox—due partly to its untimely arrival and partly to Whitehead's own contrasting and inversive reasoning. This leaves us with a fascinating picture. Husserl and Heidegger taught at the same time that Whitehead was leaving for Harvard. Existentialism and phenomenology attacked metaphysics and logical positivists like Carnap disavowed Whitehead when he *turned* to metaphysics. Wittgenstein, himself a student of Whitehead's colleague Russell, changed the philosophical outlook yet again right when Whitehead had found his cosmological voice. All sides of the philosophical empire took turns in directions *counter* to Whitehead's intuitions, which, in turn, diminished a perceptive framework for his reception for decades.

Alternatives with credibility—such as American pragmatism—were marked by James, Dewey, and Bergson, rather than Whitehead. Why? Because of the *paradoxical* nature of Whitehead's contrasts. Although denigrated as a realm of rationalism or, alternately, unbridled fantasy, Whitehead's metaphysics emphasizes *empirical* endeavor (like the pragmatists), interpretation (like hermeneutics), decision (like existentialism), experience (like phenomenology), coherence (like the analytic tradition), and symbolism (like language philosophy). Yet Whitehead subversively counters them with equally disturbing contraries: while empirical, his metaphysics remains stubbornly speculative (a horror for pragmatists); while hermeneutical, it remains stubbornly systematic (a horror for Continental thinkers); while close to phenomena, it resists the primacy of consciousness (a horror for followers of Kant and Husserl); while coherent, it prioritizes life's chaotic character over the limited instrumental usefulness of logics (a horror for analytic philosophers); while deeply engaged with matters of language, it insists on pre-symbolic reality (a horror for almost every philosopher since the 1960s). How peculiar Whitehead's philosophy is!

Nevertheless, these paradoxes may prove vital. Embedding the symbolisms of mathematics and logics in the actual life of the cosmos may add an interesting voice to the current discussion of their foundations. Emphasizing topology, mereology, and extension-theory may hold hidden treasures given the mutual inconsistencies of current physical theories that still await a revolution of understanding. Including aesthetic purposes in an organic theory of evolution and complexity might prove quite visionary given the current research within life sciences and the ecological sensitivities of our time. Envisioning a cosmos of infinite, rhythmic cycles, pulsating through the subjectivity of their chaotic lives, fits well with current concepts of "eternal inflation," and remains attractive because of its retained impulse toward novelty. Finally, including the sacred in a universal scheme of contrasts may prove superior to both religious fanaticism and irreligious indifference for a future civilization that neglects its spiritual dimension only at its own risk.

Regarding Whitehead's legacy, it is hard to estimate the depth and breadth of its true influence because it always reaches far beyond any limited boundaries imposed by disconnected disciplines. The vastly diverse contributions of his students, and the students of his students in their diverse fields, are worth thorough research.

Time forbids name dropping. So I will summarize Whitehead's presence with a flavor of the unexpected: Who else would enjoy long walks with him than Gertrude Stein? Who would write poems on him other than Charles Olson? Who else could appear in an essay on creativity by Arthur Koestler? Who else could be "spoken" through the dialogue of both a dragon and a blind priest, as in John Gardner's *Grendel*? Who else could Aldous Huxley have quoted in support of his hopes for a more liberated society? And in what other context would we expect Whitehead to appear than in the science fiction vision of a future universe of interconnected organisms from Van Voght's pen?

A Whiteheadian Future

Let me, in my final section, risk a look into the future. What could or should we project for the next 150 years? Based on the present, we can say that Whitehead's voice is alive and is being heard. His work is being taken up by many fellow travelers, who themselves are often visionaries, creatively transforming it in their own fields or using it to establish connections beyond classical boundaries. In virtually every discipline of the sciences and humanities, philosophy and education, theology and literature, we find kindred sojourners engaged in Whitehead's universal vision, or at least utilizing its insights for their own projects.

While never imprisoned in any area of thought, over the decades Whitehead's legacy has persistently been held up by adherents of process philosophy and process theology. Yet it was never removed from innovative movements in education, psychology, sociology, economics, ecology, physics, and interreligious thought. Its current proliferation in China was foreseen by Joseph Needham in the 1950s and intuited by Whitehead's suggestion that his philosophy might be more congenial to Indian and Chinese thought. The East-West and North-South dialogues are engraved in its very outlook: the overcoming of inorganic thought and dehumanizing economics. Its influence on emancipatory movements on all continents is increasingly recognized. And the fundamental *eco*-logical, instead of a mere logical, character of his cosmology has inspired environmental movements.

Probably the most important event in this newer history of the Whitehead-reception was the untimely and rather unexpected influence of Whitehead's work on the now famous French philosopher, Gilles Deleuze, who names Whitehead's *Process and Reality* one of the most important works in philosophy in the twentieth century. Not only did he reframe Whitehead's universe by knighting it with a name from James Joyce ("Chaosmos"), but he was instrumental in developing a fresh access to Whitehead via a tradition that had labeled and filed him away too early. As Michel Foucault once proclaimed the twenty-first century a Deleuzian one, maybe something also rings quite true when David Griffin imagined it to become Whiteheadian.

Certain of new philosophies—such as Bruno Latour's philosophy of cosmic community, the new Object Oriented Realism of Graham Harman, or Judith Butler's more recent ecological work—no longer overlook the profound paradigm shift Whitehead initiated; rather they recognize him as part of the heritage from which they depart. This is a new situation, indeed, and it can be expected to continue to unfold.

What is it then that makes Whitehead's cosmology attractive today, catalyzing a new vision of the future of humanity and the planet, for new thought and lines of action? I will hint at just three reasons.

First of all, like physical cosmology today, it embraces the very small, the grain of reality, and the very large, the infinite universe with an organic and evolutionary organization. In many overlapping layers, contingent unifications of multiplicities of processes initiate all kinds of ecological rhythms at large. Becoming and fading—pulsating, really—on all levels between infinitesimal events and vast cosmic epochs of organization, this chaosmos comes forth from unimaginable pasts and ventures into unimaginable futures, relentlessly striving through its complexities, building and releasing infinitely varied forms of social organization and the dissolutions of life. Gathered from its depth, we are no strangers to it.

Second, *pervading* the simplest puff in empty space and the physical and biological organisms that build up planets or are harbored on their crust like fragile foam, as well as the astounded human beings who wonder over their existence, Whitehead finds an inherent *Eros of adventure*. This world will never be the same, never become again what it was; it will never concede to eternal return. This made Whitehead's universe distinctly interesting for Deleuze, because it can always be reformed or reinvent itself and create new worlds of unforeseen intensities and harmonies. Every creature is in its peculiar way responsible for this enactment. What if the majestic laws of nature, and their beauty, are neither mere mechanical devices nor decrees of an external Deity, but the communal effect of the myriads of creatures, a matrix of their passionate *feeling* of causality, creativity, and novelty? For Whitehead, this passion also expresses the presence of an eternal depth of their potentials that always incarnates itself anew in all events and cosmic epochs. This is a vision that makes us meaningful in a meaningful All.

Its ecological depth makes us earth-bound, cosmos-bound, and its spirit seduces us to contribute to its never-ceasing production of life through all tragedies of its perpetual passage.

Third, Whitehead's metaphysics presents us with a model of experience in which all abstract opposites meet to assist us in becoming creative. It does not seek a world-formula, à la Stephen Hawking, but presents us with living sculptures, breathing through the poetry of their pulsation. Hence, Whitehead's thought balances polarities on the pivot of poetics—sharing "patterning" with mathematics, but also inviting intuitions of depth alongside philosophy. Where both mathematics and philosophy may cling to the wonders that only their abstractions make possible, discovering order upon order, poetics reminds them of the rugged beauty of the multiplicity of experiences upon experiences in which those structures are steeped. It is in their very *reciprocity* that we escape the sterile binaries of the oppositions to which we have become accustomed. For Whitehead, this poetics is *divine*. And it is through its *contrasting* embrace that a social process may begin to vivify "the good sense which we term civilization" (MT, 174).

Herein lies the reason for Whitehead's juxtaposition of positivism and speculative metaphysics. He was distressed, even annoyed by the tenets and even the very inception of positivism; it is so because of the missing imagination and the muted sense of depth and unprecedented future. If reason becomes reduced to that which is, and the "is" becomes reduced to that which only a method of exploitation through narrow concepts *imitates* as a purely material reality, one perpetuates not only a reductive primacy of being over becoming, but moreover a reality of merely external particles of matter and a lifeless logic of their mapping—virtually everything Whitehead endeavors to overcome.

Like a testament, Whitehead ends his last book *Modes of Thought* with the imperative that only a philosophy that is sensitive to mystical "depths as yet unspoken," will allow us "to maintain an active novelty of fundamental ideas illuminating the social system" (MT, 174). No wonder, then, that "trust in metaphysics," however "slight, superficial, incomplete" its insights may be, is the one "presupposition" without which "there can be no civilization" because it harbors that which "guides [its] imagination and justifies [its] purpose" (AI, 128).

The "evil of the future," Whitehead says, is the "suppression of aesthetic creativeness" (SMW, 204). He once confessed that he owed this insight to the "vivid life" of his wife, Evelyn. This insight must be considered the very motive of Whitehead's work and the impulses it hopes to release. In Whitehead's words, "aesthetics is the aim of existence" and "kindness and love, and artistic satisfaction are among its modes of attainment" (AN, 8). As in the more poetic passages of *Process and Reality* and *Adventures of Ideas*, Whitehead confirms in his conversation with Charles Lindbergh, in the midst of the most devastating war that humanity had ever witnessed, that the very force that alone is meant to withstand the violence of destruction and the decline of the civilized world is the very force that at the heart of the universe operates "slowly, and in quietness" (PR, 343). May we nourish it!

Part I

Mysticism and Multiplicity

CHAPTER ONE

The Mystical Whitehead

Philosophy and Mysticism

IT IS ONE OF Joseph Bracken's persistent insights that, if one engages with Whitehead's text, one cannot avoid finding a voice that is not only irreducible to mathematical and metaphysical rationalism, but is, in its critical accompanying of theological and religious matters, of a quite mystical nature.[1] By implication, at least, this means: Whitehead was a mystical thinker, if not, although in a somehow hidden way, himself a mystic.[2]

Bracken's contention seems to be far from Whitehead's reception in general,[3] even if it is of a theological nature, however.[4] Where does the "mystical" Whitehead really show himself? Maybe it is just a projection into Whitehead's text, originating with certain religious agendas? As the word "mystic" enshrines the image of a closed mouth, the significance of a hidden nature, and silence, Whitehead's mystical inclination might not be obvious at first. But maybe, this "silence" will precisely reveal the mystical character of his thought. Indeed, with Bracken, I would claim that Whitehead's thought is not really silent on mysticism, but leaves us with hints of a mystical significance hidden behind the closed mouth of the text, of a meaning that actually and deeply shapes Whitehead's thought.[5]

The reason for Whitehead's (general) "silence" on mysticism will be found in a peculiar ambivalence within the term "mysticism" and its use as a way of relating to the world through *experience*.[6] In principle,

1. Bracken, *Divine Matrix*.
2. Faber, "The Infinite Movement," 171–99.
3. Lucas, *Rehabilitation of Whitehead*.
4. Hosinki, *Stubborn Fact*.
5. Refer to chapter 11, current volume.
6. Teasdale, *Mystic Heart*.

as Whitehead tries to avoid the implication of any term hinting toward something that is *beyond* the "articulation" (language, thought, or propositions) of experience or any "appearance" within experience per se, he accuses the use of "the mystical" of simply pointing at a reality that in any experience remains unarticulated and inconceivable *beyond* experience,[7] and even more, that as hidden reality (beyond experience) is claimed to be the true or real or ultimate one.[8] "The shadows pass—says mystical Religion," thereby giving in to the "temptation to abandon the immediate experience of this world as a lost cause" (AI, 33–34). Based on such "mystical intuitions" (ibid., 37) "metaphysical assumptions" become "dogmatically affirmed" and free themselves "from criticism by dogmatically handing over the remainder of experience to an animal faith or a religious mysticism, incapable of rationalization" (ibid., 118).

This is the theme of Whitehead's "rationalism"[9]: to not abandon *this* world, the invaluable importance of which lies in the fact that, in Whitehead's analysis, it is *its* experience and *its* process of becoming as that of experiences that create the values by which creative process exists in the first place.[10] Hence, Whitehead's apodictic formulation which reformulates "the mystical" in his thought: "that apart from the experiences of subjects there is nothing, nothing, nothing, bare nothingness" (PR, 167). Since all creative togetherness is that of experience (creative concrescence), Whitehead's deflection of a reality beyond the creative process of experience receives its most profound formulation in terms of a matrix of relationality that cannot be broken, or only by the fantasies of mystical irrationality. On the contrary, ultimate reality necessarily exhibits *only* such relationality and such relationality *is* (the philosophically sought) rationality.[11] Hence, "what does not so communicate is unknowable, and the unknowable is unknown" (PR, 4).

If mysticism addresses a reality beyond the relationality of experience and, hence, beyond the possibility of rational articulation—Whitehead objects.[12] Whatever such a reality is called, assuming it as "an ultimate reality which, in some unexplained way, is to be appealed to for the removal of perplexity, constitutes the great refusal of rationality to assert its rights" (SMW, 92). Instead, although Whitehead accepts this search to lead "into depths beyond anything which we can grasp with a clear apprehension,"

---

7. Franklin, *Speaking from the Depths*.

8. Lundeen, *Risk and Rhetoric in Religion*.

9. Griffin, "Process Theology as Empirical, Rational, and Speculative," 116–35.

10. Faber, "'Gottesmeer,'" 64–95.

11. Faber, "Surrationality and Chaosmos," 157–77.

12. Griffin, *Reenchantment*.

he demands that it "should disclose the same general principles of reality, which we dimly discern as stretching away into regions beyond our explicit powers of discernment" (ibid., 92–93).

What seems to become a methodological closure that avoids the very possibility of mysticism, however, leads Whitehead in his final analysis back to (a very important reformulation of) "the mystical" as, in fact, *indispensable* in his philosophy.[13] Because if philosophy seeks the "essence" (PR, 4) of the relationality of the universe *as* its rationality and if this relationality is fundamentally *processual*—avoiding static being, closure and fixation in a block universe—then the *place* that this non-closure occupies in Whitehead's philosophy is as vital as its very *assertion*. In asserting a *basic structure* by which *all* actualization of processes occupies itself with their generation, Whitehead not only identifies something of "eternal greatness incarnate in the passage of temporal fact" (AI, 33), but paradoxically a *constancy* that creates and lives from the flux of the world process by being *in itself discontinuous*, unexpected, and innovative. The maxim that there is only "a becoming of continuity, but no continuity of becoming" (PR, 35) holds equally for creativity, potentiality and God, such that all three of them do not primarily appear as justifications of constancy, but as naming *organs of novelty*.[14]

Here, mysticism enters Whitehead's work again, as expression of the hidden reality of what is "unknowable" and, hence, "unknown" (PR, 4), not because it is simply hidden from our ability of articulation, but because it is *not*—in the sense of *not yet*. The "not yet" is essential for novelty to constitute the fabric of relationality (and, hence, to structure rationality) and, hence, the unknowable in the form of the *unprecedented* is constitutive of the matrix of becoming.[15] It is in this sense that Whitehead embraces mysticism: If the "use of philosophy is to maintain an active novelty of fundamental ideas illuminating the social system," it also must be said that "philosophy is mystical" (MT, 174). The reason is that the *processuality* of the world is only "saved" *if* we allow for "mysticism" as "direct insight into depths as yet unspoken" (ibid.). Now Whitehead understands the "purpose of philosophy" not to resist mysticism, but "to rationalize mysticism" (ibid.). Instead of "explaining it away" by rational or relational closures, its character as an *unarticulated beyond* can now be understood as the "not yet" of novelty that *initiates* philosophy in its "introduction of novel verbal characterizations,

---

13. Faber, *Prozeßtheologie*, §§7, 19.
14. Faber, "Amid a Democracy," 192–237.
15. Faber, *God as Poet*, §17.

rationally coordinated," countering "the slow descent of accepted thought towards the inactive commonplace" (ibid.).

The Mystical and the Apophatic

Similar to Bracken, I have emphasized "the mystical" in Whitehead in my own work, mediated especially through Nicolas of Cusa's apophatic method.[16] Why, however, would one care about a (re)discovery of the mystical Whitehead? In my case—and I gather that this is not far from Bracken's motives[17]—this interest is guided by the aim of finding a philosophical and experimental matrix of communication that would allow us to mediate or facilitate a transformation between the multiplicity of theistic and non-theistic religious systems.[18] This "mystical" is meant to express the *one* truth of ultimacy, as complex as it may be for us to understand and to categorize, ultimately for one aim: the realization of universal (religious) peace.[19] Yet, as *interruption* of a web of interrelationality, this "mystical" ultimacy would reintroduce Plotinus' *unnamable* in the heart of everything, the *apophatic*.[20]

The alert reader will have already realized the paradoxical nature of this formulation of "the mystical" in Whitehead's work. Doesn't Whitehead repeat what he wanted to avoid: that the unknowable that is unknown regains its reign in the heart of things; that communicability is in its origin destroyed; that rationality at its very place of operation has faltered? If Whitehead wanted to avoid this mystical "irrationality" for a relationality that justifies its own reason of existence, how can his reintroduction of the *apophatic* in the form of the temporal fissure of novelty—being yet unknown and, hence, unknowable—avoid its *negation* of communicability?

Yet Whitehead's reorientation of the apophatic makes all the difference. While for classical negative theology, *apophasis* categoreally or apodictically addressed the unknowability of the essence of the divine or ultimate reality, Whitehead situates the apophatic in the *future* of becoming, as the source of the novelty of the not yet.[21] While the approach of negative theology was to name only what *cannot* be said about the divine, Whitehead's *nothingness of the future* is filled with the infinite potentials for that which is not yet

---

16. Faber, "De-Ontologizing God," 209–34.

17. Bracken, *Divine Matrix*, 1–7.

18. Faber, *God as Poet*, §36.

19. Refer to chapter 7, current volume.

20. Wilmot, *Whitehead and God*.

21. Faber, "De-Ontologizing God."

actual and, hence, cannot be known in the mode of its actualization.[22] This apophatic *instigates* with its potential the actualization of events that in their creativity are becoming *from* their unknowability.[23]

The function of the mystical in Whiteheads *Modes of Thought*, as cited above, is the introduction of novelty in such a way that it becomes the sole source instilling communication *with life*—no communication can do without it. Its apophatic nature is complex, as it is a mode of not yet (nothingness of possibility) and a potential for actualization (the nothingness of actuality). Yet, in its suggestive, seductive, and activating role, it is essential for communicability not to freeze to death the repetition of the same. Hereby, Whitehead has rediscovered an essential (and easily overlooked) characteristic of the apophatic nature of "the mystical": that it does *not* want to release us from this world (for a world-less heaven, or serene peace beyond the troubles of this material world), but that it wants this "Kingdom of Heaven" (RM, 72), as Whitehead says, to be *with* us, reinvigorating the process of the community of existence (ibid., 87).

Not unlike Plotinus' One, Whitehead's God is in this spot of inexhaustible novelty from which it constitutes relationality.[24] The apophatic God of Whitehead, named the *primordial nature*, is the All-One, present in all events as their very origin in the nothingness of their not yet (PR, 244). Note: The function of the apophatic is not a withdrawal from this world (leaving it to its own evil and robbing it of life to be transported to another one), but the *affirmation* of the relationality of the world.[25] This *reversal* of the meaning of the apophatic (although it is in odd consonance with Plotinus) finds "the mystical" not aiming at the *infinite*, but at the heart of the *finite* as the very *place* in which the infinite gains meaning, worth and importance.[26]

If "the mystical" is not identical with the apophatic, understood as a negative move of the not (yet), it is because it also negates the positivity that would be identified with the One. If it rather remains (at least for us) the undefined infinite that embraces all positions and negations, it has to be (conceptually) "equidistant" from the many *and* the one. It is *neither* one nor many, and hence, is the potential of novelty for either. It avoids identification not just by negation of any meaningful position, but by

22. Suchocki, *End of Evil*, ch. 8.
23. Faber, "Zeitumkehr," 180–205.
24. Plotinus, *Enneads*, V.2.1.
25. Refer to chapter 5, current volume.
26. Faber, "Infinite Movement."

affirming the wealth of these positions.[27] The coincidence of opposites of Nicolas of Cusa, for instance, is only *apparently* apophatic, but in fact (in its deeper essence) *universally affirmative* of the wealth of the multiplicity excluded by *any* unification.[28]

Unity is *always* exclusive, *except* only when it is affirming the very multiplicity which it emanates and collects. I take this to be the secret of Plotinus' One: "The One is all things and no one of them; the source of all things is not all things; all things are its possession—running back, so to speak, to it—or, more correctly, not yet so, they will be."[29] I take that to be empirically true for many religious traditions in their metaphysical imagination of the divine or ultimate reality.[30] And it is central to Whitehead so as to allow his thought to function as a transformational matrix between these traditions.[31] The apophatic "unity" of the not yet or God as "organ of novelty" (PR, 67) is the *universal affirmation of multiplicity* that any finite unification must exclude.[32]

In Whitehead's view, any finite event, by constituting meaning, must "valuate" everything in such a way that it *must always exclude* things from its process of unification—that makes it finite and worth *something*. Only the divine or ultimate reality is able to include and affirm *everything*, by envisioning it in light of its own infinite potential and regarding the body of realization in which the finite event was housed[33] and by complementing it with the excluded.[34] This is the aspect of God that Whitehead names the *consequent nature*, the all-receptive activity of God, saving everything that actually happens such that nothing may be lost (PR, 346).

"The mystical," for Whitehead, then, is complex and only inadequately identified with the apophatic, although it would be equally untrue to say that Whitehead does not know of the essentially (and exclusively) apophatic nature of "the mystical," in the first place. Paradoxically, both the apophatic "not yet," originating from the primordial nature *and* the universal affirmation of the actual *coincide* in Whitehead's notion of God. With God's primordial and consequent natures, Whitehead situates God at the spot of apophatic novelty and the universal affirmation of relationality,

27. Faber, "Whitehead at Infinite Speed," 39–72.

28. Faber, *God as Poet*, §40.

29. Plotinus, *Enneads*, V.2.1.

30. Momen, *Phenomenon of Religion*.

31. Faber, *God as Poet*, §32.

32. Faber, "Apocalypse in God," 64–96.

33. Maassen, *Gott*.

34. Ford, *Transforming Process Theism*.

at the same time.[35] Even more: both aspects become *mutually* apophatic and affirmative: apophatic novelty is the affirmation of the infinite potential space of a new becoming, and affirmation of the actual is an apophatic process of transformation of this actual in light of the All of all collected actualities in God's nature. The mystical Whitehead, we could say, is about *this* coincidence of opposites.

The Divine Matrix Revisited

As this "mystical" notion of God is itself related to a wider *multiplicity* of interconnected concepts, it will be the mystical use of this multiplicity that will allow us to address ultimacy as aiming at, appealing to, and being radiant of a universal peace of religious, spiritual, and philosophical traditions caring about this matter.[36] It is this *interrelated* mystical multiplicity which, in a still very formal sense, I name the "divine matrix."[37] While it resonates with Bracken's approach, it is based on a different perception of Whitehead's work and addresses different connections.[38] Yet, in the final analysis, it lays out, as for Bracken, an ontological and an epistemological approach to ultimacy that facilitates interreligious dialogue between different traditions, demonstrating their ultimate communicability, although not suppressing their mutually surprising novelty.[39]

To begin with Bracken's "divine matrix": It is based on perhaps the most profound "contextualization" of Whitehead's notion of God in his own work, as it appears in his differentiation between God and creativity.[40] While the mystical flux of life in and out of primordial and consequent nature, of future instigation of becoming (breathing out) and of the reception of the actual happenings as they pass (breathing in), remind us of Plotinus' circle of creation and salvation, Whitehead, in an irritating move, and perhaps contrary to many theistic and non-theistic traditions (though not Plotinus!), does *not* identify the One with its own activity (of breathing),[41] but differentiates it as *creativity*—as the mystical breath of God that extends and rebounds *beyond* the divinity.[42]

35. Faber, *God as Poet*, §§28–29.
36. Griffin, *Deep Religious Pluralism*.
37. Faber, *God as Poet*, postscript.
38. Faber, *God as Poet*, part III.
39. Faber, *God as Poet*, §32.
40. Bracken, *Divine Matrix*, 4.
41. Neville, *God and Creativity*.
42. Cobb and Griffin, *Process Theology*, ch. 3.

Bracken uses Whitehead's solution of the mystical contextualization of God, in which the *activity* of creativity is not exhausted by God and, hence, is not only God's "nature," but the genuinely inherent activity of *all* creatures alike, thereby emphasizing the formal difference between God *as actuality* and *as universal activity* (of Godself and all else).[43] The "connection" of this differentiation exhibits yet another characteristic of "the mystical" in Whitehead—besides apophatic novelty and affirmative relationality—namely, that of *non-duality*. In fact, in many mystical and philosophical writings of eastern and western religious traditions, non-duality appears in such a form that, thereby, their notions of the ultimate *transcend* the difference between subject and object.[44] Yet *this* transcendence is, at the same time, its non-dual *closeness* to the transcended. What transcends *our* striving for the divine in the *object* of this striving "names" the unnamable of this transcendence *as* its immanence that is closer to any of its creatures than they are to themselves.[45]

Suddenly, the differentiations in East and West between God and Godhead (as in Eckhart), God and ground of God (as in Schelling), *Dasein* and *Sein* (as in Heidegger), *brahman* and *atman* (as in the *Bhagavad Gita)*, Saguna and Nirguna Brahman (as in Advaita Vedanta), the named and un-namable *tao* (as in the *Tao Te Ching)*, *samsara* and *nirvana* (as in Nagarjuna) or *pratitya-samutpada* and *tathagatagarbha* (as in Mahayana Buddhism), the non-dual togetherness of personal and the hyper-personal divine or ultimate, all fall into place.[46] Nevertheless, in exploring the examples from East and West, Bracken—and many others with him who have used this model[47]—is faced with a serious problem. Whitehead apodictically avoids identifying creativity as divine;[48] quite contrarily, he presupposes the very *secularity* of this metaphysical ultimate so as to allow him to generate a new understanding of the creative self-becoming of all actualities as their *own* activity,[49] which releases God from being identified with the oppressive powers.[50] However, as it is per se *not* destructive (RM, 96), it helps to secure a *new gentle conceptualization* of the "power" of God and the creatures that re-leases our temptations to use it in oppressive ways. As God is the "primordial

43. Bracken, *Divine Matrix*, ch. 4.

44. Huxley, *Perennial Philosophy*.

45. Griffin, *Deep Religious Pluralism*.

46. Bracken, *Divine Matrix*, chs. 3, 5–7.

47. Griffin, "Religious Pluralism," 3–38.

48. Griffin, *Reenchantment*, ch. 7.

49. Faber, "'Über Gott und die Welt," 118–42.

50. Case-Winters, *God's Power*.

superject of creativity" (PR, 32) in Whitehead's language, this means that God's activity is precisely the *prime effect* on a formless creativity that *characterizes its creativeness* instead of its destructiveness.[51] *This* "power" can only effectuate an *ideal* lure for creatures, *arousing* potentials for actualization; *deciding* among them remains the creative activity of the creatures, and their response may be creative or destructive (RM, 155–56).

It is for this divine *structuring* that Bracken turns to the term of the "divine matrix," and this is where his concept begins to differ from mine.[52] Bracken seeks to secure *in* this universal activity (that he identifies with the Godhead, *Sein, nirguna brahman,* and *dharmakaya*), which is per se formless (PR, 20) and blind, a *structural termination of divine origin and content* that will *inherently* include a saving relationship with all existents because of its very non-duality.[53] It must embrace all actualities, shaping it into its own *structured activity* in order to propel them forward and ever deeper into a "divine society" of which this matrix forms the *common structural field* of creation and salvation alike.[54] This is the reason that Bracken, instead of seeking the common mystical, that is, formless ground of novelty and relationality, coordinates Whitehead's formless creativity with the "extensive continuum" (PR, 61), Whitehead's notion for the structured *field of continuity*[55] that spans its realm *with* the actual happenings, stores their structural relationships, and defines the powers of their effective future in the mirror of their past accomplishments or failures.[56]

While Bracken's "matrix" is really a *structured* field—in his specific Catholic analysis representing the common divine essence of the Trinity[57]—my own rendering of the "divine matrix" strives for the *unbecoming* of such structural limitations: an un-structuring field of *pure life* or spirit, engendering nothing short of a process of an ontological "unknowing" of ourselves into the unknowable mystical/divine reality along the lines of Meister Eckhart and Nicolas of Cusa.[58] If we were allowed *not* to seek for notions of *order* as the primal goal of mystical analysis of Whitehead's text, but instead find its prime expression in *apophatic novelty,* then we will find

51. Faber, *God as Poet,* §§27–28.

52. Faber, *God as Poet,* §§30–32.

53. Bracken, "Energy-events and Fields," 153–65.

54. Bracken, *Society and Spirit.*

55. Nobo, *Metaphysics.*

56. Bracken, *The One and the Many,* part II.

57. Bracken, "Process Philosophy and Trinitarian Theology," 217–30; "Process Philosophy and Trinitarian Theology-II," 83–96.

58. Faber, *Prozeßtheologie,* part IV; Faber "'Gottesmeer.'"

a very different mystical matrix of non-duality, namely, *a nexus of mutual immanence that defines itself not through structures, but as process of pure life*.[59] This, in my work, is the "divine matrix" as the realm of the spirit.[60] And it is the multiplicity of indications of appearances that this mystical spirit makes in Whitehead's work that for me, instead of its structural definition and limitation, creates the aura of a real "matrix" of interreligious transformation, as it engenders the very potentials of a *lived* (religious, interreligious and universal) *peace from* the mystical/formless (or hyperformal) *life-process of* essential relationality.[61]

The Khoric Manifold of Life

In my approach, "matrix" is a misnomer: it is not a structure, but that which un-structures or cannot be captured by structure. All of Whitehead's ultimate notions harbor such a force of un-structuring, and it is precisely this force that makes them the center of "the mystical Whitehead." Embracing apophatic novelty, renewing relationality, and non-duality—the three basic elements of Whitehead's mysticism (as mentioned before)—they flow together in the complex notion of *khora* or emptiness. I have written extensively on this matter elsewhere and will confine myself here only to immediately necessary hints.[62]

Plato's notion of *khora* or space (emptiness) appears in Whitehead's analysis of its alternative Platonic name, *hypodoche* (receptacle), ultimately in three interconnected areas in *Adventures of Ideas*, which immediately generate the main characteristics of my understanding of "the mystical life" in Whitehead's work. The first context introduces *khora* as the notion of ultimate relationality, as the space that, since it is empty of itself, harbors the intercommunication of everything (AI, 134). The second context introduces *khora* as formless receptive power harboring the life of events as they happen such that it becomes the very expression of what "personhood" means: namely, a formless unity of a strain of happenings in the universe closely interrelated, but ultimately, as an expression of unity in the universe per se, only a focal point of universal intercommunication (ibid., 187). In its third appearance, *khora* names *the* ultimate of ultimates; that which remains if one strips everything else (physically and metaphysically) from

---

59. Faber, "O bitches," 200–219.

60. Refer to chapter 8, current volume.

61. Faber, *God as Poet*, §§26, 38.

62. Faber, "Khora and Violence," 105–26; *God as Poet*, §§15–16, 24, 32, 40, postscript; Faber, *Prozeßtheologie*.

the scheme of existence; that which is the ultimate condition of becoming and being, unity and multiplicity; that which, beyond all laws and rules, is unavoidable for any kind of existence: namely, the *mutual immanence* of everything with everything (ibid., 201).

Mutual immanence is, in fact, "the mystical" in Whitehead.[63] As intimation of the formless nexus of everything with everything as being the *condition* for any kind of order, it is not even mere (or pure) chaos, since it is essentially *relationality*. Therefore, *khora* is not the opposite of process, as in mere receptivity instead of activity, or inertia instead of activation, since it hinders no process, no novelty or *apophasis*. It does not resist creative change, but facilitates and propels it, such that Whitehead also names it "transcendent creativity" (PR, 88), that which carries the memory of factual happenings beyond themselves (their Selves) into a transcending and transcendent future.[64] Other than Brackens *constructed* togetherness of creativity and extensive continuum (as it never appears directly in Whitehead's text), Whitehead, indeed, relates *khora* and creativity himself in the last pages of *Adventures of Ideas*. As the mystical, that is, non-dual connection, the activity of un-structuring becoming is *non-different* from (but not identical with) any becoming (as its activity), but also *non-different* from (but not identical with) the All as involved in that particular becoming (the "adventures of the Universe as One"), as well as *non-different* from (but not identical with) the divine ideal, that is, the Eros and lure of final Beauty that instigates and collects this whole process (AI, 295–96).

If one looks closely enough, one will find *khora* mirrored in a manifold of Whitehead's concepts in which it reflects "the mystical (life)" (PR, 248). Perhaps the most obvious example is the concept of the "entirely living nexus" (ibid., 105) in *Process and Reality*. It stands for the *formless relationality* of a nexus that is "characterized" *only* by its activity of creativity, that is, its *apophatic novelty as it is communicated* among the members of this nexus. Here, amidst all structural limitation of organization of organisms, "the mystical" appears as *coinciding* with the life of a nexus whose life-spirit it is to become what it is (will be) from an origin that is entirely beyond structure and, hence, in the most intense way its organism's life as togetherness of novelty and relationality.

Once discovered, this "pattern" of un-structuring appears at the heart of all of Whitehead's ultimate concepts and notions. Creativity is formless and, hence, the non-different activity of all actualities (PR, 20–22). In the same way, God's natures are "empty," that is, *formlessly alive:* the primordial

---

63. Faber, *Prozeßtheologie*, §21
64. Garland, "The Ultimacy of Creativity," 212–38.

nature is not a set of ideas (eternal objects), but a relational life of divine valuation relative to every becoming (ibid., 31–32); the consequent nature is not a historical record of what has happened, but a transformation of the actual in light of its (missed) potentials and in light of its interrelationality with everything else in God's nature or the "kingdom of heaven."[65] Hence, even the superjective "impregnation" of the formless creativity through God's activity—by the "objective immortality" of the two divine natures (PR, 32)—is not conveying a fixed character, but releases the love that God has gathered (in light of the unfathomable wisdom it was evaluated by) anew into every new event of the world as *their* apophatic novelty that renews their relationality, which again enlivens the space of intercommunication with which we began these considerations (ibid., 351).

This khoric, formless life of the divine spirit expresses a unique "one-ness," namely that of the *affirmation of unrestricted multiplicity*: the mul-tiplicity of the forgotten, the excluded, the least one (PR, Postscript). This "oneness" is the unrestricted, infinite, and in this sense, *divine affirmation of difference*.[66] Borrowing "divine names" from Nicolas of Cusa, we could say that the divine matrix is *the coincidence of opposites* that characterizes the khoric manifold of the life of the spirit as "oneness" of all opposites. It does not indicate a balance of antagonistic terror, but only healing complexity. Moreover, in its utmost transcendence being *non-aliud* (non-other), this "oneness" shows itself as non-difference between opposites (such as identity and difference) by, at the same time, pointing at the mystical source and col-lective center of *reconciliation* of all opposites in the world.[67] In this sense, the divine matrix is the reconciled non-difference of the life of the spirit that differs from the world in which all differences are laid out and identities are mutually exclusive.[68] Yet on a deeper level, even this mystical *unity* ad-dresses the *reconciled* non-difference of the difference between the "divine matrix" *and* the multiplicity within the world of opposites.

Nicolas of Cusa envisions this coincidence *not* as static divine beyond the finite universe, but as dynamic breath of the spirit, as breathing out or unfolding or *explication of* the hidden wealth of the divine and as breath-ing in or enfolding or *complication* of the infinite multiplicity of its reflec-tions of its own formlessness into the non-difference of the khoric life.[69] In

---

65. Suchocki, "The Anatman and the Consequent Nature."

66. Faber, "Infinite Movement"; "O bitches"; "Introduction: Negotiating Becoming," 1–49.

67. Faber, "De-Ontologizing God."

68. Faber, "De-Ontologizing God."

69. Keller, *Face of the Deep*, chs. 11–13.

Whitehead's text, this spiritual dynamic of the "divine matrix" is expressed by *non-difference between God and the world*. Summarizing his famous Six Antitheses at the end of *Process and Reality* with the last one—"It is as true to say that God creates the World, as that the World creates God" (PR, 348)[70]— Whitehead demonstrates not only that we *cannot make any difference between any predicate* that could be "characteristic" to God in difference from the world, but also that this non-difference between God and the world is of a *creative dynamism of in/differentiation* in which "God and the World are the contrasted opposites in terms of which Creativity achieves its supreme task of transforming disjoined multiplicity, with its diversities in opposition, into concrescent unity, with its diversities in contrast" (PR, 348).

This is the concept of the "divine matrix" I develop in my work, namely, the ultimacy of the mutual immanence of the manifold in the process of in/ differentiation, the dynamic process of the mutual immanence of the *enfolding of* any difference of difference and identity in the *unfolding* of itself *in* the differences of differences and identities.[71]

Mystical Unbecoming

While Bracken's "divine matrix" addresses the *structural pattern* of a non-duality of divine (creative) activity besides the duality of the "entities" of God and the world,[72] it is my intention with the breathing spirit of khoric life to *avoid* the remaining dualism of non-dual ultimate reality and a world of opposites. In my understanding, Bracken's activity of creativity that stands for non-difference (between God and the world) remains in *structural distance* from the difference it implies from God and the world alike. Conversely, I am seeking the non-structural life that is *the non-different spring of the very difference of actuality and activity*.[73] Other than Bracken,[74] I want to name *the source of the remaining difference* between the non-difference of divine actuality and creative activity, on the one hand, and the difference between all of them in the world, on the other.[75] This is where I find Plotinus' One meaningful (as nothingness of the All) and Cusa's non-difference of non-difference and difference insightful. Both of them name the *spiritual breath of in/differentiation* as the *mutual immanence* of the manifold of its elements

70. Cf. Faber, *God as Poet*, §31.
71. Faber, *God as Poet*, §40
72. Bracken, *Divine Matrix*, chs. 4–5.
73. Faber, *Prozeßtheologie*, §31.
74. Refer to chapter 10, current volume.
75. Faber, "De-Ontologizing God."

of ultimacy as they are oscillating because of their immanent dialectic of emptiness and wealth, nothingness and the All.[76] It is this emptiness and nothingness of khoric life that is the ultimate balance of the dynamic of breathing out and breathing in, of becoming and un-becoming.[77]

This leads me to a last "characteristic" of "the mystical"—*nothing-ness*. It names a last hindrance for understanding Whitehead as a mystical thinker, because Whitehead abhors "nothingness."[78] Nevertheless, in my view, nothingness (even in Whitehead) is that which is (always already) presupposed in exploring the manifold notions of the divine matrix: *Khora* is nothing, or empty, so as to be the unobstructed, activating receptacle of becoming and relationality (PR, 134–35); creativity is protean activity (RM, 92), empty of itself (PR, 21); God's natures are empty of self-interest and distortion, yet full of affirmation and transformation;[79] the realm of potentials is empty, it has no structure but offers itself as mere multiplicity for any arrangement wished for; actualities are empty insofar as they con-stitute themselves from relations to other actualities, potentials, creativity and God, from the apophatic nothingness of their Selves. Yet, Whitehead rejects the notion of nothingness.[80]

Yet, in Whitehead's final view on mysticism, "the mystical" becomes an expression of "nothingness," situated in the heart of his whole philosophy, namely, at the apophatic place of the nothingness of novelty (RM, 174). This is the spot where God resides (PR, 67), as formless life (ibid., 339) out of which creativity acts (ibid., 21) and in which all of them coincide (in/differ-ently) in their mutual apophatic "grip of the ultimate metaphysical ground, the creative advance into novelty" (ibid., 349)—the highest expression of self-emptying nothingness (and, at the same time, of the infinite wealth of foldings upon foldings).

A second look, however, reveals that Whitehead's understanding of nothingness is much more complicated and, thereby, opens a space for its mystical interpretation.[81] Two sentences seem to end the discussion on "nothingness" in Whitehead before it has even begun. "Nonentity is noth-ingness" (PR, 36) and "you cannot approach nothing; for there is nothing to approach" (ibid., 93). Neither can there be a creation from nothing (AI, 236), nor can "fact . . . float into the world out of nonentity" (PR, 46) or

76. Faber, "Tears of God," 57–103.

77. Faber, "Immanence and Incompleteness," 91–107.

78. Cobb and Ives, *The Emptying God*.

79. Suchocki, *God, Christ, Church*, part II.

80. Faber, *Prozeßtheologie*, §33.

81. Odin, *Process Metaphysics and Hua-Yen Buddhism*.

anything be said besides "actual entities, because besides actual entities there is nothing, mere nonentity—"The rest is silence'" (ibid., 43). Yet, on the other hand, it is the nonentity of "creativity" (ibid., 21), which is the very activity of actualities that only because of its own emptiness, that is, its own nonentity, fulfills its function as all-pervasive ultimate. The same could be said for *khora*, the "realm" of possibilities, which as pure multiplicity is nonentity (ibid., 31) or of God's consequent nature in which all actualities are becoming a "consequent multiplicity" of salvation (ibid., 349). In fact, instead of signifying an empty notion without meaning, nothingness/nonentity names the *apophatic origin/nature of becoming* at the heart of all of Whiteheads notions of ultimacy.[82] Hence, "nothingness" is, in its own *apophatic* way, an integral part of the divine matrix or the process of in/differentiation or mutual immanence.[83]

The meaning of its apophatic nature becomes obvious when we follow the process of un/becoming in Whitehead more closely. In Meister Eckhart, "unbecoming" means the spiritual breathing in by which the world of differences (including God) un-becomes *when we follow it backwards into the Godhead*, against the gist of its de facto becoming, into its non-difference from/within the Godhead.[84] In Whitehead, we can do the same by *inversing the arrow of becoming*, in which creativity operates as generating a multiplicity in becoming of the one and the many. But when we *reverse* the process,[85] we ask: What happened *before* the many became one? What *was* the event that just will happen if it will happen? What we find, in Whitehead's analysis is interesting: we find a "disjunctive multiplicity" (PR, 21) and an urge of the past to propel itself beyond itself;[86] we find a sphere of possibilities projected into the future of what a new event might look like (AI, chapter 12); and we find an "initial aim" from God's primordial nature of what a potential becoming might be like (PR, 244). The creative act that issues from these (future) ingredients is—a *mystery!* It is utterly unknown (yet) and, hence, in principle utterly unknowable (ibid., 4)—and yet, it happens. The question of how events happen out of nonentity is, *asked in reverse*, to ask for following the event in its *unbecoming* of itself into its "before," its nonentity, its "not yet having begun to become," its true nothingness, in which it was *enfolded* before it became.

82. Faber, *Prozeßtheologie*, §§31, 33.

83. Faber, *God as Poet*, §40.

84. McGinn, *The Mystical Thought of Meister Eckhart.*

85. Faber, *God as Poet*, 190.

86. Frankenberry, "The Power of the Past," 132–42.

From this insight, we can now build a chain of unbecoming from Whitehead's divine matrix into the heart of the mystery of nonentity, nothingness, or in/difference in its *utter enfoldment in itself,* hidden in its own mystery. This is the mystery of the nonentity that is *unmanifest.* It is, as the Islamic *hadith* says, a "hidden treasure" before its inception or after its evanescence.[87]

What is an event *after* it has unbecome and perishes into the world and into God since it is not anymore itself and its Self is beyond itself only in divine perception? It "un-becomes," it "un-manifests," in/differentiates, enfolds itself (again) in the consequent nature of God. Yet, what is the consequent nature of God *before* it perceives any such actuality into itself? It *is not,* is not manifest, "is" nonentity, or nothingness, "is (not)" an enfolded mystery of itself. And what is an actuality *before* its becoming of its Self? It is unmanifest, routed in the primordial nature of God, enshrouded in its nothingness of becoming, in/different from God's call into becoming.[88] And what is the primordial nature *before* it evaluates potentials for new becomings? It is *unmanifest.* And what happens before the primordial act of the envisagement of eternal objects happens? Whitehead says that, since the "general relationships of eternal objects to each other, relationships of diversity and of pattern, are their relationships in God's conceptual realization," that "[a]part from this realization, there is mere isolation indistinguishable from nonentity" (PR, 257). What unbecomes or enfolds or in/differentiates in this act? Everything—unbecoming nothing! *Before* the act of divine synthesis, no eternal objects are differentiated from nonentity. Since this is the *first* creative act of God (we can still "name"), there is no creativity yet that would be "characterized" by the divine superject. Since creative act and ideal form are not yet differentiated, before this act, no God can be named.[89] God has unbecome! But has God disappeared in this "nothingness"? Or is *this* nothingness *the* ultimate reality because it is, in its essence, unmanifest, enfolded, enshrouded in the "hidden treasure" beyond/before/in any articulation?

While *this* mystery is the silence before the word, utter in/difference—yet, at the same time, it is *nothing but* the mystery of becoming. In/differentiation is the "at one-ness" or the "at one-ness" of becoming and unbecoming, manifestation and un-manifestation, unfolding and enfolding, explication

---

87. Corbin, *Alone with the Alone.*

88. Faber, *God as Poet,* §20.

89. Ford, "Neville on the One and the Many," 79–84; Faber, *Prozeßtheologie,* §34; *God as Poet,* §35.

and complication.[90] Moreover, it is their mutual immanence in which all mu-tuality finds its origin and nature. Although we might think of the unmanifest ultimate or divine as utter nothingness *or* enfolded wealth (both positions are held throughout the history of eastern and western philosophy and theol-ogy), we might also say that "it"—in either of its interpretations—is "nothing" without its manifestation or unfolding.[91] Even if, as in Plotinus, the unmani-fest One is needless and without possession[92]—and in this sense is indepen-dent of its manifestations—its effluence and manifestation is a necessity of its utter perfection.[93] And even more: It remains *nothing in* its manifestations or, conversely, its manifestations are "nothing" in relation to the utter wealth of the enfolded nothingness of the unmanifest One.[94]

In the sense in which this apophatic in/differentiation enfolds mutual immanence, we should take the mystical Whitehead very seriously—the one that claims that "God is the primordial creature" and "at once a crea-ture of creativity and a condition for creativity," a "double character" that God shares "with all creatures" (PR, 31). In the divine matrix, everything conditions and evokes everything. The divine matrix is their co-arising. Hence, in all expressions of mutual immanence, reciprocity and its dynam-ics of oscillation, we should hear the *mystical* Whitehead *speaking* when he says that "there is no meaning to 'creativity' apart from its 'creatures,' and no meaning to 'God' apart from the 'creativity' and the 'temporal crea-tures,' and no meaning to the 'temporal creatures' apart from 'creativity' and 'God'" (ibid., 225).

---

90. Faber, *God as Poet*, §35.
91. Faber, "Immanence and Incompleteness."
92. Plotinus, *Enneads*, V.2.1.
93. Plotinus, *Enneads*, V.1.6.
94. Plotinus, *Enneads*, V.1.7.2.

CHAPTER TWO

A New Mystagogy of Becoming

ALFRED NORTH WHITEHEAD'S WORK exists, it seems, always anew, only in the form of its rediscovery. In fact, it is self-situated in between philosophy, science, and religion in such a form that it always arises in their interstices, today especially (as odd as it might seem) in the context of both poststructuralist philosophy and theology.[1] What at first glance looks dangerously inoperable and mutually exclusive has lead me to think intensively about the rhizomatic connections between Whitehead and Deleuze, on the one hand, and points of contact "at the interstices" of poststructuralism and theology, on the other.[2]

Given that these relations of renewal have recently gained some excellent attention,[3] addressing the strange mutual attraction between French philosophies and matters of metaphysics and theology,[4] the Deleuzian potential of Whitehead,[5] the subversive poststructuralist strand in Whitehead's work,[6] and a poststructuralist sensibility for the (ancient) theological dimensions of philosophy,[7] I want to explore further whether, and if so, in what sense, the work of Whitehead and Deleuze resonate in this mutually reactive multiplicity. It will be my thesis that a mutually attractive trace of mystical language remains vital in both Whitehead and Deleuze and that it must not be viewed as a contamination of their thought by dogmatics, but

---

1. Faber, *Prozeßtheologie*.

2. Faber, "O bitches."

3. Robinson, *Deleuze, Whitehead, Bergson*; Faber, Krips, and Peltus, *Event and Decision*; Faber and Stephenson, *Secrets of Becoming*.

4. Caputo, *Prayers and Tears of Jacques Derrida*.

5. Williams, *Encounters and Influences*, ch. 5.

6. Bracken, *The One and the Many*, ch. 3.

7. Keller, *Face of the Deep*; Faber, *God as Poet*.

as a genuine expression of their respective philosophies.[8] I will further explore whether the *theoria* of their philosophies of becoming also indicates a new experiential and experimental praxis (a philosophical life)—in the sense of a mystagogy of becoming.

The Platonic Trilemma

The first thing to recognize about the strange triangle of connections indicated before, in which to situate the resonance of Whitehead and Deleuze and to detect the novelty of Whitehead's philosophical reception today, is that it is not a new turn of things at all. It rather indicates the very story of the birth of (Greek) philosophy as such. Since Plato's differentiation of two discourses from philosophy proper—namely *theology* and *sophism*—this birthplace must be considered a constitutive, although strained triangular relationship. While Plato considered poetry (with theology), the articulation of the divine (from myths of the old ages), as precisely that which philosophy has to tame and overcome,[9] he fought sophism as a powerful opponent of philosophy.[10] Ironically, both have survived and remained unloved sisters of philosophy ever since. While, at one point, theology not only married itself to philosophy, but also made it an instrument of dogmatics,[11] sophism has reappeared as philosophy precisely in the form of the relativism and pluralism of certain postmodern modes of thought.[12]

In this triangle, the watershed between Whitehead and Deleuze appears to be Whitehead's stubborn clinging to the poetic moment of transcendence (and the divine as its expression) as a vital element of philosophy,[13] while Deleuze became profoundly convinced that theological language has to be eradicated because it negates precisely what defines philosophy—namely, immanence itself.[14] On the other hand, Deleuze seems to embrace the relativism of the sophistic attitude toward truth that Plato despised,[15] hence shifting the epicenter of the force field again.

Nevertheless, things are far from being that obvious. Doesn't Deleuze curiously engage philosophers who were far from abandoning divinity?

8. Refer to chapter 5, current volume.
9. Naddaff, *Exiling the Poets*, 3.
10. Noburu, *Unity of Plato's Sophist*.
11. Celenza, "The Revival of Platonic Philosophy," 73.
12. Pickstock, *After Writing*, 47.
13. Stengers, *Thinking with Whitehead*, ch. 24.
14. Bell, *Philosophy at the Edge of Chaos*, ch. 6.
15. Deleuze, *Difference and Repetition*, 66–69.

Hasn't he studied medieval philosophy and learned to value mysticism through his teacher Maurice de Gandillac?[16] And isn't his invocation of, for instance, Spinoza and John Duns Scotus indicating a kind of theological discourse in its own right?[17] Conversely, hasn't Whitehead studied theology over many years and then left it disappointed because of its dogmatic presuppositions?[18] Doesn't Whitehead always warn us against introducing God only to justify our little metaphysical systems (see RM, 148–49)? And isn't Whitehead always suspicious of transcendence in light of his emphasis on immanence (see AI, 236)?

In fact, on second thought, Whitehead and Deleuze form a strange alliance in how they articulate the Platonic trilemma of philosophy, theology and sophism. They do not give them up, but rather affirm all of their spheres: thought (the creation of concepts), mystery (the ineffable), and multiplicity (the khoric space). While Whitehead is still widely conceived as a rationalist with inclinations toward theology, he is, in fact, a profound pluralist for whom there is no ultimate order preforming becoming, but ultimate fluency that, hence, expresses a deep mystery that can never be rationalized.[19] Deleuze, on the other hand, although conceived as a poststructuralist pluralist, in his turn never gave up interest in systematic thought[20] and never feared to engage theologians and mystical thinkers like Duns Scotus, Nicolas of Cusa, and the like.[21] Things are complicated, indeed!

Finally, in direct reception, Deleuze always exhibits a deep appreciation of Whitehead's empiricism and pluralism,[22] Whitehead's categoreal scheme with its creative relativism,[23] the strange "vitalism" that connects both philosophies (PR, 102),[24] and even Whitehead's profoundly processual divinity in a processual world.[25] Whitehead was, in a new form, embracing the whole force field, and Deleuze did not deny the creativity of this move but instead mapped out its complexity and great importance for the formulation of his own work.[26]

---

16. Deleuze, *Two Regimes of Madness*, 262.

17. Deleuze, *Expressionism in Philosophy*.

18. Price, *Dialogues of Alfred North Whitehead*, 6.

19. Faber, "Surrationality and Chaosmos," 157–77.

20. Deleuze, *Negotiations*, 135–55.

21. Deleuze and Guattari, *What Is Philosophy?*, ch. 2.

22. Deleuze, *Two Regimes of Madness*, 304.

23. Deleuze, *Difference and Repetition*, 284–85.

24. Deleuze, *Negotiations*, 143.

25. Deleuze, *Fold*, 81.

26. Faber, "Whitehead," 302–4.

The Ultimacy of Becoming

If there is a focus revealing the synchronicity of their philosophies, it is probably their claim of the ultimacy of becoming over against all metaphysical principles, cosmological orders, or epistemological categories.[27] Whitehead articulates this ultimacy of becoming with his concept of "creativity"—as "the ultimate behind all forms" (PR, 20) that "makes process ultimate" (PR, 7). Deleuze again engages the concept of "difference for that which cannot be repeated as order and, at the same time, is what alone repeats as difference itself.[28]

Insofar as their respective philosophies of becoming integrate the Platonic trilemma of philosophy, mysticism, and pluralism, they profoundly transform its meaning to express a resistance against three of its original characteristics: unquestionable givenness of presuppositions, preordained order, and determined teleology. Instead, "becoming" gears toward three alternatives: infinite process (never beginning, never ending, never settling), chaos (movement "beyond" all organization), and immanence (without transcendently controlled aims).[29]

If we ask, "Why becoming?" the answer is as simple as it is surprising. "Becoming" is not primarily set against "being" as stabilization of power, logocentric order, the illusion of ultimate structures, or the preformation of reality. Although these reasons are prominent in poststructuralist discourse, both Whitehead and Deleuze have a different agenda. Their motivation is a metaphysical one—the conceptualization of novelty.[30]

While Whitehead's "creativity" *is* the "principle of novelty (PR, 21), Deleuze redefines the whole philosophic project by reversing its quest from "attain[ing] eternity"—which remained its very motivation despite the Platonic expulsion of poetry/theology—to its radical reversal: "the production of novelty." Despite the different reorganization of the classical Platonic triangle, it is essential for both philosophers that the "best of all worlds is not one that reproduced the eternal, but the one in which new creations are produced, the one endowed with the capacity for . . . creativity." Deleuze understands this shift as nothing less than "a teleological conversion of philosophy."[31]

---

27. Faber, "Introduction: Negotiating Becoming," 1–49.
28. Deleuze, *Desert Islands*, 32–51.
29. Faber, "O bitches."
30. Faber, "Whitehead at Infinite Speed."
31. Deleuze, *Fold*, 79.

The Shakespearian Question

Since "philosophy of becoming" not only expels the theological from the philosophical, but also the theological quest—the search for Truth—from the philosophical by becoming more akin to sophistic relativism, the grounding power of "transcendence" and "vertical Being"[32] must fade, and philosophy of becoming must find consolation in Nietzsche's divination of becoming itself against the forces of "being." After this conversion we never go back behind Nietzsche's "Death of God."[33] How could we ever again want to reestablish any (language of a) "divinity" expressing givenness, order, and teleology instead of becoming, novelty, and creativity? Eternity versus novelty—this is the Shakespearian philosophical question. This alternative most certainly forces us to side with either affirming or excluding novelty or eternity and hence to affirm "divinity" in, or to expel it from, the philosophical endeavor. This seems again, after Plato, to become a question of self-identity of the philosophical project.

Yet, while Deleuze, on first glance, seems to draw this conclusion, Whitehead obviously ignores the whole framework of mutually exclusive alternatives and—ironically—in a Deleuzian-empiricist manner says "Yes, AND."[34] In fact, Whitehead avoids the alternative by understanding divinity as the very expression of creativity whereby it becomes a moment of the metaphysical situation of the production of novelty—not its enemy.[35] Whitehead had a price to pay: not only did it ruin his reputation among philosophers; against all theological dogmatics, it also radically altered his understanding of divinity—from transcendent substance to an event of immanence, from an eternal being to a process of becoming, from a *logos* of compatible order to an *eros* "affirm[ing] incompossibilities."[36]

Athough Whitehead and Deleuze may differ on how to evaluate novelty in relation to the very possibility of any affirmative language regarding divinity, in viewing novelty as the signature of a world of infinite becoming, they *remain aware of the "place" where divinity has left the stage* and in its disappearance (or its "disfiguration" from the standpoint of classical theology and theistic philosophy), left a trace that still must be addressed. It is crucial to note that this "place" is important for Whitehead and Deleuze *not* as a site to wage an old battle for the reinstatement of eternity in

32. Deleuze and Guattari, *What Is Philosophy?*, 43.

33. Deleuze, *Nietzsche*, 152–56.

34. Deleuze, *Difference and Repetition*, 57.

35. Faber, *God as Poet*, pt. 3.

36. Deleuze, *Fold*, 81.

the form of any notion of divinity, or even by reinstating "theology," but rather because of its philosophical function: it remains a moment of the constitution of novelty, and conversely, it is here, within the demands of the paradigm of genuine novelty, that traces of this "place" in the evocation of mystical language resurface.

Therefore Whitehead identifies the function of novelty *as* novelty in his philosophy with the perhaps at first surprising claim that it is that by which "philosophy is mystical" as he defines mysticism as "direct insight into depths as yet unspoken"—that is, as the evocation of the unprecedented (MT, 174). Deleuze, on the other hand, addresses these depths of novelty with his concept of "pure difference,"[37] which, in only repeating itself, creates "that which cannot be replaced." It differentiates "non-exchangeable and non-substitutable singularities,"[38] which cannot represent anything given or eternal. Yet, such novelty needs a language that employs the traces of the disappearance of eternity (even in the form of repetition).

In fact, Deleuze articulates novelty in a language with mystical allusions that hardly avoids reminiscing the language of Meister Eckhart, Nicolas of Cusa, and Giordano Bruno.[39] For one, he adopts *their* notion of the divine "movements in immanence—*complication* and *explication*."[40] But even more prominently, he grounds his whole book *The Fold* in the underlying mystical concept of the "fold" in order to make novelty feasible in a world of becoming. And it is in the midst of this move that, as we know, Deleuze's Whitehead appears.[41]

A dramatic example of this trace of mysticism of novelty can be found in *Difference and Repetition*, where Deleuze claims "pure difference" in a language that is nothing but an expression of the very function of mystical language—namely, to manifest the very differentiation of the ground (of thinking) *from* any difference that can be named (and hence already "is") and *from* mere non-difference of silence that would not be productive of a world philosophy wants to understand. Hence, in Deleuze's mystical account of pure difference, it means "a ground in relation to which it no longer matters whether one is before . . . a beginning or an end, since the two coincide in this ground which is like a single and unique 'total' moment, simultaneously the moment of evanescence and production of difference,

---

37. Deleuze, *Difference and Repetition*, 42.

38. Deleuze, *Difference and Repetition*, 1.

39. Deleuze, *Difference and Repetition*, 280–81; Deleuze and Guattari, *What Is Philosophy?*, 44–45.

40. Deleuze, *Two Regimes of Madness*, 261.

41. Deleuze, *Fold*, ch. 5.

of disappearance and appearance . . . the moment at which difference both vanishes and is produced."[42]

The Dilemma of Infinite Becoming

The connection between novelty and mysticism will become more obvious when we further explore the problem of genuine novelty in a world of in- finite becoming. In short, it is the function of the mystical articulation of infinite becoming (which both Whitehead and Deleuze employ) to save its inherent essence of novelty from a twofold neutralization (self-annihilation) into either mere temporality or eternity.

On the one hand, if infinite becoming has no *telos* or final state, every "state of affairs" must, in light of every new becoming, perish. How, in such a world of "perpetual perishing," can genuine novelty be expected when everything disappears in Heidegger's *lethe*, the stream of eternal oblivion![43] If there is no attainment in becoming, nothing can genuinely become some- thing of importance.[44]

On the other hand, if the world of becoming and perishing is seam- less, that is, if it is infinitely becoming and perishing, how can we say that it harbors anything creative at all? This is Nietzsche's problem of the eternal return. If an infinite process of becoming must repeat infinitely what it has created infinite times before, novelty is just an illusion (working as long as we keep our scope small enough).[45] We may well end up with Ecclesiastes' statement that "What has been is what will be; and what has been done is what will be done; there is nothing new under the sun."[46]

The question is: How can novelty escape these two pitfalls of perpetual perishing and worthlessness on the one hand, and eternal repetition of the same, on the other? The first neutralization demands an interpretation of novelty as *a kind* of persistence in the midst of change that allows for at- tainment; the second neutralization demands an interpretation of novelty as "production of new creatures." While the first qualification of novelty is *importance*, the second one is *creativeness*.

42. Deleuze, *Difference and Repetition*, 42; cf. Faber, "Infinite Movement."

43. Refer to chapter 3, current volume.

44. Heidegger's *a-letheia* addresses this rescue from eternal oblivion. Cf. Heidegger, "The Essence of Truth," 111–38.

45. This is the reason that Deleuze reinterprets Nietzsche's eternal return (also the "place" of the disappearance of the divine in a world of becoming) as prime expression of difference that aims at genuine novelty. Cf. Deleuze, *Desert Islands*, 117–27.

46. Ecclesiastes 1:9.

The Paradox of Life and Death

One way of solving these two neutralizations is barred: the invocations of eternity against which the paradigm of novelty was set. This implies that the mystery of genuine novelty in the world of infinite becoming cannot be articulated as a mystery of existence.

The *locus classicus* of this mystery is Wittgenstein's famous dictum in his *Tractatus* 6.44 that "It is not how things are in the world that is mystical, but that it exists." Since for both philosophers "becoming" is ultimate, "being" must always be an abstraction from becoming.[47] Hence, neither of them is interested in dividing reality into existence and essence or into Heidegger's ontological difference, for that matter.

Over and against Shakespeare's "to be or not to be," we find that Whitehead and Deleuze focus on novelty in the context of life and death. One the one hand, novelty is the event of life in a world of infinite becoming; on the other hand, however, since becoming is also always an infinite process of passing, it is a world of death. In fact, for Whitehead and Deleuze, the mystery of novelty addresses the coincidence of life and death.

For Whitehead, "Life is a bid for freedom"; the problem it presents is not "endurance" but "How can there be originality?" (PR, 104). It gains its pure expression in what Whitehead calls the "entirely living nexus," which is not an enduring structure "at all, since 'life' cannot be a defining characteristic. It is the name for originality, and not for tradition" (PR, 104); it constitutes an "element of chaos" (PR, 111). This is the paradox of life and death: the more vivacity organic structures develop, the more life becomes destructive of the organization protecting its chaotic nature (see PR, 103).

In confessing that his philosophy is about "events, life, and vitalism," Deleuze emphasizes bursts of "orgiastic" originality over against organic structure. It is "nonorganic life"[48]—rather than being the life of organisms, in its pure expression, it is their death. In fact, Deleuze acknowledges that "you can't ever reach it, you are forever attaining it, it is a limit,"[49] the very limit where life and death coincide, where difference "*as such* is cruelty"; where "all forms . . . cease," where "the ground rises to the surface" and "the human face decomposes."[50]

In so differentiating the mystery of novelty from the mystery of existence both Whitehead and Deleuze effectively undermine a theological

47. Roland Faber, "Tears of God."
48. Deleuze, *Negotiations*, 143.
49. Deleuze and Guattari, *Thousand Plateaus*, 150.
50. Deleuze, *Difference and Repetition*, 28.

language that unavoidable becomes part of Plato's affirmation of given-ness—the divine initiation of existence; preordained order—the divine realization of essence; and determined teleology—a divine set of final aims (see PR, 111).

However, in the assessment of this differentiation, Whitehead and Deleuze differ greatly. For Whitehead, embracing the mystery of novelty avoids the identification of the divine with eternity. Although Deleuze has recognized this Whiteheadian shift, in which "God desists from being a Be-ing" and "becomes Process,"[51] he resists such a move in order to avoid a corruption of novelty. While Whitehead's divinity now names the process of "intensity, and not preservation" (see PR, 105), for Deleuze it remains an "*illusion of transcendence*,"[52] tied to the paradigm of existence.

The Mutuality of Persistence and Creativeness

Nevertheless, their different assessment of what follows from the refusal of the mystery of existence does not yet explain their deeper synchronicity in expressing novelty with mystical language. This seems to be related to the fact that, on a deeper level, the extradition of the mystery of existence (the divine gift of existence) leaves a trace in the mystery of novelty that alerts us to the problems of *persistence* and *creativeness*. But, while in the paradigm of eternity they were tied to a divine coincidence of existence and essence and a contingent creation striving for eternity, in a paradigm of novelty they must be articulated in the coincidence of life and death.

If the coincidence of life and death means that it is chaos that "grounds a world of becoming in which genuine novelty can arise, it must also stand for the death of all organisms that harbor novelty in any meaningful sense.[53] Novelty out of chaos can only avoid this problem if it names something that is neither pure chaos nor pure eternity. That which allows chaos to generate novelty instead of sheer meaningless change, or infinite return of the same, is the mystery that "defines" novelty as such.

Let me explore what it must accomplish. First, it must avoid *worthless-ness* in the event of becoming. Second, it must avoid infinite repetition that equals an eternal sea of the same. Since it must address creativeness, the sought "worth" cannot be something that *actually* fulfills it eternally—an *actus purus*.[54] Given these parameters, it must achieve what Whitehead calls

51. Deleuze, *Fold*, 81.

52. Deleuze and Guattari, *What Is Philosophy?*, 49.

53. Deleuze, *Negotiations*, 143.

54. Ford, "Whitehead's Transformation of Pure Act," 381–99.

"novelty without loss" (PR, 340), or the "permanent elements apart from which there could be no changing world" (RM, 9).

In other words, if novelty is to be neither change nor repetition, it must be about attainment of worth in the midst of change that is not eternally pre-given. In the mist of the chaos of becoming, it must in a new way address a moment of persistence or importance; and in the midst of the infinity of becoming, it must articulate a moment of creative difference. In the paradigm of life and death, genuine novelty must name a creativeness that generates persistence and a persistence that generates creativeness.

Interestingly enough, both philosophers conceptualize a medium of "persistent creativeness" or "creative importance" that is neither a permanent loss of the Singular nor a permanent repetition of the Same. Whitehead calls this reality "Value" and Deleuze "Virtuality."[55] Their Shared function is to address precisely the horizon of novelty, the possibility of novelty as such, or the transcendental condition of the possibility of novelty.[56]

Value and Virtuality

It is significant that while Whitehead introduces the term "Value" affectively in the context of the concept of "the possible"—his infamous "eternal objects"[57]—Deleuze, from the first appearance of the "Virtual" on, juxtaposes it to "the possible."[58] However, if we follow the respective function of these terms in their philosophies, we will find that Whitehead's "eternal objects" precisely function *as* "virtualities" and conversely that Deleuze's "virtualities" *do not* subsume Whitehead's "eternal objects" under the otherwise rejected "possible." In fact, both Whitehead's "possibility" and Deleuze's "virtuality" address the problem of novelty in such a way that in both cases the *classical* notion of "the possible" is rejected.[59]

Deleuze juxtaposes the virtual to the possible because for him "possibility" is an expression of the paradigm of *existence*—that is, of the divorce of existence from an eternal essence in different modes of existence: it must be; it can be; it is in fact; it might be or is not or will be. Thereby, the possible

---

55. Only recently have scholars of Whitehead and Deleuze realized the close proximity of Whitehead's concept of "Value" and Deleuze's concept of "Virtuality." Regarding their respective function in their philosophies and the mutual connotations, see Faber, "De-Ontologizing God"; Williams, "Deleuze and Whitehead," 89–106.

56. Marks, *Gilles Deleuze*, ch. 4.

57. Kraus, *Metaphysics of Experience*, 43.

58. Deleuze, *Bergsonism*, 43.

59. See chapter 5, current volume.

preforms novelty by naming an already fixed "form" to which "existence" is added or from which it is subtracted.[60] This is the "possible" of classical universals—that is, representations of the Platonic forms of givenness, order, and preordained aims. Instead, Deleuze's "virtualities" are neither universals nor individuals, neither forms nor structures, but universal singularities, pure differences, multiplicities, infinitely moving, and thereby indicating the novelty of un-preformed events.[61]

Whitehead's "eternal objects," however, although they *seem* to indicate this realm of universals (essences) of which facts (existents) are only actual variations, in fact neither function as "forms," nor do they lack reality. On the contrary, they are "pure possibilities" insofar as they are real in their own right by being "unrealizable" as actualities.[62] Hence, they do not repeat the Platonic distinction of Idea and simulacrum, whereby the image appears only as a variation of the essence of the Idea (as many still misunderstand Whitehead's possibilities), but invoke a field of instigation of that which is *not* (or other than) a possibility, namely a concrescing actuality of actualities mediated by possibilities, which remain other, different (differentiating), and dispossessed. They can only be invited; they are real, but they do not "become" actual; and they are not wholly abstract (mere mental abstractions) either, but the very *relations* mediating actualities (cf. the structure of subjective forms in Whitehead, AI, 183).

Furthermore, Whitehead's "pure possibilities" are not in any way a master-plan for, or even like, a potential house built up from possible bricks where every free spot is plastered (another misunderstanding of Whitehead's possibilities). On the contrary, as infinity of pure possibilities (and their relations among themselves and to all actualities, as well as being these relationships), they cannot be fixed in any meaningful sense. Although they seem to be "complete," their completion is not finite (countable or uncountalbe) but comprises an *infinity* (of possibilities) which per definition cannot be circumscribed.[63] Since they cannot represent a pre-given order

60. Hardt, *Gilles Deleuze*, 16–17.

61. Besides the classical Platonic instantiation of this scheme of possibility, which *lacks* actuality but in actualization only "realizes" the essence of the possibility actualized, a contemporary affirmation of the possible is David Lewis's view of "possibilities" as the *actuality* of all possible worlds. Even if they do not indicate any preformed order, because of the infinity of actualized alternative worlds, they allow for no novelty at all: in this multiverse, every possibility is already realized and actual. In both cases, however, it is crucial that the possible is defined either as "realized" or "unrealized" while this "realization" of the actual possibility executes an eternal essence. Cf. Lewis, "Possible Worlds," 96–102 and Lycan, "Possible Worlds and Possibilia," 83–95.

62. Leue, *Metaphysical Foundations*, ch. 3.

63. Faber, *God as Poet*, 92–93.

(which Whitehead secures in the image of a divine act of valuation and ordering), they are among themselves unordered and do not exhibit any "unit" or represent any "entity" or form any "class" of structures; rather they are pure *multiplicities* (see PR, 31).

Precisely insofar as the becoming of any actual event includes the "(infinite, chaotic) whole" of this pure multiplicity without unity, it offers *infinite differentiation* of actual events and, hence, the sought creativeness of unprecedented novelty instead of an infinite variability of the eternal.[64] In Deleuze's assessment of Whitehead's "pure possibilities" in *The Fold*, he correctly identifies them not only as "pure Possibilities" but (in Deleuze's critical sense directed against the Platonic possible) *as* "pure Virtualities."[65] This interpretation of "eternal objects" is the reason that Deleuze, in the preface to the American edition of *Dialogues*, can confess that he always has "felt that [he is] an empiricist, that is, a pluralist," who follows Whitehead's "search [that] is not for an eternal or universal, but for the condition under which something new is created."[66]

The Realms of Multiplicity

Although both philosophers develop these concepts over the course of the body of their whole work, their mystical inclination is best observed in their very last works—Whitehead's "Immortality" and Deleuze's "Immanence: A Life." Both works are a resume of a life's work as they formulate concisely the relationship between mysticism and novelty by way of the very reference of Values and Virtuals, as well as events and processes of becoming to their one "essence"—namely, as their folding-together as pure multiplicity, or as the play of multiplicities of interactions (of events, processes, values, and virtuals).[67]

In "Immortality," Whitehead differentiates between two worlds, one of Actuality and one of Value. While the former indicates the processes of the concrescence of actual events (from actual events), the latter names the very medium by which actualities in "the infinitude of possibility" (Imm., 689) realize themselves as concrete values, instigated by the "World of Value" (ibid., 686). While value is an extremely complex notion throughout Whitehead's work, here, it indicates four moments:

---

64. Leue, *Metaphysical Foundations*, 91–106
65. Deleuze, *Fold*, 79.
66. Deleuze, *Two Regimes of Madness*, 304.
67. Williams, *Encounters*, 79–85.

1. "Values" are about the importance of actual becoming because they are "not rooted in passing circumstances." They allow the "World of Activity" to become "valuable because it shares in the immortal of some value" (ibid., 684). Hence, values cannot "become" actualities. They name a multiplicity of relations (or a relational multiplicity) that *as* multiplicity can instigate novelty when invited into actualization of events.

2. The "World of Value" "has an essential independence of any moment of time" but "it loses its meaning apart from any necessary reference to the world of passing fact" (ibid.). Although a multiplicity of potentials, values can be generated by processes of valuation, which are actualizations.

3. Because *any* World—the world of "Mortality" and "Immortality"—for "an adequate description . . . includes characterizations *derived* from the other" they are *mutually exploratory* (emphasis added) (ibid., 683–84). In this *mutual* "process of modification," they generate creativeness without perpetual repetition (ibid, 685). Potential multiplicity and actual multiplicity meet without ever exchanging their respective perspective, necessary to mutually differentiate multiplicities (instead of unities or many unities, or a unified many).

4. The process of creating Values "includes 'incitement toward' and 'deterrence from,' a manifold of possibility" by an "active coordination of the various possibilities of Value" (ibid., 687). This activity Whitehead identifies as "the concept of God" (ibid., 694). Hence, this (concept of) the divine in Whitehead offers a path to the open space in which the sensitivity for multiplicity as relational folding of pre-identical (or not yet identified) processes unfold/fold together in mutual interdependence, immanence, and processual actualization, valuation, and dramatization.

In "Immanence: A Life," Deleuze also relates Virtually and Actuality in exactly such an intricate manner. Although he could be expected to shy away from any language invoking a divine dimension, he does not, in fact, avoid expressing novelty in terms of a mystical language. This essay shows the traces of theological language, even as it alludes to its very disappearance into apophatic indifferentiation. And it employs the same four moments as Whitehead's text.

1. Virtuality indicates the *medium* and *meaning of* actualization insofar as its multiplicity cannot be unified to any entity (a thing, a person, an actual actor, a god) but is viewed as an (impersonal, non-entitative,

non-actual/particular) "transcendental field"[68] by which universal singularity is conditioned and, hence, *only* multiplicity is generated.

2. Yet virtual reality is also independent *from* actualizations since in their "non-actualized (indefinite)" state, the "virtual events" are "lacking nothing"—although they are "engaged in a process of actualization."[69] Hence, its multiplicity can always initiate actual becoming without being "dependent" on it as it generates the unprecedented as its very "nature" a multiplicity.

3. Hence, the virtual "exists" *before* its actualization as *pure* multiplicity, while also coexisting with all creative events of actualization in time. While the virtual initiates actualization, it is not dependent on it, and hence, beyond time-events a multiplicity of events of indifference.

4. Again employing mystical language, this virtual reality can "no longer be dependent on a Being or be submitted to an Act."[70] Its "own" reality is not only beyond actualization, but beyond subject and object, indifferent to these differences (but creative of them). Hence, in the most clearly mystically motivated move in Deleuze's work, he now dares name this multiplicity (beyond identity and difference, a language he learned from Nicolas of Cusa and Giordano Bruno) as "absolute immediate consciousness," "consciousness without a self," and "pre-reflexive, impersonal consciousness."[71]

In comparing these four moments of Value and Virtuality in Whitehead and Deleuze, respectively, we must first recognize the important resonance: that of the interaction of multiplicities to generate multiplicities, that is, realms of novelty instead of imperial unifications of eternity. Yet we must also realize a subtle but nevertheless ever-growing bifurcation in the progress of the series of their respective four aspects of the two realms of multiplicity. The first moment of (the medium of) "meaning" allows both concepts—Value and Virtual—to rescue the moment of "importance" in their respective thought. Yet the second moment of *independence* and *involvement* already diverts both philosophers. Whitehead understands Value as multiplicity because it is conditioned *by* actualities so that neither can be viewed as a preformation of novelty.[72] Deleuze, on the other hand, is more interested in the *self-sufficiency of the virtual* reality beyond actualization,

---

68. Deleuze, "Immanence," 31.

69. Deleuze, "Immanence," 29–30, 31.

70. Deleuze, "Immanence," 27.

71. Deleuze, "Immanence," 27, 25.

72. Whitehead, "Immortality," 685.

which comes (much more than Whitehead at this point) close to a classical allusion to the eternal (divine), and is only kept from becoming its revival as long as the Virtual can be shown to indicate a pure multiplicity. The third moment regarding the *interaction* of the two realities (worlds) reifies this difference because where for Whitehead their multiplicity is recurred by their mutual *exploratory interdependence*, for Deleuze their ability to instigate novelty is secured by their mere *coexistence*.

Finally, the fourth moment implies the most obvious manifestation of the employment of a *mystical* move for the uncompromising directedness toward novelty through multiplicity. Yet, in both thinkers, it leads to almost opposite conclusions. Whitehead's *mutual immanence* of both realities allows him to conceptualize the World of Value *in terms of* (its "other," namely) Activity (as the World of Creativity is described in terms of valuation). It is here, in this interaction, that Whitehead sees the necessity to explicate his mystical language of mutuality as inducing divinity (although a very different one).[73] Deleuze, on the other hand, refuses to understand the Virtual in any form as an *act* because he views such a move as a dangerous subordination of multiplicity to (unifying, occupying, imperial) transcendence. Instead, in order to save novelty from occupation, he invokes a *different* mystical image, namely that of the "absoluteness of an immediate consciousness."[74]

The Mystery of Novelty

So what in these explorations of the mystery of novelty (with the allusion of mystical language and as secured by the intricacies of multiplicity) exactly differentiates Whitehead from Deleuze? What differentiates Whitehead's "active coordination" of the infinite manifold of "possibilities of Value" (Imm., 687) from the "flow of absolute consciousness"?[75] It is not that one needs divinity and the other shuns it; it is not that one seeks the eternal and the other the novel;[76] it is *how*, for them both, realities are mutually interwoven.

While both philosophers can use common terms in order to describe *either* reality—Whitehead talks of the act *of* valuation and the value *of* actualities; Deleuze of *virtual* events and actualizations *of* virtualities—Deleuze carefully insists on the saturation of both realities (against the lack of

73. Faber, "De-Ontologizing God," 217–18.

74. Deleuze, "Immanence," 29.

75. Deleuze, "Immanence," 25.

76. Faber, "O bitches," 218–19.

reality of the virtual over against the actual) while Whitehead points to their abstractness in isolation without mutual immanence. Hence, for Deleuze, novelty occurs in the *coexistence* of both multiplicities as processes of differentiation, while for Whitehead novelty occurs in the intricate *mutuality* of these processes (by which they are and remain multiplicity).

Therefore, what Whitehead views as an *act* of synthesis *within* both Worlds is also that *of* both Worlds; Deleuze, on the other hand, views any synthesis of both Multiplicities only as one *within* both Multiplicities (by which they do not become unified against possible and actual novelty). What Whitehead considers the condition of novelty—mutual immanence through an act of synthesis, although not as an imperial occupation—Deleuze denounces precisely as that: "a unity that is superior to all things or a Subject as an act that brings about a synthesis of things."[77] This is why Deleuze cannot accept any notion of divinity in addressing novelty—as it would hinder multiplicity—and Whitehead expresses novelty with a notion of divinity—the act of upholding multiplicity. Yet, Deleuze does not indulge in such a negation of "theology" at the heart of philosophy, but instead, affirms its traces in the form of his embrace of the mystical move of indifferentiation: he *transfers the mystical function of divinity to* the "plane of immanence" to which he attributes its most delicate characteristic—namely, absolute consciousness, undifferentiated by the subject-object split (of ordinary consciousness and naive notions of god).[78]

Yet, on deeper analysis, we realize that Whitehead's *divine* act of coordinating Value is not so far from Deleuze's *absolute consciousness*. As the latter, the World of Value has no Subject; rather Value is always outside of subjectivity. As in Deleuze, it is a pre-reflexive and impersonal multiplicity (by all standards of personality Whitehead employs).[79] In this sense, it is also "*pure consciousness*" exactly insofar as it is not a subject synthesizing the World of Creativity, but names the pure immanence *of* the World of Value itself as it generates it as multiplicity. And in the mutual immanence of the two Worlds, this "divine consciousness" must not be understood as a *synthesis* of them, but as the Eros toward novelty by which these multiplicities remain (never the same) multiplicities that, against meaningless change and the boredom of endless repetition, generate difference in form of novelty.[80]

Ironically, while Whitehead's "immanence" is always *mutual*—and hence is purely relative—Deleuze's immanence is only immanent *to itself*—and

77. Deleuze, "Immanence," 27.

78. Deleuze, "Immanence," 31.

79. Faber, *God as Poet*, §22.

80. Whitehead, "Immortality," 687.

hence becomes *absolute*. While Whitehead's "active coordination" of Values is accused as repetition of the theistic past, it is, contrarily, *most immanent* in the production of novelty in the World of Creativity, only producing multiplicity. Deleuze's "flow of immanent consciousness," on the other hand, although one would expect his thought to function as the denial of such a theistic move, is indeed "absolute" and hence, in some sense repeats the classical content of the conceptualization of divinity. It avoids this "classical" implication only insofar as it remains a means to address multiplicily. But it does so with the mystical move for which it is typical that its reality does not lack of anything, which makes it indifferent to actualizations.

This presents us with an interesting paradox: the criticism of White- head's invocation of the divine in his *philosophy* (not as a reinstated theology)—a criticism in which Deleuze did not participate—does not appreciate the function it gains as expression of a multiplicity of genera- tion of a chaosmos of novelty. The accusation of a blindness with which Deleuze is seen to repeat Nietzsche's dismissal of divinity, on the other hand, does not take into account the very thinly veiled mystical language with which Deleuze secures multiplicity and novelty by employing one of mysticism's most cherished images: that of the indifferent reality of abso- lute as consciousness, being beyond differences (of subject and object) or not of being or "being" not-being at all.

While I agree that "the issue here is not whether Deleuze should have a place for God in his metaphysics" but "whether his idea of the virtual can provide the kind of permanence sought by Whitehead in the face perpetual perishing,"[81] I will add that in light of the two "characteristics" of novelty— namely, the sense of *importance* and *creativeness* inherent to multiplicity— both philosophers equally allude to (even have a systematic necessity to refer to) a mysticism in their work that can be acknowledged *philosophically.* Without subscribing to any "theology," their respective articulation (and the tension of their respective approaches) might be vital for any future restate- ment of the triadic Platonic force field of the relation among philosophy, sophistic/relativism, and poetic/theology.[82]

A Mystagogy of Becoming

At this point—that is, the acknowledgment of a mystical move at the very core of the philosophical conversion of a world of eternity into a that of novelty in Whitehead and Deleuze—we may even begin to realize that this

81. Williams, "Deleuze," 105.
82. Faber, *Divine Manifold.*

common move is not only about "thought"—a reminder of the isolation of the *ego cogito*—but, as Plato imagined himself, about the meaning of philosophy, about a *philosophical life*. In this sense, Whitehead's and Deleuze's novelty that is about the novelty of the multiplicity of the chaosmos may initiate nothing less than a *mystagogy* of becoming. That is, in the exploration of the thought of Whitehead and Deleuze regarding the mystery of novelty, we can find hints for a certain philosophical *praxis* by which one can, in a certain way, approach the mystery that makes one (and should never only make one) think. I will name four tentative moments for such a *way into* the mystery.

First, in choosing becoming instead of being, the world we live in becomes overturned. This is an experience of conversion, as Deleuze mentions. In seeking novelty instead of eternity, we become sensitive to the liberating force of life, chaos, creativity, and difference over the forces of Law, order, repetition, and sameness. It will overturn not only our attitude towards Life but also any articulation of a divine dimension: whether and where we seek it, what it implies, and the intention of its invocation.[83]

Second, since this different horizon of life will also change all the categories with which we frame our existence, we will be enabled to confront anew a cruel paradox, the paradox of life and death. Where we hail becoming, we also see perpetual perishing; where becoming is seamless, we should not expect salvation from contingency. Where life and death coincide, the "human face," as Deleuze states, "decomposes."[84]

Third, both philosophies indicate that the only way to live novelty will always lead us beyond the stabilizations we seek to escape into: being, permanence, identity, and eternity. While we still might seek attainment in the event and creativeness in restriction, pure life also indicates the death of subjectivity, individuality, personality, and Self. This is what the mystery of novelty shelters: importance *dispossesses* life of subjectivity and objectivity; creativeness is the death of all forms. With Deleuze, we have to find the infinitive of "a Life" in the midst of "the Life"[85] we possess.[86]

Fourth, this reality can be experienced and conceptualized only on the border of language as complication, as in-and-out-folding, beyond difference and indifference (without ever leaving their differentiation of language). In this context, what is conceptualized resembles a mystagogy

83. Faber, "Introduction: Negotiating Becoming," 1–49.
84. Deleuze, *Difference*, 28.
85. Deleuze, "Immanence," 29.
86. Refer to chapter 5, current volume.

of the "mystical death" and an absolute immediacy beyond subjectivity and objectivity.[87]

A final thought: whether this mystical move is best conceptualized philosophically with the presence or absence of divinity is secondary. What remains in question, however, is whether genuine novelty in a world of infinite becoming *must* invoke such a reality as its transcendental condition.[88] In any case, in my view, in the contrast of Whitehead and Deleuze, any future mystagogy of becoming will never be less than the expression of this problem and perhaps never be more than its affirmation.

87. Faber, *God as Poet*, 112.
88. Deleuze, "Immanence," 26.

CHAPTER THREE

God's Absence of Listening

WHAT DO "PRESENCE" AND "absence" mean? More particularly, what can one make of claims surrounding the "presence" and "absence" of God? The *presence* of God has an important relation to the question of the "omnipresence" of God, but even more to that of the presence of the Holy that might reside (or contract) in certain places (the Shekina in the Temple of Jerusalem) or at certain times (Sabbath), allowing for the *experience* of God.[1] Always more than a philosophical question, it is, therefore, a question of meaning, salvation, and existentiality. Precisely in this combination of elements, God's *absence* became a major point in the atheism debates of the twentieth century, not only in the context of a theoretical strategy, but also that of an "experience" in society,[2] backed up with the mechanicism of scientism.[3] There was, of course, another tradition that spoke about Divine presence/absence, namely the mystical tradition of, e.g., Meister Eckhart and its philosophical ablation in, e.g., Heidegger.[4] This tradition was not so much interested in a doctrine of God's presence/absence, but in an understanding of "presence/absence" *as such*—its absoluteness to the ultimate mystery of reality—for which the language of its articulation and its function (what it addresses) became important.

What indeed can we say about metaphysical claims of divine "presence" and "absence"? In using A.N. Whitehead, Jacques Derrida, and Martin Heidegger for considering this question, I will follow their impulse to reconstruct the philosophical preconditions of "classical theism," its modern alterations (mostly) in Thomism, and its postmodern derivate. And I will connect them to the Swedish playwright, August Strindberg. One may

1. Otto, *Idea of the Holy.*
2. Morgan, *In the Absence of God.*
3. Haught, *God and the New Atheism.*
4. Yannaras, *On the Absence and Unknowability of God.*

immediately ask, at this point, "what do Strindberg and philosophy have to do with one another?" Despite a seeming arbitrariness, there is an essential connection that will become more obvious when I restate the question: "How do poetry and philosophy relate?"[5] In fact, it is their nexus in which I want to situate the question of the presence and absence of God as a question of philosophical metaphoric and theopoetics.[6]

"Philosophy is akin to poetry," says Whitehead, because in "each case there is reference . . . beyond the direct meanings of words" (MT, 174). Against what Whitehead calls the "fallacy of the perfect dictionary" (ibid., 173), his refutation of exactly definable meanings of words has led him to believe that "no language can be anything but elliptical, requiring a leap of the imagination to understand its meaning in its relevance to immediate experience" (PR, 13). In other words, elliptic images are ill-conceived as second-rate substitutes for philosophical concepts. Instead, philosophical language is metaphoric in itself.

Derrida agrees. It is precisely the *problem* of "philosophy's *unique thesis*, the thesis which constitutes [and repudiates] the concept of metaphor" that introduces "the opposition of the proper and the nonproper, of essence and accident, of intuition and discourse, of thought and language, of the intelligible and sensible."[7] If philosophy lives from this distinction, its collapse would mean "the death of philosophy"[8] insofar as it *defines* itself in distinction from poetry.

However, if there is no "great Beyond" of concepts justifying "*the Truth*" *beyond* metaphors—as Whitehead and Derrida believe[9]—then the Being of beings, or the "true" meaning of metaphors, must be *immanent*

5. This is a perennial issue from the *constitution* of philosophy in Greece from its conception out of, and rivalry with, the poetry of mythology, theology, and sophistic relativism. See Levin, *The Ancient Quarrel*; Haines, *Poetry and Philosophy*; and Baker, *Extravagant Crossings*.

6. Faber, *God as Poet*.

7. Derrida, "White Mythology," 229.

8. Derrida, "White Mythology," 271.

9. This might not have been so obvious as long as the discussion on Whitehead's missing "linguistic turn" was concentrated around a Platonist interpretation of Whitehead, presupposing that he held a "Beyond" (of Platonic realities) that can be approached directly, without interpretation; cf. Franklin, *Speaking from the Depths*. In fact, Whitehead's insistence on a "beyond" of language is based on the fact that symbolic transfer is deeper than human language, reaching back to the ontological structure of reality itself and *not* that there is any un-interpreted reality; cf. Lachmann, *Ethik und Identität*, 74–95. In the end, Derrida's conviction that there *is* reality beyond language that still is a "text" might correspond to Whitehead's conviction that there is a "texture" of reality of which language is a civilized mode; cf. Derrida, "Back from Moscow," 26–27; Whitehead, PR, 4, 9.

in its "incarnations" so that apart from the poetic multiplicity of its "accidental embodiments,"[10] Being (or meaning) would be empty. Hence, only
in its *poetic differentiation*—Whiteheads "creative advance" and Derrida's
relentless *différance* of *never present* meanings—can we find the khoric
"place" in which philosophic meaning occurs.[11] *This* philosophic quest,
however, is *always* "a passage"—as Whitehead concurs with Derrida.[12] "In
its turn every philosophy will suffer a deposition" (PR, 7) because of the
infinite elliptic nature of its appeal to the novelty of immediate experiences
"as yet unspoken" (MT, 174).

Presencing/Absencing

It is with this *distinction* between poetry and philosophy that we face the fundamental problems inherent in the tandem concept of "presence/absence"
and its application to God. According to Derrida, their bifurcation belongs
to "the great immobile chain of Aristotelian ontology, with its theory of the
analogy of Being."[13] Because of its inherently *binary* scheme of "the proper
and the nonproper, of essence and accident, of intuition and discourse, of
thought and language, of the intelligible and sensible,"[14] this "analogy of
Being" amounts to a *division of reality* in essential and accidental elements,
in reality and appearance, in Being and *doxa*.

Obviously any "essentialism" of this kind always privileges the One
over many, mind over matter, the intelligible over the sensible, persistence
over change, eternity over time, man over woman, God over the world,
presence over absence.[15] While "true reality" must always be *substance*—
changeless, timeless and self-present—the multiplicity of elliptic images
only expresses accidental appearances—inadequate, changing, death-in-
fected and deceiving.[16]

10. Whitehead, PR, 7.

11. Derrida, "Difference," 1–28; Derrida, "Chora"; Whitehead, AI, 134. For my interpretation of Derrida's and Whitehead's understanding of the *khora*, refer to ch. 5,
current volume.

12. Not only is Derrida's *différance* naming the inability to realize a static *nunc
stans*, but Whiteheads "events" (or actualities, actual occasions, occurrences) are always
"passing" and *are* a passage. Cf. PR 7, 22 (Cat. Expl. I) and 25–26 (Cat. Oblg. IX).
For explorations of the deep connections between Derrida's difference and Whiteheads
becoming. Cf. Keller, *Process and Difference*.

13. Derrida, "White Mythology," 236.

14. Derrida, "White Mythology," 229.

15. Grosz, *Space*, ch 3.

16. For the poststructuralist critique of substantialism based on Derrida and akin to
Whitehead's much earlier criticism, cf. Butler, *Gender Trouble*.

We end up with a twofold impasse: While the divorce of poetry from philosophy constitutes and haunts any "metaphysics of *presence*,"[17] its implied concept of "substantial presence" ultimately reaches, as I will demonstrate, its paradigmatic expression in a concept of "*God's* presence" that marks all theologies influenced by Aristotelian substantialism.

Nevertheless, we should not forget that essentialism is *not* itself a timeless necessity but the child of a local spirit of certain strains of Greek metaphysics. And while the urge for changeless presence already inherently suggests a *certain* notion of God, the essentialist notion of God, far from being universal, is also a *cultural variable* of a time for which salvation was identical with the ascent to a world-less One, a non-material Mind, a powerful King, and a timeless persisting, eternal Law.[18]

Today, instead of promising salvation, the *stasis* of this "spirit" destines us to remain subjects of its binary imperatives—leaving us in a hell of a world that is nothing but change, inconstancy, time, multiplicity, matter, and finitude.[19] Its symbol may be Plato's *me on*—"that what should not be"—for which salvation finally can only be destruction.[20] Interestingly, in Dante's *Divine Comedy*, the only element that, of the whole universe, has this kind of static gravity is not God but—the Devil![21]

In fact, there are *other* philosophic traditions for which "presence" is *not* defined by binary structures.[22] Moreover, there are *other* streams of theo-

17. For a sound introduction to the diverse directions of this Derridian critique of metaphysics as substantialism (of presence), cf. Gutting, *French Philosophy*.

18. For a reconstruction of the influence of the Greek metaphysics on the Christian concept of God, which became the metaphysical standard and its revision in contemporary theology, cf. Faber, *Selbst-Einsatz Gottes*.

19. This soteriological dualism is the basis for the never-fading Manichean and Gnostic tendencies in Christianity to abandon this world for a new world, or a heaven, extinct of all that is worldly. For a dispute between this kind of platonic thinking and one that does not give up the world, see the dispute between Gisbert Greshake and Josef Ratzinger on matters of "the end of history (as we know it)" in Faber, *Die neue Zukunft Gottes*.

20. Of course, Plato's notions of *me on* and *ouk on* can be interpreted, and have been used in different ways; cf. Plato, *Timaeus*, 28a. While in Christian theology, e.g., in Tillich, *ouk on* was equated with the *ex nihilo* of creation (pure nothingness, nothing at all), *me on* represents the *khora* of "no-thing." In Plato, however, the *me on*, since it is not simply nothing, means that which is the basis for being in a way that makes it not eternal, not changeless, and not-present and, therefore, remains somehow a moment of contingency that *should* not be. Cf. Russell, *Cosmology*, 96–97. For a criticism of an apocalyptic understanding of the destruction of the world as precondition of true salvation in the context of soteriological dualism, cf. Faber, "Gods Advent/ure," 91–112 and passim.

21. Dante, *Divine Comedy*.

22. For a good definition of binary structures and their relation to Logocentrism

poetics for which God is *not* determined as self-present, world-transcendent "substance," but as self-emptying love for *this* world—as a God who *incarnates* to *become world*; who is present *in* its change and passage; who loves it for its *becoming*.[23] This God *embraces finitude* with its passage and passion.[24] Whitehead's plea for the love of finitude, instead of a reverence of a world-transcendent, self-present infinity, is still breathtakingly radical:

> The superstitious awe of infinitudes has been the bane of philosophy. The infinite has no properties. All value is the gift of finitude . . . Spinoza emphasized the fundamental infinitude [of the Divine] and introduced a subordinate differentiation by finite modes . . . Leibniz . . . based [finite monads] on a substratum of Deistic infinitude. Neither of them adequately emphasized the fact that infinitude is mere vacancy apart from its embodiment of finite values . . . [Hence we must, instead, be] concerned with the characterization of the infinite in terms of finitude . . . , the limitation of deity. (MG, 674–675)[25]

This Deity, for whom pure infinity is empty, vacuous and devoid of worth, must be fundamentally different: deeply immanent, finite, many, becoming, interrelated with everything, and touched by it—a *feeling* God who is reacting to, building on, conditioned by, suffering from, and becoming by God's beloved world.[26] Against the binary privilege of timeless presence, this God is what I call *polyphilic*—the God who loves manifoldness.[27]

---

and the basic binary of presence and absence in Derrida, cf. Gutting, *French Philosophy*, 293–94 and Derrida, "Violence and Metaphysics," 79–153.

23. For a discussion of contemporary theological positions on Christian resources for correcting Greek-metaphysical presuppositions of a substantialist God, particularly through reconsidering the primordiality of doctrines of Incarnation and *kenosis*, and by understanding them as the expression of the Trinitarian *movement* of Divine love, cf. Faber, *Selbst-Einsatz*, part II and III.

24. In general, the differentiation of ways to express this embrace is usually called "Panentheism." For the different ways to express this Divine embrace of finitude, including the Hegelian and Whiteheadian strands of a "becoming God," cf. Clayton and Peacocke, *In Whom We Live*.

25. For an interpretation of this late thought of Whitehead, see Faber, "'Infinite Movement.'"

26. For a discussion of the suffering (and becoming) of God in contemporary theology, cf. Fiddes, *Creative Suffering* and Faber, *Selbst-Einsatz*, part II. In process theology, this has become a standard interpretation; cf. Hartshorne, *Divine Relativity*; Cobb and Griffin, *Process Theology*; and Faber, *God as Poet*, part IV and V.

27. For my notion of "polyphilia," cf. Faber, "Ecotheology," 75–115; Faber, *God as Poet*, postscript; chapter 5, current volume.

The *presence* of this God, then, is not unilaterally transcendent, but responsively immanent; not static, but dynamic; not isolated, but compassionate; not reigning, but suffering. This God is, in *perichoretic mutuality*, infinite *and* finite, eternal *and* temporal, one *and* many, transcendent *and* immanent and, as Whitehead boldly states, creative *and* created.[28] This God is not substance, but *event*, not a noun, but a verb. The verbal presence of this God is not a "presence" but a process of "presenc*ing*."[29]

Back to Derrida. What he repudiates as "metaphysics of presence," excluding the metaphors it builds on, is precisely a metaphysical edifice erected with *nouns*. Nouns are verbs taken *in abstraction*, i.e., in "atemporality."[30] The "presence" following from this abstraction precisely abstracts from the verbal flow of "presencing." In their *atemporal presence*, nouns always indicate *substance*. Atemporal presence *is* substance![31] And substantialism is built on the oblivion of the *event* of "presencing."[32] Derrida here only follows Heidegger, and Heidegger calls this oblivion that *constitutes* the metaphysics of presence—*Seinsvergessenheit*.[33]

Indeed, Heidegger has built the case against Greek metaphysics by uncovering its enclosed *equation* of substance with timeless presence to be based on a *loss*: the loss of the difference between *presence* and *the present*: "presence as *Anwesenheit* and the present as *Gegenwärtigkeit* (presence in the temporal sense of nowness)";[34] presence as "presencing" *(an-wesen)* and

---

28. PR, 348. For a differentiation of this mutual *perichoresis* from other forms of Panentheism, one that employs *strict* mutuality of immanence and transcendence of infinity and finitude—what I call "transpantheism"—cf. Faber, *Divine Manifold*, ch. 13; *Becoming of God*, Exploration 11.

29. This, if at all, is what Whitehead meant with his otherwise problematic identification of God as an "actual entity" in his scheme of concepts, namely that utilizing the category of substance cannot think God, but if God is not an "abstraction," God must be understood as an actual process of becoming. Whitehead was well aware that God is not fitting the categories he otherwise developed to understand the worlds events of becoming; cf. Ford and Kline, *Explorations*. For a critique of process theologies that try to "fit" God the into the categorical scheme instead of developing the resonance between them, see Faber, *Prozeßtheologie*, §29.

30. Derrida, "White Mythology," 238.

31. Derrida, "*Ousia* and *Gramme*," 32. The privilege of presence is to be substance *(ousia, Anwesenheit)*.

32. This is the central argument Derrida takes from Heidegger in order to deconstruct not only the metaphysics of presence and its binary of presence/absence, as developed in Derrida, "*Ousia* and *Gramme*," 29–68. I use this connection as the central argument for the deconstruction of the metaphysical presupposition in the notion of the presence/absence of God. Cf. Caputo, *Deconstruction*.

33. Young, *Heidegger's Later Philosophy*, 23.

34. Derrida, "*Ousia* and *Gramme*," 64.

presence as "present" (*anwesend sein*). From Heidegger's *Being and Time* on, Derrida notes,

> it seems more and more that *Gegenwärtigkeit* (the fundamental determination of *ousia*) itself is only a restriction *of Anwesenheit* . . . And the Latin word presence (*Präsenz*) will connote rather another narrowing of *Anwesen* under the heading of subjectivity and representation. These linked determinations of presence (*Anwesenheit*), which are the inaugural determination of the meaning of Being by the Greeks . . . , are giving us to think it as a closure, as the Greco-Western-philosophical closure.[35]

For Heidegger, the Gift of Being is this *Event* of "luminous rising and decline *(lichtendes Aufgehen und Untergehen)*."[36] Like the rise and decline of the Sun, "presencing" is a "rising up into and passing out of manifestness, coming forward into unconcealment and departure back into concealment" as John Caputo puts it.[37]

The Gift of Being is the *event* of becoming! That event, in which the Being of beings comes forth and departs, is what "presencing" means. "Presencing," Heidegger says, is *ver-weilen*—"lingering for a while." "Presencing" is a "Whiling" of Being as "a transition (*Übergang*) from arrival *(Hervorkommen)* to the departure (*Hinweggehen*) from (sic!) presencing."[38] The *Event* of Being—this whiling, lingering, becoming and passing—is always "a transitory interlude in the realm of the unconcealed."[39]

Because the "while occurs essentially as the transitional arrival in departure," Heidegger says, "the presencing of all things that lingers occurs" only "between this twofold absence."[40] Presencing is the "junction"[41] of the twofold process of *ab*sencing. Hence, "presencing" is *never* "present," "*in* the present," or "*the* present." In the "now," there is only *absence*, i.e., the process of arrival and departure.

As an immediate consequence, Heidegger understands Anaximander's reference to *the* "injustice" (*adikia*) of things to indicate their *claim* that their presence be present. The price for this collapse of presencing into the

---

35. Derrida, "*Ousia* and *Gramme*," 64–65.

36. Derrida, "*Ousia* and *Gramme*," 342.

37. Caputo, *Heidegger and Aquinas*, 188.

38. Derrida, "*Ousia* and *Gramme*."

39. Ibid. For the connection between "Place" (*khora*) and "Becoming" (becoming) as more basic than space and time and, thereby, allowing for such a fragile understanding of "whiling" as in Heidegger, cf. Malpas, *Heidegger's Topology*, ch. 5.

40. Heidegger, "The Anaximander Fragment," 41–42.

41. Heidegger, "The Anaximander Fragment."

present—according to Heidegger's Anaximander and Derrida's Heidegger—is the closure of Greek thought into substance with its substantial present as timeless *nunc stans*. Injustice is the robbery of time, taking the process of presencing hostage to timeless substance. Since the oblivion of the Gift of Being consists in the fundamental *loss of the distinction* between Being and beings, the "penalty" for this injustice is a world of "things"—of timeless objects with present existence (*Vorhandenheit*).[42]

Against the "crime" of substantialism—the "present presence" of atemporal essences with their present existence—justice can only be served by *differentiating* between presence and the present, which "permits Heidegger"—as Derrida notes—"to invoke presencing as *non-present presence [ungegenwärtig anwesende]*."[43] With *the Event never present*, we regain *the* "difference" that, as Derrida claims, is even "older than Being itself,"[44] namely *that there is no analogy of Being based on the grades of present beings*, but only the *différance* of events of becoming. In other words: the event of presencing is what Deleuze calls the "univocity of Being"[45] and Whitehead, the "ultimacy of creativity" (PR, 20–22).[46]

Beyond Self-Presence

At this point, I think, it becomes obvious how this criticism of substantialism relates to Whitehead.[47] Against the binary structure of a metaphysics that "hinges round the difficulty of describing the world in terms of subject and predicate, substance and quality, particular and universal" (PR, 49), Whitehead's philosophy of becoming insists on "creative passage" (CN, 73) as a crucial remedy against the oblivion of the event of "presencing."

42. For an analysis of this connection between substantialism and "injustice," cf. Caputo, *Heidegger and Aquinas*, 186–92.

43. Derrida, "*Ousia* and *Gramme*," 64.

44. Derrida, "*Ousia* and *Gramme*," 67. Derrida's reconstruction Heidegger's "ontological difference" is *différance*.

45. Deleuze, *Difference and Repetition*, 35–42. For the connection between Deleuze's understanding of event and difference in relation to his reception of Whitehead, see Deleuze, *Fold*, ch. 6.

46. For a connection between Whitehead's "creativity" and Deleuze's "difference," cf. Keller, "Process and Chaosmos," 55–72 and Faber, "De-Ontologizing God," 191–208.

47. For an analysis of Whitehead's critique of substantialism as the basis of the revolution of thought, cf. Kraus, *Metaphysics of Experience*; for an early, but in no way closed, discussion of Whitehead's relation to Heidegger's thought, which developed at the same time in great independence from one another, cf. Ford, "Whitehead and the Ontological Difference," 148–55, and Cooper, *Heidegger and Whitehead*.

> Events become and perish. In their becoming they are immedi-
> ate and then vanish into the past. They are gone; they have per-
> ished; they are no more and have passed into not-being. Plato
> terms them things that are "always becoming and never really
> are" . . . Thus we should balance Aristotle's—or, more rightly,
> Plato's—doctrine of becoming by a doctrine of perishing. When
> they perish, occasions pass from the immediacy of being into
> the not-being of immediacy. (AI, 237)

For Whitehead, being is a form of non-being and becoming a juncture
of non-being: the non-being of the past that was and could be again; the
non-being of pure potential that is not yet; and the non-being of becoming
that never really "is."[48] As for Deleuze, the event *is never in the present* but
already past and ever future, always arriving and departing.[49] The "brooding presence" (SMW, 83) of the whole universe in every event—Whitehead's
"romantic" experience—really is *the presence of what is absent*: the *past*—the
"presence" of the absent: the *future*—the appetition of what is not; and the
present—not self-presence, but always the feeling of *other* presences.[50]

In order to understand Whitehead's critique of the history and constitution of metaphysics, it is fundamentally important to realize his claim
against its substantialism to be in striking accordance with Heidegger and
Derrida.[51] Whitehead finds the mark of any substantialist metaphysics—of
substance and essence (Aristotle and Plato), of mind and matter (Descartes
and Newton), of reflection and deduction (Kant and Hegel), and of perception and impression (Locke and Hume)—in its infection with "self-presence"
(AI, 273). Against this preference of what Whitehead calls "presentational
immediacy" (PR, 178),[52] he insists on *another* non-substantial, fragile and
suppressed mode of experience. Instead of being "clear, distinct and certain"
(PR, 8), in the presence of self-present consciousness, it is

> vague, not to be controlled, heavy with emotion: it produces
> the sense of derivation from an immediate past, and of passage
> to an immediate future; a sense of emotional feeling, belonging

48. For a formal analysis of nothingness in Whitehead, which has often been ne-
glected in his conceptual landscape, cf. Faber, *Prozeßtheologie*, §33.

49. Deleuze, *Logic of Sense*, 63–64.

50. For Whitehead's analysis of events in relation to the modes of past, present, and
future, cf. AI, ch. 12

51. Keller and Daniell, *Process and Difference*. For the early recognition of such a
common critique of Heidegger and Whitehead within French philosophy, especially,
Jean Wahl, cf. Rockmore, *Heidegger and French Philosophy*, 54.

52. For a standard analysis of "presentational immediacy" *versus* "causal efficacy,"
cf. Kraus, *Metaphysics of Experience*, 75–93.

> to oneself in the past, passing into oneself in the present, and passing from oneself in the present towards oneself in the future: a sense of influx of influence from other vaguer presences in the past, localized and yet evading local definition, such influence modifying, enhancing, inhibiting, diverting, the stream of feeling which we are receiving, unifying, enjoying, and transmitting. (ibid., 178)

In *this* experience of "presencing," nothing is self-present; all is event—becoming, flowing, passing—the gift of time! It is only through "*violence* to that immediate experience which we express in our actions, our hopes, our sympathies, our purposes" (PR, 49, italics mine)—the *crime* of substantialism—that for Whitehead a metaphysics of presence takes self-presence as more fundamental.[53] By depriving presence of absence, and in fear of it, the present fills itself with *projections of infinite self-presence and fantasies of timelessness.*

"Presentational immediacy," Whitehead says, "is the superficial product of complexity, of subtlety; it halts at the present, and indulges in a manageable self-enjoyment derived from the immediacy of the show of things" (SY, 43). Since "orthodox philosophy," Whitehead says, "can only introduce us to solitary substances, each enjoying an illusory experience" (PR, 50), it leaves us with the "solipsism of the present moment" (SY, 29). Whenever we *substantialize the world in the present moment*, we begin to think that the "present moment is . . . all in all. In our consciousness it approximates to simple occurrence" (ibid, 42). Its "simple location" (SMW, 50) leads us into the impasse of any metaphysics of presence, namely the objectification of the world into self-contained "things" that exist in the present.[54]

So, how does God fit into this picture? When Derrida's caution against the *analogy of Being with its grades of self-present beings* dies unheard, its unfortunate fate unfolds itself by penetrating the concept of the "(self-) presence of the Divine."[55] Heidegger captures this turning point precisely

53. For an analysis of this violence of binaries in Whitehead, refer to Faber, "Amid a Democracy."

54. The injustice of substantial presence leads not only to *Vorhandenheit*, as we will see later, but even worse, to the pure *um-zu*, the *Zuhandenheit*, of objects for manipulation. It not only negates the basis on which it is possible, the In-the-World *of Dasein*, but also the *event*-character of this presencing/absencing. For a connection of the loss of the event-character in Heidegger's notion of *Zuhandenheit* in the creation of a world of objects with Whitehead's analysis of events *versus* objects as abstractions from the relationality and processuality of events, cf. Harman, *Tool-Being*, 33.

55. For Deleuze's resistance against this "analogy of being" that Derrida found in Aristotelian substantialism, and his insistence on *univocity* instead (although not in the sense of "there are only things" and God is one of them) as being based on Whitehead's

by diagnosing that when the "distinction" between "what is present and presenting" "is obliterated," i.e., when "presencing appears as something present *(das Anwesen wie ein Anwesendes erscheint)*," this self-present present "finds itself in the position of being the highest being present *(in einem höchst Anwesenden).*"[56] In other words, while the event of becoming *possesses no present self-presence* in the chain of analogue, beings *a substance that possesses its present*, is "permanently present,"[57] which alone qualifies it as the *"highest being present."*[58] Moreover, in the analogy of Being, the "highest being present" qualifies as, and becomes viewed as, "pure presence *(rein Gegenwärtiges)"* and, therefore, as being *the* being "in the most authentic sense *(das eigentlich Seiende)"*[59] or the highest being.[60]

A lively example of this shift is Boethius' definition of "eternity." In *The Consolation of Philosophy*, he declares: "Eternity . . . is the complete, simultaneous and perfect possession of everlasting life; this will be clear from a comparison with creatures that exist in time."[61] Although it is not true that this "eternity" is plain timelessness, since it is *life*, Boethius understands "life" in terms of *simultaneity* of past and future as contained in an *atemporal, changeless, and immutable present*. Eternity, then, is not primarily the *absence* of time but—much worse—*absolute possession of the present as self-contained self-presence.* This God exists *in the mode of presentational immediacy* and does not know of the event.

Atemporality and possession are deeply connected. While the Gift of Being is the Event in which Being *gives time*, not timelessness, to the present moment, this event must appear as *nothingness*.[62] Because the presence of a substance can always *only* be present, its *absence* indicates that it does *not exist*. Consequently, "presencing" *(An-wesen)* becomes *divided* into

---

understanding of the univocity of creativity as "ground" of events, cf. Deleuze and Guattari, *What is Philosophy?*, chs. 1–2. As in Heidegger and Derrida, Deleuze's and Whitehead's analysis of the "analogy of being" lead them to the resistance against onto-theology as an extension of the logic of the One; cf. Faber, "O bitches."

56. Heidegger, "Anaximander Fragment," 50–51.

57. Heidegger, *Introduction to Metaphysics*, 162.

58. Heidegger, "Anaximander Fragment," 51; italics added.

59. Heidegger, *Being and Time*, 48.

60. For the analysis of this chain of substitutions of presencing with presence, which *is* "substantialism," as the birthplace of onto-theology in Heidegger, cf. Derrida, "Ousia and *Gramme*" and Caputo, *Heidegger and Aquinas*, ch. 6.

61. Boethius, *Consolation*, V.V1.

62. If, from the perspective of the present as presence, time is experienced as passing, it is also understood as *non-being*. *This*, for Derrida (and Heidegger), frames the whole discussion of "time" from Aristotle on. Cf. Derrida, "*Ousia* and *Gramme*," 50.

essence (*Wesen*) and existence (*Vorhandenheit*).[63] Even more important, essence becomes *divorced* from existence.[64] Consequently, the chain of analogue beings of self-presence necessitates a "highest being present" that not only owns all of its properties *in* its present, but *possesses its present*, i.e., it cannot *not* exist.

This situation of a bifurcation of essence and existence becomes obviously prevalent with appropriations of Avicenna's distinction of essence and existence.[65] It was still disguised as long as the reasoning behind Thomas Aquinas' *ipsum esse subsistens*—i.e., being "possessed by no other nature but ... itself [as its] very ... essence"[66]—was striving for mystical plenitude beyond formal essence."[67] The substantialist bifurcation becomes obvious, however, as soon as this "coincidence" disintegrates into "essence" as form *an sich* and "existence" as a form *that exists* so that God could be *only* identified as "highest being" insofar this being is the *x that in its essence necessarily exists*. Now *existence* becomes an expression of the self-possessive necessity of the highest *essence*.[68]

It is on this background that Anselm of Canterbury's "ontological argument" becomes unavoidable. In fear of nothingness in the midst of "presencing," the "highest being present" not only must possess all of its *essence* in its own self-presence (Boethius), but also its own *existence* (Anselm).[69]

63. Both—essence and existence—are already derivatives of the event of becoming in its denial by the present presence and its permanence; cf. Heidegger, *Kant*, 178–79.

64. With the erection of *ousia* as true being and the divorce of essence from existence, existence degrades to pure "x exists" (*Vorhandenheit*) as a passive being there, i.e., it loses the *processual* nature of its original unity of essence/existence in *ousia*, while *ousia* has lost its original vitality as *process of presencing/absenting*—precisely what Whitehead, Heidegger and Derrida are reconstructing.

65. For the differentiation of Aquinas with his understanding of God's existence as being beyond essence (and therefore not as part of the bifurcation) from other distinctions between existence and essence based on Avicenna, cf. Caputo, *Heidegger and Aquinas*, ch. 4.

66. Aquinas, *Summa Contra Gentiles*, 1,26/129.

67. Thomas was not an "essentialist." His notion of existence was more basic than the reduced notion of formal essence or essence as form, but has already surpassed essence with existence by overcoming a problem of formal essence or essence as form. In this sense, Thomas' non-essentialist view of God plays into the hands of the bifurcation. This becomes obvious only when *esse* and *ens* reunite in his final concept of God.

68. In this sense, Thomas never reached beyond the essence/existence distinction as did Nicolas of Cusa, with his highly original notions of God—*coincidentia oppositorum*, *non aliud*, *possest* and *posse ipsum*—through which Cusa situated God not only beyond any formal essence, but beyond being itself, thereby avoiding the bifurcation. cf. Bond, *Nicholas of Cusa*, introduction.

69. Hartshorne, *Anselm's Discovery* and Plantinga, *Ontological Argument*.

The "perfect being" *must possess its own existence as a property*! We became accustomed to calling this highest, self-present being—God.[70]

Unfortunately, the glory of this "perfect being" balances over the denial of *creative passage*—of becoming and perishing, of time and death, of the Event as passage.[71] Since "the original anxiety in existence is usually repressed"[72] and "only anxiety originally reveals this nothingness of the creative passage,"[73] the metaphysics of presence gives birth to a God who is a projection compensating the *fear* of the Event of "presencing."[74] The properties of this God—timelessness, infinite self-presence, omnipotence, self-subsisting existence—are but anthropomorphic pipe dreams pressed by the repressed anxiety of the fluidity of the creative passage of the Event, invented to gain absolute *independence from the event of time in fear of its nothingness*.[75] For this dream of the "presentational immediacy"[76] of an unmoved "prime mover, [who,] as 'pure act' *(energeia he kath' hauten)*, is pure presence,"[77] however, we pay the price of the descent into the nightmare of *absolute possession*. This move away from being "held out into nothingness"[78] is sealed off by the contention that the "Being that Pos-

70. But, in fact, it is not "God" we are talking about (and certainly not the God that would be necessitated by Christian thought), but a "highest being" hovering over the bifurcation of essence and existence that is already based on the *loss of the event of presenting/absenting*. In light of this reconstruction, this "highest being" is but an idol, a misplaced concreteness; cf. Wieman, *Wrestle of Religion* and Kaufman, *In the Beginning*, 60.

71. It is the "creation" of the onto-theological God of the highest being or the Ground of being (both sides of the same problem!). Cf. my lecture Faber, "Sounding the Depth of Things?" and Kessler and Sheppeard, *Mystics*, 38–74.

72. Heidegger, "What Is Metaphysics?," 106.

73. Heidegger, "What Is Metaphysics?"

74. It is one of Heidegger's insights in *Being and Time*, §§46–53, that it is the *fear of death* and, in a wider sense, the fear of nothingness, that leads to substantialism, but also that in re-discovering the nothingness of death in our life we are re-opened to Being, i.e., the nothingness of becoming and perishing, i.e., the event of presencing and absencing.

75. In order to understand the argument, here, it is important that this nothingness appears as nothingness only to the present presence insofar as it has itself already sealed off from presencing/absencing so that time becomes the nothingness of the present presence (*Gegenwart*), of substance (*ousia*), of existence (*Vorhandenheit*); cf. Derrida, "*Ousia* and *Gramme*," 50.

76. The irony of "presentational immediacy" in Whitehead is that it is *constituted* by the passage of the presencing/absencing or becoming/perishing it *excludes*; cf. PR, 176.

77. Derrida, "*Ousia* and *Gramme*," 52.

78. Heidegger, "What Is Metaphysics?," 106.

sesses its Own Existence" essentially also possesses the power to grant existence to everything else."[79]

At this point, Whitehead objects![80] Where even existence becomes a property, we should not be seduced by our awe for absolute power but rather be embarrassed by the very barbarism it expresses.[81] Where one's very existence is someone else's property, we have defined slavery! Here, the Aristotelian analogy of Being, with its substances (be it the free citizen or the perfect being) possessing attributes, just mirrors the sociology of slavery (see PR, 209). In the sense in which slavery is the "barbarous substratum [that] had to be interwoven in the social structure, so as to sustain the civilized apex" (AI, 168), God owns the world as the substratum of "His" imperial will. For Whitehead, this concept of God is nothing but a

> sublimation from its barbaric origin. He stood in the same relation to the whole World as early Egyptian or Mesopotannan kings stood to their subject populations. Also the moral characters were very analogous. In the final metaphysical sublimation, he became the one absolute, omnipotent, omniscient source of all being, for his own existence requiring no relations to anything beyond himself. He was internally complete. Such a conception fitted on very well to the Platonic doctrine of subordinate derivations. (ibid., 169)

Indra's Ear

Enter Strindberg. In his drama *A Dream Play* (1901), Strindberg created a famous theopoetic counter-image to the self-possessive God of the Greek-Western-philosophical closure. In this Play, he imagines the God, Indra's daughter Agnes, to incarnate in order to experience human becoming and suffering.[82] In the wake of her progressing immersion into human flesh, she allows elected human beings to witness a unique place—"Fingal's Cave."

79. Indeed, the medieval development of the bifurcation of essence and existence shows that the discussions of the power of God to grant existence were framed in a way that the omnipotence of God was not that of *Love*, but that *of annihilation*, hence, of the power of God's possession of existence. Cf. Casey, *Fate of Place*, ch. 5.

80. It is known that Whitehead refused for many years the notion of God as creator until he found a way to state it creativity without making it a possession of a "highest being" and "the accidents of will." Cf. AI, 168.

81. Cf. my explication of this connection in Whitehead in Faber, "Amid a Democracy."

82. Strindberg used this as a counter-image to the Trinitarian image of Father and Son. In Strindberg's counter-conceptualization, it is not the will of the Father to

In one encounter, the stage instruction reads: "The waves of the sea wash under the basalt pillars, producing a choir of wind and waves."[83]

LAWYER: Where are we, . . . Agnes?

DAUGHTER: Don't you hear – ?

LAWYER: I hear . . . drops . . . falling.

DAUGHTER: When people cry, there are tears . . . What else do you hear?

LAWYER: Sighing . . . wailing . . . moaning . . .

DAUGHTER: The complaints of mortals . . .[84]

In another encounter, Strindberg writes: "Fingals Cave. Long green waves toll gently into the cavern . . . The music of the winds. The music of the waves. The Daughter and the Poet onstage."[85]

POET: Where have you brought me?

DAUGHTER: Far from the murmuring and moaning of human beings – to the outermost edge of the world and the sea – to this grotto we call Indra's Ear. For it is said that here the god of the skies and the sovereign of the heavens listens to the pleas and petitions of mortals.[86]

The poetic images of "God's Ear" and "God's listening" are, of course, multilayered; they form a *palimpsest*, a multiply overwritten text. In any case, the metaphoric elliptic of the image of the "listening God" directly confronts the "absolute . . . source of all being, for his own existence requiring no relations to anything beyond himself, [being] internally complete" (AI, 169). While this "He-Man," in fear of time, appears under the paradigm of *absolute self-possession*, the God of the event, in the act of "presencing" uniting and multiplying time, is not a-temporal but

---

sacrifice the Son (as was a widely accepted soteriological interpretation of atonement at his time), but the urge of the Daughter to become flesh, to feel human flesh and the world of senses in order to *bodily understand* its misery.

83. Strindberg, *A Dream Play*, 67.

84. Strindberg, *A Dream Play*.

85. Strindberg, *A Dream Play*, 108.

86. Strindberg, *A Dream Play*.

time-*related*.[87] This God—Indra and Indra's Daughter Agnes[88]—touches *and* is touched by the finiteness of becoming and perishing. In *un-possessing* time, God *embraces* the passage of the world; in *releasing* time, God *listens*. What does that mean?

First of all, this means that the Listening God does not count property, but traces the *becoming and passing* of the world.[89] Instead of being self-contained in "His" perfectly possessed self-presence, God is self-released, perceptive of, and sensitive to, the Other—the creative passage of the world (PR, 346–51). Instead of clinging to "His" own presence, God—in the act of *listening*—is *constituted* by the traces of the multiplicity of the world. This God cannot function as *actus purus*, which always already *is* all that ever *can* be.[90] Rather, the listening God vibrates with Nicolas of Cusa's *posse ipsum*, the potential that arouses the appetite for becoming, unfolding, and growing.[91] This God is "defined" by the influx of *what is not God as the moment of God's becoming* (RM, 87–88).

Secondly, the Listening God is not Eye but Ear.[92] Only the God who "exists" in the mode of presentational immediacy holds everything in "His"

87. For an early and profound feminist criticism of this whole image of patriarchal power, cf. Ruether, *Sexism*; for the poststructuralist discourse, cf. Butler, *Bodies That Matter*.

88. "Agnes" is a hint to the fire that will consume the Daughter, being the essence of *God's* sacrifice to the world at the end of the Play.

89. This "receptive physicality" of a time-sensitive God is one of the central insights of Whitehead's understanding of God, preserved and developed in all diverse directions of process theology. Cf. Faber, "Prozesstheologie," in *Theologien der Gegenwart*, 179–97.

90. Ford, "Whitehead's Transformation of Pure Act." If the act of being is not understood in a substantial model as "transeunt" act of a constituted substance, but as a process of "concrescence" of the growing together of a multiplicity, as a receptive act, then God's "power" is that of receptivity in the first place; cf. Faber, "Apocalypse in God," 64–96. God, then, *traces* the passing world; cf. Faber, *God as Poet*, §39.

91. Here a Thomist and a Cusanic view of "power" differ greatly. While for Thomists, God's power is that of *existence* (in relation to their finite nature), for Cusa, the *potestas* (power) or *posse* (potential) of being is the origin of existence not only in God as *posse ipsum* but in all beings as being "empowered" in their own posse within the "*Posse* of all *posse*." Cf. Nicolas of Cusa, *De apice theoriae*, §12, in Bond, *Nicholas of Cusa*, 298. While for Thomists, God's power is that of granting existence (with all implications of absolute power), in Cusa, it is about the gift of self-creativity.

92. Of course, as a palimpsest, this image is not meant in an exclusive sense, but aims to sharpen differences that have defined our fabric of perception in a way that it influences our conceptualization of God. The fact that God cannot by "Visualized" did not prevent (especially Western) art from depicting God as the "All seeing Eye." This imaginary is, indeed, part of the patriarchal stratum of the independent (objective) and controlling power. Cf. Staeheli, *Mapping Women*, 95.

present, which otherwise would fall apart or vanish into nothingness.[93] "He" is the all-seeing Eye, the public Eye, the Big Brother, the Voyeur.[94] The all-penetrating Eye does not love secrets but tortures them out of its victims. The listening Ear, on the other hand, is blind to the interiority of the events in their becoming.[95] Instead of the radiating Eye that captures all, whether it wills so or not, the listening Ear gently lets come forth what wants to become.[96]

Thirdly, the Listening God is not the Word, but Silence.[97] Only the self-present God is destined to absolutely express "His" Self.[98] This God must *always* speak—of "Himself"—and all the world must *only* speak of "the One who *is*."[99] This is the God of Derrida's logocentrism and Judith Butler's phal-

93. If the all-presence of God is the ground of being, which otherwise would vanish into nothingness, it is only the exemplification of the *exclusion* of nothingness in this presence, instead of being its own nothingness (of which the mystical tradition and all process philosophy has had a sense; see Cusa, Hegel, and Heidegger) on the basis of creativity, so that creation must be all-seen in order to exist. The problem of control is inherent.

94. For this "ever-present policeman," cf. Ford, *Attentive Life*, 35.

95. An irreplaceable element of the image of the Listening Ear is that it is *receptive* instead of penetrating. Therefore, it is a congenial image of Whitehead's God, who "listens" to every event of becoming in its own creativity, not by being "in the present" of its becoming, but "in unison with" its becoming; cf. PR, 345.

96. This is the reason that God, in Whitehead, does not "know" (see) but lures to a process of self-creativity ("initial aim"), God has to listen to (hear) in order to "know" (receive); cf. Hosinski, *Stubborn Fact*, 158–59.

97. This is also to be understood as a layer of the palimpsest-image. While the Word is normally understood as the primary image of God's immanent Trinitarian, and economic, creative act, the mystical tradition, e.g., Meister Eckhart, knows of a *silence in the Godhead* that is as original as the Divine activity to give birth by the word (in God as Son; in the world as Son in the soul); cf. McGinn, *Mystical Thought*, 86–87.

98. While, on the basis of the oblivion of the Event of presencing/absencing, the traditional concept of the highest being must be seen as an all-powerful *self* that, therefore, can only be self-expressive of "his" power, Whitehead's God has no "Ego-Self," but is the becoming of Tragic Beauty (tragic from the standpoint of the Event of presencing/perishing); see Kraus, *Metaphysics of Experience*, 177. God's "creative ground" is not an Ego but creativity; PR, 105; and God's origin of subjectivity, the divine "subjective aim" is not power of self-possession, but pure Love, the Gift of Beauty and the Eros towards the Good. This does not mean that God, as being most concrete, cannot be personal or is without "internal Life" but that this Life is not based on a substantial view of subjectivity. Cf. Faber, "Personsein am Ort der Leere," 189–98.

99. It is a classical *topos* of theology (in the context of classical theism) to answer the question of the reason for the existence of the world with the "glory of God;" cf. *Catechism of the Catholic Church, Second Edition*, sec II. ch. 1, §4/IV: "The World was Created for the Glory of God." Any re-covering of the Event of becoming as, e.g., in "Open Theism," will, then, naturally be experienced as an attack on God's glory; cf. Ware, *God's Lesser Glory*.

logocentrism.[100] The listening God, on the other hand, in silence, can actually *hear* the world, can be touched by it, and can react to it.[101] This God is *passio pura*—the "pure passion" that desires and suffers a world to which it relates, as Whitehead's says, in "mutual immanence" (AI, 168).[102]

Finally, the Listening God is not Substance, but Event (PR, 18–19). This God "harbors," as John Caputo puts it, "an event that is at best a 'weak force,'" but may be "nonetheless, the only thing that is strong enough to save us"[103]—like Walter Benjamin's "weak messianic force,"[104] which steers up the lost past—and Catherine Keller's "eros," which emits "a lure to novelty" like "prevenient grace."[105] This is Schelling's unruly ground of *an-arche*;[106] Samuel Alexander's Deity, collecting itself out of space and time (see MT, 102); or Feuerbach's absolutely non-possessive event of love.[107] This is Cusa's infinite "complication" in which the All is infinitely enfolded and from which everything unfolds.[108] This is Meister Eckhart's beyond-the-difference of God and World, or Johannes Damascenes' "infinite sea."[109]

---

100. For Derrida's interpretation of logocentrism as phallogocentrism, cf. Sosnoski, "Deconstruction in America," 30–31. For Butler's criticism of phallogocentrism in relation to Luce Irigaray and Julia Kristeva, and in relation to the formation of "monotheism," cf. Butler, *Gender Trouble*, 37–38. For the connection of Derrida's logocentrism to Whitehead, cf. Bracken, "Whitehead and the Critique of Logocentrism," 91–110. Whitehead's differentiation of God and Creativity directly undermines this phallogocentrism of controlling power and God as ego-word; cf. Hufeaker, "Feminist Theology in Process Perspective," 177–87. For the "logic of the One" behind this onto-theological move, cf. my lecture Faber, "In the Wake of False Unifications."

101. In a technical sense, this receptivity of Whitehead's God is not only an expression of the Consequent Nature that receives the actual world when it has happened, but is part of a larger paradigm of God's activity as being receptive (instead of substantially active) in its grounding. Hence, the Primordial Nature is a process of the constitution of eternal objects by the activity of reception; cf. Ford, "Neville on the One and the Many," 79–84; cf. PR, 257. Moreover, in God's "foundational process of creativity" (ibid., 105), God is the "primordial creature" (ibid., 31) of creativity, thereby fulfilling the "definition" of the creative act as being a concrescence of many into a new togetherness (ibid., 21).

102. "Mutual Immanence" is Whitehead's remedy against the substantialism of *actus purus* and the act of power; cf. Faber, *Prozeßtheologie*, §21. For the Divine *passio ad intra* as new paradigm of God's activity as receptivity, cf. Faber, *God as Poet*, §§29, 35.

103. Caputo, *Weakness of God*, 36.

104. Caputo, *Weakness of God*, 7.

105. Keller, *Face of the Deep*, 181.

106. Keller, *Face of the Deep*, 180.

107. Feuerbach, *Essence of Christianity*, ch. IV. cf. my lecture "God's Love without God?"

108. Faber, "De-Ontologizing God," 191–208.

109. Faber, "'Gottesmeer,'" 64–95.

Back to Whitehead. In fact, Whitehead's God possesses nothing! None of the ultimates in Whitehead's philosophy are created or possessed by God (RM, 131). On the contrary, they name *un*-possession: "Creativity"—the self-creative ground of becoming—is neither created nor controlled, but inspired by God (PR, 31); the "potentials"—themselves neither Platonic "forms" nor predestined "aims" but a chaotic fluid[110]—are neither created nor crafted by God into a hierarchical realm of forms, but offered as stimulations, appetites, and desires (PR, 257).[111]

God possesses not even Godself! The so called "primordial nature" is more like Schelling's "*Ungrund*," an *anarchic depth* of potentials, constantly revolving and refiguring itself in light of the so called "consequent nature," which is, of course, another name for "Indra's Ear"—God's listing to the world.[112] Against Hartshorne's unfortunate transubstantiation in which God became a substance again—possessing a *fixed character* with accidental states of affairs[113]—in Whitehead, God's primordial aspect functions as stimulating "initial Eros" (AI, 295) for the self-creation of events and God's consequent aspect, as "infinite patience . . . tenderly saving [its] turmoil . . . by the completion of [God's] own nature" (PR, 346). In neither of these aspects is God simply atemporal stasis, but always *infinite movement*.[114]

In the end, I want to opt for an understanding of God's "presence" as *the event of un-possessive listening and un-possessing silence*. In light of the reconstruction of the event of presencing/absencing, in which we are called to experience the Event of God, this Event unsettles our substantialist expectations and, in destabilizing our ego-structure, it also unsettles our understanding of God's presence as stability, our understanding of salvation as overcoming of fluency, and our understanding of God as power. Especially in a postmodern society that has lost these stabilities, only to feel left with experiencing the

110. Against the tendency to understand the "initial aim" as "orderings" that preordain the becoming of events, I think of them as chaotic potentials, with which God lures to empower the self-creative becoming of events and to disturb settled orders; see Faber, *God as Poet*, §§15–16. For the chaotic multiplicity of eternal objects cf. Leue, *Metaphysical Foundations*, part I, ch. 3

111. For the function of eternal objects in God as erotic appetites, cf. PR, 347–48.

112. Faber, *God as Poet*, §§33–34, 38.

113. Hartshorne, "Whitehead's Idea of God," 513–60. This "substantial" view of God as a "fixed character (primordial nature) of a society of states (consequent nature) is still very influential in Griffin, *Reenchantment*. Cf. my critique in Faber, *God as Poet*, §34.

114. Faber, "Whitehead at Infinite Speed." Deleuze's term of an event as "infinite speed" (Deleuze and Guattari, *What is Philosophy?*, 20–21) replaces the ideas of any fixed character and a substantial view on an event as passivity and non-activity. As such it reconstructs the *nunc stans*—if an event is an infinite movement, so is God.

absence of God, I want to indicate the implications of this counter-image for a God of self-possession with four final thoughts.[115]

First, if possession is a mark of a substance with properties, un-possession is an image of the *presencing* of the *event*. Since the presence of an event is always the juncture of absence, it is *un-presenting presenting*. The presencing, then, of an un-possessing God, is always the *trace* we cannot *see* "in" our present, but have to *listen* to—like we listen to a piece of music that is always already gone when we hear it, or anticipated before we hear it.[116] It is always *absent* to our "Eye" (Gaze) and "I" (Self) because our Eye is blind to its nothingness and our "I" (the Ego) is too preoccupied with self-possession.[117] But if we *listen*, in our silence, we hear—its nothingness. In the most intense way, God's presencing must seem to us as utmost absence of "*a* God"![118] God's listening remains always an *event of silence*.[119]

Second, the sounds "Indra's Ear" traces are the traces of God's listening to *us*—*our* sorrows, tears, and impasses. If God's presencing is God's listening—what do we hear *God* listening to? As in Strindberg's Play: if we listen beyond our Ego, we hear what God hears—the waves of *our* sorrows and the drops of *our* tears.[120] God's presencing is that of the "fellow-sufferer who understands" (PR, 350).[121] But stuck in our preconceptions, God's *absence of listening* might mean *nothing* to us.

Third, God's "presence" cannot be *enjoyed* "in" our present—as our "present" is empty of "presence"[122]—but arises only as its disturbance. That is, God's silence is not still; it is *creative* (Cf. PR, 244).[123] It creates *us as*

---

115. Howe, *Faithful to the Earth*.

116. See the musical images in MT, 83–85 and Whitehead's concept of "Harmony of harmonies" for God in AI, 296, with Deleuze's explication of Whitehead's event with a concert in Deleuze, *Fold*, ch. 6, and his concept of harmony as the "polyphony of polyphonies," ch. 9. Cf. Faber, "O bitches,"128.

117. Stambaugh, *Formless Self*.

118. This reflects Meister Eckhart' *Abgeschiedenheit* in which to "experience" the Godhead—the sea of silence—is not set against the Word, but *is* the silence of the Word; cf. McGinn, *Mystical Thought of Meister Eckhart*, 87.

119. Even so, extreme experiences of the "absence" of God as "silence" as in Mother Teresa's confession to have lived almost fifty years in such a desert of the absence of God may be intense experiences of the presencing of God as listening; cf. my lecture "Forgotten Among the Lillies."

120. Here is an interesting connection to the Buddhist experience of awakening to the feeling of the whole ream of *samsara* as dependent co-origination, i.e., as the realm of suffering that we experience with compassion; cf. Abe, *Zen*.

121. Cf. also Cobb and Ives, *Emptying God*.

122. Hart, "The Experience of Nonexperience," 188–206.

123. With the "initial aim," God's Priniordial Act constitutes any new event as

absent, i.e., as *absenting our Self* for the feeling of the Other. Levinas is not far here.[124] Nevertheless, I think, the creative silence is not *demanding*; it is *arousing*. It releases the creative forces that are hindered by narcissistic self-presence. It is not Imperative, but Appetite (AI, 148, 198).

Finally, consider Whiteheads saying, "The image – and it is but an image – the image under which . . . God's nature is best conceived, is that of a tender care that nothing be lost" (PR, 346). I want to close by augmenting this statement with this thought: "The image – and it is but an image – the image under which God's presencing is best conceived, is that of a *creative silence* expressing that *nothing be possessed*, but *everything be seduced to become self-creative beauty.*" The beauty of anything, of course, is always precisely what cannot be possessed; it can only be listened to; it becomes present only when we let go of it.[125]

Here, Whiteheads elliptic image of God as the "poet of the world" (PR, 346) fits: the poet, in creative silence, listening to the Event, its "luminous rising and decline," *touches* everything—as distorted as it may be—in its beauty. "While" we might be concerned with necessities, in this "while," a graceful lingering may occur, "which discloses to every creature its own greatness" (RM, 155).

---

self-creative in disturbing its repetition of the past with novelty. This is also what God's Consequent Act seeks: *intensity of novelty*, not preservation; cf. PR, 105 and Faber, *God as Poet*, §17.

124. Faber, *Prozeßtheologie*, §25 and "De-Ontologizing God."

125. For this understanding of Beauty in Whitehead (and Kant) cf. Sayer, *Wert und Wirklichkeit*, part II, ch. IV.

CHAPTER FOUR

The Touch of Reality

GRAHAM HARMAN'S "ON VICARIOUS Causation" explores an object-oriented philosophy *in nascendi* that, to the exact correlations, mirrors Whitehead's understanding of the "touch" of real things (and there are only real things, and besides that, things as sensed) in his organic refutation of mechanicism with "prehensive" connectivity. Although this connection only exists vicariously in my mind and in contiguous independence, that is, in mutual incompleteness, the sensibility of resonance it insinuates may give rise to certain (real) objects such that they can be meditated on and which are as "strange" as Harman defines his realism. Since "allusions" in Harman suggests such connections, I could not resist following their "tunneling" through the very "blasphemy" that Harman's buries by his non-theological recapitulation of the occasionalism of Malebranche and al-Ghazali. Hence, in relation to Whitehead's secular divine, my "object" of meditation will finally flow into the question of the status of the intentional/prehensive "space" in which the constitution of Self might point to its internal "molten core" as an allusion to that in the midst of its intentional constitution as real object, which it must always "really" exclude in order to touch, be touched, and vicariously facilitate the touch of real things.

Crash

"It's the sense of touch. Any real cities you walk, you know, you brush past people, people bump into you. In L.A., nobody touches you. We are always behind this metal and glass."[1] Such is the beginning of the 2004 movie Crash: touch and the impossibility of touch—on a local basis. You are in the "center" of non-touch! The "metal and glass" not only hints at life in

1. Opening lines of the movie *Crash*, directed by Paul Haggis (2004).

a non-space of isolated buildings, along with their missing "in-between" of common places of touch, but points at the very medium of this non-relationality in form of isolating cars, bound only by their common streams of highways, freeways, or neighborhood labyrinths—the "rhizomes" of non-touch, together alone, disentangled in one's own path, "out of touch" with the distanced sojourners. If you touch them, you create a crash. In fact, the only contact, the break-through into, and of, reality, is a crash—and its consequences: an awakening to real isolation dismantled, connected in insurmountable distance.

Yet, touched we are not in a crash, not even when slowed down to eye's sight. When we must leave our shells, we only become a new crust of disentanglement and retreat. Touched we are only when we don't crash. But how? Touched we are when we do not touch. But how? Touched we are only from within, in what Graham Harman poetically names the "molten core"[2] of the hidden other, beneath the crust of infinite distance, and without resolving it. But how?

Meditation

I am profoundly "touched" by Harman's "On Vicarious Causation"—as it is a meditation on the "touch" of things, that is, really every-thing. This world of Harman's is a world of objects, in fact, two mutually exclusive, but related kinds of objects: real objects and sensible objects. In their interplay, Harman explores a general "ontology" of our world in which touch happens without the elevation of any special "metaphysical" entities—such as God—as exceptions or exceptional causes or initiators of touch. Moreover, while alluding to, but avoiding, a theological highjacking of connectivity, Harman also disputes the other extreme, the secularism in form of naturalism, materialism, mechanicism, and skepticism.

In viewing the connectivity of real things without any presupposed scheme of necessary, effective causality—instead seeking "something closer to what is called formal cause"[3]—Harman reclaims not only philosophy from science, but also a philosophical approach that profoundly transcends an analytic reduction of philosophy to arguments and proofs of the obvious. Instead of a "procedure [that] does no justice to a world where objects are always more than they literally state," he seeks the allusions of depth unspoken. Since those "who care only to generate arguments almost never generate objects," I will use the form of a meditation in order to appreciate Harman's

2. Harman, "On Vicarious Causation," 210.
3. Harman, "On Vicarious Causation," 190.

intention to seek the release of, or allure to, the life, ineffability, and creativity hidden in the world's objects. When Harman muses that new objects "are the sole and sacred fruit of writers, thinkers, politicians, travelers, lovers, and inventors,"[4] I will forego "analysis" for a "sympathy" with the internal infinity of objects to which we, at best, can only allude.

As "meditation" is already philosophically claimed—for instance, by Descartes's Meditations and Badiou's Being and Event[5]—my use of the term will not be independent from their implicit, but conscious, theological or anti-theological ruminations—such as the ones invoked by Harman: the occasionalism of Malebranche and al-Ghazali.[6] We might say, as Harman puts it, that meditation seeks the "soul animating . . . from within."[7] This anima of things cannot be analyzed without initiating their retreat into an internality that is inaccessible. While the objects of "nature can never be grasped,"[8] we can allude to it "by brushing its surface in such a manner as to bring its inner life into play."[9] This may be the very meaning of "speculation." "There is no speculation in those eyes," Whitehead quotes Shakespeare, alluding to the very soul of the retreated object, the very "it" that refuses to give itself away in a push or crash. By "'speculative' demonstration," (CN, 6) Whitehead wants us not to witness a forced "description" of stubbornly withdrawn interiority, but to experience our retreat in which we might become witnesses of the anima of things—but only by becoming ourselves as a new contrast of real connection of real objects.

In adopting this approach, I want to aim at three goals at once. First, in leveling Harman and Whitehead, I consider both of them (with one of Harman's modes of relationality) as "contiguous."[10] Distinct, but related in my intentional space, they come together without a reigning scheme of superiority or preordained structure of composition. Rather, much like a Deleuzian "plane of immanence,"[11] they swirl around and over one another with their own internal, infinite movements within my intentional space, as a by-product of my "real object I."

Second, I consider each approach profoundly absorbed with a speculative demonstration of the touch of real objects, but in somewhat

---

4. Harman, "On Vicarious Causation," 212.

5. Badiou, Being and Event, 18.

6. Frank, Al-Ghazali and the Asharite School.

7. Harman, "On Vicarious Causation," 216.

8. Harman, "On Vicarious Causation," 208.

9. Harman, "On Vicarious Causation," 220.

10. Harman, "On Vicarious Causation," 217.

11. Deleuze and Guattari, What Is Philosophy?, 21.

complimentary ways. Hence, giving both Harman and Whitehead the advantage of the judicial *in dubito pro reo*, I judge neither philosopher as right or wrong, or more wrong than my own contrast of them. Rather, their modes of addressing the depth of objects and the mystery of connectivity strike me as mutually incomplete and, hence, enriching such that their respectively more temporal or spatial approach seems to allow certain aspects of objects to become more convincingly to the forth than others. While I am not seeking a "synthesis"[12] of both, without any doubt, in my mind, both together seem to me more deeply "in touch" with things, yet in somehow fortunately underdetermined ways.

Third, like a child's strange preoccupation with certain objects rather than others and details rather than the big picture, I will attempt to draw out a too-little and a too-much in their demonstrative gestures. Their respective "occasionalism," or their secularized versions of it, retains or hides certain theological impulses, still shining through. While I don't want to take anything away from the grand proposal of such a secular, but not naturalistic, sacred, but not religiously motivated occasionalism of their creative pen, I think these theological roots must be openly witnessed. The respective too-little or too-much of their respective secularization may not yet reveal how in a universe of only "occasions" of connectivity (PR, 207) we should designate any ontological status of real objects. Instead of following a line of thought that prejudices the invocation of a "divine" as but another "metaphysical" misconception of an exceptional entity "out there," physically causing all touch,[13] I will treat the enveloped theological allusions of both thinkers—Harman's secularized allure and Whitehead's divine "a-lure" within the "real I"[14]—as constitutive of touch.

Realism(s)

Before I further explore Harman's ingenious concept of "vicarious causation" as perhaps the real content of an "object-oriented philosophy"[15]—to the extent it resonates with Whitehead in releasing touch from causality—let me demonstrate the obvious synergies or shared sympathies of Harman's and Whitehead's version of "speculative realism"[16] or "organicism."[17] If speculative

12. Faber, "Immanence and Incompleteness," 91–107.
13. Harman, "On Vicarious Causation," 204.
14. Harman, "On Vicarious Causation," 219.
15. Harman, "On Vicarious Causation," 202.
16. Harman, *Towards Speculative Realism*.
17. Kraus, *Metaphysics of Experience*, 41–46.

realism, in fact, privileges realism, it must be asked: against what? The answer is deceivingly simple: against idealism and materialism alike.[18]

Idealism—such as Heidegger's and Husserl's, on which Harman bases his objectivist reorientation—has done little to engage objects from the perspective of their integrity as objects besides making them function as moments of human presence, use, or means of acting out—as in Heidegger[19]—or mental products of states of intentionality, by which they become "phenomena [rather than] real objects"—as in Husserl. Realism, instead, refuses any elevated station of cognition, mentality, or human subjectivity. Yet, in the midst of this phenomenalism, Harman finds another layer, a hidden[20] "novel concern with specific, concrete objects" such as "hammers, cigarettes, and silk garments"[21] that, against idealistic reductions, abandons the "gap between humans and the world."[22]

In the same way, Harman disposes of the *materialistic* reduction of objects by refusing to accept the age-old atomism of Democritus, Empedocles, and Lucretius, collapsing real objects into a *"dull realism of mindless atoms and billiard balls that is usually invoked to spoil all the fun in philosophy."* Instead, Harman defends a "weird realism"[23] that doubts "the power of [any] scientific explanation, which employs nothing but naturalistic theories,"[24] by refusing its underlying "naturalism" as again privileging "human access to the world," by treating "human consciousness" as *excluded* from being brought on "the same footing as the duel between canaries, microbes, earthquakes, atoms, and tar."[25]

Whitehead's realism is strikingly congruent with such considerations. In the poetic chapter V of *Science and the Modern World*, Whitehead expounds his "organic mechanism" (SMW, 80) as evading both naïve vitalism and scientific mechanicism in humanization, or reduction of every "thing" to a dull bundle of dead bodies. "The only way of mitigating mechanism," Whitehead muses, "is by the discovery that it is not mechanism" (ibid., 76). His *organic* view, instead, builds on a fresh presupposition, namely: a "mysterious presence of surrounding things, which imposes itself on" (ibid., 83) us from beyond. The *exception* of human perceptivity and consciousness is

18. Harman, *Prince of Networks*, 101.
19. Harman, "On Vicarious Causation," 192.
20. Harman, "On Vicarious Causation," 194.
21. Harman, "On Vicarious Causation," 192.
22. Harman, "On Vicarious Causation," 188.
23. Harman, "On Vicarious Causation," 187.
24. Harman, "On Vicarious Causation," 194.
25. Harman, "On Vicarious Causation," 195.

precisely avoided by "including . . . our acts of cognition" as "*in themselves* the elements of a common world" (ibid., 88).

Whitehead squares his distinction of idealism and realism with that of subjectivism and objectivism, and adopts a position of *objectivist realism*. While for the *subjectivist*—idealist or realist—"the things experienced only indirectly enter into the common world by reason of their dependence on the subject who is cognizing," Whitehead's "objectivist holds," like Harman's, "that the things experienced and the cognizant subject enter into the common world on equal terms" (ibid., 89). While for *subjectivist idealists* all things are mere phenomena within the human or divine mind, objectivists—idealists or realists—"agree that the world disclosed in sense-perception is a common world, transcending the individual recipient." While the *objectivist idealist* "finds that cognitive mentality is in some way inextricably concerned in every detail," this is precisely "the position the realist denies" (ibid., 90). Hence, the *objectivist realist* treats all things as *objects*, their interiority as all-pervading, and their mentality as emergent, and being in the world *as* real object. Similar to Harman's "speculative realism," Whitehead calls this "a position of provisional realism" (ibid., 91).

So far, this comparison signals agreement. Yet, *precisely at this point*, a disturbing, surprising, ingenious departure from this seemingly "common realism" arises by which Harman not only reveals one of its yet undisclosed presuppositions, but differs from Whitehead. This presupposition is *relationalism*.[26] In Harman's somewhat surprising *denial* of the view that real objects are "naturally" connected and, hence, are constituted *by relations*, he distances himself not only from all subjectivist and idealist positions of connectivity, which abandon *real* objective connection among things for *mental* ones, but also from all objectivist and realist positions that *expand* relationality to *physical* realities and their perception, including Whitehead's. Hence, what is called for in Harman's objective realism is not causation *from* relation, but *vicarious* causation without touch—a "touch without touching."[27] To say it in even stronger terms: The very condition of Whitehead's objective realism—universal relationalism[28]—is at the *very center of Harman's denial*—this denial being *the very condition* of his definition of speculative realism.

For a moment—this gives one a pause—or, at least, it should!

Whitehead's relationalism is meant to pose a "warrant of universality throughout all experience." That which "does not so communicate is

26. Shaviro, "The Actual Volcano," 279–90.
27. Harman, "On Vicarious Causation," 220.
28. Weber, *Whitehead's Pancreativism*, ch. 4.

unknowable, and the unknowable is unknown." If, in fact, only a "universal-ity defined by 'communication' can suffice," any connection, causation, and touch must express "an essence [of] the universe which forbids relation-ships beyond itself." "Speculative philosophy," Whitehead affirms, "seeks" nothing but "that essence" (PR, 4).

Not so for Harman! Not only does Harman not seek such a relational "essence"; rather, he explicitly *avoids* it and *thereby* establishes real connec-tivity! That which Whitehead excludes is, in fact, precisely what Harman affirms: that real objects are *unknown and, hence, unknowable*. Hence, real objects only connect *occasionally*, but by no means or in any sense necessar-ily. It is *because* things are not in touch, or, at least, not "naturally," that they are *real* objects. While Whitehead's relationalism reconstructs the solip-sism of isolated substances as interconnected events of change and limited permanence,[29] Harman courageously readopts the notion of substance as that which expresses real disconnection.

Object(s)

To get to the root of this profound opposition, we must first seek to ex-clude potential simplifications that might release the forces of antinomy too early and from the wrong places. Obviously, Harman's and White-head's terminologies are not the same—how could they be, since both philosophers strive for novelty through a reconfiguration of traditional philosophical concepts. Hence, we must test whether their ontological antinomy is not based on a loss of translatability. In order to exclude pre-mature places of departure, I will only name some of the most obvious conceptual transferences, leaving the more obscure and subtle elements to further confirmative or inhibiting clarification.

For Harman, real objects have no relations and, for the most part, do not seek them. If sought, these relations seem to be only *apparent*, that is, they do not give rise to a direct physical or mental grasping of the *interiority* of the reality of real objects. Rather, utilizing Heidegger's tool-analysis, real objects retreat under pressure, refuse to be grasped, withdraw from any pre-supposed, imposed, or desired relation. Real objects are hidden in their own internal infinity.[30] They are—and hereby Harman begins to use the classical terminology—inaccessible "substances" with their essential attributes and accidents of change. Hence, if there is any connection between real objects, it can be established neither by direct physical contact nor direct clairvoyance

29. Leclerc, *Whitehead's Metaphysics*.
30. Harman, "On Vicarious Causation," 211.

of an object's inner core. Rather, such connection exists occasionally, mediated by something else, which is not a real object. Harman finds this *vicarious* connection in a different kind of object, the sensible object, situated *within* the interior of the perceptive real object.

Would Whitehead disagree? Of course, when we take Whitehead's explicit abandonment of the substance/attribute/accident-scheme as a starting point—but then we would only state the obvious, namely the very opposition we want to understand. Moreover, Whitehead *agrees* that "substances" are isolated instances of solipsism (PR, 152). Yet, while this is part of Harman's explanatory scheme, the fact that Whitehead abandons this does not imply that he adopts a position of universal relationalism that would *eo ipso* fall into the trap of Harman's "fanatic mirror holism"[31] by which he might have counted out Leibnitz. Whitehead does *not* hold the view of a panoptic holism in which everything is a mirror of everything, unobstructed, in mutual public view and control. Yet, he also does not hold the view that any "contact" is purely external, a crash of steel, glass, and meat. When Whitehead expresses relationality by hinting at physical field-theory—after all, he did work on Maxwell's field-equations for his dissertation—for which any particle is somehow distributed throughout the whole field (SMW, 125), he immediately counters this incomplete picture with allusions to quantum-physical discreteness and atomicity (PR, 245). Indeed, Whitehead contrasts atomism, but not in form of a digital seriality of purely external relation (the crash), with *organicism*, but not in form of a universal continuity through purely internal relationality (the mirror) (ibid., 36).

In fact, then, like Harman, Whitehead asks the profound question, how a substance can be *in* another substance (ibid., 50). He concurs with Harman that connection between real objects can neither be a crash nor a mirror; that touch cannot be a point of shock or a reflection. Instead, touch—and with it the notion of causation—must name some kind of *mediation* between disconnection and convergence. Real connection must be engaged in *mediating between externality and internality*. It must translate the *disjunction* of mutually external real objects, disconnected among themselves, into a *conjunction* that is *internal* to the constitution of *another* real object, the "real object I." This is, of course, a rendition of Whitehead's vision of the fundamental creative relationship of events in the production of novelty as condensed in his Category of the Ultimate (ibid., 21), technically unfolded with the neologism of "prehension" (SMW, 103).

Harman extracts the distinction between real and sensible objects from the idealist and empiricist tradition, that is, a milieu in which always

---

31. Harman, "On Vicarious Causation," 200.

some doubts as to the reality of causal efficacy of material objects prevailed. It is remarkable, how under Harman's wizard rod their descendants—Heidegger and Husserl—transform into veritable realists! While Heidegger's *Dasein* is frustrated by the withdrawal of real objects, which accounts for Harman's view of disconnection,[32] Husserl's subjective intentionality of the human "I" becomes the very place in which sensible objects appear on the inside of a real object, the "real I."[33] At the same time, Harman's antianthropocentric enthusiasm diffuses *Dasein's* infinite internality among *all* real objects as their "molten core,"[34] and claims intentionality as the very structure of its internal perception of externality.

This double expansion is crucial for Harman. It is an *expansion* because it infuses withdrawal, internal infinity, and perceptivity into all possible real objects, only including, not elevating, human beings. It is a *double* expansion because of the real objects' *independence* from the sensible objects' population of an intentional interior, by which the latter remains *distinct* from the externality of the former. It is crucial because, now, Harman has a way to connect the outside of disconnected real objects per *mediation* of sensible perception with the *inside* of another real object, the "I"—both without the crash of mutually external billiard balls, and without the mirror of a mutually internal arrest within an all controlling mind.[35] In other words, this complex connectivity between objects has reached *ontological* universality, while discarding metaphysical—human or divine—exceptionality.

Again, this does not establish any *essential* bifurcation from Whitehead. In fact, Harman's double expansion circumscribes rather exactly both outlook and intention of Whitehead's "prehension."[36] Like Harman, Whitehead retrieves its directional (external–internal) structure from the idealism and empiricism of the likes of Hume, Berkeley, Locke, and Leibnitz by transforming their anthropocentric inclination into a realistic outlook with universal reach (PR, 119). In avoiding the models of crash and mirror, "prehension" envisions a connectivity of real objects as a *modal concern* of an internal standpoint with a perspective on external objects (SMW, 64). As for Harman, connection is threefold: it is an objectification of a *real* object's internal, inaccessible becoming via a *modal* transfer to another object-in-becoming (PR, 23).

---

32. Harman, "On Vicarious Causation," 192.
33. Harman, "On Vicarious Causation," 194.
34. Harman, "On Vicarious Causation," 210.
35. Harman, "On Vicarious Causation," 187.
36. Rose, *Whitehead*, ch. 2.

Like Harman, Whitehead does not view this "democratization" of perception among all "fellow creatures" (ibid., 50) as vitalism, but as a recognition of internality and sensitivity in all things.[37] Using Francis Bacon of all sources, Whitehead affirms that "all bodies whatsoever, though they have no sense, yet they have perception. . . ." (SMW, 41).

Like Harman, Whitehead transforms "causal efficacy" from an external necessity into a kind of *formal* causality.[38] In *Symbolism*, he states that we must inquire how in "any one individual . . . other individuals . . . enter 'objectively' into the unity of its own experience"—the "unity of its own experience" being "that individual existing formally"—and, conversely, "how it enters into the 'formal' existence of other things. . . *objectively*, that is to say—existing abstractly, exemplifying only some elements in its formal content" (SY, 26–27). The inaccessible, formal interiority of a real object remains *disconnected* from its *objectification* in other real objects. Yet, in its objectification it is perceived *modally*, that is, through a "subjective form," (PR, 26) in the formal constitution of the becoming-itself of a new real object.

Like Harman, Whitehead differentiates the *external* real objects prehended, which remains always external, from the *internal* process of prehension. The prehending entity cannot recover the formal wholeness of the prehended real object, but only reinterpret its physicality by *mentally* abstracting a fragmented *modal form* of this real object, internalizing and projecting it, so to say, as its "sensible" object—which in a prehension appears as a complex of form and feeling (ibid., 88.)

So far, we may say that the respective differentiation between objects as well as their relations and contrasts do not give rise to the profound opposition that we were seeking to understand. On the contrary, Whitehead and Harman seem, although through different terminologies, to say that there *is* a connection between real objects despite various forms of disconnection; that the overcoming of disconnection does neither discard the inaccessibility of real objects nor the internal infinity of their core; and that any overcoming of causal isolation is not of efficacious necessity, but somehow of formal nature, and hence, vicariously stimulated. So, then, where does their divergence come from?

---

37. Faber, "Amid a Democracy," 192–237.
38. Harman, "On Vicarious Causation," 190.

Allure/A-lure

A hint lies in the yet-undisclosed mystery of the *initiation* of connectivity.[39] The center-piece of Harman's move toward the overcoming of the disconnection of real objects among themselves—since their obvious, undisputed connection must be explained somehow[40]—via the vicarious presence of sensible objects in the "real object I" is enfolded in the question, how the skepticism of disconnection (as in Hume) and the premature reintroduction of God as agent of connectivity (as in Malebranche) can be avoided.[41] Harman's answer is not yet complete with the introduction of the mediation of vicarious sensible causes because the vicarious presence of real objects per sensible objects leaves the door wide open for internal solipsism. Maybe, there are no real objects at all—only projections of the only *immediate* real object, the "I"? Descartes *ego cogito* still lingers, raising the still open question of *realitas objective* (PR, 49).

Harman tries to escape this calamity with this fourfold disentanglement: between the function of vicariousness and the two kinds of objects; between relation and connection; between the "real object I" and all real objects; and between the hidden substantiality of real objects and their substantial qualities. First, as real objects are vicariously connected by sensible objects, so are sensible objects vicariously connected through the "real object I."[42] Second, as there are many different kinds of relation— the *intentional* space of sensible objects and the "real I," the *contiguity* of sensible objects in this space, the *sincerity* of the occupation of the "real I" with sensible objects, *real* connection, and *no* connection[43]—it is only through "sincerity" by which the "real I" in its intentional space transforms a sensible into a real object and connection occurs.[44] Third, the question of the *production* of real connections elevates the "real I"[45] over all other assumed real objects since it is the *exceptional experienced place* in which sensible objects are converted into real objects[46]—still only *assuming* the others' own "molten core." Fourth, the transformation in both directions and, hence, the *differentiation* between real and sensible objects in the

---

39. Harman, "On Vicarious Causation," 212.

40. Harman, "On Vicarious Causation," 199.

41. Harman, "On Vicarious Causation," 219.

42. Harman, "On Vicarious Causation."

43. Harman, "On Vicarious Causation," 199–200.

44. Harman, "On Vicarious Causation," 210.

45. Harman, "On Vicarious Causation," 198.

46. Ibid.

sincerity of the "real object I" happens by a procedure of "coupling and uncoupling,"[47] namely: by *allure*.

While Harman's original intention for the introduction of the disconnection of real objects may have been his insistence on the inviolable reality and infinite interiority of things against the possessiveness of human subjectivity, power, and manipulation,[48] the introduction of *substantiality* as expressive of this independence becomes necessary only for solving *another* problem, namely: the *purely internal production* of real objects by the "real object I"[49]—the counter-piece of Descartes's *ego cogito*, Heidegger's Dasein, and Husserl's *intentional Ego*. However, the Aristotelian and Western congruence of essence and essential qualities does *only* answer to the former, but not to the latter intention. Why? Because as long as the essence of a sensible object is *identical* with its sensed essential qualities,[50] its "reality" is still stuck in a potential solipsism of the "real object I" of which it might still represent an imagination (a unicorn).[51]

It is in *this* context and with *this* latter intention that Harman takes the audacious move to leave Aristotelian substance, instead establishing a *disassociation* between the "essential qualities"[52]—even the unity-quality to *be* an essence[53]—as being part of the *sensorium* of the "real object I" and the "essence" of the real object itself, which is *inherently withdrawn, hidden, unknown, and unknowable*, only leaving a subtle trace of its real exteriority beyond any interior projection. This is the function of "allure": *in* an "analogous event"[54] of transference, this dissociation becomes a trace for how real objects connect in their hidden interiority. Hence, only by *metaphorically alluring*[55] to the infinite depth of objects as such,[56] beyond signification (qualification),[57] somehow "brushing its surface,"[58] we come somehow, *je ne sais quoi*,[59] in touch with its *anima*, the internal life of its "molten core."

47. Harman, "On Vicarious Causation," 213.
48. Harman, "On Vicarious Causation," 211.
49. Harman, "On Vicarious Causation," 209–10.
50. Harman, "On Vicarious Causation," 214.
51. Harman, "On Vicarious Causation," 215.
52. Harman, "On Vicarious Causation," 213.
53. Harman, "On Vicarious Causation," 214.
54. Harman, "On Vicarious Causation," 215.
55. Harman, "On Vicarious Causation," 212.
56. Harman, "On Vicarious Causation," 211.
57. Harman, "On Vicarious Causation," 215.
58. Harman, "On Vicarious Causation," 220.
59. Harman, "On Vicarious Causation," 214.

Whitehead, who completely abandons the category of substance, instead builds on the interplay of *events* and *objects* (CN, 143). First, instead of the mutual vicariousness of real and sensible objects, Whitehead establishes the interplay of real objects (objectified events) and abstract objects (forms), in which both mediate their respective function—the inaccessibility of the formal interiority of real objects and their accessibility through (subjective) "forms" (pure objects) of objectified events (facts). Second, relation is a mere abstraction of contrast, which is the very *becoming of connections* of actual events per prehensions. Third, prehensions, in their own turn, constitute the internalization of objectified events in actual events, which are the very *becoming* of the "real I." Fourth, the differentiation between real and sensible objects *in a process of becoming* a real object reflects the difference between real and abstract objects in physical and mental prehensions as *they are synthesizing their own* "real object I" (the subject-superject).[60]

Yet, while Harman's "allure," built on a transformed category of "substance," addresses the *je ne sais quoi* of disconnection as well as connection, Whitehead's conceptual counterpart—"symbolism"—is but an interference of two pure modes of prehension, a causal and presentational objectification—partly reconstructing Harman's claim of the feeling of reality in the distinction between real and sensible objects and their mutual inaccessibility and inherence.[61] Hence, in Whitehead's paradigm of events and objects, "symbolism" or "allure" *does not yet* point at the mystery of the *je ne sais quoi*. Is it missing then, missing because of presupposed relationalism that—as Harman seems to imply—explains its mystery away?

Not at all! For Whitehead, *because* of the event and object–structure, the *je ne sais quoi* appears *from another place*, namely *the process of becoming* a "real object I" itself in which the modes of prehension (the interplay of real and sensible objects) are *creatively* connected. Since, for Whitehead, the "real object I" is not a "given"—as it is for Harman—the question of the inexhaustible "depth of objects"[62] is *transferred* from the "occasions" of the vicarious interplay of real and sensible objects in the intentional space of the "real object I" to the *sundering of all relationality in the becoming* of such an "occasion" from its real and sensible objects, that is, *in the very appearance of its unprecedented novelty*.[63] This—Whitehead calls the "initial aim" of an *event yet-to-become from objects*. It names the *je ne sais quoi* of real connection. And it is at this point that Whitehead's occasionalism introduces

---

60. Faber, *God as Poet*, part 2 and 3.

61. Faber, "Introduction: Negotiating Becoming," 1–49.

62. Harman, "On Vicarious Causation," 211.

63. See Faber, "O bitches."

God[64] in the "thundering depth"[65] of things, "a-luring" to the *becoming* of real connections and objects (PR, 85).

Occasionalism(s)

The theological turn of Whitehead's occasionalism must not surprise.[66] Or, it will only surprise if we forget that it was the obvious basis for Harman's secularization all along. Yet, instead of posing "God's power as the shared space of all entities" as in Malebranche—thereby either presupposing "God as a real object" among real objects or as a substitute of the "intentional agent as the vicarious case of otherwise separate phenomena"[67]—Whitehead's God does not substitute any object, but becomes *that* vicarious cause of otherwise separate, divergent phenomena that causes nothing, touches nothing, substitutes nothing—but *is* the "nothing" of becoming itself, the *je ne sais quoi* of the self-creative occasion of connectivity.[68] Whitehead's divine answers the question *from where*, if the real objects are the *outcome* of creative connections,[69] the "real object I," which holds the mystery of such novelty, is itself *arising*. Whitehead's occasional God does not address any transcendent physical force or universal mental space of relationality, but the *sundering novelty* of the very Self of becoming in its becoming *as* Self of connectivity by which it is self-immanent.[70]

Whitehead's occasional God names the same "thundering depth" of the "real object I" that, for Harman, is the very ground on which he builds his substantialism—saving the independence of real objects and the ineffability of their interiority from any (human) "presence" of manipulation or (scientific mechanicism of) causal power. Admittedly, Harman's "substance" as inaccessible essence, *dissociated* from its essential qualities and any claimed attributive unity, is itself based on such a theological presupposition. While Malebranche would not have yielded the concept of "allure" as the *felt unknowability* of real objects other than the "real object I," the invocation of the Ash'arite substantialism does the trick.[71] Yet, here, Harman follows al-Ghazali's refutation

---

64. See Faber, *God as Poet*, part 3.
65. Faber, *God as Poet*, 193.
66. Faber, "Surrationality and Chaosmos," 157–77.
67. Harman, "On Vicarious Causation," 219.
68. See Faber, *Prozeßtheologie*, §33.
69. Harman, "On Vicarious Causation," 208.
70. See Faber, *God as Poet*, §17.
71. Harman, "On Vicarious Causation," 209.

of Aristotelism and his exploration of the Islamic concept of *tawhid*—God's oneness as absolutely unknowable essence.[72]

Two peculiarities differentiate al-Ghazali's occasionalism from Malebranche's. First, Malebranche, firmly in the Aristotelian, Western, and Christian tradition of the identity of God's essence and attributes, formulates occasionalism under the perspective of God's omnipotence and, hence, God's activity as substitution of physical causality. Al-Ghazali, while teaching the absolute *dissociation* of God's inaccessible essence from its attributes as part of creation, understands his occasionalism under the perspective not of power, but of divine emanation, compassion, and beauty. For both Sufi metaphysics and the official Islamic doctrine, the beginning of creation is, as Henry Corbin has demonstrated, enveloped in the *bismilah ar-rahman ar-rahim*, in the name of God as compassion and all-pervasive love.[73] Second, while for Malebranche all existence is *lacking* power and hence, in ontological *need* of God, al-Ghazali is an early representative of the doctrine of *whadat-al-wujud*, as developed by Ibn Arabi after him, which states that, because of God's unity, nothing exists *except* God. Not that nothing really exists, since the attributes and names of God exist, but nothing is something besides or independently from God's unity *with* everything. Hence, God does not replace, but initiates connectivity by empowering inexplicable interiority.[74]

In light of this background, it is not only meaningful that Harman finds his understanding of substance through al-Ghazali rather than Malebranche, but its very heart, the "democratization" of its theological inaccessibility, placed into the interiority of all real objects, begins to resonate with Whitehead's divine release of, and *dissociation* from, any occasion of becoming. An occasion "is constituted by its living aim at its own self-constitution" that in its "initial stage . . . is rooted in the nature of God," while "its completion depends on the self-causation of the subject-superject" (PR, 244). While Harman expresses infinite depth of real objects with an "allure" that both hides and reveals the inaccessible essence of real objects in any real connection, Whitehead seeks the irretrievable immediacy of events in their very *becoming* as a real object, in their *irrelational* beginning.[75]

72. Corbin, *Alone with the Alone*.

73. Corbin, *Alone with the Alone*, ch. 3.

74. The intricacies of the debate between the orthodox and Sufi schools and, partly, between them (especially between Ash'arties and Mi'tazilites), is far beyond this article, and, hence, the "being with" of God reflects my own understanding of their differences as an inherent potential for this philosophical conundrum. Cf. Rahman, *Islam*, 85–99.

75. Faber, *God as Poet*, §20.

Both the "allure" of the hidden essence of the event (or real object) and the "a-lure" of the hidden beginning of the becoming of its Self may be necessary or at least complimentary in their expression of an ontological occasionalism. Moreover, both apophatic moves might not only address this same intention, but, in fact, *be* of the same nature. Maybe "allure" alludes to the very reason for the *infinite depth* of the becoming of events (or real objects) *in themselves* and the *hidden essence* of objects in other *events* (or "real objects I") *because* it alludes to the "a-lure" of the infinite depth and hidden essence of the becoming Self *in its very "conception."*

This sundering of relationalism may not just point at the hidden interiority of real objects, which, therefore, is vicariously mediated through sensible objects and itself vicariously mediating them, but it might also already name a sundering *within* the Self of the becoming "real object I." Whitehead's occasionalism indicates that the becoming Self at the "molten core" of any real object may be like a heart with two chambers, that is, released into its own becoming by being *detached* from its own infinity. The "essence" or "realm internal constitution" (PR, 25) of real objects may even be inaccessible *because* of their Self being *inaccessible to themselves*. And they *become* relational, connective, and Self as *new* real objects by becoming *disconnected* from their own infinite depth. The mystery of the Self of real objects is, indeed, their *hiddenness from themselves.*[76]

Here, Harman and Whitehead cross over into one another's conceptuality. While Harman's concept of "substance" occupies the place of an initial independence and non-relationality of real objects, he finally poses real objects *as the result of connections.*[77] Does this not mean that all connectivity creates objects? But from where, then, is relationality sundered, if not from the *je ne sais quoi* of the *becoming* of the interiority of the "real object I"? Conversely, Whitehead's all-relationality—in the form of universal "mutual immanence" (AI, 201)—is not caught up in efficient causality, and only *seems* to exclude the inaccessibility of the unknown and the unknowable as impossibility (PR, 4) because it is *based* on a "creativity [that] transcends the world already actual" (ibid., 237) *in the very becoming of the Self* of a new event (or "real object I"). Does this not mean that any event or real object is in its Self irrelational, sundered from the "ontological principle" of connectivity (ibid., 244), *unknown* in its "conception" and *unknowable* in its becoming Self?

76. Faber, *God as Poet*, §48.
77. Harman, "On Vicarious Causation," 208.

Gnothi seauton

The inscription at the Apollonian Temple of Delphi might not be obsolete, after all. If we take the question of "touch" as that of a connection in any actual events or any real object's interior subjectivity, and this *subjectivity* as that of the mystery that "apart from the experiences of subjects there is nothing, nothing, nothing, bare nothingness" (PR, 164)—the "Know thyself!" may well be its hidden essence. Maybe the opposition between the occasionalism of Harman and Whitehead is, then, one of a too-little and a too-much, of an unnecessarily "pure" muting or articulating of its respective theological initiation. When Juvenal, the poet, alluded to its prescription as coming *de cealo*, he might well have struck a middle way: We may *only* be able to allude to the very apophasis of the Self, in which we touch the other, when we *desist* from *explaining* its self-exclusion, its hiddenness to itself away, but also desist from understanding it as *already explained* by merely naming its infinite interiority "God."[78] If the two chambers of the heart of things becomes porous, it might well be poisoned and become insane.

For me, at this point of my meditation, this has four implications—with which I will end. First and foremost, in the question of "touch" the *hidden depth of the Self* is unavoidable; it is irreplaceable. It is *it* that is touched and that touches—in me and the other. Far from indicating an external crash of efficient causes or the purely internal mirrors of human or divine minds, it finds otherness only in the intensity of recognizing its *inward and outward dynamics of intimation and detachment*—as the same move toward the mystery of its creative core of connectivity and, in it, from a receptiveness for otherness. If one enters this—what Meister Eckhart calls—*Abgeschiedenheit* (detachment), one may intimately encounter one's Self in the *sphere of touch*, the nameless, the unspeakable, the void, khora, or—in Whitehead's words—the "common function exhibited by any group of actual occasions," namely "that of mutual immanence" (AI, 201).

Contemplating this intimacy with every "thing" in the exploration of the infinite interiority of detachment, its "molten core" may strike us as an encounter of the "appearances as they really are, neither upside down, nor moving, nor receding, nor turning, just like space, of the nature of nothing, cut off from the course of all words and expressions, unborn, not coming forth, not arising, nameless, formless, really without existence, unimpeded, infinite, boundless, unrestrained, only existing by causation and produced through the perversion of thought," as the *Shaddharma-pundarika Sutra* (the Sutra

---

78. Faber, "Tears of God," 57–103.

of the Lotus Flower) says.[79] Or, one may become absorbed into al-Ghazali's experience of *fana*, the annihilation of the released Self, and *baqa*, the paradoxical subsistence in the oneness of God with everything.[80]

Maybe Feuerbach was right that this "God" is only a projection of the infinite interiority of Self—wrong only in his restriction to humanity—because "everyone believes in a god according to what he has subjectively posited in his mind. God . . . is dependent on the subjective act of positing . . . Thus a man of this kind sees (in the form of God) only his own self and what he has posited in his mind."[81] Yet, these words are not from Feuerbach, but from Ibn Arabi, addressing the inexpressible nature of the "hidden treasure" of Self. Second, enfolded in the first implication is another one, namely, that of a universal relativism. I fear that, as long as we confine ourselves to Descartes and Hume, Malebranche and Leibniz, Kant and Hegel, we drag with us a certain unspoken claim of the superiority of Western philosophy—conditioned by Greek origin and Christian mediation. Have we forgotten that Ibn Arabi was a European thinker, an Andalusian, who may seem so far away, temporally and culturally, because he was not in the Christian realm of things? Have we forgotten that Derrida was of African descent, a Sephardic Jew, culturally situated in Arabian Islam? I fear that as long as we, in general, take our inspiration only from the likes of Heidegger and Husserl, we might forget that we also transmit a particular and particularly restricted view of the superiority of the Greek and German tradition. And we know where this led Heidegger.

Hence, I value highly the fact that Harman has chosen to desist from only claiming the occasionalism of Malebranche, but also to at least hint at the Ash'ari school. And I understand Whitehead's insistence to seek approximations of his "philosophy of organism" more within "some strains of Indian, or Chinese, thought, than . . . western Asiatic, or European, thought" (PR, 7) as prescription to embrace otherness without the exclusion of 4/5th of human thought. What other traditions contribute to the other, objects, the Self, intimacy, and detachment is legion, indeed. It might reach from the Zen meditation on the "original face"[82]—the infinite interiority of Self before it was procreated—to the Sufi meditation on the "Face of God"[83]—as the only thing that remains, or maybe just as the last

79. Kato and Tamara, *Threefold Lotus Sutra*, ch. 14 (A Happy Life).

80. Momen, *Phenomenon of Religion*, 236.

81. Ibn al-Arabi, *Fusus-al-Hikam*; quoted in Izutsu, *Sufism and Taosim*, 254.

82. Clearly, *The Original Face*.

83. Corbin, *Face de Dieu, Face de l'homme*.

illusion. In any case, the understanding of "touch" may implicate the multiplicity of all of these others.

Third, again as an implication of the antecedent point we may want to expand this relativity of the "touch" of inaccessible objects even further. Consider this: Why is it that we might implicitly think that the "molten core" of all objects is anything *like* our Self, our "real object I"? The infinite interior of our Self guarantees only that we cannot name its hidden essence. Moreover, its infinite imaginary activity might rather point toward a *rigorous unknowability of the very character* of other Selves of objects. Have we not already, in our meditation on Harman and Whitehead, presupposed that this otherness is only one of "other subjectivity" *like* ours, *like* mine, thereby ironically remaining caught in an anthropic paradigm? What is the common feature of the otherness of non-human objects, non-living objects, maybe even non-human-like minds?

Terms like panpsychism, animism, or pan-subjectivity may not really be helpful to overcome the paradox of such generalities that only restrict our perceptibility and imagination of such otherness.[84] Maybe—to use Harman's differentiation here—there is not any common "ontology," but— to use Deleuzian terminology[85]—only a plethora of metaphysics of singularities and *their* universality? The paradox may well be that we must—as Whitehead says—want to face a "universality of relativity, whereby every particular actual thing lays upon the universe the obligation of conforming to it" (SY, 39). It may be our obligation to release this infinitely diverse mystery of multiplicity from any schemes of generality to get to the "molten core" in our Selves—with radical openness for the unprecedented that it hides from and with which it touches every other thing.

Fourth and finally, I am aware that my meditation has led me "off track," so to say, far away from its initial figures and their thoughts, yet not without unfolding their own impulses. One might level the allegation that philosophy is not mysticism—suspect as it seems. And hasn't Whitehead so eloquently drawn the line between both by, indeed, not excluding mysticism, but, nevertheless, by giving philosophy a direction *away* from it? While he affirms—and I claim for my philosophic meditation—that "philosophy is mystical," he also (we remember) insists that "the purpose of philosophy is to rationalize mysticism" (MT, 174). Yet, Whitehead also warns us from "sterilizing philosophic thought" (ibid., 173) and views its "adventure" (ibid.) as the *care* for a "wonder" in which philosophy "begins" and that, "at the end, when philosophic thought has done its best, . . . remains" (ibid., 168).

84. Griffin, *Reenchantment*.
85. Deleuze, *Difference and Repetition*, 3.

In this sense, the character of the philosophic meditation, that I have employed here, might best be circumscribed with Nicolas of Cusa's *docta ignorantia*, as learned unlearning. I now know less that when I began, but I know its unknowability as surrender to the world's "creativeness" (SMW, 111), as capitulation in the face of what Whitehead calls "depths as yet unspoken" (MT, 174). In fact, "touch" might not be accessed as crash or mirror, reduced by our limited imagination of the human or divine. Yet, it might be vicariously facilitated in the depth of Self and the other, and the other of any Self and its other; not as "given," but as always unprecedented; as an *apophatic living of creative uncertainty in the face of sheer multiplicity.*

Part II

Multiplicity and Divinity

CHAPTER FIVE

Bodies of the Void

WHAT IS AN "APOPHATIC body"? Is there a phenomenology of "apophatic bodies"? Probably not! Instead of an essentializing definition, let me try this: The "apophatic body" is a paradox that lives from a *negation*, an "un-naming" or "un-signifying" that is a twofold process of "negating bodying" and "bodying negating." What is negated? *What is un-, and in this way, embodied?* It is the "What"—essence—itself! This *What* that cannot be named or signified, is *un*-bodied. However, in un-naming "essence," we do not negate the process of "bodying," but "what" is negating it, fixating it, pre-stabilizing it as the *That* of the body. That *body* is negated; and *that* body is un-said: its individuality as *this* body and its generality as *some* body. In this negation, what is embodied? What the *What was* before it was fixated, before it was identified as *that* body and that *body*. The double process of "negating bodying" and "bodying negating" does not negate the process of "bodying," but "what" negates its un-preformed singularity; and it does not embody negation (as such), but "what" negates its bodying (as such).[1]

The thesis is that apophatic negation works in two directions: It *can* negate the bodying itself, carrying with it the peril of a negation, which, embodied again, destroys the body; but it can also *negate what negates* the bodying, thereby freeing the process of "bodying." In uncovering the first apophasis as "peril" (especially of negative theology), I will mark some of the "characteristics" of the second apophasis as *pure affirmation*, especially with the help of Butler's, Derrida's, Deleuze's, Kristeva's, and Whitehead's

---

1. The language of "bodying" indicates the necessary openness of the otherwise problematic introduction of a hidden dualism of body *and something else* included in the metaphor of "embodying" and "un-bodying"—like a "soul" or an "essence" that is *embodied or unbodied*. Countering any dualism, the apophatic move—as will be elaborated in the following considerations—precisely *inscribes itself* and not by negating or realizing "something Else" like an essence that is negated or realized.

respective accounts of concepts that indicate, imply, or can be directed toward an understanding of what I mean by "apophatic Bodies."

Infinite Un-Bodying and Bodying the Infinite

What is un-said in negative theology is any "attribute" that could grasp deity. Although we may start with positive characterization, for example, knowing, in un-saying knowing, we negate the finite character of knowing in which we live, and we project its absolute negation as the position of the deity: as absolute knowledge beyond any creaturely restriction. This method of negation is a process of "un-bounding," of "de-limiting," in proposing that the deity is in its "essence" un-bound and in-finite. In relation to the cosmos, the theology after 1277, the theological decisions published by the Parisian faculty about the orthodox notion of God in the medieval Church, named this the *immensity* of God, which led to a "spatialization" of the infinite deity and a deification of infinite space.[2] Although this "sea of infinite substance" has been conceptualized since Gregory of Nazians (*pelagos ousias apeiron kai aoriston*) and John Damascenus (*est enim deus pelagus infinitae substantiae et per consequens indistinctae*),[3] it was implanted at the heart of negative theology by John Duns Scotus. In his *Quotlibetal Questions*, he writes:

> Damascene confirms this corollary when he says that the essence is an infinite and limitless sea of substance. Substance, then, insofar as it represents what is absolutely first in the divine, he calls a sea, and as such it is infinite and boundless. But substance in this sense does not include either truth, or goodness, or any other attributable property. Therefore, infinity as such is a mode of essence more intrinsic than any other attribute it has.[4]

For Duns Scotus, this bound-less infinity is the "innermost attribute" of the essence of the deity, which is *in se* beyond *any* "character"—even Goodness or Truth. Its infinity is the expression of pure negativity, the negation of any finiteness. It cannot, therefore, be embodied at all. It is the negation of embodiment, of bodying, of the body. It is the expression of pure transcendence, unsaid, unheard, silent, empty of whatever it may characterize. Paradoxically, although it is without essence, its essence is Infinity itself. Whatever "embodies" this pure negativity must die! No body can "see" this infinite substance. And as Meister Eckhart has taught us, in the ecstasy of "mystical

---

2. Casey, *The Fate of Place*, 103–29.

3. Beierwaltes, *Identität und Differenz*, 104 n. 34.

4. Duns Scotus, *God and Creatures*, 112.

unknowing," which can be equated even with a "mystical death" of the soul, one may enter this silence, but only by losing any embodiment—be it that of World or God.[5] In his German sermon *Nolite timere eos*, Eckhart states that to enter the Godhead is to *un-create creation* and *un-god God*.[6] This negativity ends in *pure indifference*, pure un-bodying.

Yet, there is another way to look at this negating of bodying in negative theology. Rooted in a certain view of Plotinus and the Neoplatonic tradition, Nicholas of Cusa was not only engaged in the un-bodying infinity of the indifferent deity, but also in the embodying of this infinity in the difference, which would be *deity's relation* to the world. Quoting Eckhart's *Sermo IV* of the *Sapientia Commentary*, he states that "*Deus autem indistinctum quoddam, est quod sua indistinctione distingitur*,"[7] that the indistinct God is precisely *distinct* by this indistinctness. But distinct from *what*? In order to be able to engage in the negativity of the un-bodying in mystical discourse, Nicholas insists that this is possible only if it is *already* constituted by a *relation* of God to the world, which, in the indifference of the Godhead, is not interrupted but rather *posited*. Here, the indifference of God is not a negation but an *affirmation* of the world as the creation of God.

With the "trinitarian formulary" of *De veneratione sapientiae*—a peak of apophatic unsaying—Nicholas states that the indifference is not nothingness beyond any bodying, but in the middle of its process: "The *non aliud* is *non aliud* than *non aliud*."[8] That the Non-Other is nothing other than the Non-Other, means two things: that the Non-Other is *before* the difference of anything, even the difference of "identity" and "difference"; and that, in its very relation to anything, it *creates* its identity and difference.[9] Thereby, the *non aliud* is even beyond (the difference and identity of) unity and plurality; and, of even more importance here, it opens a *process* of differentiation: The *non aliud* is *non aliud* than *non aliud* which is *non aliud* to *non aliud* . . . indefinitely differentiating. In proper Deleuzian terms, not being a differentiation of actual beings (between "things" already constituted as "unity"), because it is prior to "identity" and "unity"; this is a "differenciation" of the real—that which is not yet "identical" or "unified."[10] In other words, the

5. Carlson, "Postmodernity's Finitude," 33.

6. See Meister Eckhart, "Nolite timere eos," In *Deutsche Predigten und Traktate*, Sermon 26, 273.

7. Beierwaltes, *Identität und Differenz*, 117.

8. Gabriel, *Nikolaus von Kues*, 65.

9. Faber, "'Gottesmeer,'" 64–69.

10. Deleuze, *Difference and Repetition*, 207–20. The differentiated presupposes unity, as in the difference of things from one another; differenciation does not, intellectually, conceptually, or materially, presuppose any "unity," it is the pure process of difference that is "prior" and constituting shifting "unities."

non aliud is a process of *infinite embodying* of difference before identity, not against identity, but rather actualizing itself as the identity and difference of subjects and objects of the world.

While the negativity of the first account is infinite un-bodying, the negativity of this second account is a process of *infinite embodying*. What does it negate, then, if it is *not* the positioning of bodying? It negates any identity and unity as being *prior* to the process of embodying. It negates any essentialism that understands the process of bodying in this world as the permanent positing of a substance or essence with accidental change; it negates any subject or object as the cause of its changing actions. Instead, it is an astonishing account of the *affirmation of the body* as being prior to any given "identity" or "unity." In this second sense, negativity does not negate bodying anymore; it negates the *presuppositions* that preform the becoming of the body; it frees the body in its bodying. The "negativity" becomes that of an embodied becoming before any indication, any being, any signification, any stabilization. It embodies the *event of becoming* of bodying.

Negative Bodies or Embodying Negation?

It is, of course, not uncommon to characterize the poststructuralist tradition as emphasizing precisely this twofold critique of the "inscription" of allegedly pre-given structures of stability upon the body, which—for Michel Foucault more than Judith Butler—may indicate inevitable social power but—for Butler more than Foucault—may also hold resources of resistance.[11] Alain Badiou's critique may have been launched against the inability of this poststructuralist attack against the subject as *effect* of its (social) body, namely that it unsettles the ability to think of both the *identity* and *agency* of the so deconstructed subject.[12] But it forgets the poststructuralist's affirmation of a *body-apriori* as basis for *identity* and *unity* that, indeed, resembles the visionary thought of Nicholas of Cusa. However, it differs precisely in that now the apophasis is said and unsaid of the human (and social) body—unmediated by any deity.

With the *same* characteristic of the human "apophatic body" as its *becoming* (before identity) and its *difference* (before its unity) in both accounts—the theological and the poststructuralist—they also coincide in the *same* critique of negativity or "negating bodying." With Derrida's reconstruction of the *logocentric* negation of the body and Kristeva's *phallogocentric* localization of the universal negation of the body, we enter the critique

11. Butler, *Gender Trouble*, chs. 1, 5.
12. Badiou, *Infinite Thought*, 3–4.

of the "metaphysic of presence"[13] with its seemingly neutral universals and its oppressive binaries, resituating the discourse on the body in the context of gender, race, and social power. The universality of the mind, ideas, and consciousness ever seeking identity and unity, cannot and does not want to undercut its own presuppositions of oppressive sexual and social inscriptions in the body.[14] Here the body itself becomes negated, bodying is substituted with the substantiation of universals of mind and consciousness. The body becomes "apophatic," a purely negative body, emptied of everything except Cartesian "extension,"[15] a hull of the Phallus/Logos. And in its connotation with the idea of the one, transcendent God, the master of infinite identity and unity, Derrida and Deleuze warn us that negative theology is afflicted with this negation of the affirmation of the body.[16]

Against this *active negating* of bodying in the interest of oppressive generalization, stabilized identity, and transcendent unity, various attempts have been launched to convert the apophasis of the "negative body" of phallogocentrism into an embodying of an apophasis. This embodying of apophasis, this "bodying of negativity" would not negate the body, dissolving it into mere generality, but rather would deconstruct the structures that maintain the fake neutrality of phallogocentric negation of the body. There is Irigaray's reconstruction of the female that cannot be represented by male generality. Its subversive realm is beyond language at all—negative, but concrete bodying.[17] And there is Kristeva's reconstruction of Lacan's universal symbolic structure as "law of the father," which *negates* the matrix of the mother, a pre-symbolic realm of the body (of the mother). In equating this *semiotic* realm of irregularity, non-identity, and pre-unity, with the "poetic" account of concrete bodily processes and with Plato's *khora*,[18] she recovers bodying as the prevalent process of becoming and of the "uncoming" of male neutrality and generality. Very much does this recovery— as Catherine Keller has shown—also relate to Whitehead's discovery of the *body-apriori* in what he calls "causal efficacy," the often negated primordial mode of perception of our bodying:[19]

13. Irigaray, *Sex*.

14. Laquer and Gallagher, *Making of the Modern Body*.

15. Casey, *Fate of Place*, 151–61.

16. Deleuze and Guattari, *What Is Philosophy?*, ch. 2. For Derrida cf. Almond, "How *Not* to Deconstruct a Dominican," 329–44.

17. Irigaray, *Sex*.

18. Kristeva, *Revolution*.

19. Keller, "The Process of Difference," 16.

> It is evident that "perception in the mode of causal efficacy" is not that sort of perception which has received chief attention in the philosophical tradition. Philosophers have disdained the information about the universe obtained through their visceral feelings, and have concentrated on visual feelings. (PR, 121)

Instead of negating the body, the apophasis, now speaking through "causal efficacy," begins *positing* the body as the pre-conceptual, presignified, pre-identified mode of our existence in concrete difference. In Deleuze's conceptualization of Whitehead, the multiple vibrations of events in their interrelation, that is, their rhythmic pulsating, is the bodily pre-conceptual connection of this "causally effective" nexus, "us" being the *effect* of its *vibrating multiplicity of becoming* from which is extracted what we call "my Self (Moi)."[20] "Bodily experiences, in the mode of causal efficacy," happen to us when we lift those negations of bodying, when

> in the silence, the irresistible causal efficacy of nature presses itself upon us; in the vagueness of the low hum of insects in an August woodland, the inflow into ourselves of feelings from enveloping nature overwhelms us; in the dim consciousness of half-sleep, the presentations of sense fade away, and we are left with the vague feeling of influences from vague things around us. (PR, 176)

In this "visceral philosophy"[21] of Whitehead, Deleuze, and Kristeva, we encounter the other side of apophasis, the embodying of a negativity that erases not the bodying but the oppressive unifications and identifications that hinder understanding and politically demands its liberating difference, its unoccupied diversity and indispensable becoming-differently. The "great divide" of the "apophatic negation of bodying" and the "apophatic positing of bodying" is where generality negates becoming and becoming embraces difference, where multiplicity negates pre-given identity and unity.

In his analysis of Heidegger's ontological difference as a sexual difference, Derrida gives an important account of a common ground for the departure of both directions of apophasis from the profound *neutrality* of *Dasein*.[22] When Heidegger understands *Dasein* as prior to sexual difference, or any difference (except the ontological difference by which it is constituted), for that matter, he proposes its

---

20. Deleuze and Guattari, *Thousand Plateaus*, 84.

21. Lorraine, *Irigaray and Deleuze*.

22. Derrida, "Geschlecht," 65–83.

peculiar *neutrality* [to be] ... essential, because the interpretation
of this being must be carried prior to every factual connection
... [However, its] Neutrality is not the voidness of abstraction,
but precisely the potency of the origin, which bears in itself the
intrinsic possibility of every concrete factual humanity.[23]

On the one hand, this seems to say that a negating generality is at work
here, which instantiates precisely the phallogocentric apophasis of bodying
as the neutrality of *Dasein* in relation to any difference, especially sexual
difference: it erases the sexual difference in the ontological difference. On
the other hand, this neutrality does not want to "abstract," to "void" (sexual)
difference; rather, it wants to open a path for the *positing* of Dasein as *pleroma*, as the origin of potency for indefinite differentiation. *This* neutrality
"strongly [indicates] a negativity,"[24] that, as Derrida notes, is itself an apophatic process of *affirming* apophatic bodying.

> By means of such manifestly negative predicates there should
> become legible what Heidegger doesn't hesitate to call a "posi-
> tive," a richness, and, in a heavily charged code, even a power.
> Such precision suggests that the a-sexual neutrality does not
> desexualize; on the contrary, its *ontological* negativity is not
> unfolded with respect to *sexuality itself* (which it would in-
> stead liberate), but on its differential marks, or more strictly
> on sexual duality.[25]

Other than the neutralization of difference, this apophasis is pure affirmation of the multiplicity of the process of bodying as pure *excess*, the
pleroma of potency. Its negativity erases the generalizing binaries, thereby
liberating the event of the bodying for infinite differentiation. Its negativity
removes the oppressive oppositions and dualities that stabilize identity and
unity, thereby un-creating "transcendence" as a possessive unity under a Law
and re-creating it as that which becomes only "in difference." Following this
second apophatic negation as affirmation of bodying, Derrida now envisions
"a multiplicity of sexually marked voices . . . this mobile of non-identified
sexual marks whose choreography can carry, divide, multiply the body of
each 'individual,' whether it is classified as 'man' or 'woman.'"[26]

23. Heidegger, *Metaphysical Foundation of Logic*, 136–37.
24. Derrida, "Geschlecht," 71.
25. Derrida, "Geschlecht," 72.
26. Grosz, *Space*, 78.

Bodying the Apophatic

It is ironic that although the logocentric reduction of the body is part of Kant's transcendental approach, in his early work (and largely forgotten and not even taken up later by himself), he already had made first steps for a fresh philosophical recognition of the body. In his mature *Critique of Pure Reason* he followed Hume's *Treatise* in reducing the body to a mere constituent of consciousness in which bodying is transcendentally reconstructed as a mere condition of space and time for thought, devoid of any "causality" or effective and affective reality. In his early dissertation *On the Form and Principle of the Sensible and Intelligible Word* (1770), however, and in his essay on "The Ultimate Ground of the Differentiation of Regions in Space" (1768), Kant already had re-discovered a *bodyapriori*. Following the old philosophical axiom of Archytias that "to be is to be somewhere," Kant realized the body to be *the* precondition for any discourse on the sensible and the intelligible, phenomena and noumena.[27]

Yet, it was Whitehead who (among a number of other philosophers of his time) contested *systematically* the negation of the body in philosophy. His "philosophy of organism" is, indeed, a *philosophy of the body*.[28] In his vision of infinite nested hierarchies of bodies and their environments, which are themselves bodies in other environments and altogether an interfused multiplicity of bodies, the (human) body becomes the presupposition of all knowledge and experience of the world. In *Science and the Modern World*, Whitehead states that

> we have to admit that the body is the organism whose states regulate our cognisance of the world. The unity of the perceptual field therefore must be a unity of bodily experience. In being aware of the bodily experience, we must thereby be aware of aspects of the whole spatio-temporal world as mirrored within the bodily life. (SMW, 91)

The bodily life is so important for everything we might be inclined to substitute for it (and which we cannot substitute, therefore) that *all* of our knowledge, internally and externally, is mediated by our body. It is the membrane of both our "direct knowledge of the relationship of our central intelligence to our bodily feelings" and our understanding of "other sections of the universe [which] are to be interpreted in accordance

---

27. Casey, *Fate of Place*, 202–10.

28. Cf. PR, 113, where Whitehead in relation to Kant's *Critiques* makes the paradigm shift by inversion of their interest in the transcendental subject and proposing a "critique of pure feeling," which is nothing but a systematic statement of the *body-apriori*.

with what we know of the human body" (PR, 119). It is the membrane of perception, which

> takes place where you are, and is entirely dependent on how your body is functioning. But this functioning of the body in one place, exhibits for your cognisance an aspect of the distant environment, fading away into the general knowledge that there are things beyond. If this cognisance conveys knowledge of a transcendent world, it must be because the event which is the bodily life unifies in itself aspects of the universe. (SMW, 92)

This "event which is the bodily life" is a becoming of the whole world in it so that the "world for me is nothing else than how the functionings of my body present it for my experience;" and yet, "the body is merely one society of functionings within the universal society of the world" (MT, 163–164). The reason for *not* recognizing this "mutual immanence" (AI, 197) of the body and the world and all nested organisms in one another is precisely the substantialism that haunts the history of philosophy—a symbol of the phallogocentric generalizations and abstractions that fulfill Heidegger's "voidness of abstraction" and Derrida's "a-sexual neutrality" as the apophatic negation of bodying (in the first sense). Whitehead conceptualizes his critique with the *Fallacy of Misplaced Concreteness*, which does not point to the use of (neutral) abstractions as such but to our "mistaking the abstract for the concrete" (SMW, 51). A basic indication of this replacement of concrete difference by abstract oppositions is what Whitehead calls "simple location," which takes everything just to be where it is in space and time. Whitehead, instead, proposes

> the entire abandonment of the notion that simple location is the primary way in which things are involved in space-time. In a certain sense, everything is everywhere at all times. For every location involves an aspect of itself in every other location. Thus every spatiotemporal standpoint mirrors the world. (ibid., 91)

While the generalizations of "simple location" indicate the "neutrality" of the phallogocentric "bifurcation of nature" into static binaries (of male/female, mind/matter, soul/body) that indicate the vanishing point of the body, their entire abandonment frees (our recognition of) the body from pre-stabilized stability and recovers it as a *universally diffused becoming of the multiplicity of the world*. It establishes the other apophasis (in the second sense) of a pure affirmation of the plenitude of differentiation before and beyond any identification, unification, or stabilization, of its existence and meaning by negating its priority.

Part of the problem of the first apophasis lies in the constitution of the subject, part in the social determination of the body. If the body is subjected to a (private) subject, this subject becomes unable to understand itself as the body's emergent *effect* and instead projects itself as its *possessor* (I and my body) or even *origin* (my soul as original and actual form of my body). Yet, substantializing itself, this subject follows only the social power that inscribes itself by internalizing the pre-formation of environmental societies. While Foucault saw the soul as a mere surface effect of this social inscribing of the body,[29] Butler deconstructs the (socially logocentric) "matrix of intelligibility" that erects the regulative boundaries of identification and unification of which the self-identifying identity of persons is an effect.[30] But Whitehead deconstructs the substantiation of the subject in relation to its body in a reconstruction of consciousness, namely, the effect of the same bodily life that undercuts its socially preformative character.

The bodily paradox of consciousness and life unfolds when we hold them together as "contrasting opposites." Consciousness, for Whitehead, is a *late evolutionary product* of bodily life that *heightens its intensity* by *interrupting its stability*; but the "stream of consciousness" (MT, 162) is also *cloaking* the "infinite complexity of our bodies" by "the selectiveness of enjoyment" through which structures of the environment are highlighted, while consciousness, at the same time, negates "its dependence on detailed bodily functioning" (ibid., 29). The body becomes apophatic in the *first* sense: It loses its visceral dependence and the multiplicity of the causal efficacy working in it as pure multiplicities of myriad processes. Life, on the other hand, develops for Whitehead where the "defining characteristic" of a society, which is the body and the social (and natural) environment sustaining it, is *interrupted* by non-determination arising from the difference of bodily actualization in differentiation from what is or could have been otherwise.[31] Then, it is precisely the interruption of "conformity" that elicits consciousness as effect of the originality of bodily life.

> Life is a bid for freedom: an enduring entity binds any one of its occasions to the line of its ancestry. The doctrine of the enduring soul with its permanent characteristics is exactly the irrelevant answer to the problem which life presents. That problem is, How

---

29. Foucault, *Überwachen und Strafen*, 41–42.

30. Butler, *Gender Trouble*, ch. 5.

31. For the interaction of life and consciousness and also the mutual evolutionary dependence of both modes of mutual obstruction in Whitehead, cf. Kraus, *Metaphysics of Experience*, 65–75.

can there be originality? And the answer explains how the soul
need be no more original than a stone. (PR, 104)

With this bodily view of life and consciousness in Whitehead, we
need a critique of the "negating bodying" of consciousness in its stabilizing,
unifying, and identifying effect, which (through consciousness!) regains
the multiplicities veiled behind its creation of seamless unity, of identifying
things and oneself as subject. Such "vivid conscious experience is a return
to the concrete" (MT, 214) multitude of becoming. This is the regaining of
the "bodying of the apophatic." In Butler's words, it is the uncovering of a
"subversive matrix of disorder" and the "heterogeneity" of the body that
liberates to new and alternative potentials.[32]

Multiplicities and Void

With the differentiation of the two forms of negation operating in this reversal of apophasis, namely neutralization *as* abstraction, on the one hand,
and neutralization of the *negation* of abstraction, on the other, we can now
see how both modes of apophasis correspond to the "bodies" they instanti-
ate or liberate. The first apophasis can be found to be articulated by the
atomism of Epicurus, Democritus, and Lucretius; the second apophasis
may reveal itself by the "interconnected emptiness" of the "place" in Plato's
Timaeus.[33] Both traditions address the two kinds of negativity their bodies
populate, respectively: The atomistic approach presupposes "simple location" and, therefore, negates the becoming of the body; it knows only of
external relation of identified "units" in "empty space," the void, the *kenon*.
It is precisely this approach which lived on in Descartes's "extension" and
Newton's "geometrical space." In its phallogocentric negation, it neutralizes
all relation except that of "pushing." The Platonic approach situates everything in its becoming in an unidentified space of vibration, of *pre*-symbolic
non-identity, and *ante*unified multiplicity. This negation is the *khora*, the
"origin (without origin)" of *becoming—becoming as such*.

It is not without reason that Whitehead, Derrida, and Kristeva attacked the first apophatic negation of bodying as being simply the located,
presented, and symbolized realm of the Phallus/Logos, and adopted the
second apophatic negation of unity, identity, and stability in the image of
the *khora*. While the *khora* names the pre-symbolic, semiotic, concrete,

32. Butler, *Gender Trouble*, ch. 5.
33. Casey, *Fate of Place*, 79–84.

material poetic for Kristeva[34] and the un-signifying of the negativity of dif-
ferance for Derrida,[35] for Whitehead, it names unpreformed, unidentified
"mutual immanence."

> In itself, with the various actualities abstracted from it, the
> Receptacle participates in no forms, according to Plato. But he
> designates it as "the fostermother of all becoming." Later in the
> same Dialogue he calls it "a natural matrix for all things." It re-
> ceives its forms by reason of its inclusion of actualities, and in a
> way not to be abstracted from those actualities. The Receptacle,
> as discussed in the *Timaeus*, is the way in which Plato conceived
> the many actualities of the physical world as components in
> each other's natures. It is the doctrine of the immanence of Law,
> derived from the mutual immanence of actualities. It is Plato's
> doctrine of the medium of intercommunication. (AI, 134)

In being the *negation* of the "form" as medium of identification and
unity, and in being the *negation* of the stabilization of "being," it frees the
body as *pure becoming, differentiating,* and process of *intensity*.[36] While the
first apophasis creates a stabilized being *out of* or *in* the void (*kenon*), the
second apophasis fosters bodying as becoming *of* the void (*khora*). While
the negation of bodying presupposes an *empty void* of pure externality and
transcendence of everything in it—indicating sheer plurality—the negation
of abstraction as affirmation of the bodying, on the other hand, is embraced
by the *void of pure intensity and immanence*—indicating pure multiplicity.
Becoming is the *multiplication of this (second) void.*

When Deleuze invokes Nicholas of Cusa's and (following him)
Giordano Bruno's concept of *complication/explication* to indicate the understanding of his pairs "difference/repetition," "intensity/extensity," and
"enfolding/unfolding," he follows the second apophasis of plenitude for
which identity is neither prior to difference nor the point of reference in
its understanding—for example, as difference between "identified" things.[37]
On the contrary, it relates to Cusa's series of notions for the deity that are *apophatic affirmations* of becoming and multiplicity. This can be witnessed by
the relentless overthrowing of his terms of apophasis by increasingly strip-
ping away any negation that would create opposition. From the *coincidencia*

---

34. Kristeva, *Revolution*, 19–106.
35. Derrida, "Khora," 89–127.
36. Deleuze and Guattari, *Thousand Plateaus*, 260.
37. Deleuze, *Fold*.

oppositorum and the *non aliud* to the *possest*, his way ended with the *posse ipsum*, the pure *potential for complication and multiplication*.[38]

There is, however, another approach to the void as introduced by Badiou in his *Being and Event* (2005), which I refer to here to highlight an important aspect of the void introduced here, which would otherwise go unnoticed, namely that it indicates that which is "unaccounted for" in any form of unification. For Badiou, the ontological difference is that between unification—"counting-as-one"—and a sheer multiplicity that is unified. In the process of unifying, becoming a being, the Being (multiplicity) is always already unified, although in itself it must be considered an *inconsistent multiplicity*, devoid of any unity—it is multiplicity of multiplicity all the way down. This "void" is a "nothing" that

> [b]y itself . . . is no more than the name of unpresentation in presentation. . . . The nothing names that undecidable of presentation which is its unpresentable, distributed between the pure inertia of the domain of the multiple, and the pure transparency of the operation thanks to which there is oneness.[39]

What in the counting-as-one is "not there" but is the "nothing" that ontologically allows for it to "be" is therefore the *uncounted* multiplicity and the *act* of uniting. This void is "present" as "nothing" in the counted one. In this sense, *every* "being" is an "apophatic being," a creature in and of this void; everything is a body in and of the void; everything has an apophatic *aspect*.

The problem with Badiou's void—in contrast to those of Whitehead and Deleuze—is that it *presupposes* unity and identity as given for events to happen. Although it hints at the *process* of counting-as-one, it voids this process in the light of its "being (already) counted." This is important: what goes "uncounted" in Badiou, but is aimed at in Whitehead and Deleuze, is the *becoming* of this being (one); and what is postulated is that this becoming is always *intending* unity and identity.

Whitehead's account of the same "ontological difference" as presented by his *Category of the Ultimate* avoids the presupposition that we find in Badiou because the *act of becoming* is, at the same time, creative uniting *and* creative multiplying—the "becoming-one-of-many" and the "increasing- many-by-one." Its aim, now, is not only *unification*—as in Badiou—but also *multiplication*.[40] Other than the way "being" is for

38. Faber, *Gott als Poet*, §40.
39. Badiou, *Being and Event*, 55.
40. Faber, "Whitehead at Infinite Speed," 39–72.

Badiou, for Whitehead "being" here is a *disjunction*, a potential, an infinite divisibility of infinite perspectives, an infinite depth of the multiplicities from which the becoming is the *process* that is *not* countable (PR, 21). It is not countable ("counting-as-one"), because in Whitehead's ontology, *becoming* is neither in space and time, nor *is* it at all, that is, "one" or "identical." It does not per se create *identity* because it is always a unique becoming *and* perishing. It is only "countable" insofar as it "accounts for" a unification in space and time that is a *repetition of attainment* (of becoming) in building a "defining characteristic" (counted-as-one) which is that of a "society," an "organism," a "body." Only as *counted*, the character of "becoming" *in a nexus* will *define identity* (AI, 203). With Kristeva, its "pattern" may now function as the *symbolic structure* that creates identity (an identical subject) in negating (or neutralizing) the *process of becoming*, the semiotic disorder, that underlies this "being."

Consequently, although Badiou's void enables us to speak of the apophatic nature of *every* body, what—in the light of the contrast between Badiou and Whitehead—happens in such an apophasis must be *differentiated* into the void of the "apophatic negation of bodying"—the *empty void* of the atomists (that Badiou favors)—and the void of the apophatic negation of this "*dualistic* marking of identity"—the *plentiful void* of Plato (that Whitehead favors). To say it in terms of multiplicity: while the first negation Badiou employs neutralizes difference (counting-as-one), the second negation, the one we find in Whitehead's concept of becoming as multiplication (which always goes unaccounted) seeks multiplicities in their depth, their becoming, their heterogeneity, their intensity, in their radicality "*before*" any counting of unity as identity.

Apophatic Life

In Whitehead and Deleuze, there are two *direct* accounts of such "bodies of the void," that is, of "apophatic bodies," that conceptualize the "bodying of the apophatic" (in the second sense). One is Whitehead's strange notion of an "entirely living nexus" (PR, 103–107), and the other, Deleuze's odd notion of a "body without organs."[41] Both concepts undercut any negation of bodying, but negate its dualistic construction of identity and unity.[42] Furthermore, in sensitivity to Derrida's "multiplicity of sexually marked voices," we may even recognize their complex sexual connotations: In a fundamental sense, both concepts in their recovering of the "orgiastic" over against the "organic" are

41. Deleuze and Guattari, *Thousand Plateaus*, 149–60.
42. See Roland Faber, "O Bitches," 117–28.

seeking pure "life" and indicating pure "desire."[43] Like the "body without organs," which "discovers in itself the limits of the organized,"[44] the "entirely living nexus," although it can arise only in a highly structured society, "is not properly a society at all, since 'life' cannot be a defining characteristic. It is the name for originality, and not for tradition" (PR, 104). Freed from any social "defining characteristic," its pure intensity may be

> perhaps some thread of happenings wandering in "empty" space amid the interstices of the brain. It toils not, neither does it spin. It receives from the past; it lives in the present. It is shaken by its intensities of private feeling, adversion or aversion. In its turn, this culmination of bodily life transmits itself as an element of novelty throughout the avenues of the body. Its sole use to the body is its vivid originality: it is the organ of novelty. (ibid., 339)

It is pure apophatic negation, since it has no "correspondences" to any identity, unity, or fixation by "character" or "form." It is not defined by its possibility (as pre-formation). It is the negation of any unification that may substitute its multiplicities of becoming. It is "apophatic life." Since it does not "correspond" (or repeat) any "origin," it is, indeed, the expression of *pure becoming*—thereby only "responding" to the "*Eros* of the Universe" of which originality, novel potential, and creative intensity is an incarnation (PR, 11, 198, 253). It is the incarnation of pure life! They are pure *intensities!*[45] This is the singularity of "apophatic body" we may look for when we try to understand the "resurrected body."[46] This might also direct us to the singularity of an apophatic deity that is not negating bodying but, as in Cusa, is the pure *posse ipsum* of apophatic life.

We would, however, misunderstand the "orgiastic" and "erotic" nature of this "pure life" of an "orgiastic body" or an "entirely living nexus," if we become tempted to equate or identify it with pure *subjective* life or pure subjectivity (devoid of any objectivity). On the contrary (and maybe counter-conceptual at first glance), "pure life" is always beyond, before, and after subjectivity. The pure becoming of the "entirely living nexus" is always *satisfied* by its (subject's) death—as is true for any organic becoming (AI, 25–26; Category of Explanation, xxv). Its "orgiastic" striving is not "possessed" by any subject; it is pre-subjective. Herein, it functions quite similarly to the presubjective process of *desiring* and *intensity* of the "body

---

43. PR, 103; Deleuze and Guattari, *A Thousand Plateaus*, 165.

44. Deleuze, *Difference and Repetition*, 42.

45. Deleuze and Guattari, *Philosophy*, 32.

46. 1 Corinthian 15. Biblical references are to the New Oxford Annotated Bible (= NOAB; based on NRSV).

without organs" in Deleuze and the pre-symbolic *semiosis* in Kristeva. What Kristeva, Deleuze, and Whitehead indicate is the *body of the void*. A better way of phrasing it might be that they uncover bodying in its apophatic dimension of becoming, and they insist on multiplication as the veiled event in all structuring and subject-creating of the body. This void is pre-subjective and pre-objective, it is all-relative and non-exclusive, it is non-formal and in a plentiful sense "neutralizes" its phallogocentric binary markings. In this void, both the "entire living nexus" and the "body without organs" are unpossessed and unrepresented by the social constructions they un-structure or de/construct—both *de-* and *con*struct at the same time, ever new, ever the event of their becoming-multiple. In bodying the apophatic, these bodies live only by the traversing multiplicities of their becoming. Apophatic bodying, hence, is the caring about multiplicity, the love for the multiple. Its event of becoming is *polyphilic*.

With polyphilic bodying we may encounter the pre-subjective, preoccupied dimension of our bodily relationship to the world as *pleromatic* and the *world* in all its interrelatedness as *the bodying of the void*—as a moving, fluid concourse of forces, emotions, feelings, energetic movements, rivers of tensions—what Merleau-Ponty names "the flesh"[47] and Glen Mazis calls "e-motion," that which "neither [is] just matter or spirit, neither physical nor mental, but something between and in motion,"[48] and that is the experience of Whitehead's non-localizable, all-relational body insofar as it "is to be conceived as a complex 'amplifier'" (PR, 119) of an all-pervading vibration of apophatic energy. Bodying the plentiful void of the *khora*, the "body without organs . . . [reveals itself as] an effective, intensive, anarchist body that consists solely of poles, zones, thresholds, and gradients."[49] In the freed movement of the event-field of polyphilic bodying the body exhibits a "complex energy" of becoming, at the same time physical and "emotional and purposeful" (AI, 186), which is the *apophatic event of becoming*. Because it cannot be restated as "being" with its unity and identity, the *apophatic event of polyphilic bodying* can never be reconstructed from either the subjective/objective or the individual/social binaries. In the void, it is always traversing all bodying as Life—personal, cultural, ecological, or cosmic.

Polyphilia, the practice of the *pure life of the body*, however, is *dangerous*. Since this life is apophatic by being "*non*-social," as in Whitehead, it always corrupts the "organic" by becoming "orgiastic." It is dangerous, because it "answers to the notion of 'chaos'" (PR, 72) and "tumult, restlessness

47. Merleau-Ponty, *The Visible and the Invisible*, 133–34.
48. Mazis, *Emotion and Embodiment*, 129.
49. Deleuze, *Essays*, 131.

and passion underneath apparent calm. It rediscovers monstrosity."[50] It is dangerous because it is its "existence" to *interrupt* unification for unoccupied multiplicities. It can, indeed, *destroy* the organic (natural, cultural, or social) matrix that allows it to proliferate. But neither Deleuze's nor Whitehead's (nor Kristeva's) apophatic negation in the concepts of a "body *without* organs" or an "entirely living nexus" (or the poetic semiotic body) negates the organic body or the social organization of life (or the symbolic body) as such by indicating the becoming of an "un-social body" or an "un-organic body" or "organless body" (or a purely nonsymbolic body). They urge, however, for an interruption that denaturalizes the account of this "organicity" as expression of the pre-given Law they understand as the secondary process of sedimentation.

That is to say: against any dualistic account of the first and second apophasis, which to differentiate was necessary conceptually, it is now important to see their intricate interaction: Because of its *endangered fragility*, the *apophatic body of pure life* exists only *with* the "organic body" (the "social body," the "symbolic body"), and its unifications of subjectivity; and its polyphilic practices come only *with* a certain ontological *neutralization* of itself. This is to say that the first and the second apophasis may after all not be viewed as dualistic alternatives (they are not forming a new binary), but in bodily practice only as interwoven *directions of bodying*. While the "organic" bodying aims at unification, thereby exercising the *unifying bodying* (with the danger of oppression), the "orgiastic" seeks the multiplication beneath, before, and after all unification, thereby exercising the *polyphilic bodying*. The "orgiastic" direction may become ecstatic, but it can never become undifferentiated and existing on its own (in Cartesian self-sufficiency).

Polyphilic bodying realizes pure difference, but its actualization is never "pure." This is also the reason that the organic, and with it, the apophasis as neutralization of bodying, can never be totally overturned; nor might we wish to overturn it. Pure life would be instant death! Nevertheless, the uncovering of this bodying of multiplicity or the bodying of the apophatic plenitude, or the seeking of the "orgiastic" (in this sense) may be understood, as Deleuze does, as the "greatest effort of philosophy."[51] And it is here that we enter the mystical tradition again: Only the dead can "see" the "living God"[52]—only in the "mystical death," beyond subjectivity, beyond the difference of God and Creation, are we approaching the apophatic life of God. However, as in Eckhart, the "un-godding" of God, the indifference of God

50. Deleuze, *Difference and Repetition*, 42.
51. Deleuze, *Difference and Repetition*, 262; cf. PR, 156.
52. Exodus 33:20–23.

and World *in* the Godhead, is always already a process of self-differentiating, of the creative differenciation *of* God and the World *out* of the Godhead: creating and "godding"—polyphilic bodying.

Mining Polyphilia or Bodying Immanence

One of the most interesting aspects of Deleuze's and Whitehead's treatment of polyphilic bodying—which differentiates them equally from mystical monists and Cartesian dualists—is *how* they conceptualize the pre-structural and pre-subjective voidness of apophatic life *in relation* to the organic and unified construction of (natural, human, social, and cultural) bodies. By a bold move against any hermetic isolation of apophatic negation, they intimately interlock the organic and the orgiastic dimensions of bodying by indicating their abstract *incompleteness* for themselves and, hence, their *mutual* determination. Especially in their last essays, Deleuze's "Immanence: A Life— . . ." (1995) and Whitehead's "Immortality" (1941), they distinguish the polyphilic Life as the apophatic dimension *of* bodying, which is "pure immanence" and "value"—realities of nonsubjective importance and meaning.

Instead of the negating bodying inherently related to *real* individuals and their *possible* generalities (first apophasis), Deleuze differentiates apophatic bodying in terms of *virtual* singularities and their *actual* universality (second apophasis). Instead of the individual with its subjective unity and objective (general) identity, in the (second) apophasis, we learn to experience the pre-individual singularities that in becoming reformulate the event of unique existence with its universal importance.[53] With this differentiation and the restatement of the "body without organs" as "field of consistency"[54] or "plain of immanence" that "traverses the organism,"[55] Deleuze enables us to discriminate the *subjective* life, which is individualized and possessed, from the *apophatic* life, which is "absolute immanence."

> Absolute immanence is in itself: it is not in something; it does
> not depend on an object or belong to a subject. . . . [T]he plain of

53. Deleuze, *Difference and Repetition*, 1: "The exchange . . . of particulars defines our conduct in relation to generality . . . By contrast, we can see that repetition is a necessary . . . conduct only in relation to that which cannot be replaced. Repetition as a conduct . . . concerns non-exchangeable and non-substitutable singularities . . . Generality, as generality of the particular, thus stands opposed to repetition as universality of the singular."

54. Deleuze and Guattari, *Thousand Plateaus*, 154.

55. Deleuze and Parnet, *Dialogues*, xxxvii.

immanence [cannot] be defined by a subject or an object that is
able to contain it.—We will say of pure immanence that it is a life,
and nothing else. It is not immanent to life, but the immanent that
is in nothing is itself a life. A life is the immanence of immanence,
absolute immanence: it is complete power, complete bliss.[56]

What we encounter in the event of such singularities is that they appear only in the *indefinite* form of the verb—of "bodying" (going, smiling,
greeting, and so on). This indefinite verbal process resonates with the *infinitive* form of Whitehead's "values." In his differentiation of a "World of
Multiple Activities" from a "World of Value," Whitehead sought to articulate
that neither the orgiastic nor the organic direction of bodying can be sepa-
rated because "[e]ither World considered by itself is an abstraction." But
while in Deleuze the virtual and the actual are both "real" and don't lack
anything in relation to each other, Whitehead's "Worlds" of subjective life
and apophatic life must for their "adequate description include . . . characterizations derived from the other, in order to exhibit the concrete Universe"
(Imm., 684). While the one World articulates "the multiplicity of finite Acts"
(Deleuze's actualizations of the real), the other World is "grounded upon the
unity of active coordination of the various possibilities of Value" (ibid., 687)
(Deleuze's virtual potentials).[57]

In Whitehead's view, however, infinite Values (abstract potentials) must
become "*realized* values," that is, become *actualized* in multiple becomings.
They must become *events of valuation* in order to become what they are: singular, important, immortal. In this "persuasive coordination of the essential
multiplicities of Creative Action" (Imm., 694), it is Value, and not the Creative
Act, that represents the *singularity* (and universality) of "*a* life" over against
the individuality (and generality) of *the* subjective life. In its "*active* coordination," Value actualizes the singularity of Creative Acts. Whitehead's World of
Value, again, in its "modification of creative action" (ibid., 686), which realizes
the apophatic life rather than the subjective life of creative action, begins to
unravel its uniqueness when we see it through the eye of the pre-individual
and pre-subjective singularities of Deleuze's "Virtuals."

> A life is everywhere, in all the moments that a given living sub-
> ject goes through and that are measured by given lived objects:
> an immanent life carrying with it the events or singularities that
> are merely actualized in subjects and objects. The indefinite life
> does not itself have moments . . . it offers the immensity of an

56. Deleuze, "Immanence," 27.

57. Despite his critique of the scheme actual-possible, Deleuze was inclined to
subscribe to such a resonance. Cf. *Fold*, ch. 6.

empty time where one sees the event yet to come and already
happened, in the absolute of an immanent consciousness . . . The
singularities and the events that constitute *a* life coexist with the
accidents of *the* life that corresponds to it, but . . . they connect
with one another in a manner entirely different from how individuals connect.[58]

For Deleuze, the apophatic life takes place in the "immensity of empty
time," in *connecting* intense singularities (which are neither subjective nor
objective) in a *virtual event* that might become actualized in an extensive
individual, and for Whitehead "the essential character of the World of Value
. . . [is intensive] *coordination*" (Imm., 695–96; my emphasis). But, while
for Deleuze the virtual and the actual do not *change* one another, although
they *become* as virtual and actual event, for Whitehead, Value and Actual
determine one another mutually—as *activity*. Thus Values resonate with
Deleuze's "timeless immensity" or are otherwise of *immortal intensity*, but
since, other than in Deleuze, they require *mutual determination* with the
"World of Active Creativity (ibid., 694), this determination is also an

activity [that] consists in the approach to the multiplicity by
the adjustment of its many potentialities into finite unities,
each unity with a group of dominant ideas of value, mutually
interwoven, and reducing the infinity of values into a graduated
perspective, fading into complete exclusion. (ibid., 692–93)

Both thinkers conceptualize *polyphilic* bodying. The Virtuals and
the Values are pre-individual, pre-subjective, and immense or immortal
realities, which represent singularities of universal importance that group
together in the event of virtual or actual becoming. In other words, the
bodying of the singularities *in the event* is the apophasis of the bodying.
It *becomes* a constantly changing "coordination" of singularities/intensities
which is profoundly veiled in the substantiated individual/extensive body.
In this insistence of the *event* of the constantly changing coordination of
immortality and immensity of Virtuals and Values lies the character of the
second apophasis as plenitude, as the *event of polyphilia*.

Nevertheless, both thinkers conceptualize *different* polyphilic events
of apophatic bodying. Deleuze understands the event as the virtual reality
of groupings and changing regroupings of singularities as potentials of
becoming, whether they are actualized in an actual becoming or not.[59]

58. Deleuze, "Immanence," 29–30.

59. The mutual determination between virtuality and actuality being differentiation
and differenciation. Cf. Williams, "Deleuze and Whitehead," 89–106.

Whitehead, on the other hand, allows for the *event* of polyphilia to occur only in *mutual* completion of Value and Actuality. In other words,
this event occurs in *both* Worlds, as in Deleuze, but only in their mutual
determination so that in both Worlds the event is an *activity* of realization,
not an activation of a virtual reality.

If there is a deeper difference between their understandings of the
event of polyphilic bodies, it is that for Deleuze *becoming is a change in
the event* (which is virtual),[60] and for Whitehead, the *event is a change in
becoming*.[61] While the virtual event is pure immanence and in its virtuality
is independent of actualization, Whitehead's event needs to be *actualized* in
becomings of which it is a *nexus* that exhibits no social character. But since
such an event can be said to be either "the *difference* between actual occasions comprised in some determinate event" (ibid) or to be taken in as "a
nexus in its formal completeness" (ibid., 80), the *form* of an "entirely living
nexus" will precisely be its *formlessness*, its being a body (out) of the void.
Hence the Values of the event are the togetherness of *actualized* singularities
in the difference of each of the becomings of the event—its actualized Immortality as Void or as actualized Multiplicity. They *are* not just Multiplicity,
but are driven by its actualization. In the Void, the actualized multiplicity of
singular event-valuations, they become the event-field of polyphilia.

Theoplicity

The difference between the conceptualization of polyphilic bodying in
Deleuze and Whitehead implies that Deleuze's Virtuals are real but not
actual, that they need nothing, are pure immanence, and remain in their
empty time of pure consciousness, and that Whitehead's Values, although
also in immortal timelessness, only "exist" as immortal *activity*, an activity
he names God: "The World of Value exhibits the essential unification of
the Universe. Thus while it exhibits the immortal side of the many persons, it also involves the unification of personality. This is the concept of
God" (Imm., 694).

While the event of virtuality of the togetherness of singularities is Deleuze's polyphilic bodying, or the bodying of the apophatic, which happens
in pure immanence and timeless, empty time, this togetherness of Values
is immortal in the *activity* of God. Neither can, for Whitehead, the "character" of a living person nor the "character" of the "living nexus" of any

60. Stagoll, "Becoming," 21.

61. PR, 73: "I shall use the term 'event' in the more general sense of a nexus of actual
occasions."

society (cultural or ecological) be restated as a "defining characteristic" (of a soul or a world-formulary) so that the "maintenance of character is a way in which the finitude of the actual world embraces the infinitude of possibility" (ibid., 695). Rather, it is the togetherness of singular Values without organization, the "orgiastic nexus," which is then, in the realm of Value, "immortal." As in Deleuze, this timeless Virtuality or Immortality is neither about subjectivity (e.g., of a person's immortality) nor any objectivity (e.g., the life of an event beyond itself or the permanence of a world-structure)—immortality is unpossessed—but about its *apophatic life*! It is "*a life*" that becomes immortal or, in other words, is the *event of immortal becoming*. That for Whitehead this World of Value, which is determined by the "concrete values" attained in the actualization in the World of Creative Action and Change, not only constitutes the "immortal side of the many persons," but also "involves the *unification* of personality" as such (in its *event*!), is a consequence of the immortal event as *activity*, which "is the concept of God" (ibid., 694).

This difference is so profound that for Deleuze a concept of God arises only when the pure immanence is broken by a "One" that is a "transcendent that might contain immanence."[62] Then, it would be precisely the apophatic body of pure life, the "'body without organs' that God has stolen from us in order to palm off an organized body without which his judgment could not be exercised."[63] With this transcendent, the first apophasis would reappear as an "*Omnitudo realitatis*, from which all secondary realities are derived by a process of division."[64] For Whitehead, on the other hand, apophatic life would be broken if we destroy the *mutually determining activity* of the two Worlds, which in "mutual immanence" is *pure immanence*—not transcended by a deity but insisted on by the *activity* of the pure *posse ipse*.

God, for Whitehead, is not the transcendent One, not the "apophatic body" *of* the World of Creative Action (first apophasis). Rather God, in Whitehead's account, is the apophatic body *of the World of Value*. In "seeking intensity, and not preservation" (PR, 105), God, then, is the *immanent* bodying of the apophasis of Immortality *of* the World of Creative Action *in* the World of Creative Action; that is, God's bodying immortalizes its "pure life" beyond its subjectivity or objectivity (second apophasis) only by becoming the polyphilic "Eros of the Universe," the *lover of the multiplicity* of the World of Active Creativity. This Divine apophatic activity I would like to name "theoplicity." In God's *apophatic activity*, God is the

---

62. Deleuze, "Immanence," 30.

63. Deleuze, *Essays*, 131.

64. Deleuze and Guattari, *Anti-Oedipus*, 13.

event of theoplicity, of insistence on multiplicity, in being the apophatic bodying of multiplicity, in being the polyphilic Eros of *initiation* and, at the same time, the polyphilic *salvation of the self-created multiplicity of the World of Creative Act*, thereby (by the Immortality for the World of Change) insisting on its *diversity*. Indeed, this invokes Cusa's apophatic "bodying" of God (the World of Value) and the World (of Change) with the pair of *complication/explication*, which is the *event* of becoming-God and becoming-World in the *same* act, which, in Whitehead, appears as the *mutual, completed activity* of the two Worlds.

Whitehead's biblical association of this activity with the "kingdom of heaven" (PR, 350) is easily misleading: It is not the collection of the subjective life (*the* life) in its individuality, but the immortality of the Value, the *singularity* of the *apophatic* life (*a* life) of our bodying. And it is not a fugitive collection *out of* and aiming *beyond* the World of Creative Activity, but the activity for *its* intensity, *its* importance, *its* Immortality as *event of its becoming*. It is the activity of *theoplicity*: the insistence on *its* "essential multiplicity of Creative Action" (Imm., 694). It is with the "kingdom of God" as with "*a* life" of "very small children [who] all resemble one another and have hardly any individuality, but they have singularities: a smile, a gesture, a funny face—no subjective qualities. Small children, through all their suffering and weaknesses, are infused with an immanent life that is pure power and bliss."[65]

Perhaps it is this apophatic life, this immanent life of "our" singularities, in which we are bodying the void, pure life, pure immanence, pure unique connectivity—thereby, in this apophatic bodying, becoming immortal *as* the event of God's activity. Perhaps the becoming-immortal in the "kingdom of God," then, is our unique importance for the World of Active Creativity, in which "the kingdom of heaven is with us," because "the love in the world passes into the love in heaven, and floods back again into the world" (PR, 351). And perhaps, this is the meaning of the biblical saying that it is to such as little children "that the kingdom of God belongs,"[66] because "a life" is the becoming of the apophatic body, the body of apophatic life—a smile, a gesture, a funny face. It is perhaps here that we might begin to understand the *activity* of God: the "coordination of the many personal individualities as factors in the nature of God" (Imm., 694) and "the transformation in God's nature . . . beyond our imagination to conceive" (ibid., 698). Perhaps it is this "power [that] lies in its absence

---

65. Deleuze, "Immanence," 30.

66. Luke 18:16. In some Gnostic gospels, like the *Gospel of Judas*, Christ appears to his disciples as a child! Cf. Kasser, Meyer, and Wust, *Gospel of Judas*, 20.

of force" (RM, 57), this "suffering and weakness"[67] of "a life," that is God's "pure power and bliss"[68]—"the Tragedy, the Sympathy, and the Happiness" (Imm., 698). And perhaps this is the "resurrected body," the *soma pneumaticon,*[69] the apophatic body of pure life, that is immortal, infinitely important beyond objective death and subjective life.

67. Deleuze, "Immanence," 30.
68. Deleuze, "Immanence,."
69. 1 Corinthian 15:44.

CHAPTER SIX

Polypoetics

AT THE END OF *Adventures of Ideas*, exploring the profoundly de/constructive implications of the "principle of limitation," Whitehead's divine *explodes* into a polyphilic multiplicity of open concepts in mutual suspension—Supreme Adventure, initial Eros, final Fact, Harmonies of Harmonies, Adventure of the Universe as One, the union of Zest with Peace, final Beauty, tragic Beauty, the Great Fact (AI, 295–96)—where theopoetics becomes both multiple and experimental at the same time.[1] As the divine is *diffused* into the process of the becoming-manifold in such multiple and experimental ways, so does its "poetics" become this *multiple and experiential diffusion*. The spacing (mapping) of the traces (*poietics*) of this multiple divine (*theios*) is the task of *theopoetics*. The "traces" it leaves sensed in polyphilia; the "map" unfolded as divine *comedia*; its expressions steeped in irreducibly many poetics—is *theoplicity*, "demonstrated" by mapping the symbolic traces of disappearance, "played" on the enfolded exclusion or subtraction. This is the concept of "polypoetics" of the *poiesis* of the divine *in* multiplicity.

Polypoetics in this sense is, however, not a theoretical construct to satisfy metaphysical "games," but a serious instrument of analysis of our world of power and its "games" of oppression. Polypoetics is a de/construction of such games of power in terms of the *comedia divina*, its revolt against a dualism (AI, 190) that, in its many forms, guides or justifies religious, social, cultural, and political violence. The "constructive" mechanism of power either omits the divine *in* multiplicity (for the free game of power) or controls it with the One, the Two, and the Many (as justification of power). Instead of the oppressive implications of these two alternatives of reduction, abstraction, and legislation, polyphilic polypoetics radically articulates the *infinite foldings of becoming* for which "God" *symbolizes* the mystery of their dignity.

---

1. Deleuze, *Two Regimes of Madness*, 304.

The "poet" is the *insistence* on "walking in the recesses" of the infinite chaos-mos²—neither its enemy nor its Lord, but its *importance*.

The true adversary of this *poetics of multiplicity* is the obsessive "rationality of power," the *logos* in which *abstractions* of oppositions are "cut out" of the manifold as real instruments in the justification of violence. In obscuring their suspension in multiple folds, their abstractions serve as *instruments of oppression* not only because their *logos* generates a reductionism in which these folds become "invisible." Rather, since these folds always live *in sight of the least ones* from which they were taken away in the first place, polypoetics with the *diffusion* of the divine *in* multiplicity is not interested in a disappearance of the divine, but *in regaining the sight* of the many folds in the "visibility" of the least ones to which they belong in the first place. In this poetic process of liberation, the divine disappears as *logos* of the One and leaves traces in the *multiple* (pluralist) and *experimental* (empirical) symbolization of the dignity of the complications of "the many"—we all are. "Be multiplicities!"³

Polypoetic Nomoi

Polyphilic symbolization is a production of difference in which we can witness *theoplicity insisting on/in multiplicity*. Within multiplicity, theoplicity is the infinite invitation to create in/finite symbolizations of the gift of self-creativity, which expresses itself in the *suspension* of ultimates. This can readily take the form of the Sixth Antithesis in *Process and Reality*: In the sense that it "is as true to say that God creates the World, as the World creates God" and, therefore, that "God and the World are the contrasted opposites in terms of which Creativity achieves its supreme task" (PR, 348); *it is true to say* that the "aim" of polypoetic symbolizations is the in/finite becoming of "contrasts" and "contrast of contrasts" (ibid., 22) that is nothing less than the emergence of a multiplicity of *suspended* "ultimates."

While *polyphilic* polypoetics resides in a creative evocation of an *infinity* of "ultimates" in suspension, it is the *mutual suspension* of "ultimates" *and* the process of suspension itself that Whitehead—as "ultimate non-ultimate"—calls "adventure." Neither in need to "exclude" the divine as "Supreme Adventure" nor to "identify" God within these "Adventures of the World as One" (AI, 295), the adventure rather diffuses the divine in such a way that, in fact, the *divine insistence* on subtractive affirmation of pure multiplicity and the *mutual immanence of this insistence* in all events of

2. Keller, *Face of the Deep*, ch. 7.

3. Deleuze and Guattari, *Thousand Plateaus*, 25.

"ultimacy" become *in/different*. Theopoetic in/difference addresses the final *creative incapability* to ever bring this process of adventure to a hold; hence, a polyphilic theopoetics must insist on the importance of the multiplicity of projective symbolizations as precisely expressing the *love* of multiplicity that *saves* it. Whether we symbolize this adventure which *saves multiplicity* as "God's" adventure, *or* as that of the multiplicity of mutually immanent creatures of creativity, becomes a matter of skillful suspension. Since the reference is that of the "ultimacy" of the events of their happening-together, salvation (of multiplicity) is an unending process of in/finite becoming in which this process *as* process poses them as always in/different and this process *is* process only in their in/difference.

This "game" of suspension of ultimates (in the process of the becoming of their events of manifestation) is, however, not merely a release into mere chaos of indeterminacy.[4] It is rather an adventure of emergent *nomoi* of indetermination, resisting the *logos* of the One, the Two, and the Many. Like Deleuze's *nomos*, this "structuring" of indeterminantion only designates an "occupied space, but one without precise limits."[5] It is with such a "no-madic *nomos*," which is "without property, enclosure and measure" that we no longer seek logical "divisions of that which is distributed but rather a division among those who distribute *themselves* in an open space."[6] These "rules" of self-distribution of the "players" of the "ultimate game" among the mutual suspension of themselves (the events of ultimacy), offer a surprising depth of *self*-suspensive features, of which I will name five.

First, since all ultimates in suspension are *incomplete* with regard to their "definability," they *always invite other ultimates to join them.*[7] Like Deleuze's "concepts," they move in an ever self-differentiating and overlapping complex of "planes of immanence," in the crossing of which they alone make sense, momentarily and as events.[8] Hence, no "list" of "ultimates," Whitehead ever offers, is complete. So does, for instance, the "category of the ultimate" lack abstractive patterns or "eternal objects" (PR, 21–22); "creativity" lacks the "extensive continuum" (ibid., 61–82); and "universal relativity" lacks "process" (AI, 201).

Second, since all ultimates are "coherently" within one another—coherence being the mode of necessity in universality (PR, 3–4)—they are *complications of one another*, folds of one another, irreducible to one another, but

---

4. Refer to the next chapter.
5. Deleuze, *Difference and Repetition*, 309.
6. Deleuze, *Difference and Repetition*, 36.
7. Faber, "Immanence and Incompleteness."
8. Deleuze, *What Is Philosophy?*, ch. 2.

always in mutual processes of enfolding implicit folds of the other and folding together the others in themselves. Hence, "one" is always the unification *of* multiplicity and "many" is always the relativization *of* "ones" (ibid., 21); "coherence" is *empirical* (ibid., 6–7); "mathematical structures" are *relative* to the body of events (ibid., 89); "societies" are *no less* concrete than "actual entities" (ibid., 18); "categories" *are* "principles" and vice versa (ibid., 25–26); and necessity (relationality) *mirrors* freedom (novelty) (ibid., 4).

Third, in their mutual complication, suspended "ultimates" demand *their* "region" of irreducible uniqueness of *perspective* on the process, but it is their trans/unification that *creates* process as the Open. Such perspectives are the *events* of the Whole. They do "not exclude complexity and universal relativity"; rather, every perspective designates actuality as "a system of all things" (ibid., 36). *Immersed* in these perspectives, the universe is enfolded in them in such a way that it is always *perspectively distorted* in them. Not that such perspective distortion would be a *lack*; rather, it is the refutation of the transcendent-observer view. All "ultimates" are only in their *perspective incompleteness* encoding all others so that from one such perspective all other "ultimates" *are different* than lived through from any other perspective. There is no universal bridge for the (ex)change of perspectives; it happens like a quantum leap or appears like an effect of quantum tunneling. Hence, their "relations" are only the *becoming* of togetherness as "concrescence" (ibid., 189); "objective" reality, the past disjunctively, is only given in "interpretation" as "objective datum" (ibid., 240); a theory is an event;[9] becoming never "is" (AI, 237).

Fourth, suspended "ultimates" *are created*, that is, they are *emergent features* of novelty in the relational process of mutual immanence. Since novelty is always "emergent" (PR, 36)—irreducibly "concrescing" out of its collected relations—every event is such an emergent "ultimate," that is, not just an *instance* of (the "ultimacy" of) "creativity," but itself the *self-creative "ultimate"* of which "creativity" is an abstraction (ibid., 21). Because the business of a philosophy of multiplicity is not to explain the concrete, but instead to understand "the *emergence* of the more abstract things from the more concrete things" (ibid., 20; emphasis added), their "ultimates" are abstractions. In Whitehead's logic of multiplicity, this process implied the *distributive arbitrariness of abstractions*[10] in creative events of "contrasting" opposites. "Contrasting" again is a process of complexification that cannot be reduced to the binaries it complexifies. Hence, Whitehead understands his "doctrine that a multiple contrast cannot be conceived as a mere disjunction of dual

9. Faber, "Whitehead at Infinite Speed," 64–71.

10. Faber, "Amid a Democracy," 192–237.

contrasts . . . [as] the basis of the doctrine of emergent evolution" (PR, 229). Two daunting implications are, first, that *"ultimates" are always created on new levels* of complexification, and, secondly, that, therefore, *all "ultimates" are complex* (ibid., 267). Hence, continuity is always *becoming* (ibid., 35); all actualities *are* nexuses (ibid., 28); causes are causes only by being actualized *in* events (ibid., 84); *togetherness* is ultimate (ibid., 22).

Fifth, the infinitude of connectivity and complexity invites an *infinite multiplicity of "ultimates" in mutual suspension*. Hence, Whitehead's "categories of existence" are, first, actually infinite since their last category—"contrasts"—"includes an indefinite progression of categories [of existence], as we proceed from 'contrasts' to 'contrasts of contrasts', and on indefinitely to higher grades of contrasts" (ibid., 22). But second, even the seemingly "basic" categories of "actual entities and eternal objects [that] stand out with a certain extreme finality" (ibid.) are not "simple" either, but are always *complexities* of relations of nexuses and multiplicities of abstractions and their mutual actual inherence. "Ultimates" are no transcendent grounds! Hence, Whitehead was not opposed to Zeno's "infinite series" of mutually co-arising realities (*reductio in infinitum*), because they are not in need of a "foundation" of the whole series; rather, "ultimates" are only ultimate in the *event* of their *complex togetherness*, which is groundless (ibid., 69).

Divine Polyphilia

If we infuse the notion of "God" into this "game" of the suspension of ultimates with its five self-suspensive features, we will find "God" exhibiting the following astonishing *"characteristics" of indetermination and diffusion* in multiplicity—which again are mutually immanent to each other—that will present us with the polypoetic *nomoi* for the use of the polyphilic concept of God. Differently stated, instead of determinations of "functions" of "God" in a system of divine dominion, we will find a trace of theoplicity as active indetermination of such systems.

First, since God in the suspension of ultimates is *incomplete* with regard to God's "definability," the concept of God always invites *other ultimates to join its indeterminateness. In this nomic production of difference, God is understood as diffusing Godself as expressive of a radical receptivity for the Other.* Whitehead calls this activity God's *synthesis* ("concrescence") of the infinite multiplicity of abstractions ("primordial nature") and actualities ("consequent nature"). But this "synthesis" is not aiming at the One anymore, it is not an expression of God's dominion as the power to "create" or as an image of the "creation of power," but becomes a *polyphilic region of "invitation"*—inviting the *manifold* (ever differentiating and ever becoming) to be ultimate.

Second, since God is "coherently" in the other "ultimates," God is a *complication of and in all other "ultimates"* that fold together in God. The concept of God, then, becomes irreducible as the process of a divine that folds together the implicit folds of ultimacy. Conversely, God is irreducibly unfolding Godself with the enfolding of ultimate realities in themselves and all others. Hence, *God's diffusion in multiplicity is the enfolding of multiplicity in God's self-relativization in others.* God's "coherence" *is pluralistic, empirical, and surrational.* God is always *in mutual immanence* with all other "ultimates" so that God's synthesis is God's *transition* (as witnessed by the claim of the objective immortality of the natures of God) (ibid., 32). God's trans/unification *"collects" the other by being diffused in the other.* God's polyphilia always *complicates* matters for Godself and all others.

Third, God's "region" of complication is an *irreducibly unique perspective* on the process of mutual suspension, but is in trans/unification a diffused "region," diffused in multiplicity, which only in all of its perspectives *creates* process as the Open. As such a perspective, God is the *event* of the Whole. By "not exclud[ing] complexity and universal relativity," God is actually "a system of all things" (ibid., 36) among infinite other events. *Immersed* in God's perspective, God, as all other ultimates, enfolds the others by always *perspectively distorting* them in Godself. God's perspective distortion is, however, not a *lack*, but the refutation of the transcendent-observer view. *God's diffusion among the multiplicity of "ultimates" is their perspectively incomplete encoding of all others so that from God's perspective all other "ultimates" are different than when viewed from any other perspective.* Whitehead's metaphor for the *uniqueness* of this divine "region of perspective distortion" is to name God's *difference* from all other "ultimates" *in relation to* all others: the view of the Eros of appetition in the "primordial nature" and the "perfected system" of salvation in the "consequent nature" (ibid., 348–349); of the "harmony of harmonies" (AI, 296) and the "super-jective nature" (PR, 88) in the cyclic love of the infinite process of becoming (ibid., 351). However, there is no universal bridge for the (ex)change of perspectives; it happens like a quantum leap, that is, *immersed in* other perspectives, or a quantum tunneling that cuts through impossibilities. Hence, Whitehead can speak of God as a creature *of* creativity (ibid., 47) and "in the grip" *of* creativity (ibid., 349) *or* of creativity as *self*-actualization of God (AI, 236). Whitehead can understand God as an *abstraction* of permanence from the world process (PR, 347) *and* as the *world's* Eros (AI, 158). He can metaphorically picture the world's salvation *in* God (PR, 348) *and* of its *apotheosis* as God (PR, 350).

Fourth, God, like all other "ultimates," *is created*, that is, is an *emergent feature* of novelty in the relational process of mutual immanence. Since novelty is always "emergent" (ibid., 36)—*irreducibly* "concrescing" out of its *collected* relations—God's event is such an emergent "ultimate," that is, God is not just an *instance* of "creativity" (ibid., 31), but itself the *self-creative "ultimate"* of which "creativity" is an abstraction.[11] *God's diffusion into multiplicity is God's emergence from multiplicity that can only be addressed in poetic transgression of the differences in their mutual suspension.* This diffusion is theoplicity: God is not only *complex* but, even more dauntingly, God is *always recreated and differentiated on new levels of complexification.* Hence, in such complex diffusion, God might disappear as "God" and might reappear as "activity," as "entity," as "matrix," as "person," as "interrelation" itself, as "change," or as nothing at all.[12]

Fifth, God's infinite connectivity and complexity always *invites an infinite multiplicity of "ultimates" in mutual suspension.* God's self-diffusion in multiplicity can only be expressed *in* this infinite multiplicity, that is, it can never be expressed in any reductively unified way, because it is always escaping any determination and, even more, is the activity of indetermination itself. Its articulation is in need of a polypoetics that expresses nothing less than the awareness of the inclusion of all levels of emergent complexity of "ultimates," which is at the same time beyond any articulation. Hence, that "God does not exist" is one of its expressions. In other words, "God" *cannot be expressed within* Whitehead's "categories of existence" (PR, 22), which are actually infinite in the category of contrasts. Hence, we cannot express God by "identifying" God within the process of all such inclusions of complexities since they always "proceed from 'contrasts' to 'contrasts of contrasts,' and on indefinitely to higher grades of contrasts" (ibid., 22). Since "ultimates" are no transcendent grounds, God is *not* beyond Zeno's "infinite series," but the *reductio in infinitum* as it manifests itself *in the mediation of the impossible event* of their complex togetherness ("principle of concretion") in which what is groundless—happens.

> Thus the universe is to be conceived as attaining the active self-expression of its own variety of opposites—of its own freedom and its own necessity, of its own multiplicity and its own unity, of its own imperfection and its own perfection. All the 'opposites' are elements in the nature of things, and are incorrigibly there. The concept of 'God' is the way in which we understand this incredible fact—that what cannot be, yet is. (PR, 350)

11. Franklin, "God and Creativity," 237–307.
12. Faber, *God as Poet*, 178–79.

If these *nomoi* of indetermination are not a mere chaos and anarchy in disguise—although they are "chaos" as life[13] and *an-arché* in the sense of the suspension of any Archimedean, foundationalist ultimate:[14] What, then, are the *criteria* for a polypoetics in which the infinitely multiple suspensions of metaphors for the "divine *in* multiplicity" become *skillful means* of articulating the multiple divine? I will name three such criteria.

First, *within* always infinitely many interwoven "ultimates" that are only found in a process of being folded together and folded apart, we can only address the divine by a *poetic transgression* of all abstractly stabilized ultimates, which are otherwise; that is, as victims of the Logic of the One, the Two, and the Many used to "identify" God in the process.

Second, since God's reality must always be addressed *against* the Logic of the One, the Two, and the Many, the introduction of the divine in the process of multiplicity must be the expression of the *de/construction of all concepts of power*, which are always a sedimentation of a "logic of fear," and are only mitigated by the favor of polyphilia, the *love* of pure multiplicity.

Third, insofar as the multiplicity-diffused divine is irreducible to any "ultimate," it must be addressed *in theopoetic difference* from all "ultimates" without ever being considered outside their universal relationality. This is the *subtractive affirmation* of the *poiesis* of God.

With these polypoetic *nomoi* in mind, we can now revisit the two series of ultimates proposed earlier, as their understanding will now be shifting—given their wide use in process thought, and also the tendency to substantialize them[15]—to name their polypoetic nature. The implications for the concept of God through the lens of the indeterminacy of ultimates in their *skillful suspension* will become obvious insofar as their duality includes mutual suspension of each other. One series designates the Category of the Ultimate—"one," "many," and "creativity" (PR, 21); the other the distributive actors of the Six Antitheses—"God," "world," and "creativity" (ibid., 348).

First, "God"—in the fluent movement of the "ultimates" through one another—*cannot* be "identified" with the "one" (as a reflex of logocentrism would like to have it). Not only is "God" in the second series introduced in the context of the Six Antitheses that explicitly avoid this identification (neither is God simply "one" nor "many"!), but the poetic transgression of all "ultimates" of the one series must flow through all of the others by which procedure all are complications of the others.

---

13. Faber, *God as Poet*, §§15–16
14. Caputo, *Weakness of God*, 13–17.
15. Griffin, "John Cobb's Whiteheadian Complementary Pluralism," 45–51.

Second, "God" cannot be used as a *source of power of induced divisions in the process* that would *reserve* something for God's power alone, since in mutual suspension of the two series, the "functions" of all "ultimates" can be claimed by *all* of them. Even more important, the second series can be "replaced" by the first one without naming "God" at all, yet without losing anything (which would be of interest to power). While God becomes anonymous, polyphilia shines.

Third, since the insistence on both series *at the same time* can be understood as expressing the theopoetic difference, the *vibration between* both series exhibits the *subtractive affirmation* of multiplicity for which Whitehead has only one word that he consequently explores following the second series: Love.

By following these three criteria, neither is God "identified" *in difference to* all other "ultimates" (and beyond their inherent "metaphoric") nor is God found *as* any of the (myriads of metaphoric) expressions of "creativity," which are always expressions of power. It is in *this* complex differentiation *in* infinite multiplicity that the theopoetic difference is a *poetic in/difference*; that is, the "divine *in* multiplicity" will always only be voiced as complex *poetic transgression of difference and identity.* Since theopoetic in/difference is *the subtractive affirmation of love as that for/in/as multiplicity,* the "super-criterion" by which to differentiate the polypoetics of the diffused divine *in* multiplicity from any other approach to "ultimates" in the form of a logic of the One, the Two, and the Many is its *in-sistence on/in (the salvation of) multiplicity.* This is the task of polyphilia as a polypoetics of theoplicity.

Polyphilic Pluralism

As a consequence of the "pluralism" and "empiricism" of polypoetics, we must now situate "religious pluralism" in their context, insofar as it is one of the essential questions of polypoetics as to how to understand *the relation of the divine manifold to the ultimacy of multiplicity.* In this context, polypoetics may distinguish itself through the *nomoi* of "skillful suspension (of ultimates)" as its *polyphilic* logic of multiplicity—as elaborated above. It is neither prepared to give up its insistence on a language of the divine, nor does it want to compromise with (always) remaining residues of the Logic of the One, the Two, and the Many. In echoing Deleuze's appraisal of Whitehead's insistence on multiplicity, polypoetics is in its *polyphilic* sense a "pluralist" and "empiricist" account of the divine *in* multiplicity.[16]

---

16. Faber and Keller, "Polyphilic Pluralism," 69.

This line of thought, if it is situated among current positions on "religious pluralism," can begin by discerning positions, which obviously follow the Logic of the One, the Two, and the Many from other positions that try to avoid it. In an outright dismissal of positions that desire to find the *one Logos*, namely "exclusivism" and "inclusivism," we can discern two outspoken "pluralist" approaches: a "monistic" or "mystical" pluralism and a "pluralistic" or "differential" pluralism. *Polyphilic* pluralism (and empiricism) wants to *affirm* pluralism and empiricism by avoiding the problems associated with monistic/mystical and pluralistic/differential pluralisms *insofar as* their appeal to the divine and to multiple ultimates *remains bound to modes of dualism.* The process by which to lose these dualistic sedimentations can be structured with the account Whitehead gave of divine multiplicity and ultimacy in his last article, "Mathematics of the Good," that readily mirrors and transcends the dualistic fallacy.

> Spinoza emphasized the fundamental infinitude and introduced a subordinate differentiation by finite modes. Leibniz emphasized the necessity of finite monads and based them on a substratum of Deistic infinitude. Neither of them adequately emphasized the fact that infinitude is mere vacancy apart from its embodiment of finite values, and . . . finite entities are meaningless apart from their relationship beyond themselves. (MG, 106)

This urge for radical pluralism and empiricism mirrors Whitehead's recapitulation of his own way to reformulate "coherence" *as* suspension of ultimates from the dualism of Descartes, Spinoza, and Leibniz in *Process and Reality*. Spinoza abandoned Descartes's "incoherence" ("disconnection") of two substances with the introduction of "one substance" in which multiplicity enters as individualized modes of its "essential attributes" (ibid., 6–7). Leibniz again de/constructed these "modes" as monads or mutual world-mirrors with God remaining the one transcendent Monad. Whitehead, as Deleuze after him (although in a different way), de/constructs these "monads" into "sheer actualities" (ibid.,7) (or Deleuzian "nomads"). Their "coherence" ("solidarity") consists in their *mutual immanence as emergent ultimates that generate the empirical movement of the Whole as the Open.*

Precisely at this point Whitehead introduces "creativity" as immanent self-creativity by which events become events. Since creativity is ultimate only by being "actual in virtue of its incidents," events in their becoming always "involve" all other events. Hence, this is also the point at which he introduces the "theopoetic difference" that does *not identify* God with either such an event or its creative activity (ibid., 7). This way of overcoming dualism is the place that gives birth to the "category of the ultimate" with its *suspension* of ultimates.

In his final move, in "Mathematics and the Good," Whitehead de/constructs "ultimacy" into an *open series of sheer actualities* that underlies any possible rationalization. Where monistic/mystical and pluralistic/differential pluralisms remain bound to the *primacy of infinity*—paying "reverence" and "compliments" (SMW, 179) to infinity—they also remain entrapped in a dualism that re-instantiates a Logic of the One, the Two, and the Many. Based on such a *reversal of the assumption of transcendental completeness* that is presupposed by the primacy of infinity (and the paradigm of eternity), *polyphilia* gives primacy to *in/finitely becoming finitude* (and the paradigm of novelty). From the *generative* energy of this *intersection* of *immanent infinitude* in open *multiplicities of actualities*, polyphilic pluralism will now poetically *derive* all "ultimates" *from the process of their mutual suspension* in which their symbols mutually de/construct each other.

In symbolizing the divine in terms of "the fundamental infinitude" that "introduced a subordinate differentiation by finite modes" (MG, 106), *monistic/mystical pluralisms* in some of their (mostly Christian) philosophical and theological manifestations—for instance, in John Hick[17] and Perry Schmidt-Leukel[18]—tend to understand the divine as infinitude that becomes (easily misunderstood as) the *hidden "unity" of all appearances of the divine in different religions.* As "ultimate reality" *that is fundamentally unknown (or even unknowable),* it *grounds* the plurality of experiences and symbolizations of "God" so that either there is a true symbol of ultimate reality while no religion is able to recognize it because of the natural inability of the human intellect, or out of sin, *or* such symbols apply *only* to the sphere of the temporal world and *not* to the divine sphere, which is considered totally beyond any symbolization. Since this monistic pluralism often draws on, and insofar as it assimilates itself to, apophatic theologies of Christian inheritance, it can be called a *mystical* pluralism: the unification of both the plurality of experiences and symbolizations of the divine *within a nameless ultimate reality.*[19]

Most contemporary "religious pluralisms," insofar as they take seriously the multiplicity of revelations in diverse religions,[20] obviously prefer such a mystical framework for the divine in multiplicity, as can especially be witnessed in the context of reflections on *comparative theology,* represented, for

17. Hick, *Problems of Religious Pluralism.*

18. Schmidt-Leukel, "Das Pluralistische Modell," 353–64.

19. Refer to chapter 12, current volume.

20. Ward, *Religion and Revelation,* 23–24.

instance, by Keith Ward,[21] Frances Clooney,[22] Daya Krishna,[23] and Raimon Panikkar.[24] While they seek to *pluralize* the *monological* implications of inclusivism/exclusivism by suggesting that we always already stand within more than one belief-system that we can access or are, in fact, committed to, they also strongly suggest that there must (in this or another way) be some *mystical* "unity" manifesting itself in all the diversity of religious experiences and symbolizations of the divine and ultimacy in different religions. This becomes evident by the following quote from Perry Schmidt-Leukel.

> Not relativism, but perspective realism is proposed here. It is the one reality, which is perceived by different people in different contexts—and in this sense differently. Transferred to revelation, respectively the experience of transcendent reality, this means that, in religious history, we encounter different experiences of the same transcendent reality.[25]

Regarding the "pluralism" and "empiricism" of the monistic/mystical pluralism, this leads to the unfortunate implication that its *integration* of both the monistic and the pluralistic traits *weakens both*. In light of the hidden ultimate reality, its "pluralism" is born out of intellectual or moral *deficits* that will be revealed or healed in the divine Eschaton. Hence, *either* its "pluralism" is a version of "rationalism" for which the pluralistic alternatives will finally fall away—as in Nicolas Rescher's "orientational" pluralism[26]—*or* its "empiricism" is a *fake* since the nameless and silent ultimate reality cannot be experienced *at all*—as in John Hick's Kantian "transcendentalism" that forbids any experience of the *ignotum x* as being beyond our mental categories.[27]

Pluralistic/differential pluralisms, on the other hand, lay emphasis on "the necessity of finite monads" that leads to *a plurality of "defined ultimates."*[28] Nevertheless, they either remain in peril of operating under the assumption of "a substratum of Deistic infinitude" (MG, 106) or of using its *logos* to "stabilize" these "ultimates" so as to be able to "identify" religions against one another.[29] In the first form—as proposed by Mark Heim—it

21. Ward, *Religion and Revelation*, 3–49.

22. Clooney, "Current Theology," 521–55.

23. Krishna,"Comparative Philosophy," 71–83.

24. Panikkar, "What is Comparative Philosophy Comparing?," 116–36.

25. Schmidt-Leukel, "Das Problem divergierender Wahrheitsansprüche," 52–53.

26. Rescher, *Pluralism*, chs. 4–5.

27. Hick, *Interpretation of Religion*, 241–45.

28. McDaniel, *Gandhi's Hope*, ch. 3.

29. Griffin, "John Cobb's Whiteheadian Complementary Pluralism," 45–51.

produces the idea of *multiple salvations*.[30] Because this "plurality" of ways of salvation toward different aims—for instance, a theistic Heaven in Christianity and a non-theistic nirvana in Buddhism—does not want to fall apart in a pluralistic substantialism of isolated regions of salvation into which one will find oneself after death removed, it must *mediate* itself through another *unifying* logic; for instance, through that of the Trinity, to address the mutual relationality of such "regions" of salvation.[31] Hence, either it remains pluralistically *substantialist* or it reintroduces a *particular* religion's symbolism as mediation of a new logic of relationality, which remains within the *logos* of the One and, hence, becomes a subtle form of "inclusivism."[32]

In its most promising form—without either dismissing "God" altogether or making the divine the only form of ultimacy—such pluralistic/ differential pluralism comes in the shades of process theology's differentiation of ultimates with Whitehead's "category of the ultimate" (PR, 21–22). With John Cobb, David Griffin, and Jay McDaniel, we find a theological interpretation of the *plurality of symbolizations* of ultimate reality ("pluralism") in different religions as expression of a *plurality of experiences* of such ultimates ("empiricism"): "God," "creativity" and (sometimes) the "world" (or even adding the "present moment"). As in Hick, in its basic form, this differentiation of "ultimates" allows identifying religions that tend to symbolize the ultimate in personal ("*personae*") or non-personal ("*impersonae*") terms[33] as a distinction, for instance between Christianity and Buddhism. In a more elaborate sense, this differentiation allows us also to find intersections *within* religions by which these religions accept *both* ways of articulating ultimate reality—such as the Hindu distinction of *saguna* and *nirguna* Brahman, the Buddhist distinction between Buddhas and Buddha nature (*buddhadhatu* or *tathagatagarbha*), or the Christian distinction in mystical lore between God and Godhead (Meister Eckhart). Unlike Hick, however, Cobb's *complimentary* pluralism (of two ultimates) or Griffins *differential* pluralism (of three ultimates) unmasks the Kantian presupposition in Hick's ultimately "Real." Since Whitehead's does not accept the Kantian epistemology—that there can be any absolutely unknown we can, nevertheless, relate to (PR, 4)—the Real beyond divine *personae* and *impersonae* is *neither* pluralistic, if it desires the *one* Real, *nor* empiricist, since it cannot be experienced at all. This leaves Hick's pluralism on the side of "*identist* pluralism,"[34]

---

30. Heim, *Salvations*, ch. 5.

31. Heim, *Salvations*, ch. 6.

32. Panikkar, *Intrareligious Dialogue*, 6–7.

33. Hick, *An Interpretation of Religion*, 162.

34. Griffin, "Complementary Pluralism," 24.

which is not pluralistic at all. In fact, it seems to re-instantiate the Logic of the One-Beyond. "*Differential* pluralism,"[35] then, seems to demonstrate itself to be much more suited to the recognition of *plural experiences and symbolizations* of ultimacy in and between multiple religions.

Nevertheless, in light of the "theopoetic difference" between multiplicity and theoplicity, which does not lend itself to an "identification" of the divine in terms of symbolisms of "many ultimates" either, but to a *suspension* of ultimates and a *diffusion* of the divine (in) multiplicity, differential pluralism may also fall short in both its pluralistic and empirical inclinations in at least three ways: First, in a stabilization of the two series of the "category of the ultimate,"—one, many, creativity (PR, 21) and God, world, creativity (ibid., 348)—"God" seems to represent the "one," and the world, the "many." This move, however, would imply a clear re-instantiation of the Logic of the One, the Two, and the Many with regard to the notion of God. Although this move would still indicate a "deep pluralism," insofar as it does not elevate God to the position of the One-Beyond, it *remains monistic by the identification* of God with the ultimate of the "one." Second, "deep pluralism" remains bound to the *identist* pluralism it despises, because it *identifies religions by the ultimate it attaches to them*, be it theistic or non-theistic, and, thereby, robs religions of their *experiential* development and *inner* pluralistic differentiations that escape such identifications. In this sense, "deep pluralism" remains resembling a colonization of fixed categories instead of employing the arbitrary distribution of such abstractions in polyphilic intention. Third, whether differentiated into two, three, four or even more "ultimates," the *stabilization of "ultimates"* transforms them back into *abstractions* that can be used to exert power over the *lived* and *experienced* religious phenomena and societies as well as their as of yet unprecedented novelty. In undermining the remaining *dualistic stabilization of the difference between "ultimate reality" and "ordinary reality,"* the suspension of ultimates in polyphilic intention, instead, assumes the *infinity* of "ultimates" in suspension, the *mutual* suspension of "ultimates," a *process* of suspension itself, and the *emergence* of ultimates in this process.

In its most *radical* form, differential pluralism, that is, a pluralism that suspends "ultimacy" altogether, will *abandon* the "superstitious awe of infinitude [that] has been the bane of philosophy," because the "infinite has no properties" and will, instead, seek its "embodiment of finite values" (MG, 106). It will find itself at the *embodied-suspended intersection of infinity and finitude* by precisely meditating the "gift of finitude" (ibid., 105) in which multiplicity becomes a process of folding and valuing, revealing the *dignity*

---

35. Griffin, "Complementary Pluralism."

of the folds. This "conversion of philosophy," as it appears in Deleuze and Whitehead, does not, however, *per se* amount to polyphilic symbolization of the divine in multiplicity, but might instead, in *another* logic of multiplicity, lose any language of the divine altogether. By excommunicating "unity" as an oppressive concept over against difference, this *deconstructive* pluralism will follow Derrida's appraisal that *différance* never unifies, but always diversifies in processes of differentiation.[36] Instead of finding polypoetic symbolizations as they arise in "skillful suspensions" (*upaya*) of multiplicity *useful* for the articulation of the divine (in) multiplicity, this *other* pluralism will tend to *restate truth with liberation* and, hence, articulate itself in freedom from symbolizations altogether.[37]

While *différance*, in its infinite deferral of stabilization of "ultimates" as expressions of a fulfilled "presence," must deconstruct *all* symbolizations *as* expressions of the Logic of the One, the Two, and the Many and, hence, defer any language of the divine *indefinitely*, polypoetics, conversely, in its *different* logic of multiplicity, expresses precisely the *gift of finitude*. As genuine *polyphilia*, it seeks *polypoetic "incidents" of "plural" and "empirical" evocations of the divine (in) multiplicity in the multiplicity of its symbolic expressions.* Although (as considered earlier), there is no *logos* that could be used to decide *between* such different logics of multiplicity. From the point of view of a polyphilic logics of multiplicity, the surrational theopoetic difference makes sense as an *insistence on the difference between power and love.* The *suppression* of *this* difference, however, might amount to *another hidden logocentrism* for which the infinite suspension of "ultimates" *must exclude* polyphilia as "trace" of the divine *in* multiplicity and the virtues of its polypoetic symbolizations.

It is the tendency of forms of *mystical* and *deconstructive* pluralism to avoid any "identifications" of the divine either by radical *apophasis* into absolute unknowability or through radical *différance* (and perhaps they meet in their movement). Here, ultimacy tends to *disappear in namelessness* and the many symbolizations of this nameless will be equivalent to the *disappearance of the divine itself in the process of apophasis/différance*. Such a tendency is, however, not without presuppositions of its own, since both movements operate under the assumption of the (absolute) *passivity* of (the concept of) the divine/ultimate. The consequence of this seclusion is that the *symbolizations* of the plurality of experiences of the ultimate/divine become virtually non-discernable from their mere *infinite interpretation* that might not have any implication of reality or, at least, any reality

---

36. Welsch, *Vernunft*, 260–75.

37. Refer to chapter 12, current volume.

we can know of anything at all. This pluralism is less a form of "debilitating relativism,"[38] for which no measure of differentiation remains, but a mute apophaticism with regard to ultimacy. What separates *polyphilic* pluralism from such muteness is that it insists on *both* sides, mystical monism and differential pluralism. The remedy of its polypoetics against this weakness of *absolute passivity* of the disappearing ultimacy is its understanding of polyphilia as a *gift* of *self-creative events of symbolisms*, in which the divine *in* multiplicity appears as the *poietic* mystery of creative passage.[39]

Instead of a mourning over the alleged "weakness of projection" of the polypoetic process in symbolizing the divine *in* multiplicity, polyphilic pluralism understands its theopoetics as *subtractive affirmation of multiplicity* in which it would be "surrationally" possible to understand the virtually infinite, but always finite, *empirical plurality of symbolizations* of ultimacy (SMW, 179) as the *gift of/for the self-creative process of passage*. As *poietic revelation* of ultimacy, and not the merely apophatic incognito and permanent deference, it evokes the notion of *theoplicity*. The symbolisms of ultimacy, then, don't indicate somehow distorted projections, *failing* to reach the One-Beyond (as in Hick), yet stabilizing the mythopoetic content of "ultimate reality" (over ordinary reality). On the contrary, unknowability and deferral indicate the *revelation* of *novelty* within this relativity and ultimacy itself.[40] The multiple images of ultimacy are, then, not indispensable projections of an inescapable relativism and, ultimately, agnosticism, but *revelations* of in/finite perspectives of the *poietic process of suspension* of ultimacy *in ever-new events* of *their* experience. Theoplicity is the theophony of *polyphilic poiesis* within the process of creative passage.

---

38. Griffin, "Complementary Pluralism," 4.

39. Faber, *God as Poet*, 244–51.

40. Refer to chapter 12, current volume.

Chapter Seven

Divine Para-doxy

Orthodoxy and the Doxa of Multiplicity

ACCORDING TO A QUALIFIED theological "opinion" (*doxa*), the alpha and omega of theology, is *doxology*: The functionless evocation of divine *doxa*—powerful beauty—for its own sake.[1] In Luke 2:4, the doxological invocation of divine *doxa* is equivalent with her shining over the ones who live in peace. However, in recollecting the history of religion, would it not be just as easy to claim that religion is the last resort of violence, a "record of the horrors," of "human sacrifice . . . the slaughter of children, cannibalism, sensual orgies, abject superstition, hatred as between races, the maintenance of degrading customs, hysteria, bigotry," or in one phrase, "the last refuge of human savagery" (RM, 37)? Is it not with deep disgust that we must admit that "the name of God" has become equivalent with any number of reasons for war?[2] And is it not with deep embarrassment that we must be stupefied by the fact that while we might (want to) confess that *God* becomes *flesh*—*doxa* has become *orthodoxy*—our orthodoxies are considerably implicit in our religious divisions? How, and in what sense, then, could the doxological arousal of the divine become an evocation of peace?

If the only means of "peace in heaven" is the inhabitation of a single, true *orthodox* realm, its doxology only suggests a subjugation to an orthodox One. Consequently, the equivalent of *doxa* on earth becomes "war." The question is this: can we save "the name of God" from war—"in heaven" and "on earth"—by saving divine *doxa* from orthodoxy?[3] Could we, perhaps,

---

1. Pannenberg, *Systematic Theology*, 1:55.

2. McTernan, *Violence in God's Name*.

3. Revelation 12:7–9. "War in heaven" is associated with a logic of the One: the origin of sin as fall from the One; it is used as explanation of the "war on earth"—as not being one under the true One—and it companions the eschatological restitution of peace—a peace through war as peace of the One. Since in such a war one side is always

resist the *ortho-dox* One—the only true measure "in heaven"—and instead evoke a *para-dox* multiplicity as an expression of "peace on earth?"[4] Could, perhaps, an understanding of divine *multiplicity* before and beyond any "true orthodox essence" be key to envisioning the overcoming of perpetual generations of religious wars? Could the *doxa* of such *divine love of multiplicity* shine over us, instigating a profound *sense* of peace, that is, the imagination of its *real* possibility?[5]

Like a paranoid disorder, religious "opinion" (*doxa*) tends to find in itself such *absolute* truth that, if it really were the shadow of God's *doxa*, it makes God *only* the expression of the power of war. Is the reason to abandon religion altogether, for many, a disenchantment with the sanctification of someone else's idiosyncratic horizon that, in its own turn, justifies itself as the expression of the one, absolute God "himself"? What is such an "orthodoxy" that seduces to a "doxology of war" other than *fanaticism*—the *exclusive* expression of *being right*, righteous, justified, sanctified by *being on the right side*, namely God's side?[6] If only these orthodox ones are meant to survive the war against all others, "orthodoxy" becomes a synonym for *exclusion*; the exclusion of the unwilling ones who (even by God's will or damnation) cannot find the right side; the untruthful; the evil ones—or are they perhaps just the others, the aliens, the poor, the different, the nonconformists, the lawless? *Paradoxically*, would such a fanatic orthodoxy not have excluded all in whom, in Matthew 25, God's presence *anonymously* resides with its hidden desire for, and sense of, peace?[7]

Religious fanaticism always erodes the earth and its inhabitants. The unmasking of its war-soul is a theological imperative. In order to generate "peace-making propositions,"[8] we must dissociate *doxa* from fanaticism. And in order to generate at least a *sense* for the possibility of peace among humans and of humanity with the eco-cosmos in which it is embedded, we

---

excluded, it is a war of orthodoxy, of segregation, and destruction of "the other."

4. Schneider, *Beyond Monotheism.*

5. For the introduction and exploration of these terms, cf. Faber, *God as Poet*, postscript, and idem, "Ecotheology," 75–115.

6. I suggest that this and not "atheism" was the reason for Feuerbach to abandon any "entitative" (substantial) notion of God instead of the pure act of love that avoids fanaticism and always creates peace. His reformulation of Christian orthodoxy may be nothing but such a reconstitution of "theology" under the auspices of love. Cf. Feuerbach, *Essence of Christianity*, ch. 4; cf. also Faber, "Ecotheology," 99.

7. The overwhelming biblical topos of God's "presence in" or even "siding with" the lost ones may be a good starting point to approach an understanding of peace that is not built on the rightness of the One, but a mutual engagement for a common future that envelops the respect, justness, and "divine nature" of the other as other.

8. Stengers, "Beyond Conversation," 254.

must dissociate *doxa* from self-designated "orthodoxies." We must name a *difference* of *doxa* from the *function* of orthodoxy in religious fanaticism; namely, as the reason and expression of one of the most fundamental binaries in human existence: the exaltation of "better ones" and the enslavement of the other. This master-slave mechanism is the foundation for all kinds of binarisms that signal power structures and their omnipotence. Pushing Michel Foucault, we might say that the only reality in fanatic enthrallment that is, in fact, omnipotent, is not God, but the power of the elected.[9] In other words, whenever we seek an "eminent reality" from which to explain and reconstruct our own fragility, such that it issues a legitimate reason for the domination of others, this reality fairly regularly ends up being named "God." God is power and to be in power is to be like God; that is, in God's service: *vicarii potestatis Dei*. Participants in the power of God's vicars are bereft of their own *potestas* and they are given back to themselves as inventions of the omnipotence of the better ones *ex nihilo*. Fanatic participation is a subtle machine for the production of slavery.[10]

Various orthodoxies have had their fair share in the perpetuation of fanaticism and slavery.[11] Whenever they became (and become) used as an instrument of legitimating any variety of religious violence, religious aristocracies intrude into the bodies of people (in the singular and plural sense).[12] There is an interreligious resonance between religions not just in their effort to seek and find peace and justice—as Hans Küng has demonstrated[13]—but a companionship of war against one another. As war is a *regular* means of religious communication, violence is its generalization throughout experience, and the use of orthodox measures often its script. In fact, in any analysis of warfare as an intra and interreligious medium of conversation and conversion, orthodoxy must be reckoned with *as the very medium* of the reign of fanaticism and enslavement on various levels of bodily and mental existence. As orthodoxy becomes a medium for the canalization of righteousness and a domination of access to salvation, the poetic complexity of religious myths become the harbinger of the

---

9. Foucault, *Power/Knowledge*.

10. Faber, "'Amid a Democracy of Fellow Creatures,'" 192–237; cf. also Keller, *Face of the Deep*. The *ex nihilo* manages to deconstruct the relational "other" into either nothing or evil (opposite), such that the One is always the winner of this war (that is, its redemptive impulse, although it might simply hide the interests of orthodox control).

11. Hilkert, "Experience and Tradition," 69; cf. also Ferguson, *Backgrounds of Early Christianity*.

12. Garland-Hill, *Slavery and Christianity*.

13. Küng, *A Global Ethic*, 114–53.

justification of subjection. In numbing resistance, orthodoxies universalize the internalization of fanaticism as such.

In Whitehead's analysis of the fanatic function of Christian orthodoxy, it becomes the expression of a power-driven confusion of God and Caesar—based on imperialistic fantasies of the divinization of power and its dialectical companion: subjection into physical and mental enslavements. In its fanatic use, orthodoxy not only legitimizes the power of domination, but also attaches itself *as* the Law to the notion of God per se, such that the only possibility to relate to this divine Law is by orthodoxy. "When the Western world accepted Christianity," Whitehead concludes in the final section of *Process and Reality*, "Caesar conquered; and the received text of Western theology was edited by his lawyers. The code of Justinian and the theology of Justinian are two volumes expressing one movement," of the *legalization* of the "deeper idolatry, of the fashioning of God in the image of the Egyptian, Persian, and Roman imperial rulers." In fact, according to Whitehead, the "Church gave unto God the attributes which belonged exclusively to Caesar" (PR, 342).

Its alternative, the "brief Galilean vision of humility," which is not based on the Law and its power, but on the "the tender elements in the world, which slowly and in quietness operate by love," just appeared as an aberration that only "flickered throughout the ages, uncertainly" (PR, 342–43). Maybe, however, it is precisely in this *uncertainty* of the ever-fragile endangerment of the movements of love through power that *doxa* reveals her place as the "other" of orthodoxy *within* its domain—that which cannot be grasped from within the binary of orthodoxy and heterodoxy (or heresy); that which in Law will only appear as outside of any lawful behavior; the event that must be ignored or, if this is not possible, must be destroyed. A living connex that is not bound by the certainties of any Law, but by the uncertainties of relativity and relationality, does not operate through the power of domination. In its domain, the tenderness of mutuality will always only appear as a disturbance of the Law. This *doxa* becomes the mirror that reveals the terror of the Law of power and, if it is confused with God, the violence of the righteous. Against its very insistence on *that which cannot be defined by power*, this *doxa* will *paradoxically* always arouse orthodox violence of expulsion and destruction. Its sense of peace always arrives *sub contrario*: not as *power* to create peace, but as mischief; not as peacemaker, but as the sufferer of the violence of domination; not as king, but as pariah. Rene Girard is right about the "function" of the Lamb—to take the sin away.[14]

14. Girard, *Violence and the Sacred*.

In its most sublime form, the "vampirism" of orthodox fanaticism will appear as a reconstruction of mutual relationality from the *participatory* sovereignty of an all-creative sovereign: everything is created by "his" despotic act and everything only participates in it.[15] The logical (logocentric) implication of such a reconstruction of mutuality from a binary structure of elevation and subjection is nothing less than the generation of various forms of enslavement. As the elevated becomes an independent *substance*, the subjected remains only a shadow, a mere *participatory property* of the higher and highest beings.[16] In this dynamic of enslavement, its imperialism becomes the very structure of orthodoxy. It presents us with a concept of God from the perspective of the master–slave hermeneutics in which God not only stands "in the same relation to the whole World as early Egyptian or Mesopotamian kings stood to their subject populations." But in the final "metaphysical sublimation" from "its barbaric origin," becomes precisely "the one absolute, omnipotent, omniscient source of all being, for his own existence requiring no relations to anything beyond himself" (AI, 169). While this orthodox divine is "internally complete," it makes everything else dependent such that its creature must find *even its very reason of existence* in the subjection to the sublime barbarism of power.

It is interesting that this Transylvanian conception of the divine within Christian orthodoxy appears not only in Whitehead's philosophical appraisal of participatory enslavement as the "metaphysical sublimation" of God in the realm of power as it suffers from "the Platonic doctrine of subordinate derivations" (ibid) of properties from Ideas. Teilhard de Chardin, from the heart of his Christian spirituality, pointed to the same problematic Platonism as the cornerstone of the orthodox obstruction of the renewal of theology. It needs to overcome the tendency to cling to a non-relational and internally complete *ens a se* that "dangerously devaluates 'participated being' to a mere *ens ab alio*,"[17] that is, a mere subordinate derivation from the perfect being.[18] Instead of reducing the world's multiplicity to a puppet of the all-sufficient completeness of an absolute sovereign, he urges us to re-imagine God as *only* relational. But such a God "must complete [God] self in something outside of [God]self."[19] As it is this radical move that rescues the world from being viewed as a mere imitation of the transcendent original, it also frees its multiplicity from the binary of elevation (election)

15. Faber, "Wahrheit und Maschine."
16. Faber, "Amid a Democracy," 203–4.
17. Teilhard de Chardin, *Letters from My Friend*, 166.
18. Teilhard de Chardin, *Science and Christ*, 182.
19. Teilhard de Chardin, *Lettres Intimes à Auguste Valensin*, 296.

and subjection (enslavement). As a consequence, such a new theology will yield to a *genuine mutuality of God and the world*. As Teilhard speaks of a "strictly bilateral and complementary relationship of the world and God,"[20] Whitehead suggests that the "mutual immanence" of God and the world "requires that the relationships of God to the World should lie beyond the accidents of will, and that they be founded upon the necessities of the nature of God and the nature of the World" (AI, 168).

In the same sense in which the one absolute, omnipotent, omniscient One is only the sublimation of rogue power into structured Law, this logo-centric mask of power, in which its *logos* appears innocently as reflecting (a neutral and naturalized) "rationality," makes its appearance in the philosophical category of substance and its properties, attributes, and predicates. In fact, this One of power subjects self-creativity rather than releasing it. It mutes relationality rather than inventing it. And it coerces relationality into enslavements, rather than persuading, within a web of mutual relation, splitting the multiplicity into independent substances of which everything else is only its own inherent, participatory property. But does this "bifurcation" express the most profound "violence to that immediate experience which we express in our actions, our hopes, our sympathies, our purposes, and which we enjoy" (PR, 49)?

The *substantialism* underlying the development of Christian orthodoxy is not innocent, after all. On the contrary, if everything is the mere property of the One, this hierarchy of power will, in its ultimate consequence, lend itself to a total reconstruction of "creation" in terms of property and the absolutism of merely granted existence. On the one hand, if every creature is the *property* of the creator (at least in the Eschaton), its absolute subjection to orthodoxy is the *measure of its very existence*.[21] On the other hand, since the One is complete and independent of any relationship and mutuality, this God must also be *esse ipse subsistence* that *possesses "his" own existence*.[22] The outcome of this orthodox substantialism was not only the justification of the right of orthodoxy to burn its enemies on the stakes.[23] It survives in any recollection of those doctrines that convey the absolute sovereignty of God with regard to creation and redemption. The alleged power of God as one that can annihilate creation without a trace (whenever "he" pleases)[24] only mirrors the power to condemn any

20. Teilhard de Chardin, *Christianity and Evolution*, 226.

21. Faber, "Amid a Democracy," 203.

22. Faber, "Indra's Ear," 174–78.

23. Barstow, *Witchcraze*.

24. Caputo, *Weakness of God*, ch. 9.

creature that is not compliant to eternal pain or non-existence.[25] Such is the domain of the doxology of fanatical orthodoxy.[26]

What, on the other hand, would happen, if we do not follow the substantialism of orthodoxy and its doxology of power and instead invoke the *doxa* of that which cannot be named with any name of power? What if, instead of the silencing violence of the Transylvanian deity, we seek the silent traces of the tender *love* of multiplicity? What if, instead of the doxology of the One, we follow a doxology of *polyphilia*? What if, instead of the mechanisms of subjection, we emphasize the multiplicity, reciprocity, and mutuality of creative becoming? The implications would, indeed, be profound on all levels—methodologically, ontologically, and theologically. In a disentanglement of God and Caesar, we could instead cherish and worship a *divine polyphilia* in which the love of multiplicity becomes liberated from the encroachment of the love of power—even in the form of the power of love. We might, with a phrase from Laurel Schneider, just "let go (of the One)"[27] and, in doing so, find another *doxa*: the *doxa of a divine manifold* in which not only Oneness ceases to figurate as the ground of being, but—in an disentanglement of the confusion of being with unity—"being" itself might be freed *from itself* by being transformed into an *irreducible multiplicity of infinite becoming*.

With Teilhard, we could learn to replace the "metaphysics of *Esse* with a metaphysics of *unire* or *uniri*"[28] in which unity always means a process of unification, of *becoming* united. Following Whitehead, we could embark on a deeply polyphilic account of multiplicity in which *creator, creatures*, and *creativity* have "no meaning" (PR, 225) apart from each other. With Gilles Deleuze, we could relieve ourselves from the power of the participatory ontologies of the One and instead risk perceiving the world differently, as a *univocal* texture that "repudiates hierarchies" and any "One superior to being." We could trust a *doxa* in which we transgress into an "essentially anti-hierarchical world," a "world of immanence," "almost a kind of anarchy,"[29] of connectivity, differentiation, and creativity. In fact, where our love for multiplicity does not seek any unity of the One that ever would overcome irreducible complexity,[30] we might gain a new sense of (religious) peace. Not

25. Pawson, *The Road to Hell*.

26. For a classical dogmatic scheme of orthodoxy under the name of doxology, cf. Wainwright, *Doxology*.

27. Schneider, *Beyond Monotheism*, 203.

28. Teilhard de Chardin, *Christianity*, 226–27.

29. Deleuze, *Lecture on Spinoza*.

30. Deleuze defines multiplicity precisely in this way:

a peace that lives from pacification in the name of the legitimized violence of hierarchical orthodoxies, but a peace that will only make sense with a life *from* and *within* the multiplicity of uncertain, vague, complex, differentiated, and ever-new differently differentiating voices that speak with the voice of mutual immanence. This *polyphony* of voices beyond the binary of elevation and subjection, beyond master and slave, and beyond reductions of others to heterodox or heretic intruders, invokes a *doxa* that will tell a story of *polyphilia*. I will call the characteristic of this story *para-dox*. If the polyphilic insistence on multiplicity is a means of a new sense of peace, the *doxa* of multiplicity itself is para-doxical.

Multiplicities and the Paradox of Indetermination

Multiplicity is, as Deleuze muses in *The Fold*, an "irruption of incompossibilities on the same stage."[31] It names the *incompossibility* of a "divergent series (of events) in the same world" without pre-established unity. It neither constitutes a One nor many already constituted ones. It is a "harmony" only "through a crisis that leads to a broadened chromatic scale, to the emancipation of dissonance or of unresolved accords, accords not brought back to tonality." It transgresses "from harmonic closure to an opening onto a polyphony."[32] It is the polyphony of inconsistencies and inadequacies, a harmony of indeterminacies, a process of poly-harmonic indetermination of presupposed identities or mere pluralities. Instead of a divine Law that establishes a harmony of *exclusion* of the incompossible from a world of divine consistency (Leibniz), poly-harmonic multiplicity consists of any number of multiplicities of *reciprocal and reciprocally incomplete* series of events or reinventions of harmonic becoming. Since any form of generalized abstractions cannot conceptualize poly-harmonic multiplicity, it will need a new method of understanding: the paradox.

The states of things are not unities or totalities but multiplicities. That does not simply mean that there are many states of things (where each state would be a whole) or that each state of things is multiple (which would only be an indication of its resistance to unification). The crucial point from an empirical point of view is the word "multiplicity." Multiplicity indicates a group of lines or dimensions that cannot be reduced to one another. Every "thing" is made up of them. A multiplicity certainly contains points of unification, centers of totalization, points of subjectivation, but these are factors that can prevent its growth and stop its lines. These factors are in the multiplicity they belong to, not the reverse. Deleuze, *Two Regimes of Madness*, 304.

31. Deleuze, *Fold*, 82.
32. Deleuze, *Fold*.

Everyone knows the Liar's paradox: if the lie speaks truth, it is false; if it speaks false, it is true. It formulates a *contradiction* of something being *this* and *its opposite at once*, or being true and false at the same time. The claim that *some* contradictions of such a form are *true* implies that there is a *sound* reason as to why, from such contradictions, *only indeterminacies* can follow. They are not false because they are indeterminate or they are *only* false if we presuppose reality to be *determinate*.[33] In other words, their truth-value is false not insofar as it is wrong (without correspondences to a presupposed reality) but insofar as "reality" always *invokes novelty*.[34] Whitehead's version of such *paradoxical indetermination* takes the form of the claim that "in the real world it is more important that a proposition be interesting," insofar as it arouses novelty, "than that it be true." Although the "importance of truth" is not eliminated, it is that it "adds to interest" (PR, 259). In other words, the determinant of truth is not the ground of truth, but an *addition* that names a *resonance* within a multiplicity *in the process of incessant creative alteration*.

The paradox of indetermination states that any claim will be situated between the ever-fluent limits of *consistency* and *adequacy*. On the one hand, when we survey experience with some adequacy, it becomes inconsistent. On the other, when we reduce experience "to a rigid consistency" it will become inadequate to its complexity (ibid., 57). In both cases, what escapes is the paradox of multiplicity (of experiences, thoughts, or claims). *Either* we lose the *adequacy* of experience to perceive multiplicity in the process of creative renewal by the very categoreal reductions of these processes resulting in abstract unifications that cannot account for novelty, or the story these experiences tell will remain *incomplete* with regard to their *consistency* because of the sheer multiplicity that can never be suspended by any presupposed or generated unity. The paradox of multiplicity consists in this *incompossibility*: the impossibility of any abstraction to function as *a priori reason* for the participation of multiplicity as a variation of its "essence" *and*, at the same time, the necessity to formulate such *ideas* in order to *understand* multiplicities as multiplicities, that is, as an experiential a priori of any abstract unification. Any *consistent* unification has already lost the multiplicity that it was meant to control, but any *adequate* idea of multiplicity will necessarily become inconsistent. Such is the paradox of indetermination: since multiplicity is always inconsistent or inadequate, it is always *polyphonically indeterminate*. Moreover, multiplicity as multiplicity is always *a process of poly-harmonic indetermination*.

33. Sainsbury, *Paradoxes*, 107–34.
34. Faber, *God as Poet*, ch. 2.

The "logic" of the poly-harmonic multiplicity does not *state* any law under the logic of the One and Many; it names the *becoming* of multiplicities with a *paradoxal logic* for which experience and understanding are fundamentally indeterminate.[35] In the Greco-philosophical sense of the term, the *logos* of the One and the Many can always only aim at a compossibility of its premises and consequences. It impresses the world with its bifurcations of the world into true and false, this and that, determinate opposites and consistent (but undiscovered) determinations *because* it is urged (under the logic of the One and the Many) to presuppose reality as per se *determinate* (and that only the determinate is real). *Doxa*, the accompanying shadow of *this logos*, was understood as mere vanity, a mere illusion, or a mere uninformed opinion *on this otherwise determinate reality*. Hence, *doxa*, here, always follows the logic of the One and Many: it just *imitates* this *logos* of the either-or of determinate reality and only differs from it with regard to the scope it finds and embraces for the determination to be satisfying. Hence, from the perspective of the *paradoxal logic* of multiplicity, *doxa* and *logos* are not opposites between which one has to decide—as was classically believed—but *the same: determinations of identities* as criteria of understanding and reality. Contrarily, the *paradoxal logic* of multiplicity discards the very categorization of the world as reality built on determination as a ground or aim of understanding and reality altogether, and views "reality" as being constituted by *what has been lost* in such a doxic logic—a pre-original indeterminacy and indetermination of multiplicity.

What, from the perspective of *doxic* logic, must appear as the *intoxication* of Apollo by Dionysius—the indeterminacy of that which *becomes* before, after, and beyond sedimentations of unifications with their simplifications, obstructions, and suppressions of inherent differences and differentiations of becoming—is, from the perspective of *para-doxa*, a poly-harmonics of multiplicity. What "doxically" was held to be the orgiastic *Bacchanalia*, is "para-doxically" the *polyphilic doxology of the eros of becoming*, a doxology of the *indeterminacy of pure intensities*. This polyphilic *doxa* is—with Deleuze—neither cosmic (lawlike determinate) nor chaotic (merely indeterminate), but "chaosmically" poly-harmonious in the irruptive movement, through the indeterminate zones of the manifold of chaosmic bodies.[36]

It is this poly-harmonics of indetermination that makes all the difference to war between *doxa* and *logos* and its war-generating fanaticism. Polyphilic indetermination suggests a new sense of peace not because it

---

35. Deleuze and Guattari, *Thousand Plateaus*, 24.
36. Faber, "O bitches," 200–219.

omits differences or forgoes otherness by being merely "vague" (like fuzzy logic), but because it formulates *procedures of indetermination*. With Nicholas Cusa, Nagarjuna, and Deleuze's paradoxal logic of the *both-and-neither-this-and-that*, polyphilic indetermination is deconstructive of abstractive unifications, simplifications, or reductions that haunt multiplicity under the Law of the One and the Many.[37]

First of all, polyphilic indetermination is not the *opposite* of determination; it is *indifferent* toward opposites. In the paradoxal logic of multiplicity—its both-and, and neither-nor—opposites are only universalizing abstractions, substantiations of abstractions that only appear on the surface of processes of becoming-multiplicity. They become toxic when we allow them to ignore the before, the after, and the beyond of unifications by which they *determine themselves* as opposites against multiplicities. For the polyphilic para-dox, there are no determinations as differences "between" opposites, except as substantializations that establish power over multiplicities. Hence, determination, universalization, and abstraction are not "the opposite" of indeterminations; or *as* opposites, they are only illusions that abandon multiplicities for "reasons" of security. If "reasons" are about security (in order to control multiplicities), not understanding (of multiplicities), they oppose *themselves* to indeterminations only as *regressive self-determinations within* multiplicities. From the perspective of indeterminations, however, they are only *abstractions from* multiplicity, the *invention of dualism* in the midst of a sea of indetermination that for reasons of power-establishment *only ground themselves*, nothing less. And since they are only *repetitions of sameness* in the midst of difference, they *only oppose themselves* to multiplicities and indeterminations, but are *not opposed by* multiplicities and indeterminations.

Further, paradoxal poly-harmonics *"in-determines" opposites*. What poststructuralists name deconstruction of logocentric binaries is, in fact, the *suspension of opposites* of their hierarchical determination of multiplicities by uncovering them as abstractions of power, as simplifications of control. By emphasizing the paralogical indeterminacies instead, the *logos* of opposites is really the *doxa* of the logocentric discourses it was meant to oppose. The "*logos* of reasons" is only the disguised "*doxa* without reason" because the "reasons" found in the logic of determination are, in fact, groundless repetitions of *self-grounding abstraction from* multiplicities. These hierarchical contaminations of multiplicities are always a means of violence. Nevertheless, in establishing the substantial logic of enslavement, it is *not* multiplicity that is determined (like chaos that is in need of control), but only the *logos* of domination in its *own abstraction from*

37. Faber, *God as Poet*, §40.

multiplicity. The determinations of this *logos*, then, is itself nothing but a groundless *doxa* (groundless opinion of false determination). But ironically, in the same movement it also appears as a shining *doxa* of power, as ontological or even a divine halo for the very (participatory) existence of multiplicities.[38] The paradox of multiplicity remains witness to the fact that multiplicity is *not determined* by dualism. In being *indifferent* to its power, multiplicity is always the infinite resource of resistance against the logic of the One and the Many. The self-determination of the logic of the One and the Many is always already harbored *within the space* of undetermined multiplicity. This is the notion of *khora*.

Khora names the paradox of multiplicity that always escapes determination into opposites. This was already the fourfold insight of the late work of Plato. In the *Sophists*, he realizes that the world is always only one of *becoming* and that even the Ideas are not eternally frozen classes of participation but living beings. In the *Timaeus*, he realizes that it is false to think of reality in terms of oppositions of Ideas (forms, Laws) and sensible becoming (matter), but that such oppositions are embedded in the space of indetermination, *khora*. And in the *Parmenides*, Plato deconstructs the very idea of the One as enshrouded in the paradox of self-reference and, hence, as in *itself indeterminate*, that is, as not identical with itself.[39] Not only is Derrida's *différance* built on this paradox, but also Whitehead's reference to the space of mutual immanence. *Khora* is the *space of profound indetermination* through the *mutual incompleteness*, *reciprocity*, and *determination* of everything by everything in terms of the multiple multiplicities of differentiation.[40]

Moreover, the paradox of *khoric* multiplicity "*in-determines*" a space for *novelty*. "Reasons" are not grounding abstractions, but *arising conditions of novelty* that—like Whitehead's "ontological principle"—only call for *acts of indetermination* in which events of becoming become the only reasons for becoming of novelty. Like a retrovirus of their own perpetuation *as* indeterminate, such events of becoming cycle back into their own becoming *as the reason* of their becoming such that the univocity of becoming is always and only the "ground" of becoming (PR, 24–25). This is the polyphilic paradox: where only becoming is the *reason* for becoming—Deleuze's "univocity"[41]— there is *no* reason for becoming except becoming itself. Without a transcendent

---

38. This is one reason why the two classical meanings of doxa, from the perspective of indetermination, can appear as one and the same movement of the repetition of self-determining power structures that create their own power of foundation and domination.

39. Sayre, *Plato's Late Ontology*, 198. Cf. also Faber, "Infinite Movement," 171–99.

40. Faber, *God as Poet*, §15–16, 24, 32.

41. Deleuze, *Logic of Sense*, 194.

rule or law or divine decree, becoming is not geared towards, or bound by, a repetition *of* the same (determination), but liberated for the becoming of *novelty*, that is, an indetermination in which only *the unprecedented may be repeated*. Deleuze calls this process *the repetition of difference itself*.[42] "Reasons" as repetition of the same are, then, only self-determinations that always already assume the determinacy of reasons repeated in actualities for "reasons" of security and control and because of the fear of the intoxication from the indeterminate (the becoming of what has no precedence). *Novelty*, on the other hand, does not just fall from heaven—not even Whitehead's heaven of possibilities (RM, 154). Rather, it is itself introduced as *methexis*, as a kind of "participation" in the fabric of the process of *the repetition of the unprecedented into ever-new indeterminacies*. Indeterminations, by way of novelty, always appear in events of becoming-multiplicities.

In classical Aristotelian logic, such a suggestion was avoided because it seems to imply an infinite regress. Aristotle, and any theistic derivation that aimed at the *same* instead of novelty, solved this problem by the "unmoved mover," a perfect act of origin that precedes any becoming-multiplicity. Whitehead, however, as Deleuze after him, demonstrates that this solution is already based on the precondition of substantialism, that is, the elevation of abstraction to the status of an eminent reality with its participatory sovereignty. Everything that becomes is always already *something*, a substance of which becoming is only a dismissible, secondary, or evil variation (PR, 242–243). In using Zeno's paradoxes, Whitehead makes the point that *only if* we suppose that it is *something* (a substance) that (already in its essence *is* and then) becomes, infinite regress is absurd. If, however, (substantial) continuity is itself *in becoming*—namely from the passing events of multiplicities—continuity (of substantiality) is *not* a precondition for becoming, but *becomes* itself (ibid., 35). Hence, the polyphilic paradox of undetermined multiplicities implies that if becoming is its own precondition, it *has no precondition* except its becoming. Therefore, *becoming-multiplicity is always unprecedented* (ibid., 68).

While the *doxa* of the *logos* of the One and Many establishes the violence and enslavement of exclusive determination of truth, rightness, and righteousness, it is the peace-making proposition of the *doxa* of the paradoxal logic of multiplicities to invite to polyphilic embrace of the profound indeterminacies of multiplicity and to embark on a process of un-determination. In de-legitimizing hierarchical power structures employed by orthodoxies that worship with a doxology of the One and the Many, the doxology of the *paradox of polyphilia*—the *non-precedence of*

42. Deleuze, *Difference and Repetition*, 57.

becoming-multiplicity—divines only the *para-doxa*, the *pure expression of the polyphonic voices of infinite becoming.* Instead of presupposing the One that determines one (identity) and many (mere difference) with any form of pre-established harmony as its means of grounding, the paradox of *para-doxy* uses modes of communication, resonance, and mutuality that cannot be *framed* by any means of identification within structures of laws of identity, universal generalization, or classification. Instead of finding the divine in the abstractness of an eminent reality, established as the hierarchical reason for actualization such that actualizations were only instances of abstractions (ibid., 29–30), *polyphilic para-doxy* seeks the divine (in) multiplicity—a divine that *loves* multiplicity (polyphilia) and names *the poly-harmonics of multiplicity,* that is, *divine multiplicity.* In reference to Deleuze's understanding of Whitehead's God,[43] this divine (in) multiplicity names the process by which becoming-multiplicity *never determines itself per logical exclusion* (of "other" worlds of unfitting harmonics) but *indeterminately affirms the all of the polyphony of the chaosmos.*[44] The *para-doxy* of the divine (in) multiplicity worships the *divine insistence on/in/as the process of the always-unprecedented affirmation* of the rugged chaosmos of incompossible and unprecedented complexity.[45]

Polydoxy and the Problem Violence

Para-doxy does not seek orthodoxy. "Paradox is opposed to *doxa*"[46] as is paradoxy to the *doxa* of orthodoxy. Para-doxy avoids orthodoxy *if* its *doxa* views the divine from a logic of the One and Many and, hence, builds the relationship of the divine with the non-divine (or creation) on a universalized structure of abstraction *from* multiplicity that, for reasons of security and control, is invested with the eminent reality of absolute power that structures the binary functions of a world under the prerogative of a hierarchical dualism of ultimate opposites of faith and apostasy impregnated with bifurcating determinations of right and wrong, good and evil, true and false, as well as correct and insufficient.[47] The *doxa* of this orthodoxy is defined by identity and counter-identity: who is in and who is out. Its God is *esse ipse subsistence* and *actus purus,* the paradigm of absolute

---

43. Deleuze, *Fold,* 81.

44. Williams, *Encounters,* ch. 5.

45. This is the thesis of my book *The Divine Manifold.*

46. Deleuze, *Logic of Sense,* 75. Robert Scholes defines *para-* as *being against doxa as dogma.* See *Polydoxy of Modernism,* 275.

47. Gutting, *French Philosophy,* 293–94.

identity. This *doxa* starts with the *dogma* of the divine identity of essence and existence of which everything else is a derivative and participatory system of hierarchical property. It was precisely against these mythologians (God-singers and story-tellers) that Plato set his philosophy of reason as grounded in universal and universally valid Ideas. It was against such dogmas that Plato developed his *typoi peri theologias*, that is, *criteria* of naming God *rationally*.[48] Ironically, it was precisely this universal *logos* that Christian theologians began to claim for their dogma. By identifying *doxa* with *logos*, the Christian dogma became the very expression of the universal structure of Plato's Ideas by which theologians not only claimed their own rationality, but also hid their own inherently irrational *doxa* by the divination of its logocentric structure.[49] This is a lesson in two-fold colonization: the colonization of multiplicity by logocentric reason and the doxological colonization of the universal *logos* by an irrational *doxa*. This colonization holds *in nuce* the fatal oppositionalism of religious fanaticism by which all systems become "dogmatic," in the sense of a striving for their precedence over all others by immunizing against any porosity of their implied logic against the inflow of multiplicity.

Instead of seeking "orthodoxy," para-doxy suggests *polydoxy*—the proposition that the divine cannot be encroached in any logocentric binary in the form of the master–slave dualism, but instead should express the paradoxal poly-harmonics of multiplicity. This proposition is, however, only mediating the paradoxal sense of peace *if* it risks violence and avoids it, at the same time. In avoiding the colonizing identifications, polydoxy might become a mortal offence to orthodoxy. Any suggestion of the orthodox confusion of deity and power might not be seen as a friendly act, but as an offence against religious identity or even as the very blasphemy the religious dogma of orthodoxy was meant to be guarding against. On the other hand, any suggestion of schemes of understanding that avoid orthodox binarisms may ironically not liberate from such dualisms, but be in danger of exchanging them for *forced plurality*. Polydoxy may need to suffer the first violence, but it must avoid the second violence: the principle that forces everyone to believe *in* a plurality of truths, salvations, and divine realities. The paradox of polydoxy is not meant to exchange the violence of orthodoxy with a violence of a religious pluralism that is not necessarily more tolerant than orthodox fanaticism. Polydoxy is meant to avoid *any* fanaticism, and be it a counter-fanaticism against the orthodox dogma and its potentially violent implications.

48. Seckler, "Theologie als Glaubenswissenschaft."
49. Pannenberg, *Theologie und Philosophie*, chs. 1–2.

Polydoxy seeks the poly-harmonics of an interrelated multiplicity of relational differences, but it is never exempt from the seduction to introduce its own fallacy of misplaced power, that is, it is not exempt from the impact of its paradoxal claim of multiplicity on any formulation of identity—be it that of the One or that of the Many. Polydoxy will always be overshadowed by the question as to *how* its inherent refutation of fanatic orthodoxy and its desire to live in a religious world of the indeterminacy of divine multiplicity will convey a *sense of peace* that is liberating *and* non-violent at the same time. This is not only a perennial question of political philosophy[50] and of liberation theologies in their effort to overturn unjust structures of oppression "in the name of God"; it is a question of the *very possibility* of liberation from subjection, *whether this can be done non-violently.*[51]

Thereby, polydox engagement of religious complexity really touches on deep questions of resistance to, transformation of, dissociation from, and overcoming of power—questions with which Foucault and Butler are wrestling (whether power structures are omnipotent and unavoidable), whether any "outside" (a kind of paradise, kingdom of heavens, or ideal society) is a mere illusion, or whether such an "outside" might even be produced by omnipotent power to generate control over any relief from it. One thinks of the movie *The Matrix* in which machines generate a virtual world of imagined freedom in order to control human imagination as a necessary part of their main interest to use human bodies to produce energy.[52] In employing the polyphilic indetermination suggested in the previous section, polydoxy might generate a new sense of peace that undercuts any orthodox or pluralist violence precisely by employing *principles of indetermination* that avoid any dangerously war-bound paths of resistance, refusal, liberation, or transformation.

First of all, we *cannot simply exchange the logocentric world* of the law of the One and the Many, we always already live in, with *khora* as a realm of unframed multiplicity. If with Julia Kristeva and George Bataille we do not believe—as is almost unavoidable in Foucault's and Butler's early work[53]— that *khora* is an *illusionary* "outside" of the Law, we must also remain aware of the impossibility that "the expulsion from paradise" cannot be simply reverted. We have "left" the *khoric* matrix of the mother, or the animal kingdom's intimacy, for good in becoming human, developing language,

---

50. Deleuze and Guattari, *Anti-Oedipus*, 29.

51. Douglass, *The Non-Violent Cross*.

52. Faber, "Introduction: Negotiating Becoming," 40.

53. Butler, *Bodies That Matter*, 41.

consciousness, thought, culture, and religion.[54] It is precisely this expulsion from paradise that made us seek the khoric "paradise" *through* the law
of the father (Kristeva) or the manipulation of objects (Bataille)—and, of
course, hopelessly so.

Hence, we must instead *invert the effects* of this "paradise lost" *from
within*, for instance, by seeking the openings of poetic inconsistency
(Kristeva) or by a conscious consummation of the subject-object duality
(Bataille).[55] With Butler, we might engage in strategies of parody, citation,
and performance that practically achieve from within the lived logic of
the One and Many, what Plato theoretically exercised of the One[56]—its
non-identity. If identity is an abstraction that always needs the power
of self-assertion (and the assertion of its servants) of its very possibility
and, hence, is in practice always already contradicting its self-evidence,
we must rather *live* the paradoxal process of in-determination as it makes
"space" for multiplicity to become *effective* as "de-formations" all the way
up and down the ladder of material, psychological, cultural, social, and
political formations of identity.

Further, we must *transform the way we perceive, experience, and live in
the world*. This was Whitehead's and Deleuze's remedy against logocentric,
dualistic (binary), and substantialist modes of settling the power of identification. Instead of the world of isolated substances (simple location), we may
learn to *feel the multifarious complexity we are suppressing, but were feeling all
along, and transform our categoreal frameworks such that they allow for such
transformations*.[57] Instead of the violence done to our "immediate experience
which we express in our actions, our hopes, our sympathies, our purposes,
and which we enjoy," we may become aware and enabled to ecologically situate ourselves within a "buzzing world, a democracy of fellow creatures" (PR,
49). Instead of clustering the world with concepts all over, the accessibility
of such an "ocean of feeling" (ibid., 166) might open a disturbing "silence"
where "the inflow into ourselves of feelings from enveloping nature over-
whelms us," where "in the dim consciousness of half-sleep, the presentations
of sense fade away" and "we are left with the vague feeling of influences from
vague things around us" (ibid., 176). Where we invert—revert from the inside—the logocentric exclusions, we might gain an awareness of *the poetic
indeterminacy of overwhelming multiplicity*.[58]

54. Kristeva, *Revolution*, ch. 1. Cf. also Bataille, *Theory of Religion*, ch. 1.
55. Bataille, *Theory of Religion*, 103.
56. Butler, *Giving Account of Oneself*, ch. 1.
57. Faber, *God as Poet*, §41–42.
58. Whitehead describes the process of opening with an explosion of layers of

Finally, in order to access multiplicity we need not violently destroy the abstractions on which the dualistic logic of the One and Many is built, but we must non-violently *transform the function of abstractions from serving the substantialization of power*. Instead, these abstractions, insofar as they are implied by orthodoxy, must be transformed into a polydoxy that can release *their liberating potential for an experience, theory, and practice of multiplicity*. We can find such redirection of the impact of abstractions in Deleuze's "transcendental empiricism" that transforms their use from an establishment of a state of eternity into a mode of understanding the world *from* novelty and creativeness.[59] It is also present in Whitehead's profound *para-doxy of novelty* that shifts the function of abstractions in their sedimentation of an eminent reality to the evocation of the unprecedented.[60]

"Orthodoxy" is not discarded in this polyphilic approach to polydoxy. It becomes *contextualized*, that is, elucidated from the polyphony of experiences *from* which it springs. Orthodoxy must be situated in the poly-harmony of mutual relatedness. From this, it follows that religious inspiration must never be limited to a "narrow circle of creeds" because a "dogma . . . can never be final" in its "adjustment" of its "abstract concepts," but must in "the estimate of the status of these concepts" (PR, 130–131) always remain *indeterminate*. When we accept, with Whitehead, that orthodoxies "commit suicide when they find their inspirations in their dogmas," we also suggest that polydoxy evokes an "intuitive response which pierces beyond dogma" (RM, 144) into the *creative methexis of the novelty as the source of their inspiration*. In conceptualizing this indeterminacy of multiplicity, we must value the dogmatic *intuition* from which such conceptualization arises—"Prometheus chained to his rock, Mahomet brooding in the desert, the meditations of the Buddha, the solitary Man on the Cross" (ibid.,

---

experience: "In order to discover some of the major categories under which we can classify the infinitely various components of experience, we must appeal to evidence relating to every variety of occasion. Nothing can be omitted, experience drunk and experience sober, experience sleeping and experience waking, experience drowsy and experience wide awake, experience self-conscious and experience self-forgetful, experience intellectual and experience physical, experience religious and experience skeptical, experience anxious and experience care-free, experience anticipatory and experience retrospective, experience happy and experience grieving, experience dominated by emotion and experience under self-restraint, experience in the light and experience in the dark, experience normal and experience abnormal" (AI, 226).

59. Deleuze, *Fold*, ch. 6.

60. "The explanatory purpose of philosophy is often misunderstood. Its business is to explain the emergence of the more abstract things from the more concrete things. It is a complete mistake to ask how concrete a particular fact can be built up out of universals. The answer is, 'In no way.' The true philosophic question is, how can concrete fact exhibit entities abstract from itself and yet participated in by its own nature" (PR, 19)?

19–20)—but not its momentary conceptual or doctrinal expression if it postulates itself as universally determining exclusive relevance.

The *para-doxa* of a religion will inherently recognize its own polyharmonious complexity against its own simplifications *if* it is not forced to leave its own intuition behind in order to attend an anonymous "universal harmony," but if it can recognize the (interreligious) entanglement of its own unique beginnings in the world of experiences, conceptualizations, and communities.[61] The inherent polydoxy of the dogma of a religion will, then, *release* a sense of peace if the "universal harmony" it feels—through its unique sources of experiences—is felt as affirmative of its *own* experience *in* its interrelatedness with a multiplicity of experiences, that is, an awareness of a poly-harmonics it always already employs beyond all its determining conceptualizations.[62]

A Para-doxology of Divine Multiplicity

To say it again: the poly-harmonics of multiplicity will release a sense of (interreligious) peace *if* the doxology of orthodoxy is *inherently* transformed into a para-doxology of polydoxy. Polydox doxology, then, indicates *the divine multiplicity of interreligious entanglement. At the same time, it affirms the unique intuitions of religions as enveloped in a process of the renewal of unprecedented novelty that always is beyond any fixed identities of singular religions and their orthodoxies.* Since this *para-doxology* is concerned with *polyphilic indetermination*, the sense of peace it suggests may be hinted at in *procedures of indeterminacy* that live from an inherent "theopoetics of multiplicity"—of the divine manifold that loves and graces multiplicity. I will name three such dimensions of polyphilic indetermination in which we might begin to find traces of such a para-doxology of the divine (in) multiplicity.

First, *the divine (in) multiplicity cannot be "identified,"* that is, "identity" under the logic of the One and Many is not a category of experiencing the divine. The implications of this mark of the process of polyphilic indetermination are profound: neither should we identify God within the realm of the One and Many nor with any multiplicity (which otherwise would still remain its very expression). While it is understandable that many poststructuralist thinkers follow Nietzsche's "death of God" insofar as God appears to be the very expression of the rule of the One, it would also be problematic to counter-identify the divine with the *khoric* multiplicity that the logic of the

61. Refer to chapter 12, current volume.
62. Refer to chapter 11, current volume.

One has excluded. While I can follow Butler's criticism of monotheism as an expression of the Law,[63] I would not follow theologians that, with Irigaray, infer that the *khoric* realm, which is never (the) one (the male God), imagines an inexpressible (female) divine.[64] It is, perhaps, an odd commonality of Kristeva and Bataille that they have pointed in this direction when they (in very different ways) differentiate the dogmatic (logocentric) naming of God from the mystical experience of *khora* (in the form of pre-symbolic immediacy to the mother or the nothingness of immediate intimacy of animality) *that cannot be named divine.*[65] Although *khora* harbors deep religious gestures that must be saved from the reign of the One (insofar as they also appear within it), their poetic of *ecstasies* of the subject-object split is profoundly a-theological.[66] Nevertheless, by directly hinting to deep mystical practices *within* the realm of orthodox Christianity (and beyond it in other religions) they touch on such "zones of immanence"[67] as Nicholas of Cusa's poetic logic of the *coincidentia oppositorum* or Eckhart's *Godhead* beyond the differentiation of God and creation.[68]

This insistence on the non-identity of the divine with either the One (and Many) or multiplicity satisfies a para-doxology that *affirms* the singular experiences buried in orthodoxies at the same time as it *inverts* any desire for their dogmatic substantiation. This is why I suggest that in our poetics of the divine, a *divine poetics* can neither be constructed from any logocentric universalization of the One nor in opposition to these constructions by an identification with the *khoric* ream.[69] If God cannot be identified, the function of the divine to be the expression of power—a power among powers, or as *the* super-power or as a khoric anti-power—is avoided.

This is what I name the divine *subtractive affirmation* of multiplicity that *affirms* multiplicity but *subtracts itself* from any identification *with multiplicity.*[70] Instead of such identifications that, in my view, *always* arouse the ream of power and violence, the divine as polyphilic love may be *within* all powers—be they of the logic of the One or of multiplicity—but is neither *of* them.

63. Butler, *Gender Trouble*, 38.

64. Irigaray, "Equal to Whom?," 198–214. Cf. also Joy, *Divine Love*. For the discussion of the khora in Irigaray, cf. Butler, *Bodies That Matter*, ch. 2; for a discussion of Irigaray and Spivak, see Rivera, *Touch of Transcendence*, ch. 6.

65. Kristeva, *Revolution*, 24–30 and Bataille, *Theory of Religion*, ch. 3.

66. Kristeva, *Revolution*, 61, and Bataille, *Inner Experience*, part I.

67. Deleuze, *Two Regimes of Madness*, ch. 35.

68. Faber, "'Gottesmeer,'" 64–95.

69. Faber, *God as Poet*.

70. Faber, *God as Poet*, postscript.

Second, *the divine (in) multiplicity must always be "ecologically contextualized" within multiplicity*. Since *the divine polyphilia is before, after, and beyond any identification*, it can only appear in the *mutual immanence* of all contexts on which it insists as multiplicity.[71] Divine indetermination implies a process of *mutual reciprocity* and *mutual incompleteness* in which the divine (in) multiplicity only appears *in* mutual reciprocity and mutual incompleteness *with* all multiplicities. There are two ways to *avoid* such an "essential relationality" of the divine. One can either elevate God to the "highest being," a superpower player in the world among other players of less power—this is the God that fights against the devil, that uses religious hierarchies for his judgment, that micromanages the globe from "his" throne through an elected group of the faithful. The other way, disgusted with this power-play, refrains from invoking God in mundane matters—either as deistic *epoché* or (with the early Wittgenstein) as the whole of the world that cannot appear within itself.[72] It was the incarnational and kenotic dynamics of Christian *orthodoxy* that has always broken through such assumptions *by finding God in the midst of everything*—the incarnation of the infinite horizon *within* its horizon,[73] or as a desiring God at the *heart* of all becoming, or as a *complication* of God and the world *in one another*.[74] This polydox transgression of orthodoxy appears in *the mutual incompleteness and reciprocity of the divine (in) multiplicity* in Whitehead's statement that creature, creativity, and creator must find their meaning only in mutual reciprocity (PR, 25) and in Heidegger's *Geviert*. Earth, sky/heaven, the mortals, and the *divinities (as multiplicity)* transgress any identification and become multiplicity,[75] as do Whitehead's "fourfold" of the "World of Creativity" (mortals), the "World of Value" (sky/heaven) as *folded together* through "Creativity" (earth) and "God" (the divinities). In such "ecological contextualization," divine polyphilia becomes the name that names *only* multiplicities—*multiplicities as enfolded within themselves (Cusa), but even more as irreducibly making sense only through the other multiplicities—none are all, but all are all in all*.[76]

Third, we may want to seek *new conceptualities that actually can transform the function of abstraction at the heart of the avoidance of multiplicity in orthodoxy into a polyphilic multiplicity of multiplicities in polydoxy*. Such

71. Faber, "Ecotheology."

72. Wittgenstein, *Tractatus Logico-philosophicus* 6.41–45; cf. also Philips, *The Problem of Evil*.

73. Rahner, *Foundations*, chs. 1–2.

74. Faber, *God as Poet*, §40.

75. Heidegger, "Building Dwelling Thinking," 359.

76. Faber, "De-Ontologizing God," 209–34.

polyphilic "abstractions" (inverted against themselves) will be creative *only* of multiplicities instead of substantial unifications by, at the same time, remaining *internally* transformative of the doxic and logocentric use of abstractions. These paradoxal modes of indetermination must not explain reality through abstractions, but rather the very abstractions and their working in a world of multiplicities. They must transform the function of abstraction from being explanatory reasons elevated to the eminent realities of divinities into *initiators of becoming-multiplicity*. Hence, without diminishing their importance for the formulation of conceptual frameworks of experience and activity in the aesthetic, ethical, political, or religious world (and by not even denying their divine connotations), they inversely lure us into a world *constituted by novelty and creativeness.*[77]

An example of such transformative conceptual processes can be found, for instance, in Nicholas of Cusa's construction of the divine "names" of *coincidentia oppositorum, possest, non aliud,* and *the posse ipsum* that upset an expectation that their use could abstractly construct an eminent reality that controls the creativity of creatures or limits the relationality of God. Instead, God arouses the chaosmic disturbance of identity, novelty, and the change of characters of repetition.[78] In the best scenario, this use of "abstractions" will address the *indetermination of non-identity by way of their mutual reciprocity, incompleteness, and immanence.* Because the "adequate description" of such terms as Whitehead's triad creator, creature, and creativity "includes characterizations *derived* from the other" (Imm. 683–84), they are *mutually exploratory and, hence, entangle multiplicities.* In this *mutual* "process of modification" (ibid., 685), these terms begin to generate the creativeness that is not based on the eternity of the same, but always the poly-harmonies of becoming-multiplicity.

The transformation of the mindset of orthodoxy into that of a poly-doxy of religious/theological teachings and doctrine is its ever-new passage through, and exploration of, the para-doxy of its founding or "revelatory" events in which polydox formulations would withhold a determination of their identity in orthodox dogmatizations. Instead, in the internal *inversion* of the use of their dogmas, the para-doxy of indetermination would engage in new modes of universality, namely, an *ongoing re-enactment of their founding or "revelatory" event-character* in its universal importance for the chaosmic harmonics of the "open whole" of multiplicity, that is, the shared world or the ecological community. Since re-enactments of events per se express novelty, singularity, and renovation, their conceptualization can never reach a static

77. Faber, "Infinite Movement."
78. Faber, *Prozeßtheologie,* ch. 2.

universality; instead, their event-character will always elicit a disturbance of stasis. Hence, polydox conceptual expressions of singular (revelatory) events will *mediate* their universality through an open-ended poly-harmony that could only illegitimately claim "eternity." The peace-making proposition of this para-doxology of the divine (in) multiplicity is that the "eternity" in these events, in which we worship the divine mystery, should be allowed to maintain their mystery through polydox indetermination, that is, the *mutually immanent, reciprocal, and incomplete disturbances of any conceptual sedimentation.* The paradoxal sense of peace might appear when we seek the *traces* of this polyphilic mystery not despite, but because of the poly-harmonious journey on which it invites us to embark upon.

CHAPTER EIGHT

Tracing the Spirit

SPIRITUALITY IS AN ACTIVITY. It is not an area; not a field of behavior; not even a method of performing certain techniques. More radically, it rests on nothing—no ground to settle; no base to cover; no structure to appropriate. And most disturbingly, spiritual activity has no subject that initiates it and no object to which it is directed. Its activity is that of the "spirit"—like a wind that blows where it chooses (John 3:8); like water that is poured out on us (Mk 1:8); like fire that energizes us (Acts 2:3). It is an activity of the future, the coming of God, the peace we await and the life that is promised (Joel 2:28). It is the activity of what is *not* in the midst of what *is*; or better: it is the power that transforms what *is* into what *is offered* to become, of what *has* become into what *could* become.

The Spirit is a gift—*this* gift, *the* Gift. It places us into the midst of a tension: the tension Whitehead calls "becoming," or better: the tension in becoming that comes as its crisis: the crisis of becoming that opens up when we understand becoming as the Great Opening of Difference: the difference between past and future, between exterior and interior, between self and other, between public and private. Wherever this Opening arises, as it does only in becoming, it creates the difference between Life and death. The Spirit is the Gift of *this* difference and spirituality is the *crisis* of this Gift, the crisis of *this* process of becoming, the activity of the *In Between*, bridging the hiatus of the difference of Life and death, the process of the transformation that arises out of this crisis of becoming and as becoming otherwise.

Peace: Interests of the Spirit

In Whitehead's opus, a conceptualization of the process of becoming out of this Spirit appears only sparsely. Nevertheless, it has an important place in the scheme of his philosophy, namely when he addresses the ultimate categories on which he sees civilization and any deeper development of the cosmos as being based: the concept, experience, and practice of Peace. "The experience of Peace," Whitehead says famously in *Adventures of Ideas*, "is largely beyond the control of purpose. It comes as a gift. The deliberate aim at Peace very easily passes into its bastard substitute: anesthesia. In other words, in the place of a quality of 'life and motion', there is substituted their destruction" (AI, 285). Indeed, the Gift of Peace cannot be controlled; any control may transform Life in its "bastard substitute": anesthesia, which is nothing other than, and precisely, the loss of the *tension* that *is* the crisis of becoming; the collapse of the difference of Life and death into the death of becoming: the death of future, novelty, creativity, and depth.

If the experience of Peace introduces this tension of becoming against the forces of its death, it must cope with the deep differences in a way that does not take away the crisis, but transforms it into a Life of "intentionality," thereby giving tension a direction, a purpose, an aim. "Thus Peace," Whitehead further elaborates, "is the removal of inhibition and not its introduction. It results in a wider sweep of conscious interest. It enlarges the field of attention. Thus Peace is self-control at its widest,—at the width where the 'self' has been lost, and interest has been transferred to co-ordinations wider than personality" (AI, 285). The intention that removes inhibitions— always followed by the shadow of its twin, "anesthesia"—does not remove "interest," but "the Self" that hinders the tension to become productive of Life. This Peace lies always already beyond the self-interests of personality. In fact, this *interest* in Peace is the crisis of personality.

It is precisely here, with this crisis of Peace, that Whitehead situates the Gift of the Spirit, because "[h]ere the real motive interests of the spirit are meant, and not the superficial play of discursive ideas" (AI, 285). Spirituality, then, is to follow the "motive interests of the spirit" in the process of becoming that *put us into the crisis of becoming*, the crisis of the Self and of personality—the crisis in the midst of the dangers of death, of anesthesia, of the loss of the Self for nothing, of the loss of the interests of the spirit for the "peace" of the grave, the dead past. In its ecstasy of self-transcendence, the Spirit shakes the rock of the (pre)given; it unsettles the powers of Being, it destabilizes the powers of resistance to becoming in its transformation beyond our Selves.

In order to analyze this Whiteheadian spirituality of Peace, I will lay out a map of three profound elements of the Gift of the Spirit that will form a landscape of approaches to the Spirit of becoming: *Polarity*, *Eros*, and *Place*. In the interaction of these elements, a Whiteheadian spirituality will reveal itself as *experience* and *practice* of Self-Transcendence.

Polarity: Field of Difference

If spirituality is the activity of the Spirit, it always induces an experience of being in the midst of the crisis of becoming and, at the same time, in a process that transforms the hiatus, it opens into an integration that again opens up a new differentiation. Two elements appear to constitute this experience: becoming as the *opening* of difference and becoming as the *ending* of any mastering of this difference.

Indeed, in Whitehead's analysis of experience as an event of becoming, everything is situated in the *opening of differences*. First, there is no becoming that is not the Opening of the tension between past and future. Every happening is only an event of becoming because its process is the Transcendence of Being, past, history, and the "given" for an undecided future, a realm of possibilities *for* this past to become what it—when it *has* become—will *be*. Therefore, everything in experience is situated in a *field of polarities*. This field is the process of becoming. Second, every actuality, in becoming, is the Opening of the Difference between physicality and mentality: past events and possible new realizations, physical experiences of this past (actual entities) and mental experiences of abstractions from these physical experiences (eternal objects) that allow for a new realization. For Whitehead, every event exists only as an actual *entity* (unity) through the opening of the *difference* between physical experiences and mental experiences and their process of unification. Every experience is the feeling of other (past) actualities in their *being* in the space of unrealized *possibilities*, taken either from the unsettled past and drawn to its repetition, or as a gift of an unsettled future, with the offerings of unrealized possibilities to become otherwise.

Whitehead conceptualizes this opening of differences as the *fundamental "dipolarity"* of the event of becoming: the Field of Difference between a physical feeling of an external, public past (of what has become) as internal to a new event, in the horizon of its mental feeling of possibilities (as potentials for realization). "Thus an actual entity is essentially dipolar, with its physical and mental poles; and even the physical world cannot be properly understood without reference to its other side, which is the complex of mental operations. The primary mental operations are conceptual feelings" (PR, 239). An actual event of becoming is *everything* in this field of dipolarity between the physical and mental pole and *nothing* without or beyond it.

It is this *dipolarity* that expresses the fundamental *tension* which is the crisis of spirituality: the tension between *receptivity* of the world and the *valuation* of this world in a unique unification. "The bare character of mere responsive re-enaction constituting the original physical feeling in its first phase is enriched in the second phase by the valuation accruing from integration with the conceptual correlate. In this way, the dipolar character of concrescent experience provides in the physical pole for the objective side of experience, derivative from an external actual world, and provides in the mental pole for the subjective side of experience, derivative from the subjective conceptual valuations correlate to the physical feelings" (PR, 277).

In the *re-enactment*, every event is the expression of a world beyond itself as the event's own body. In the *internalization* of the world, bodily existence, in *difference* to the subjective valuation, becomes the critical impulse of becoming: we can either comply with the re-enacted world or re-evaluate it in such a way that it re-integrates uniquely in the new event. The more we integrate an ever-diverse past in its diversity and otherness into an ever more novel, unanticipated uniqueness, the more we realize the gift of the Spirit. The more we are "concerned" with the world in the process of internalizing, and the more we release novel possibilities in its integration, the more we not only intensify our own existence as events of becoming, but also liberate a world beyond ourselves, in which we transcend our Selves, transforming ourselves into moments of the enriched becoming of Others.

This *field of becoming*, which is the tension between the poles, is both: the *opening* of the difference and the *intensification* of the difference. The crisis of becoming always situates existence between the limits and on the edges of collapse or explosion: too much past or too much novelty; too much public socialization or too much privacy, too much repetition or too much novelty. Spiritual development is, indeed, the high art of balancing compassion for the Other with the stature of Uniqueness.

The field of difference is so profound that it becomes Whitehead's expression of the fundamental structure of the universe as such: it reflects the process of *becoming-one* and *becoming-one-in-the-midst-of-many*, altered by the many unifications as entities lose themselves into the world beyond their own becoming (PR, 21). It becomes the expression of the fundamental difference between God and the World as the final "contrasted opposites" (PR, 348) in the process of becoming. And it becomes the expression of the nature of God as the ur-difference of Primordial Nature and Consequent Nature, of creation and salvation, of memory and initiation. "Any instance of experience," therefore, is in *this* profound sense "dipolar, whether that instance be God or an actual occasion of the world" (PR, 36).

In the field of polarity, the spiritual process of *differentiation* is an expression of the nature of the World and God and their internal and intermediate dipolarity; and God as Spirit reveals its character as Gift. "Thus the universe is to be conceived as attaining the active self-expression of its own variety of opposites—of its own freedom and its own necessity, of its own multiplicity and its own unity, of its own imperfection and its own perfection. All the 'opposites' are elements in the nature of things, and are incorrigibly there. The concept of 'God' is the way in which we understand this incredible fact—that what cannot be, yet is" (PR, 350).

Eros: Trances of God

If *this* Gift is Whitehead's concept of God (in which we are invited to understand the process of difference), then it is precisely the *difference* in the process of God and, consequently, the difference *between* God and the World that marks its dipolarity as the process of the *Spirit*. In other words: because in "every respect God and the World move conversely to each other in respect to their process" (PR, 349), the Great Opening of the difference is not per se the dark abyss of indifferent chaos, but that of a purposeful openness. Because the "origination of God is from the mental pole, [while] the origination of an actual occasion is from the physical pole" (PR, 36), God becomes the purposeful creator of the spiritual crisis, because *only in it* we experience the trace of the Divine Eros incarnating itself into the process of differentiation as the fundamental expression of the depth of the universe.

If the "initial phase of each fresh occasion represents the issue of a struggle within the past for objective existence beyond itself," then Whitehead introduces God as the "determinant of the struggle" by being "the supreme Eros incarnating itself as the first phase of the individual subjective aim in the new process of actuality" (AI, 198). In other words: God as Eros becomes the gift of every event's "origin" in the sense of the Great Opening of Difference: the difference between the event and the world (that has become). This difference is the process of becoming, and by this *incarnation of difference* the process is characterized as a *spiritual* process.

Whitehead conceptualizes this disturbance of Being as God's gift of an "initial aim." This paradoxical notion is in itself already an expression of the spiritual field between beginning and end, initiation and purpose, origin and finale. It is not only the verbalization of the fact that every process, in order to begin, needs a horizon of purposeful unification or integration; it indicates even more profoundly that no event would *begin* to become in the first place if it was not created by the difference the initial aim initiates, as the event's possibility becoming *purposeful*. Hence "the initial stage of its aim is an endowment which the subject inherits from the inevitable ordering of things, conceptually realized in the nature of God" (PR, 244). But because the gift of the initial aim is the *act of the constitution of the process itself*, it is not an "abstraction," not just a general "eternal object" issued by God. On the contrary, in its givenness by God, the initial aim radically marks the beginning of the event *as a whole*—and this whole in its *uniqueness*. This "immediacy of the concrescent subject," then, is precisely what "is constituted by its living aim at its own self-constitution" (PR, 244). Thus, while the dipolar field of differences (between past and future, externality and immediacy, objectivity and subjectivity) is a creative process that in "its completion depends on the self-causation of the subject-superject," the truly "initial stage of the aim is rooted in the nature of God" (PR, 244). We are traces of God.

Whitehead is well aware that if God is the gift of the initial aim of the process of becoming, this becoming is in its *constitution* nothing but a *spiritual crisis*. Because Eros lures from the lost past into an intense future, the intensity to obtain, and the tension to endure, will inevitably be tied into the complexities of the *struggles of the past* that seeks recognition beyond itself. Hence, he articulates this "function of God" as gift of difference to be "analogous to the remorseless working of things in Greek and in Buddhist thought" (PR, 244). Because the "initial aim is the best for that *impasse*" of the past, the crisis may be that "the best be bad," appearing as "the ruthlessness of God [that] can be personified as *Até*, the goddess of mischief" (PR, 244).

Always in midst of this impasse, therefore, the spiritual journey will realize the trace of the Eros in the dipolar field of solitariness and solidarity. "In its solitariness the spirit asks, What, in the way of value, is the attainment of life? And it can find no such value till it has merged its individual claim with that of the objective universe. Religion is world-loyalty." Spiritual practice, Whitehead says in *Religion in the Making*, will begin with the awareness that the "spirit at once surrenders itself to this universal claim and appropriates it for itself" (RM, 60).

In *solitude* the trace of God reveals itself in the initial aim as the gift of God *only* when we dive into the *beginnings* of ourselves, where we lose ourselves in the mystical moment in which we are not yet differentiated from the World and God. The mystics have always directed us to this moment of non-difference, the gift of the *unio mystica*. It might well be that the spiritual practice of attaining this "union" with God at the depth of creation itself is only possible by losing any distraction from the noise of the world. We may look at this dark place of our own beginning with blind eyes. Only in our retreat from the world and ourselves, only in this dangerous mode of self-loss, in a solitude of which we cannot control, a *breakthrough* to the very beginning of the difference we are in our becoming, may we become aware of the Gift that we are. Only in the crisis of the missing world and the missing Self—always endangered by the abyss of anesthesia—may we be given the "union" of self-transcendence that is the moment of the creation of the Self.

In *solidarity*, however, we turn our view in another direction. Because we cannot become aware of God in Godself even in this union (if attained at all), the true Gift of this union is not the unification with God, but the *differentiation* from God, the becoming-oneself in the tension between God and the World. If this is the origin of our subjectivity, we are "born" to *follow* God's incarnation into the World. In this *metanoia*, we become the trace of God by becoming world-loyal. In this self-transcendence, now, we do not lose our selves in God, but we lose our Selves by becoming "important" *beyond* ourselves—for the development of the world, *her* intensities and harmonies.

Place: Nexus Beyond Personality

If it is true that (at least in a Whiteheadian context) the spiritual crisis always is generated from the dipolar field of differences, its transformative process takes place only when the Self that the field *creates* is, at the same time, profoundly *transcended*. Here, ethics is born from the gift of the Spirit in the midst of the spiritual crisis of seeking self-transcendence. As Whitehead in his *Category of Subjective Intensity* notes: "The subjective aim, whereby there is origination of conceptual feeling, is at intensity of feeling (α) in the immediate subject, and (β) in the relevant future. This double aim—at the *immediate* present and the *relevant* future—is less divided than appears on the surface. For the determination of the *relevant* future, and the *anticipatory* feeling respecting provision for its grade of intensity, are elements affecting the immediate complex of feeling. The greater part of morality hinges on the determination of relevance in the future" (PR, 27).

Self-Transcendence as World-Loyalty, in other words, is the "self-formation which is a process of concrescence" that at the same time "by the principle of objective immortality characterizes the creativity which transcends it" (PR, 108). Again we find the spiritual process to be a transformation in the dipolar field. On the one hand, we "become" as *self-collection* of relations of/to/within an internalized external world to which to be loyal means to respect its otherness in constituting the subjective process of becoming. It is the valuation of the self-transcendence of the Other as it constitutes the Self. On the other hand, we "become" as an act of *self-relativity* in which a future beyond the Self is not only accepted, but anticipated as a *moment* of the process of becoming itself. This is the dipolar field that Whitehead calls "subject-superject": "the emergent unity of the superject" by which an "actual entity is to be conceived both as a subject presiding over its own immediacy of becoming, and a superject which is the atomic creature exercising its function of objective immortality" (PR, 45).

In the *anticipation of self-transcendence*, the major ethical impulse is released in the midst of the spiritual crisis of the *immediacy* of the Self and the *importance* beyond the Self. This anticipation releases the transformation of concrescence into transition, of unification into multiplication, of the claim of Life into an "ethical death" of becoming, into importance beyond one Self. Whitehead's so-called "objective immortality" is not just an interpretive category of ethical self-transcendence, but in its consciously anticipatory realization, it should be considered an important spiritual practice by which we experience that we "become a 'being'; and [that] it belongs to the nature of every 'being' that it is a potential for every 'becoming'" (PR, 45) beyond itself. Here, precisely, dipolarity is realized as a process of spiritual transformation: where we dare to experience, and to practice, a "'perishing' of [the] absoluteness" of the Self by "the attainment of 'objective immortality'" (PR, 60). "In this [spiritual] sense, each actual occasion experiences its own objective immortality" (PR, 216).

Especially in the Christian context, this crisis has led to the suspicion that one of its most cherished notions of the worth of human beings is in peril of being lost: that of personhood. But for Whitehead the opposite is true. The acceptance of the gift of the spiritual crisis as a process of self-transcendence, even to the point where the Self is lost in immortality of its worth beyond itself, is the *true transformation* of a naïve notion of person into a spiritually informed understanding of personality. In one sense, personality would be lost, namely as "absoluteness of the subject," which seems to be but a variation of the sublimation of the relationless "absolute" oneness so problematic to the formation of a monotheism, in which God (the Self) is considered as "requiring no relations to anything beyond himself" (AI, 169). Instead, in Whitehead, personality can appear in the context of the "mutual immanence" of all instances of becoming, which was even the "origin" of the formation of the Christian notion of person in the doctrine of the Trinity as "a multiplicity in the nature of God, each component being unqualifiedly Divine" (AI, 168). With his transformed notion of personality, Whitehead is historically on rather firm ground, because the theological use of "person" came into being as an expression "of mutual immanence in the divine nature" (AI, 168).

If, indeed, mutual immanence is the "characteristic" of personhood, Whitehead's shift of usage of this notion in the context of the spiritual crisis, indicating the loss of absoluteness and "ethical death" of the Self as moments of the *constitution* of its own becoming, becomes understandable. Instead of

situating "person" in the realm of "identity" through a permanent "form"—
the soul (PR, 104)—she becomes the most precious expression of the realm
of the *khora*, the nexus of the Platonic "place," the profound "natural matrix
for all things," the "medium of intercommunication" whereby "the many actualities of the physical world [are] components in each other's natures" (AI,
134). Of this "place" Whitehead says that once we have lost self-referential
subjectivity and structural sustenance as basic moments of the notion of personality, this nexus becomes the expression of a "personal identity [which]
is the thing which receives all occasions of the man's existence. It is there as a
natural matrix for all transitions of life, and is changed and variously figured
by the things that enter it; so that it differs in its character at different times.
Since it receives all manner of experiences into its own unity, it must itself
be bare of all forms. We shall not be far wrong if we describe it as invisible,
formless, and all-receptive. It is a locus which persists, and provides an em-
placement for all the occasions of experience" (AI, 187).

Spirit: Gift of Self-Transcendence

Peace, Polarity, Eros, Place, Self-Transcendence—these are the elements
we have collected. In their light, we may now ask again: What is the Spirit
that informs Whiteheadian spirituality? And what, in light of this Spirit, is
Whiteheadian spirituality? If spirituality is the Gift of the Spirit, it is *how* this
gift is given that forms *what* it is (PR, 23): it is given in the form of the *crisis*
that not just accompanies the process of becoming, but is its very process,
its initiation and end. This crisis is the opening of a difference so profound
that it characterizes reality *as such* and in its most intimate concreteness
insofar as it is a process of the becoming of becomings and is a nexus of
perishing in becoming. The "essence" of the "spiritual adventure" (AI, 82),
in Whitehead's eyes, is the recognition and affirmation of the thoroughgoing dipolarity of Life and death and "becoming" as the field of difference *in
between*, which is the cosmos.

On every level the crisis of difference appears as the paradox of *antitheses* not dissimilar to, or better: precisely of the same order as the Six Antithesis between God and the World at the end of *Process and Reality* when
their metaphysical function reveals what the spiritual process is about: to
be(come) a transformation that induces "a shift of meaning which converts
the opposition into a contrast" (PR, 348). And if in the final analysis everything is embraced by the dipolar field in which "God and the World are the
contrasted opposites in terms of which Creativity achieves its supreme task
of transforming disjoined multiplicity, with its diversities in opposition, into

concrescent unity, with its diversities in contrast" (PR 348), then this is the *essence* of the spiritual adventure.

In the end, we are left with the arch-difference that characterizes everything; it is the only positive nature of the Spirit, the Gift, and its activity: the "two concrescent poles of realization—'enjoyment' and 'appetition,' that is, the 'physical' and the 'conceptual'" (PR 348). Spirituality, then, *is the actualization of the gift of becoming in/between enjoyment and appetition*, both being paradoxically differentiated in themselves and mutually intertwined: Enjoyment only provides satisfaction in transcending the Self that creates itself out of the relations it enjoys; and Appetition is the erotic urge beyond the enjoyed world that is always the beginning of the adventure of becoming. Spiritual transformation reveals this final dipolar structure of the Gift—to be a process of Self-Transcendence.

In the complexity, in which both Appetition and Enjoyment presuppose each other, are mutually immanent in one another, the process of becoming reveals itself as the process of the Spirit. It is the process of the Spirit *herself* as their transformation in *her* own nature—suggested by Whitehead in referring to God's own dipolar nature. Precisely by *embracing* the process of the becoming (that is the World) with the creative Appetition of the Primordial Nature and the Enjoyment of this becoming beyond itself in the Consequent Nature, God is Spirit. But God is Spirit *only in the process of the Gift* of God's own Self-Transcendence: the "objective immortality in respect to his primordial nature and his consequent nature" (PR, 32). *Spirit is God beyond God.* Or as Whitehead says, "this 'superjective nature' of God is the character of the pragmatic value of his specific satisfaction qualifying the transcendent creativity in the various temporal instances" (PR, 88).

The transformative realization, then, of this ultimate dipolarity of the Appetition and Enjoyment of God's nature beyond God in the creative field of the World-Process (which again is always already a new realization of the difference from God in the embrace of God) indicates the spiritual process in the World. It is the creative crisis of this difference and embrace, and the perpetual mutual transformation of Appetition and Enjoyment into a *contrast* of integration and dissolution, of Immediacy and Immortality.

In spiritual practice, this multiply intertwined field of difference and transformation becomes most visible in the most extreme differentiation of either Appetition or Enjoyment, or their integration—as the practice of self-dissolution into the non-difference of the Eros opening the process in every initial aim, *or* as the practice of the "ethical death" whereby all becoming "enjoys an objective immortality in the future beyond itself" (PR, 230). In the final analysis, it becomes the realization of the ultimate *formlessness* of the nexus of the creative field that God as Spirit opens and embraces. The spiritual adventure, then, is in experience and practice the most intense, creative, and world-sympathetic realization of the "self-enjoyment of being one among many, and of being one arising out of the composition of many" (PR, 145).

Of course, if this is what Whiteheadian spirituality is all about, it will most certainly leave us with another crisis. If, indeed, the Gift of the Spirit is the transformative differentiation of Appetition and Enjoyment, the process of Self-Transcendence will always hinder us in becoming absolute; it will always relativize us; it will always take our youth and age it; it will always have a tragic side. In a shockingly peaceful poetics, Whitehead envisions this tragedy at the end of *Religion in the Making* by remarking that the "universe shows us two aspects: on one side it is physically wasting, on the other side it is spiritually ascending. It is thus passing with a slowness, inconceivable in our measures of time, to new creative conditions, amid which the physical world, as we at present know it, will be represented by a ripple barely to be distinguished from nonentity" (RM, 160).

The spiritual crisis consists *precisely* in becoming aware of this *character of love* as self-transcendence: "It is the feeling as to what would happen if right could triumph in a beautiful world, with discord routed. It is the passionate desire for the beautiful result, in this instance. Such love is distracting, nerve-racking. But, unless darkened by utter despair, it involves deep feeling of an aim in the Universe, winning such triumph as is possible to it." Spirituality is always the Gift of *this* dipolar tension of the Becoming-In-Between. It is the Gift of "the sense of Eros, hovering between Peace as the crown of Youth and Peace as the issue of Tragedy" (AI, 289).

Returning to the beginning again—and we are always spiritual beginners—we become experimenters *in this sense of Peace*. This "sense," however, is always a crisis in which we become aware, experience, and exercise the "Adventure of the Universe [as it] starts with the dream and reaps tragic Beauty. This is the secret of the union of Zest with Peace: —That the suffering attains its end in a Harmony of Harmonies. The immediate experience of this Final Fact, with its union of Youth and Tragedy, is the sense of Peace" (AI, 296). This is what Whiteheadian spirituality is all about. Here, of course, the sense of Peace will be a consequence of our activity that desires its reality.

Part III

Divinity and Mystery

CHAPTER NINE

Theopoetic Creativity

No other topic has provoked as much discussion as process theology's understanding of *creation*.[1] Insofar as process theology itself unfolds within the context of cosmology, that is, within the context of the *relation* between God and world, God's creative love must necessarily constitute the quintessence and touchstone of its theoretical reflections. It is especially in connection with the *four phases of the creative process*[2] and the *six antitheses*[3] that process theology has developed the pronounced thesis that God does *not* create the world "out of nothing,"[4] and that the critics of process theology have found support for their suspicion that process theology *denies* God as creator.[5] Cobb and Griffin accordingly openly admit that "process theology rejects the notion of *creatio ex nihilo*, if that means creation out of absolute nothingness."[6] Pannenberg counters that the resulting idea of radical "self-creative capacity" demonstrates the irreconcilability of Whitehead's metaphysics with the biblical idea of creation and, hence, also the biblical idea of God.[7] It is clear that both assumptions—the assertion of process theology and the theological objection to it—are referring to the *theopoetic difference* of God and creativity, which thus quite justifiably stands at the center of theopoetics.[8] The interpretation of that difference will determine how God is to be understood as creator and in what sense thesis and antithesis are in fact

---

1. Küng, *Does God Exist?*; Scheffczyk, "Prozesstheismus und christlicher Glaube," 81–104; Koch, "Schöpferischer Lockruf im Prozess der Welt," 129–71.

2. Faber, *God as Poet*, §30.

3. Faber, *God as Poet*, §31.

4. Ford, "An Alternative to Creatio ex Nihilo," 205–13.

5. Moltmann, *God in Creation*.

6. Cobb and Griffin, *Process Theology*, 65.

7. Pannenberg, "Atom, Dauer, Gestalt," 194.

8. Faber, *God as Poet*, §28.

accurate. Ultimately, however, *both* assumptions (assertion and objection) can be refuted *to the extent* one interprets this theopoetic difference against the background of the *conversion of processes*[9] and *God's superjectivity*.[10] To that end, let us examine Whitehead's *central passage concerning theopoetics—* as it describes what happens *theopoetically* in the *threefold creative act*.

> The universe includes a threefold creative act composed of (i) the one infinite conceptual realization, (ii) the multiple solidar- ity of free physical realizations in the temporal world, (iii) the ultimate unity of the multiplicity of actual fact with the pri- mordial conceptual fact. If we conceive the first term and the last term in their unity over against the intermediate multiple freedom of physical realizations in the temporal world, we con- ceive of the patience of God, tenderly saving the turmoil of the intermediate world by the completion of his own nature. The sheer force of things lies in the intermediate physical process: this is the energy of physical production. God's role is not the combat of productive force with productive force, of destructive force with destructive force; it lies in the patient operation of the overpowering rationality of his conceptual harmonization. He does not create the world, he saves it; or, more accurately, he is the poet of the world, with tender patience leading it by his vision of truth, beauty, and goodness. (PR, 346)

God is the poet of the world. The first thing this means is that God certainly is the creator of the world (PR, 47, 225, 346ff). God's *poiesis*, how- ever, is a *relational* act of tender patience and saving love, not a *unilateral* act of physical production or destructive force.[11] Within the threefold creative act, God's *poiesis* appears as the unity of creative beginning and reconciling end, as the tender embrace of the self-creativity of the world with its produc- tivity, destruction, and its turmoil.[12] In its threefold structure, the creative process opens up to the world an "intermediacy" between God as vision and completeness, an *intercreativity* extending between God's creative and reconciling love, a divine matrix in which God—being world sensitive—is Godself engaged in the tender, caring concern of a "great companion—the fellow-sufferer who understands" (PR, 351).[13] This specifically *relational* understanding of creator, creativity, creation, and creature leads not only to

9. Faber, *God as Poet*, §29.

10. Faber, *God as Poet*, §28; Faber, "Zeitumkehr," 180–205.

11. Mesle, *Process Theology*.

12. Faber, *God as Poet*, §30.

13. Faber, *God as Poet*, §34: Figure 5.

the source of the negation of creation from nothing (*creatio ex nihilo*), but also—following the same line of thought—to a perspective from which one can refute the objection that this view robs God of God's creative capacity. The basis as well as the goal of process theology's thesis is not to attack God as creator, but to deconstruct the *ontotheological context of interpretation* of God's creative power.[14] Whitehead concurs with many process theologians that classical creation theology is formulated within a *context of coercive (or impositional) power*, whereas the theopoetic difference of God and creativity inhering as countermetaphor in the threefold creative act, is an attempt to reestablish the *original biblical context* for understanding God's creative power from the perspective of God's *relational love* and *alterity*.[15]

If one follows the *traces of coercive power* in the doctrine of creation, viewed from the perspective of John Cobb and David Ray Griffin's assumption that the classical doctrine of *creatio ex nihilo* "is part and parcel of the doctrine of God as absolute controller,"[16] one encounters first of all Whitehead's own *complex theory of coercive power* in connection with cosmology, religion, and creation theology. Even in his initial systematic introduction of God into his work—in *Science and the Modern World*—Whitehead rejected attributing any coercive characteristics to God. Theodicy prevents Whitehead from interpreting God as the "all-producer"[17] or from paying God "metaphysical compliments."[18] In this sense, the notion of theopoetic difference inheres in Whitehead's work from the very outset.[19] In *Religion in the Making*, Whitehead then traces the emergence of coercive power in religion through the latter's association with political-nationalistic currents (Roman Empire, state religion, national religion) and the concomitant morbid exaggeration of national self-consciousness (RM, 43), the accompanying dogmatic intolerance of its doctrines, and especially the emergence of the simple concept of an arbitrary, transcendent God beyond this world.[20] Ontotheological (nonrelational) substantialism in politics, religion, and theology transformed the "gospel of love" into a "gospel of fear," and God into a "terrifying" concept serving solely to enhance the power of "his" representatives (RM, 75). In *Process and Reality*, Whitehead *unmasks the structure of coercive power* in analyzing the notion of "his" ontotheological transcendence that

---

14. Franklin, "God and Creativity," 237–307.
15. Ford, "An Alternative to Creatio ex Nihilo."
16. Cobb and Griffin, *Process Theology*, 65.
17. Faber, *God as Poet*, §27.
18. Faber, *God as Poet*, §29.
19. Faber, *God as Poet*, §28.
20. Faber, *God as Poet*, §26: Figure 2.

resulted in specifically *unilateral* creative power being attributed to God. "When the Western world accepted Christianity, Caesar conquered," and the theology of the legitimization of sovereign coercive power formulated by "his lawyers" came to dominate the scene. The "deeper idolatry" inhering in that theology conceived God "in the image of the Egyptian, Persian, and Roman imperial rulers" (PR, 342), and "the Church gave unto God the attributes which belonged exclusively to Caesar" (PR, 342). The result was that God could appear in the threefold figure of the "imperial ruler," the "personification of moral energy," and as an "ultimate philosophical principle" (PR, 342–43). For Whitehead, the tragedy of Christianity is that against this background of coercive power, the philosophical understanding of God as "unmoved mover" and the political understanding of God as "imperial ruler" merged in the incriminating idea of an "aboriginal, eminently real, transcendent creator" (PR, 342). Whitehead amplifies this analysis in *Adventures of Ideas* by asserting that Christian theology adopted the *analogy of ruler* in which God "stood in the same relation to the whole World as early Egyptian or Mesopotamian kings stood to their subject populations" (AI, 169). The resulting ontotheological concept of God as "the one absolute, omnipotent, omniscient source of all being, for his own existence requiring no relations to anything beyond himself, constituted in effect an apotheosis of coercive power, or a "sublimation from its barbaric origin" (AI, 169).

Process theology subscribes to this deconstruction of ontotheology as an expression of *structural coercive power*. One finds hardly any version of process theology that does not direct itself in some fashion against such organized grounding of arbitrary power and against the coercive power of repression of the sort archetypically inhering in the concept of God as "transcendent creator," and there is not any process theology that has not itself formulated a *theology of non-violence* through the *countermetaphor of theopoetic difference.*[21] Whitehead himself adduces especially *three resources*—even speaking about "threefold revelation"—in carrying through a *theopoetic deconstruction* of the ontotheological, nonrelational regime of coercive power. These resources include a *philosophical* one, the Platonic conception of God as ideal force; a *religious* one, the person and message of Jesus; and a *theological* one, the early Christian doctrine of the Trinity (AI, I66f.). All three moments disclose the relational categories that should characterize a creation theology critical of coercive power.

(1) Whitehead was fascinated by the intellectual power with which Plato freed himself from the coercive impositional power inherent within barbaric conceptions of God by conceiving God's creative power not as a

---

21. Mesle, *Process Theology*; Griffin, *God, Power and Evil.*

physically efficacious, power of coercion—with its attendant implications for a concept of creation based on an analogy of coercive power—but as the *ideal power of persuasion* (AI, 166). God's creative power refers to the "power of [Godself] as ideal" of the world (RM, 156), the power that does *not* compete with physical power (nor is even analogously conceivable as such), being instead the "patient operation of the over powering rationality of [God's] conceptual harmonization" (PR, 346). Whitehead found, however, that Plato did not go far enough, insofar as instead of a "supreme agency of compulsion," he posited merely a "supreme reality, omnipotently disposing a wholly derivative world" (AI, 166).

(2) Whitehead saw in the figure of Jesus nothing less than the religious "exemplification" of the Platonic "discovery" of a noncoercive God and a concrete criticism of all claims of coercive power beyond surrendering love. The center of Jesus' fate was his challenge to the illegitimacy of coercive power and his reaction to this power, namely, the *suffering under coercive power*, on the one hand, and the *power of love*, on the other. His message was one of "peace, love, and sympathy" (AI, 167). If the essence of Christianity consists in nothing other than that the life of Christ itself is the revelation of the "nature of God and God's agency in the world" (ibid.), then that life does not belong in the context of the three ontotheological traditions of the "ruling Caesar, or the ruthless moralist, or the unmoved mover," being based instead on the "tender elements in the world, which slowly and in quietness operate by love" (PR, 343). In Jesus, God's *nature* is manifested as *love*, and God's actions are determined by precisely that love.[22]

(3) The subsequent theological interpretation of the revelation of God's nature in Jesus in the Trinitarian theology, especially of the Alexandrian and Antiochian schools, represents for Whitehead the key source of the doctrine of *mutual immanence*.[23] It represents the decisive breakthrough—after Plato's discovery of God's noncoercive agency—in its assertion that God *in and of Godself is* that particular *noncoercive communication* that *for just that reason* also reveals Godself in the world as its ultimate "wherein," as the Trinitarian communicative space of the mutual immanence of God and world. If one now expands Trinitarian immanence, over against its ontotheological restriction to the immanent Trinity, into a general metaphysics, the Platonic vision loses its final transcendent reserve concerning God's immanence, and God's own agency is revealed in its innermost essence as "persuasive agency" (AI, 169).

22. Faber, *God as Poet*, §30.
23. Faber, *God as Poet*, §34.

Whitehead's understanding of God's creative power is shaped by the notion of the noncoercive power of persuasive love, by the renunciation of such power on the part of tender love, and by the thwarting of impositional power by communicative immanence. Here God's essence (communication) and nature (concrescence) are revealed as the expression of a *necessity*. That is, God does not in some way "decide" to renounce coercive power or not to rule. God is instead *in principle* nonruling, nonviolent, and noncoercive.[24] Contrary to the *analogy of dominion*, which attributes to the God-king a creative power accessible to his (arbitrary) will (AI, 130), here God and world—"beyond the accidents of will" (AI, 168)—are related relationally and nonunilaterally commensurate with their *nature*, and God's creative power is *communicative* rather than autarchic, *weak* rather than powerful, *creative* rather than restrictive.[25] Process theology's struggle against the notion of an omnipotent God—a struggle that has shaped it from the beginning[26]—derives from its rejection of the substantialism of an ontotheologically based understanding of God's dominion, of the sort culminating in references to the "transcendent creator" or in *creatio ex nihilo*. Process theology itself counters with a creation theology based on the *theopoetic difference* of God and creativity.[27] It is in *Adventures of Ideas* that Whitehead formulates his most radical understanding of his *theopoetic alternative* of a relational creation theology within theopoetic difference as the *essential relationality* of God's creative "weakness";[28] here, without denying God's transcendence, he refers to God as the "immanent God/creator" (AI, 131, 168) conceived in *nondifference* to "immanent creativity" (AI, 236).

> There are two current doctrines as to this process . . . One is that of the external Creator, eliciting this final togetherness out of nothing. The other doctrine is that it is a metaphysical principle belonging to the nature of things, that there is nothing in the Universe other than instances of this passage and components of these instances . . . Let this latter doctrine be adopted. Then the word Creativity expresses the notion that each event is a process issuing in novelty. Also if guarded in the phrases Immanent Creativity, or Self-Creativity, it avoids the implication of a transcendent Creator, so that the whole doctrine acquires an air

---

24. Ford, "Divine Persuasion and Coercion," 267–73; Cobb and Griffin, *Process Theology*.

25. Faber, *God as Poet*, §26.

26. Hartshorne, *Omnipotence*.

27. Faber, "Zeitumkehr"; Faber, *God as Poet*, §28.

28. Faber, *God as Poet*, §26.

of paradox, or of pantheism. Still it does convey the origination
of novelty. (AI, 236)

This central passage mentions both the reason for rejecting *creatio ex
nihilo* and the sense of the envisioned alternative. The *reason* for rejecting a
"transcendent creator" is that this creator refers precisely to that particular
ontotheological ruler who arbitrarily disposes over communication. The
attendant notion of "creation out of nothing" is merely the logical expression lurking behind the mask of the transcendent creator. In this sense, the
omnipotent God is the *origin of coercive power* insofar as God determines the
conditions of communication from "his" hermetic dominion. Yet Whitehead
considers this very understanding of God itself to be an expression of actual
coercive power and a projection of the legitimization of human power. The
sense of the alternative reference to "immanent creativity" or "self-creativity"
is obviously to develop—contra the ontotheological power fantasy—a *relational concept of creation* that renounces power and violence *precisely because*
such renunciation ultimately derives from the very essence of God.[29] The
analysis of "creativity" has already identified it as the noncoercive, power-
free communion of *universal intercreativity* or *divine matrix*. The fact that in
"an air of paradox, or of pantheism" Whitehead chooses no longer to mention God as the subject of creative power is *not* to be taken as a dissolution
of God into creativity—such would constitute pantheism, which Whitehead
rejects in any case, rather than a *paradox*. What he is doing instead is addressing an important function as a signal of precise theological language.
Commensurate with the *sixth antithesis*, it is the *same* self-creativity—*as*
intercreativity—that creates God and world.[30]

Process theology did, however, choose an interesting but problematic
expression to refer to this relational and noncoercive alternative to *creatio
ex nihilo*, namely, *creation out of chaos*. Cobb and Griffin's assertion that
"process theology affirms instead a doctrine of creation out of chaos"[31] did
not fail to evoke vehement objection, its opponents suspecting it of conceal-
ing what was in fact a turn away from the specifically Christian concept of
the creator and a revitalization of Plato's demiurge, who created not "out
of nothing," but out of the unformed.[32] Jürgen Moltmann articulates the
programmatic opposition to this notion in his assertion that "[i]f the idea
of the *creatio ex nihilo* is excluded, or reduced to the formation of a not-yet
actualized primordial matter, 'no-thing,' then the world process must be just

29. Faber, *God as Poet*, §28.
30. Faber, *God as Poet*, §31.
31. Cobb and Griffin, *Process Theology*, 64.
32. Maassen, "Offenbarung," 217–33.

as eternal and without any beginning as God himself. But if it is eternal and without any beginning like God himself, the process must itself be one of God's natures.[33] In that case, however, process theology—so Moltmann—has no creation doctrine at all, but only a doctrine of maintenance and order.[34] A more differentiated assessment must first address four questions involving the metaphor of "creation out of chaos": (1) What exactly does "creation out of chaos" mean in the context of process theology's discourse concerning coercive power? (2) How do process theologians in their own turn ground the metaphor of "chaos"? (3) What does "chaos" itself mean in Whitehead's cosmology? (4) To what extent does this chaos metaphor correspond to Whitehead's theopoetic alternative of "immanent creativity"?

(1) The *sense* of the metaphor concerning "creation out of chaos" emerges from process theology's goal of providing an alternative to the ontotheological metaphor of coercive power understood as inherent in the doctrine of "creation out of nothing." If the root of creation is characterized by coercive power, then the world itself is ruled by such power. How would it reveal itself as a world corrupted by coercive power or violence in this sense? The innermost *creative motor* of the world itself would be *violence*, that is, ruthless coercion, hopeless compulsion, oppression, repression, suppression, and heteronomy.[35] The fundamental metaphor here would be the one-sided determination of the conditions of communication, omnipotent autocracy, substantiality, creation from *nothing*—an isolated (needing only itself) and relationless (absolutely one sided) dictate.[36] The *theology of nonviolence* counters "unilateral power" with "relational power,"[37] which persuades rather than coerces, lures rather than compels, liberates rather than oppresses.[38] God and world correspond in the countermetaphor of "creative chaos." God is the *Eros* of the world (primordial nature) who is attractive through God's ideas, the potentials God opens up to the world (eternal objects), the goals God bequeaths in caring concern (initial aim), the alternatives with which God lures toward freedom (AI, 233).[39] The world is accordingly never "nothing," but rather the *coming about of self-value* and for that reason conceivable only as a *self-creative happening* which God releases and values.[40] Theopoetic difference expresses the

33. Moltmann, *God in Creation*, 78.

34. Moltmann, *God in Creation*.

35. Loomer, "The Conceptions of Power," 5–32.

36. Keller, *Face of the Deep*.

37. Keller, "No More Sea," 55–72.

38. Ford, "Divine Persuasion"; idem, *The Lure of God*.

39. Loomer, "Conceptions of Power."

40. Mesle, *Process Theology*; Faber, *God as Poet*, §§15–16, 32.

notion that God determines *everything*—and is in this sense the creator of all events—*except* the self-creativity of each event.[41] In this sense, every event is free—at liberty to determine *itself*, a notion from which process theology then develops an "ontology of freedom." This "radical self-creative capacity" refers to the dignity of the irreducible freedom and unconditional self-value of every event and indeed of the world as a whole. The term "chaos" expresses this freedom and dignity of creation, its spontaneous self-creativity, which *ex nihilo* would autocratically undermine.[42] It is no accident that process theology developed further precisely as a theology of liberation, as political theology, and as feminist theology by adducing this irreducible dignity of freedom, freedom that, inasmuch as it applies to the cosmos as a whole *beginning with creation itself*, now doubtless acquires inalienable significance in *all* spheres of life.[43] "Chaos" expresses the fact that God cannot transform the world into nothing, since God never destroys freedom, albeit not because God does not want to do so, but because doing so belongs *neither* to the essence of God *nor* to that of the world. Hence "chaos" always refers to freedom contra *autocratic* order that through its repressive arrangement and with the power of its closed structure would otherwise cripple freedom. Moltmann's charge that "creation out of chaos" ultimately divinizes the world or even understands it as "one of God's natures" proves to be wrong. In fact, quite the *opposite* is the case. As the central theopoetic passage in *Process and Reality* attests, God encompasses the process with God's natures such that in the "intermediate process" of the world, the world can be *wholly world* precisely because it stands in freedom, and because in the face of this "chaos," God's creative power, rather than coercing, instead continually communicates.[44]

(2) Process theology *grounds* the metaphor of "creation out of chaos" in the paradigm of the *thoroughgoing evolution* of the universe. Here Whitehead juxtaposes *two fundamental cosmological models*—that of Plato and that of Newton—ultimately taking the side of Plato,[45] because Newton's *Scholium* "made no provision" (PR, 95) for a thoroughgoing evolution of the world and thus for evolution of matter—precisely the path taken by Plato's *Timaeus* in its understanding of the evolutive world of events emerging from

---

41. Griffin, "Hartshorne, God and Relativity Physics," 85–112; Faber, *God as Poet*, §27.

42. Keller, *Face of the Deep*.

43. Cobb, "Freedom in Whitehead's Philosophy," 45–52; Keller, *Apocalypse Now and Then*.

44. Faber, *God as Poet*, §32.

45. Rust, *Die organismische Kosmologie von Alfred N. Whitehead*; Faber, *God as Poet*, §15.

ideas (forms), the demiurge (defining act), and the "wherein" (khora).[46] Whitehead adopts Plato's cosmology at precisely the point at which, within the context of contemporary physical cosmology (in light of the theory of relativity, quantum mechanics, and contemporary theories of evolution), it provides a relational theory of the origin of the world, its development, and its grounds.[47] It offers the archetypical alternative to the notion of an arbitrary creation of this world that breaks through all relationality. Whereas Newton assumed that the world *either* "with its present type of order, is eternal," *or* "came into being, and will pass out of being, according to the fiat of Jehovah" (we know that Newton delivered the latter), Plato by contrast traced "the origin of the present cosmic epoch . . . back to an aboriginal disorder, chaotic according to our ideals" (PR, 95). Whitehead understands this position as the "evolutionary doctrine of the philosophy of organism" (PR, 95). In that sense, so Whitehead, it represents the alternative to the "Semitic theory of a wholly transcendent God creating out of nothing an accidental universe" (PR, 95). These efforts to establish a nonsubstantialist view of the world prompted Moltmann to object theologically that the metaphor of "creation out of chaos," by taking the notion of the eternity of the world as its point of departure, thereby erects the world itself as the anti-God.[48] But this objection too misses the mark. Rather, the "chaos" metaphor provides an *evolutive metaphor* of the creation of the world under the conditions of a *thoroughgoing* evolution of all types of order (including natural laws) and even of matter itself.[49] It is noteworthy that Whitehead, rather than finding the *true* alternative to the evolutive view in an eternal world, instead formulates this alternative contra *both* "creation out of nothing" *and* the "eternity" of the world (PR, 95). Even though the implication is that Whitehead allows for multiple "cosmic epochs" ("many universes"), the goal is nonetheless *not* the "eternity" of the world (PR, 91ff., 111ff., 197ff.) Notwithstanding that even process theologians themselves are occasionally less than unequivocal on this point,[50] "chaos" *actually* neither directly *opposes* the "nothingness" of the world nor *advocates* the notion of the "eternity" of the world, insisting instead on the *thoroughgoing relationality* of the world.

The *theological support* for this metaphor of "creation out of chaos" is drawn from the *biblical doctrine of creation*. As a matter of fact, the notion of "creation out of nothing" is *not* a biblical doctrine at all, but the result of

---

46. Maassen, "Offenbarung,"; Faber, *God as Poet*, §2.

47. Kann, *Fußnoten zu Platon*.

48. Moltmann, *God in Creation*.

49. Kann, *Fußnoten zu Platon*.

50. Cobb and Griffin, *Process Theology*.

the later philosophical reflections of Irenaeus of Lyon and other church fa-thers.[51] The biblical understanding of creation includes the metaphor of the *formless sea*, whose unfathomable depths represent the "beginning" of the world. Catherine Keller demonstrates how in Genesis 1:2 the sea as *chaos* is antecedent to all creation acts *through which* God, from Genesis 1:3 on, is creatively active.[52] Genesis 1:2 reads: "The earth was a formless void (*tohu-wabohu*) and darkness covered the face of the deep (*tehom*), while a wind from God *(ruach)* swept over the face of the waters" (NRSV). Two mytholog-ical terms associated with chaos characterize the act of creation, namely, the chaos of the land (*tohuwabohu*) and the chaos of the sea *(tehom)*. It is *within* them that God creates. The text *never says* that God creates them. They are instead the consistent, *unspoken presuppositions* of creation. The initial situ-ation is that of darkness, of dark, profound stillness prior to creation itself. *Moreover,* God's creative power—the spirit—is there, hovering above the abyss of chaos. This stillness is the point of departure for creation. Not until verse 3 does the action of creation itself commence, namely, "God said."[53] Here "chaos" is revealed as a *nothingness of formlessness* or, put differently, as the nothingness beyond all form or shape, as an unfathomable depth "in which" everything hovers over the abyss.[54] Creation happens biblically *in* chaos.[55] The metaphor of "creation out of nothing" occurs biblically *only* in 2 Maccabees 2:7, which refers *not* to *creatio ex nihilo*, but to re-trieving into being *that which is past*, the eschatological resurrection of that which has *already* existed.[56] Moltmann's objection that process theology's adherence to "creation out of chaos" supplies it not with a doctrine of creation, but with a doctrine of maintenance, is faulty, for it is precisely the biblical doctrine of *creation* that understands itself not merely as a doctrine of maintenance; but neither does it oppose "chaos," that is, the assumption of primal chaos does not run counter to a genuine biblical doctrine of creation. What process theology is asserting is merely that the doctrine of *creatio ex nihilo* is not biblically supported and thus, at the very least, does provide justification for theological discussion of its motives. The notion of *creation ex nihilo* in the theology of the church fathers needs to be examined, insofar as it might well imply unbiblical nonrelationality, and the metaphor of "creation out of

51. May, *Creatio ex Nihilo.*

52. Keller, *Face of the Deep.*

53. Faber, "'Gottesmeer.'"

54. Keller, "No More Sea."

55. Eissfeldt, "Gott und das Meer in der Bibel," 256–64; Kaiser, *Die mythische Be-deutung des Meeres.*

56. Faber, "Zeitumkehr."

chaos" needs similarly to be examined to the extent it might biblically reflect the relationality of divine creative power.

(3) In Whitehead's own work, the *meaning of the "chaos" metaphor* emerges from its correlation with the *essential and universal relationality* of the world, which in fact has several dimensions. "Chaos" refers first of all to the *basic chaotic nexus,* that nonsocial nexus referring to the broadest context of "existence" and alluding to Plato's *khora* (PR, 72, 94f.).[57] In that sense, it always refers to *relative chaos,* that is, although "chaos" is indeed always formless, it also always expresses *relation*, or that in which communication might be rendered possible (AI, 134). The chaotic "wherein" corresponds to the fundamental relationality of the world, which Whitehead calls *mutual immanence.*[58] And finally "chaos" moves to the center of the evolutive dynamic of creation in the mode of what Whitehead calls the *entirely living nexus,* insofar as it expresses life, which for Whitehead always develops "along the borders of chaos" (PR, 111). As such, it is essential for living beings and for the emergence and unity of persons.[59] The theological ground of this "chaos" is God's own *Trinitarian immanence* in the world, the direct immanence *in which* the chaotic nexus manifests mutual immanence.[60] As such, "chaos" is disclosed as the theological metaphor for the ultimate "wherein" of the world in its *disposition for life and communication.* Hence, Whitehead argues *against* "creation out of nothing," but rather *for* the notion that precisely *because of* God's immanence there can be no "pure chaos" indistinguishable from "nothingness," though also no ultimately static order (PR, 208ff., 339, 348f). Here Whitehead's use of the "chaos" metaphor emerges as the quintessence of a cosmology formulated nonsubstantialistically, and as such—quite in the sense of Derrida—*nonlogocentrically.* The self-fulfilled presence of a "formal" Logos is countered by "chaos" as the emphatically nonformal, freely moving, living evolution of orders and by a Logos of *living communication* based on God's own nonformal, living Trinitarian immanence. Whitehead's "chaos" metaphor is directed against *all* ontological "givenness"[61] that depends on the alternative of being or nothingness; that is, it is directed both against the notion of the *eternity* of the world and against that of *ex nihilo.*[62] Just as in Derrida's interpretation of Plato's *khora,* so also is Whitehead's "chaos" *older than*

57. Faber, *God as Poet,* §15.
58. Faber, *God as Poet,* §34.
59. Faber, *God as Poet,* §22.
60. Faber, *God as Poet,* §§32–34. .
61. Wiehl, "Aktualität und Extensivität," 313–68.
62. Faber, *God as Poet,* §13.

ontological difference, because it neither "posits" self-present being nor, for that reason, "pre-posits" or presupposes nothingness prior to creation.[63] Instead, "chaos"—*beyond the abstraction* of being and nothingness—is not an "absolute beginning," but rather *différance,* that is, beginnings within difference. Although Pannenberg objects that process theology thereby withdraws creation from God's creative power, and Moltmann is suspicious that what is actually presupposed here is "eternal matter," Whitehead in fact refers to God as the *ground* of creation (PR, 225). Because God creates *relationally,* however, creation can *neither* come "from nothing" (pure chaos) *nor* indicate material resistance ("op-position") to God. "Chaos" is instead the *formless activity of communication* that is wholly an *expression of divine perichoresis.*[64]

(4) In assessing process theology's countermetaphor of "creation out of chaos," one must also keep in mind that "chaos" is *not the same as* "immanent creativity" to which Whitehead's new initiative is referring in *Adventures of Ideas* (AI, 236). This becomes evident in the structure of the "ecological reminiscence," where "chaos" refers to that particular "part" of the divine matrix corresponding to "world," namely, the cosmologically grounding and encompassing chaotic nexus.[65] The "chaos" of the chaotic nexus, however, is *not identical* with the intercreativity between God and world to which the metaphor of "immanent-creativity" is referring. Whitehead's reference to "out of chaos," contra "out of nothing" in *Process and Reality* (PR, 93), thus does *not* have the same meaning as the reference to "immanent creativity," contra the "out of nothing" of an "external creator," in *Adventures of Ideas* (AI, 236). The discussion of "chaos" in *Process and Reality* is dealing with an *evolutive cosmology* directed against two modes of cosmological substantialism, namely, the supernaturalism of a creation from will of a transcendent God "out of nothing," and a Spinozism according to which the world emanates out of God "from eternity" by the force of natural necessity (PR, 95). Hence the countermetaphor of "chaos" exhibits a *cosmological meaning* regarding the difference between evolutive and non-evolutive cosmology. By contrast, the countermetaphor of "immanent creativity" in *Adventures of Ideas* is rejecting the notion of an "external creator" of the world and, as such, thus has a *theological* meaning in speaking about the *theopoetic difference* between God and creativity (AI, 236).

On the basis of this distinction between the *cosmological-evolutive* and *theopoetic* sense of the expression "out of nothing," some process

---

63. Faber, *God as Poet,* §15.

64. Faber, *God as Poet,* §32.

65. Faber, *God as Poet,* §32: Figure 4.

theologians, who in fact do cosmologically advocate the notion of "out of chaos," have nonetheless, with respect to theopoetic difference, identified creativity as specifically *divine* creativity, thereby rendering at least conceivable from the perspective of process theology, the notion that the world was indeed created "out of nothing." Steven Franklin has concluded that if creativity is never real without its instances,[66] then God as *primordial instance* of universal (self-)creativity must also be understood as its *origin*.[67] In his analysis of the primordial activity of God's primordial nature, that is, of the "primordial envisagement" of eternal objects,[68] Lewis Ford finds that it implies a primordial distinction *in* God between form (eternal objects) and act (creativity) without which creation is impossible.[69] Ford's point of departure is Whitehead's remark that God is "at once a creature of creativity and a condition for creativity" (PR, 31), that is, not only "exemplifies general principles of metaphysics," but also "constitutes" them in a *primordial act of creation* (PR, 40). Ford understands the *cosmologically* uncreated elements "creativity" (activity) and "ideas" (potentiality) *theopoetically*, as the result of *creatio ex nihilo*.[70] For his part, Joseph Bracken maintains that the divine matrix constitutes a field of creativity of the divine persons that God *freely creates*.[71] With such reflections, process theology precisely renders the *sense* of the ancient introduction of the doctrine of *creatio ex nihilo*, namely, that God creates the world freely, without (pre-)conditions deriving "from outside," and without any counterpart of eternal matter.

The key argument in favor of maintaining and acknowledging the reference to *creatio ex nihilo* in the context of process theology is found in the notion of *God's Trinitarian superjectivity*.[72] Within the inner conversion or *inversion* of the divine process, God's *superjective nature* is the origin of the *distinction* between act and potency, nature and person, God and world, indeed the *origin of the theopoetic difference* between God and creativity as such. From the *internally divine* perspective, creativity is God's nature, God's self-creativity: *in the world*, however, divine creativity as the "wherein" of communication renders possible the self-creativity of all events. In this sense, both the "radical self-creative capacity" (Pannenberg) and the "not-yet-actualized primordial matter" (Moltmann) are grounded

---

66. Faber, *God as Poet*, §16.

67. Franklin, "God and Creativity," 237–307.

68. Faber, *God as Poet*, §33: Trinitarian model II.

69. Ford, "Neville on the One and the Many," 79–84.

70. Ford, "The Viability of Whitehead's God," 141–51.

71. Bracken, *The One in the Many*; Faber, *God as Poet*, §32.

72. Faber, *God as Poet*, §34: Figure 5.

in the primordial act of God's superjective nature. Because of its own lack of ground, it appears simultaneously as the internally divine and world-creative *source ground*.[73] This enables the notion of God's superjectivity to express the early Christian doctrine of the Father as the *origin* "from which everything" (*ex quo omnia*) arises, for the Father is unbegotten (*agennetos*) "inwardly" (immanently) as the origin of the Trinity (*patrogennetos*) and "outwardly" (economically) as the bearing of the world (*gignomo*).[74] Within the *same* superjective nature, God is "patrogennetically" (*gennaō*/beget) the origin of theopoetic difference *as such* (and with it of the Trinity), and is "theogenetically" (*gignomai*/bear, give birth to) the origin of the world *in* theopoetic difference. In contradistinction to their unilateral view of creation, however, the creation act of God's superjective nature is a *relational* happening *within* the divine matrix.[75]

In the light of the divine matrix, the *primordial act of creation* of God's superjective nature can be understood as *relational creatio ex nihilo*. Lewis Ford describes this primordial act of "primordial envisagement," that is, of the primordial differentiation of form and act, as a *creative* happening *directed inwardly*, an act in which God differentiates so that God's "own act of concrescence would [not] exhaust all creativity,[76] and would instead, as *intercreativity*, render the world possible beyond God. Joseph Bracken speaks about an act *within* the divine matrix of the inner-Trintarian life (in God's nature) that freely allows for world.[77] Remarkably, from the perspective of God's inverse concrescence this creative act is, however, *not* an act of impositional or coercive power, nor is it comparable to either productive or destructive physical force, but instead an *act that creates "space"/"khora" inwardly*.[78] "Concrescence" is *per definitionem* an act of "receptivity within," that is, of relationality, rather than "outwardly directed production." Hence, in the *reverse synthesis*[79] of God's Trinitarian concrescence, through a self-creative act of *self-differentiation*, God first creates that "nothing" *within* the divine matrix *within* which the chaotic nexus can arise.[80] Not unlike the "zimzum" (God's "self-limitation") of the Lurian Kabbalah,[81] which Molt-

---

73. Refer to chapter 10, current volume.

74. Schulte, "Die Vorbereitung der Trinitätsoffenbarung," 49–84.

75. Faber, *God as Poet*, §§28, 32: Figure 4.

76. Ford, "The Viability of Whitehead's God," 148.

77. Bracken, *The One in the Many*.

78. Faber, *God as Poet*, §29.

79. Faber, *God as Poet*, §23.

80. Faber, *Prozeßtheologie*.

81. Scholem, *Die jüdische Mystik*.

mann introduces into the creation discourse to show that the divine act of creation *first* refers to the "creation of space" *within* the divine,[82] an understanding of *creatio ex nihilo* now emerges that takes account of process theology's discourse concerning coercive power—that is, of the relationality of the creation act—without abandoning the intentions driving the development of a doctrine of "creation out of nothing." Creation is viewed here as the gracious gift of communication directed outwardly, *not* from sovereign coercive power, but from an *inner-divine* act of tender love that allows for the *Other* (alterity) "within itself."

Given the distinction between the *evolutive* meaning of "chaos" and the *theopoetic* meaning of "creativity," the notions of "out of nothing" and "out of chaos" are not necessarily mutually exclusive. In a new interpretation of the biblical doctrine of God as the beginning and end, as alpha and omega, I understand "chaos" and "nothing" as *two aspects of the same creative happening,*[83] corresponding to a *countermovement* arising from the *external conversion* of the processes between God and world,[84] and taking place in the *four creative phases.*[85] God creates *"counter"* to the world such that the result is a conversion of *evolutive* "creation out of chaos" and *theopoetic* "creation out of nothing." *Cosmologically,* the world can be understood as a process evolving out of chaos. The alpha (α) of the world points back to a past into which its beginnings fade and to an omega (ω) of an open-ended future into which it similarly fades. In this sense, the world can be interpreted as a cosmic epoch alongside of which there can certainly be other, "older" and "future" eons, all representing larger overall rhythms of cosmos and chaos. Here there is neither "absolute beginning" nor "apocalyptic end," but only—critically similar to Derrida's *différance*—"beginnings" and "endings."[86] Here creation is "creation out of chaos." From the *theopoetic* perspective, however, God, in a *reversal* of this *"creaturely* process" (of cosmological evolution) moves toward the world as *"creative* process." In a fashion moving counter to evolutive time, God's creative process is an *eschatological process* that at once *both* opens up the creaturely process "from the front," *from the future* of the world and of every event in God's primordial nature, *and* rescues it *into the past* of the world in the consequent nature.[87] Within this creative process, there is an *absolute beginning of* the world (A) that from the perspective of

82. Moltmann, *God in Creation.*

83. Faber, "Zeitumkehr."

84. Faber, *God as Poet,* §29.

85. Faber, *God as Poet,* §30.

86. Keller, *Face of the Deep.*

87. Faber, *God as Poet,* §§17, 20, 39.

process theology represents the locus *of creation ex nihilo*, and an *absolute release* (Ω) (in the sense of a *release* of limitations) in God's consequent nature, in which God transforms the "old" into Godself and renews it "back" into the world, in that sense creating it *ex vetere* (from the "old").

Unlike the notion of Whitehead's cosmological difference between "chaos" and "nothing" in *Process and Reality*, the theopoetic difference between "external creator" and "immanent creativity" in *Adventures of Ideas* provides a key reference for the abiding meaning of the notion of "creation out of nothing" in the context of process theology. The characterizing feature of creativity is to be the "origination of novelty," and it is precisely this "absolute novelty" of the creative process that represents the genuine content of *"ex nihilo."*[88] Process theology can thus refer meaningfully both to the notion of "out of chaos" within the creaturely process and to that of "out of nothing" within the creative process—namely, as the *countermovement* of *creaturely* and *creative* processes. Ultimately the two processes coincide within the innermost feature of both "nothing" *and* "chaos," namely, the *absolute novelty* expressed by *"ex nihilo."*[89] "Chaos" is based on the absolute beginning expressed by nothing—the absolute beginning of creation within the Trinitarian matrix, that is, within the creative primordial act of the superjective nature, in the novelty of potentiality (future) of the primordial nature itself, and in the novelty of release of the consequent nature. And precisely this is God's "poetics"; instead of renouncing the idea of a creator God, it represents a nonsubstantial, relational, and noncoercive grounding of universal creative power.[90] It takes nothing from God in the way of God's "absolute novelty" (*ex nihilo*), yet with no detriment to relationality (out of chaos). Within God's "poetic weakness," God's creative power is nonetheless "overwhelming" ("overpowering"); in God's "tender patience" it is nonetheless "rational"; and in its "conceptual harmonization" it is "persuasive" rather than "coercive." As the "origination of novelty," God is that particular "absolute beginning" who, within God's *creatio ex nihilo*, nonetheless remains a *relational creator*—God's *poiesis* maintains the self-value of the creature, bequeaths to it its self-creativity, and presupposes ("pre-posits") the world for itself for creative communication.

88. Faber, "Zeitumkehr."

89. May, *Creatio ex Nihilo*; Haught, *What Is God?*

90. Faber, *God as Poet*, §28.

CHAPTER TEN

Trinity as Event

THE FOLLOWING IS A deeper comparison of possible connections between the development and concerns of trinitarian theology and process theology to show how they can indeed supplement each other. The main thesis is that the concepts of *analogy* and *coherence* make it possible to translate each tradition in terms of the other, and in so doing, shed light on peculiar problems within each tradition. For trinitarian theology, the problem is often understood as the problem of the "three" and their relations to each other and to the world. For process theology, the problem is whether to understand God as a single actuality or as a society. And for both together, the problem is how to relate God and the world so that God is not a part of the world, nor just its "idea," nor solely its untouchable, transcendental ground. The common basis of comparison is the question of an internal relationship between God and world. I show how analogy represents the process of coherence in a way that allows us to express how a deep structural possibility for the trinity exists within the process paradigm. The thesis, then, as briefly touched in the previous chapter, is that it is feasible to develop a trinitarian theological differentiation within the process paradigm that understands God as one actuality in everlasting self-differentiation.

In his famous chapter 11 of *Science and the Modern World*, with the laconic title "God," Whitehead compares his attempt at a concept of God with Aristotle's metaphysical model of the unmoved mover. When Whitehead observes an "analogous metaphysical problem" in Aristotle that "can be solved only in an analogous fashion" (SMW, 174), he is not arguing for a re-appropriation of Aristotle's unmoved mover. It is not the ancient solution that determines the analogy; on the contrary, it is the structure of the process of inquiry. God is required for the essence of the universe, as principle of concretion; or better: the Principle of Concretion is named God by Whitehead.

Thus, Whitehead treats the world and God under one combined view by determining the appropriate and even necessary categories for comprehending the world. In these categories, God's being gives *expression* to itself, and for that reason, the categories frame the world. The question is not whether we need a concept of God to prevent the breakdown of the principles from framing the world (PR, 343), but which categories can be employed in a discussion of the concept of God that lead to *comprehension* of the world. The categories for comprehending the world are elucidated through the conceptualization of God. Likewise, the concept of God is illumined through the comprehension of the world within the same categories. While Whitehead introduces God to illuminate the structures of the world, he actually understands God more as the expression of these structures, their uppermost realization, their pure gestalt. God's being embodies in itself the ground of these structures, and at the same time, as their reason, God is their actualization. This form of development of an analogy let Whitehead establish a connection to Aristotle, insofar as he can give expression to the principle that everything that is in existence represents the categories of existence. To be sure, the resemblance to Aristotle's conception is limited, because Whitehead does not try to grasp God as the ground of the universe. The conceptualization of God, rather, must have the capacity for God's radical otherness, even if God represents the principle of the world.

Developing a notion of analogy for the relationship between God and the world unfolds a coherent concept of God that is suitable and not unreasonable to the Christian experience of faith and tradition. Theology tried to understand how God is related to the world, and whether God's relation to the world is a way to think of God as trinitarian. The categories gained in religious reflection were never intended to be a positive insight into God's mystery, but rather, they made possible a new insight into the world. The aids for understanding the incomprehensible God extracted from secular reason serve at the same time to elucidate the world as one to which God is engaged. Thus, we can realize God's engagement with the world is not unreasonable.

It is this kind of development of analogy as mutual explanation of God and world that advances both trinitarian theology and a process theological view. Analogy and coherence can supplement, interpret, and criticize each other and, therefore, benefit both trinitarian theology and process theology.

Trinity

The classical way of determining theologically God's relation to the world made the doctrine of God's one, substantial essence preeminent over God's trinitarian relational being.[1] God's being in relation to the world was a "thought," or external relation in which God is not touched by the world. This leads to the separation of God and world. However, the assumption of God's intrinsic movement requires a real relation of the trinitarian God to the world. This leads to criticism of that understanding of freedom and sovereignty by which God seems to be self-sufficient, producing the world through an arbitrary act of love. But can God be eternally self-sufficient in an untouched glory? Does God not really need the one loved, in the suffering of God's love? Could a loving God ever be without a world?

This requires anew that we determine God's world-reference in such a way that it could be name a real relation, but with a non-arbitrary reason within God. This is adequately found only in trinitarian refinement. Thus, the crucial questions in a new determination of the relation of God and the world sharpen into the problem of whether, and how, and in what respect, the category of an internal relation is constitutive for reality in such a way that it can determine God and the world, precisely because God is *in se* its prime realization.

In answering this question, a trinitarian conception of God can solve the problem of interpreting God's internal relationship with the world without denying God's primordiality over against the world. To speak within trinitarianism, God as Father is not primarily to be understood as in opposition to a world, but in relation to the *Logos*. Thus, it would be possible to interpret the world-relationship of God out of the intrinsically trinitarian self-relationship, and to see in the one relation a model for the other. The history of theology specifically offers the following perspectives.

The First Ecumenical Council in Nicaea spoke of the *homoousios* of the incarnated *Logos* with the Father; this meant a decisive change from the metaphysical categories of the ancient world. It implied a revolution in thought, conferring on the category of relation an equal rank to the hitherto dominant category of substance. We can only observe this change in terms of the Middle Platonism and Neoplatonism that held sway in the time between 100 B.C.E. and the Council of Nicaea in 325 C.E. A hierarchically

---

1. Moltmann, *Trinität und Reich Gottes*, 31–32: "Seit *Tertullian* wurde die christliche Trinität immer in dem allgemeinen Begriff der *göttlichen Substanz* abgebildet: *Una substantia—tres personae* . . . Es ist verständlich, daß für *Augustin* und *Thomas von Aquin* diese eine, gemeinsame, göttliche Substanz als das den trinitarischen Personen Zugrundeliegende und ihnen gegenüber darum logisch Primare galt."

ordered world was grounded in the inaccessible One in contrast to the principles of multiplicity (namely *nous*, "world-soul," and the unformed multiplicity of *hyle*). The absolutely undifferentiated One is, thus, strongly the
prime-ground of the world, with no real relation to the other principles.
Nous and world-soul are unneeded (although, in fact, given) manifestations
in the pluralistic world with "nothing" in common with the absolute One.[2]
Although this absolute unity, standing above all possibility of differentiation, became the image for a Christian understanding of the divine oneness
of essence, in the concept of the Trinity, the notion of *homoousios* undercut
this monolithic understanding of unity.

In the trinitarian context, the possibility was open for a relational
worldview. By means of the concept of "ex-sistence;" namely—to be by being grounded in another being—the category of a relational constitution
of reality became possible. Richard of St. Victor developed the idea of the
unity of the divine persons as *ex-sistentiae*, as beings who are intrinsic to
one another, so that they are emerging out of one another. His now famous
definition of person in this context is: *persona est divinae naturae incom-
municabilis existentia*.

This concept no longer relies on a notion of a substantial *ens per se*, or
ens in se, as the founding category of thought. Its "essence" consists in being not out of oneself—tantamount to a substance—but out of the relation
with another. Each divine person is essentially only out of, and in relation
with, the other persons. This nonsubstantial, relational understanding of
God's internal, trinitarian being can now be understood as an element in the
foundation of God's internal relationship with the world.

Analogy

Analogy is that element of the tradition where the quest for the relations
in God, from that of God with the world, and within the world itself,

---

2. Refer to the profound investigation in Grillmeier, "Jesus von Nazareth," 68: "Es
ist das Bild einer hierarchisch gestuften Welt, deren oberste Spitze das 'Eine,' das 'Hen'
bildete, jenes absolut 'Eine,' das schließlich als Prinzip, als arche, ueber allem Sein
schwebte. Darunter kam der schon depotenzierte, die Vielheit in sich enthaltende Logos oder Nous . . . Zwischen diesem Nous und der Hyle, dem Inbegriff der ungeformten
Vielheit, stand an dritter Stelle die Psyche, die Weltseele. Wenn die griechische Philosophie der damaligen Zeit gegen etwas empfindlich war, dann gegen dies: als oberstes
Prinzip, als arche etwas anderes zu setzen als das exklusiv-absolute 'Hen' . . . Nous und
Psyche sollten im Grunde gar nicht sein. —Eine gottliche Einheit in Dreifaltigkeit an
die oberste Stelle als absolute arche zu setzen, war also fur die Mittelplatoniker und die
Neuplatoniker reine Torheit. Dies aber bedeutete die Annahme eines im Vater preexis-
tenten Logos und Sohnes und des Pneumas."

intrinsically appears. The only "official" definition for analogy in a theological context was formulated by the Fourth Lateran Council (1215) in
the process of determining a relation between God and the world.[3] The
Council comments upon a theological disputation between Joachim of
Fiore and Peter Lombard about the correct understanding of the unity of
the trinitarian community in God. Both the disputants and the Council
agreed that God is to be understood not only as Trinitarian, but also as
one. The problem was *how* to determine this unity of the divine persons.
Joachim reproached Peter Lombard for adding the one substance of God
as a fourth person. The Council sided with Lombard in noting that God is
one reality shared equally and totally by the three divine persons. It agreed
with Joachim of Fiore that the unity of the divine persons is fundamentally
unlike the unity of human beings within a community. Human beings
ought to be "one" as the Son is "one" with the Father (John 17:22). But the
meaning is transformed in a sense of divine analogy in which the oneness
of the three persons is ever more dissimilar to human and mundane oneness. Because the understanding of unity has to be conceived as based in
God and the assumption of the world in God's community, the analogy
itself must be grounded in God. Thus, the Council could hold tight to a
unity *sui generis*, which is not to be deduced from elsewhere, but is a natural oneness of the three persons, equal in the beginning.

Commonly, analogy is understood as a relation of similarity, a relation aimed at an abolition of dissimilarity. This understanding came to
have such enormous influence that all attempts to think non-analogously
militated against analogy itself. I want to reverse this tendency in a way that
is suggested by the Lateran definition of analogy. The formula runs, " . . .
*inter creatorem et creaturam non potest tanta similitudo notari, quin inter eos
maior sit dissimilitudo notanda.*"[4]

This is the core of the appeal to analogy: that the dissimilarity is ever-
more-vast than similarity, and that this analogy between God and world
(and internally in the world) is founded in God's relational being, in the
trinitarian community itself. In God's ever-vaster dissimilarity to the world,
unity is not determined prior to the divine relations, but through them. An
ultimately trinitarian horizon allows us to speak of an internal relationality
of the world insofar as the world derives from God.

On dissimilarity, therefore, is bestowed a self-reliant weight vis-
a-vis similarity in the "one" analogy: the dissimilarity is ever-vaster, not

---

3. Denzinger, *Kompendium der Glauhensbekenntnisse*, nos. 803– 8. I will use HD to
reference this citation as we continue below.

4. Ibid. (= HD, 806).

subsumable under similarity, inconceivable, ever-ahead of it. And this is the challenge: that this analogy between God and world is founded in God's *internal*, relational being; in the Trinitarian community itself. In God's innermost life, there must be the ultimate origin for this analogy that ultimately grounds the creational structure of being. The analogous relation between God and world is founded "in" God, *in* God's *intrinsic*, trinitarian relations, and it emerges *out* of this trinitarian origin. Because of God's intrinsic, analogous structure of ever-vaster dissimilarity, unity is not determined prior to the divine relations, but through them. And thus, the Lateran understanding of analogy realizes the classical trinitarian concept of "person" in its deepest meaning. "Person," then, means all that which is *not common* in God, all that in which the persons of the Trinity *exclusively differ*—for in everything they don't differ—they *are* the one divine essence.[5] Thus, the divine analogy is intrinsically the analogy of the dissimilar, divine persons and in their "oppositional relations" lies the ultimate root of the analogous structure as suggested.

Furthermore, the ultimately trinitarian horizon also allows us to speak of an *internal* relation of the world with God insofar as the world derives from God's dissimilarity, but is called into similarity with God. God's constitutive dissimilarity, in which God opens God's innermost self, transforms us into similarity. God remains the unsurpassable origin of the revelation of God's intrinsic life, but makes itself recognizable through similarity. Analogy can now be understood as the internal relation of God to the innermost heart of the creatures. The being of God's creatures is an analogous being-from-God as ex-sistence, which is biblically characterized as a love-relation. In God's disclosedness, the ex-sisting creature, in being dissimilar, is called into similarity, and in this, to its own self-being as free ex-sistence. Nevertheless, when God defines God in world-relations, in God's definition, God is in a certain sense always *dissimilarly* ahead of it while being *similarly* concrete within it.

Process

The structure of the universe is to be in process; all complex realities in their multiple relations to one another are processual. The entire world can

---

5. " . . . das Wort von 'drei Personen' [bringt] dasjenige noch einmal unter einen quasi-allgemeinen Begriff . . . , worin Vater, Sohn u[nd] Geist sich *nur unterscheiden,* nicht aber übereinkommen, denn in allem, in dem sie übereinkommen, sind sie auch schlechthin eins in der einen u[nd] absolut selbigen Wesenheit" (Rahner, "Trinitatstheologie," 359). In God, then, the concept of person is not univocal, but analogous.

be analyzed as a process of organic processes. Each process is the creative realization of relations out of the world into a new relational creature. The universe is the whole of all possible and actual relations, meaning not only that anything "more" is not recognized, but that there is simply nothing more. Or, seen the other way around: All that is communicable stands in connections, and is, therefore, in this sense relative. There is nothing that, insofar as it is, is *not* interconnected with all others in a permanently developing *universalis communicatio.*

In the working out of Whitehead's metaphysics of reality and actuality, this "communication in process" will find its expression in the three fundamental principles of reference for actualities: (1) the "ontological principle," where actuality leads back solely to actuality again, or that the concrete is the reason for the concrete; (2) the "principle of relativity," which regulates the universal togetherness of all actualities, and finally (3) the "principle of process," which is that being is its becoming and is not to be understood apart from it. All that is, is experienceable; whatever is not "in" experience *does not exist.* And it is the concrete that gives itself to experience; when we experience, we experience the concrete actuality, the singleness, the unrepeatable, the unique itself, and not solely the general, attributes, universals, the repeatable.

Thus, the process paradigm can clearly support elements of the Lateran analogy formula and its mode of reference: the process of the world is grounded within God in a way that can interpret the relation between God and world. And this interpretation takes the irreducible concreteness into account as it grows out of dissimilarity and defines itself in similarity. This relation is one of inexhaustible novelty in a process of self-communication, self-revelation and attachment.

Interpretation

Important elements can be named in which the coincidence of the doctrine of analogy and of Whitehead's thought will manifest itself in detail. Already in his early philosophy of nature, Whitehead drew attention to the distinction between dissimilarity and similarity in analogy. Against the conventional stress on similarity, he gave the primary weight to dissimilarity: "Rational thought which is the comparison of event with event would be intrinsically impossible without objects" (PNK, 64). Fugitive, unique, absolutely incomparable events that constitute reality as concrete are, in their concreteness, unrecognizable if there cannot be found an element whereby a comparison will be made possible. Dissimilarity has to interpret itself in similarity in order to receive durability as dissimilarity. This process is not just one of human cognition, but one of nature itself. The abstraction of thinking is just one mode of the essence of every natural interaction.

Obviously, the preeminence of actuality is due to dissimilarity; i.e., objects of perception solely exist in regard to events, because without them they are, so to speak, nothing. To be sure, a retro-reference to similarity is required. For, while each act of realization is irreducibly concrete, private, ineffable, incommunicable, atomistic, perishing in becoming, perceived repetition of events is an abstraction of the similar from the concrete, and for that reason, recognizable. Thus, neither events nor objects are independent, subsisting apart from each other. Their function to one another renders them both possible and actual. Despite a certain kind of independence from each other, one that makes them not reducible to one another, they are together or they are not at all.

However, how can such a structure of concretes and abstracts be made evident, meaning that knowledge always aims at the concrete, the unprecedented, the irreducibly dissimilar, while cognition always happens in developing similarity through abstraction?

> But an event is just what it is, and is just how it is related; and it is nothing else (PNK, 64). [F]or an entity which stands in internal relations has no being as an entity not in these relations. In other words, once with internal relations, always with internal relations (SMW, 160).

With his conception of actuality as concrete, actual, becoming, and, therefore, concrescent, Whitehead can help to master this paradox, because for him organic relationality and concreteness irrevocably presuppose each other. Each single, processual actuality is a process of becoming, growing together out of already concrete actualities. Therefore, dissimilarity is essential for similarity. Concrete past actualities are objectified in the becoming actuality.

The process of objectifying past events renders possible the passage from public objects into the privacy of concrescence, and the passage from this intrinsic subjectivity into the new publicity of transition, and with that, the passage from subject into object and reverse. In this way, the retro-connection of the irreducible, analogous difference to similarity can be made intelligible by Whitehead, and he can express the rhythmical turn from one to another as the act of process that founds every reality.

Moreover, in choosing the process paradigm as a point of departure, the opposition between similarity and dissimilarity does not get stabilized into an ultimate antagonism. On the contrary, within the relative process structure of actuality, substance becomes *dynamized* and, therefore, "unsubstantiated." The becoming of concrete actuality is the growing together of "concretes" and "abstracts" in *one* process, while the transition *between* them is an everlasting revolution. This twofold function grounds a kind of polarity in the process of every concrete actuality that has a physical and a mental side, with the physical side feeling actual entities, and with the mental side feeling eternal objects.

In the general process, the mentality of a prehended actual occasion becomes the content of the physical pole of another actuality. Just as events represent the "unique-dissimilar"[6] and objects the "universal-similar," an event intrinsically is the perception of the dissimilar and its processual transformation into the similar. Events have the feature of being real potentials in other events, and objects have an individual, dissimilar essence, because they are not entirely defined by their relations. Actual entities are perceived in physical feelings as dissimilar with reference to their importance for the process of appropriation. Therefore, they make the process, in which they ought to become consistent to one another and, therefore, similar, everlastingly go on by reason of their dissimilarity to each other.[7] On the other side, is the physical perception of nothing other than a conformal feeling of the predecessors and, therefore, the process of becoming similar (PR, 164). Within the context of Whitehead's categories, the rhythmic passage of similarity and dissimilarity into one another gets transplanted into a complex matrix in which all elements condition one another in a certain mode of indefiniteness. This, on the other hand, renders our project feasible, because it avoids every dualism within the analogous structure.

On the other hand, "analogy" does not belong to the technical terms of Whitehead's philosophy. He uses it generally and without specific intention, although he does use it in the context of the definition of congruence (PR, 331), or in connection with the question of probability (PR, 205), which does not have much in common with the issue treated here.[8]

6. The essential nature of events to be dissimilar is due to their unrepeatability, not to their quality of being different from other events. Therefore, in repetition, the similarity of events could be perfect without losing the fundamental uniqueness.

7. PR, 164–66: Whitehead named the essence of the higher phases, treating physical feelings, "comparing" (*conceptual feeling*) and "comparing of comparing" (*propositional feeling*). This can be understood as development of analogous similarity.

8. Beelitz, *Die dynamische Beziehung zwischen Erfahrung und Metaphysik*, 163–70. He follows explicitly the question whether the Aristotelian-Platonic origin of the concept of analogy binds its contents in a way that Whitehead, with his relativistic, nonsubstantial conception, would be necessarily, and, in principle, beyond it. Dorothy Emmet, on the other hand, puts together five different kinds of analogy and investigates their connection with Whitehead's thought. Cf. Emmet, *The Nature of Metaphysical*

However, an important text referring to the notion of "analogy" does appears earlier in *The Function of Reason*.

> But why construe the later forms by analogy to the earlier forms. Why not reverse the process? It would seem to be more sensible, more truly empirical, to allow each living species to make its own contribution to the demonstration of factors inherent in living things. (FR, 15)

For our context, this means that analogy has to proceed out of what is dissimilar, not out of what is common in terms of a smallest common denominator. For Whitehead, this form of analogy seems implied within the notion of participation, particularly in *Adventures of Ideas*.

> [A]n abstraction can be made and some elements of the complete pattern can be omitted. The partial pattern thus obtained will be said to be abstracted from the original. A truth-relation will be said to be objective contents of two prehensions when one and the same identical partial pattern can be abstracted from both of them. They each exhibit this same partial pattern, though their omitted elements involve the differences which belong to their diverse individualities. Plato used the term "participation" to express the relation of a composite fact to some partial pattern which it illustrates. Only he limits the notion of the partial pattern to some purely abstract pattern of qualitative elements, to the exclusion of the notion of concrete particular realities as components in a composite reality. This limitation is misleading. Thus we will speak of a pattern as possibly including concrete particular realities as components in a composite reality. (AI, 242)[9]

Analogy is the process of participation, of *methexis*, wherein individual, dissimilar actualities are related to each other in reciprocal interpretation in terms of a common pattern of similarity abstracted from them. Decisive here are two elements: On one side, the process does exactly what was emphasized already regarding the relation between event and object; namely, allowing for mutual participation of individualities though an abstraction; thus, it is about an analogous relation. On the other hand, what Whitehead criticizes in Plato (namely, that he did not take the moment of participation of concrete actualities in the constitution of new actualities

---

Thinking, 8–14. Nevertheless, all these forms of analogy are actually overtaken by the Lateran kind of analogy.

9. Whitehead named this procedure of particular defined patterns "mutual interpretation"; cf. AI, 250.

into consideration) is the reason for his giving priority to dissimilarity over similarity. If the concrete events are integrated into the participation process, the relation of participation will describe exactly the process of development of actual entities out of their world's elements. In this way, the process of the emergence of concrete actuality from concrete actuality can be described with the help of abstraction as the process of analogy.

Thus, to summarize: Reality is the process of the development of concrete actualities through reciprocal participation and interpretation of dissimilar elements of the process (prehensions), so that through "similarization," which is mutually operative in these elements for one another, the end result will appear as nothing else than united dissimilarity.[10] Process is analogous; analogy exists as a process of actualities. The beginning point is the difference of the concrete; the end result is their contrast-enriched unity whose intensity will depend on the "analogous differentiatedness" of their components. Analogy within the process paradigm is the becoming of the *res verae.*

The Principle of Concretion

> The general principle of empiricism depends upon the doctrine
> that there is a principle of concretion which is not discoverable
> by abstract reason. What further can be known about God must
> be sought in the region of particular experiences, and therefore
> rests on an empirical basis. (SMW, 178)

Whitehead proposes that that which is the last reason, or even the ultimate principle of reasoning, has no reason itself. As the ground of this world, there rules neither necessity nor reason, but freedom. Reason becomes God as the principle of freedom and of the concrete that happens historically, in all its novelty. This finding leads Whitehead far beyond Aristotle's attempt to ground the world in necessity, and thus, in rational accessibility, in which God should be the necessary ground for the general character of things. If the concrete is the undeceivable dissimilar, then God as the reason of concreteness is the ultimate reason of dissimilarity. And God is this "reason" in a way that God's being does not allow one to reason about it. On the contrary, God gives reason out of unfathomable wealth. This givenness of God is the same time God's self-giving as ground. The climax of this twist in Whitehead's thinking on analogy, then, is that God, because of God's being is the ground of concreteness, can only be known in historical concreteness.

---

10. PR, 26: *Contrasts* consequently produces in origination of dissimilarity, an *indefinite progression* of categories.

God's metaphysical rank opens this way for a historical understanding of God, and a real relation with the world without dissolving in that relation because of God's dissimilarity.[11]

In *Process and Reality*, Whitehead comes back again to speak of God as Principle of Concreteness in the context of his innovative theory of subjectivity, in a passage that allows him to establish with all desirable clarity the connection with the inquiry concerning analogy:

> The immediacy of the concrescent subject is constituted by its living aim at its own self-constitution. Thus the initial stage of the aim is rooted in the nature of God, and its completion depends on the self-causation of the subject-superject . . . In this sense God is the principle of concretion; namely, he is that actual entity from which each temporal concrescence receives that initial aim from which its self-causation starts. (PR, 244)

Subjectivity is, thus, not a "substantial" subject any more, but a "relational" subject that emerges out of its experiences, that constitutes itself within its experiences. The subject is an activity, a creative act of "becoming one" out of all its experiences, without being in advance of them (PR, 26). Thus, the subject is in a certain sense forever "outstanding" and, at the same time, in the process of its becoming, is always already present as a final cause.[12] As initial aim and subjective aim, it is in its character of being "outstanding," still leading the process (PR, 222), and is in its satisfaction perfected, and now available for the becoming of other subjects. For Whitehead, the subjective process is the original happening of the creative, rhythmical turn from object into subject, from externality into immediacy and vice versa. By this cycle, the process fulfills the ultimate motion of the universe. It is always "subject-superject," becoming, standing in the immediacy of its own becoming, *and* being, which, deprived of its subjectivity, permanently acts upon others in order to enter them. As subject, its actuality is as subjective immediacy (PR, 23), and as superject, its actuality is as objective immortality (PR, 45).

Consequently, what should be noted here is that the subjectivity of each creature is, thus, grounded in the nature of God. Whitehead discusses this clearly in the passage cited above. The immediacy of irreducible subjects is grounded in the divine gift of a subjective aim, from which the otherwise *un*derivable subjectivity "derives." In a subtle paradox, God's nature is the

11. Faber, *Freiheit*.

12. See Michael Welker's idea that we understand Whitehead's theory of subjectivity as the acting of "not-yet-beings" and in their becoming again "standing-out-beings"; Welker, "Whitehead's Vergottung der Welt," 267–68.

source of the process of self-constitution for every actuality. This notion, in which the dissimilar God grounds independence and unsurpassable dissimilarity, and, with that, the self-reliance of creatures, proves to be a new variant of Richard of St. Victor's "ex-sistence" as relation, in which the incommunicable is founded as communicable in relation with others. According to God's "intrinsically analogous" being, dissimilarity does not found similarity, but dissimilarity; not dependence, but self-reliance; not necessity, but freedom. The initial subjective aim, luring the subjective process, is in its essence a complex eternal object. On the one hand, it represents essential novelty and freedom, introducing them in contrast to the fixed reality of the world (AI, 83). On the other hand, in its dissimilarity in comparison with the past world, it is more the expression of analogous similarity, as argued above. The "underivability" of subjectivity, realizing itself in the decision-making process, therefore, paradoxically derives from somewhere else; namely, from creativity that is its process.

Thus, finally we ask: How does each becoming subjectivity originate in God's nature? Now we have arrived at that point where it is obvious how, in Whitehead's conception, the "analogous motion" of subjectivity is grounded in God, being the happening of God's essence itself. God, in God's primordial aspect, is the active synthesis of inexhaustible potentiality in a process of self-actualization. God's concrescence itself, however, is directed by a divine subjective aim (PR, 88) that is not to be derived from another ground, except out of creativity itself, herewith being the sheer expression of the undecisive primordiality and underivable disimilarity. God's subjective immediacy is not the eternal objects it unites, nor is it the creativity it enacts. Indeed, even eternal objects and creativity are expressions of God's godhead, but the ultimate root of God is God's unfathomable subjectivity that is not to be grounded in anything other than its own irreducible act. This means that in the process theological understanding of God, the Lateran preference of dissimilarity over similarity is grounded in God's nature itself, which realizes in its subjectivity the dissimilar actualization of similar objects. This is God's incomparability, providing for each analogy without being comprehended by it (PR, 47).

Whitehead acknowledged this weight of God's underivable actuality himself in designating the subjective aim not just as *expression*, but also as *limit* of the ontological principle (PR, 44). This is a remarkable assertion, if we consider the ontological principle to regulate the relation between ground (ratio) and principle, meaning that which can be grounded. One and the same reality is a concrete actuality *and* an abstract principle, realizing itself in actualities by means of being almost nothing in independence of them. Thus, God's primordial act is the ultimate reason, hence, not "reasonable" anymore. Yet such ungroundedness is not inconsistent with the system, but the proof of its ultimate consistency, because God's being is the underivable concrete, the ground of all rationality, and as such, the ultimate ir-rationality, that is, ungrounded in reason, or "sur-rationality," that is, a movement always (venturing and coming from) beyond rationality. Ultimately, the Principle of concretion is God's *actus essendi*.

Coherence

We can now apply these reflections to a process theological understanding of the Trinity. Based on the concept of coherence and its use, I ask the question as to whether there can be a way, beside the traditional trinitarian analogies in Whitehead, to establish the Trinity. Similar to the inquiry concerning the Lateran analogy, we seek not the meaning of the "three," or the "functionalization" of the divine persons for any trifold character. On the contrary, our way of proceeding has the freedom to underline elements of structure within Whitehead's categories, and their structural unity with the Lateran analogy, rendering a trinitarian theological interpretation possible and meaningful. Whitehead employs "coherence" in the following paradigmatic definition:

> "Coherence" . . . means that the fundamental ideas . . . presuppose each other so that in isolation they are meaningless. This requirement does not mean that they are definable in terms of each other; it means that what is indefinable in one such notion cannot be abstracted from its relevance to the other notions (PR, 3). Incoherence, on the other hand, is the arbitrary disconnection of first principles. (PR, 6)

Thus, analogy and coherence are structurally similar. Were abstraction not possible, there could be neither derivation nor difference from one another. The intrinsic connection to the other, of that which is ultimately not derivable from the other, involves a dissimilarity ever-vaster against each possible approximation. This nicely overlaps with Whitehead's understanding of reciprocity in which he states a presupposition of each according to their ever-vaster dissimilarity (MT, 46). In this sense, Whitehead knows that such formulations of ultimate principles are not able to be derived from each other, yet they achieve an internal, incorruptible togetherness. Examples are the polarity of events, subjectivity/superjectivity, givenness, potentiality, and freedom, and, finally, the category of the ultimate, whose three elements (many, one, and creativity) perhaps afford the final point of reference for a process trinitarian theology.[13] This ultimate togetherness in coherence itself performs a process: "Thus 'becoming' is the transformation of incoherence into coherence . . . (PR, 25) . . . Creativity achieves its supreme task of transforming disjoined multiplicity . . . into concrescent unity . . . " (PR, 348).

The process paradigm retains its final say even in the context of the concept of coherence. Process is the becoming of coherence, and this transformation is the supreme task of creativity. Coherence involves reality *incarnating* as the satisfaction of every process. The sole coherent outcome renders superjectivity possible in which coherent givenness gives itself into new processes of becoming. Coherence is the attainment of superjectivity in which every concreteness obtains an element of ongoing creative process. Process, therefore, is systematically anchored in Whitehead's thinking because of the everlasting rhythmical turn into one another of coherence *into* incoherence, which indicates the character of the ultimate givenness of the world. And this transition is again indebted to the equally ultimate character of dissimilarity of the elements of process. Dissimilarity stands at the beginning of a creative unification of the dissimilar many. And as an element of ongoing process, the unified "one," in its unique subjectivity is, again, dissimilar to other processes of unification. The ultimate is not *a fact*, the ultimate is *the process of concrete facts* (PR, 7; AI, 190).

For Whitehead, the highest expression of dissimilarity, pushing the creative process incessantly further, is the contrasting opposition of God and the world (PR, 348). This already coherently results in the ultimate irrationality; i.e., the ungroundedness of God both as primordial actuality and as the ground of this world (PR, 75), in that God is both the ever-vaster dissimilarity in opposition to the world and, at the same time, its ground. This special dissimilarity expresses itself through the differentiation of the divine process from the world's process.[14]

13. See Hans Günter Holl, who has indicated this connection in a hint to his German translation of PR, *Prozeß and Realität* (Frankfurt a.M. 1987): "'Elementar' ist hier also logisch wie ontologisch gemeint und setzt in beiden Bedeutungen eine Grenze, die nicht überschritten werden kann. Wenn man so will, könnte man vielleicht sagen, dass sich hier die christliche Trinitätslehre in säkularisierter Form niederschlagt . . ." From this point, one is justly referred to the connection with this other "Trinity," God, world, and creativity (PR, 348–49), to see the relevance of this category. This connection is expressed in Bracken, "Process Philosophy and Trinitarian Theology—II," 85–86.

14. I explicitly agree with the idea of *"reversal* of the poles" as developed by Marjorie Suchocki for a reinterpretation of Whitehead's concept of God. I do not agree with the idea of God as "society," because to think of God as one actuality seems to be more consistent *if* we are able to see the process of God as a very different process from that of other entities, without hurting the common categories through which we understand actualities. Cf. Suchocki, "The Metaphysical Ground," 237–46. Note, however,

> In every respect God and the World move conversely to each oth-
> er in respect to their process. God is primordially one, namely, he
> is the primordial unity of relevance of the many potential forms;
> in the process he acquires a consequent multiplicity, which the
> primordial character absorbs into its own unity. (PR, 349)

Significantly this *conversion* of process in God obeys the same principles and categories as any other process and, yet, subsists intrinsically in
a completely dissimilar nature in every respect. Not only a so-called "reversal of the poles" is remarkable; i.e., God's primordial origination from
the mental pole, but also the entire process progresses in the opposite manner to entities in the world and *intrinsically* conversed to it.[15] Thus, God is
not just primordial subjectivity and infinite unconditionedness, but also
the primordial superject of creativity; and God is this within the primordial, underivable, dissimilar actuality of God's subjectivity that represents
perfect unification and validity of the objects in God's equally primordial
satisfaction. For finite entities, the superjective self-giving to other processes means the loss of immediacy; but for God, God's essence is to *give
itself away* in its givenness. God's objectivity (similarity) actualizes itself
through God's immediacy (dissimilarity). Objectification (assimilation) is
not the consequence of God's process, nor its end, but its actuality in the
working out of God's subjective process. In the divine process, subjectivity
and objectivity, dissimilarity and similarity attain supreme, coherent unity
in the fulfillment of an analogous structure.

The Primordial Roles of God

Whitehead's twenty-second category of explanation now comes into play
for developing the trinitarian implications of these features.

> . . . an actual entity by functioning in respect of itself plays
> diverse roles in self-formation without losing its self-identity.
> It is self-creative; and in its process of creation transforms its
> diversity of roles into one coherent role. Thus "becoming" is the
> transformation of incoherence into coherence, and in each par-
> ticular instance ceases with this attainment. (*PR*, 25)

---

that Whitehead himself speaks of the "*conversion* of the processes." This means more
than a reversal of poles; namely, an intrinsic conversion of each aspect of the process of
God in comparison with that of the world. Therefore, I prefer the concept of "conversion" to "reversal."

15. Even for an interpretation of God as society, the "conversion of processes" will
have a conversive meaning in reference to God.

Every process is self-functional. In performance of such self-function-
ality, actuality combines self-identity and self-diversity. In such performance,
actuality constitutes itself as immediate subject (PR, 25). God's self-function-
ality is of such a structure as to project itself into a consequent multiplicity out of its primordial oneness. Thus, if the "Conversion of the processes"
really occurs, then God's process must begin as primordial coherence and
proceed into a diversity that may not be shaped out of an incoherence of
different roles, but construes itself into these roles as a sign of the dissimilar
plenitude of God's oneness. To put it differently, the realization of God's subjective self-identity subsists in its continuous movement into self-diversity.
This process is not the expression of an imperfection, of missing oneness, or
underlying incoherence, but the expression of supreme wealth: in God, the
inconsistent roles do not perish in finding coherent self-identity. In God, the
coherent self-identity gains everlasting roles as an expression of the wealth of
God's everlasting, self-diversifying, subjective process.

This is not contradictory to the theory according to which the process
results in a coherent "one," which, in reaching coherence, turns again into
"one under many," meaning new incoherence. The way of worldly being in
process, or the world's processual, everlasting essence, is not cancelled in
God through "conversion of the processes," although it is realized in a totally
different manner. Incoherence is an expression of the ultimacy of dissimilarity. In God, contrary to the process of the world, the final, coherent role
of the divine process is not shaping the *end*, but the *beginning* of the divine
process. The everlasting unfolding of this ultimate being of God into many
roles, embodying the expression of the process as incoherence, is the *expression* of coherence without losing the *meaning* of incoherent dissimilarity. To
put it differently, God's many roles are the expression of primordial coherence in the meaning of incoherence.[16] But this is not, as one might think, a
contradiction within Whitehead's categories;

on the contrary. Whitehead's concept of coherence, as explained
above, does not demand that the terms that are conceived as coherent to one
another are to be inferred from one another. In this case, God's Being is to
be understood as an everlasting, coherent process within God's roles, which
are un-deducible from one another, having *ultimate character* in God.

The origination of such roles in God's process provides a structure that
allows us to ground theologically a trinitarian interpretation within the following supporting features.

---

16. This is the remaining Heraclitan side of Whitehead's thinking. Heraclitus' famous statement says that "*struggle* is the origin of the universe," insofar as it makes the
process ongoing and grounds the world as process: "*Polemos panton men pater esti . . .*"
(*Fragment 53*).

1. The process of an actual entity constitutes itself out of those elements it objectifies through prehension from its preceding actual world, and it proceeds to integrate these elements as a requirement of coherence. Each concrescent process passes through a functionalization of all prehensions in which all reach a defined, unmistakable, self-consistent function, reaching a coherent state in satisfaction. In the "conversion of processes," God's becoming will articulate itself in such complex, self-consistent functions. With that corresponds the intrinsically divine process of the realization of trinitarian structures in which each divine person stands in an appointed, unmistakable relation with the other persons, defining them to some extent.

2. The origin and meaning of the word and concept "prehension" is explained by Whitehead with reference to the ancient word "appropriation":

> In a genetic theory the cell is exhibited as appropriating for the foundation of its own existence, the various elements of the universe out of which it arises. Each process of appropriation of a particular element is termed a prehension. The ultimate elements of the universe, thus appropriated, are the already constituted actual entities, and the eternal objects. (PR, 219)

"Appropriation" means to make of something private property.[17] This is an ancient trinitarian theological term expressing the sense in which it is possible to assign the divine actions corresponding to the world's creation, redemption, and justification, to the different divine persons, because these actions have a certain kinship to the "properties" of the persons that differentiate them from one another.[18] Theologically, in "conversion of the processes," the appropriation happens not for gaining coherence, but as the unfolding of divine plenitude within God's self-giving to the world. Appropriation is the development of primordial, coherent, multiple divine roles that represent everlasting, personal properties in God.

3. Each process runs through different phases of unification, of gaining coherence (PR, 215). Each phase then is a part-process with its own task, its own depth, and its own importance:

> [An event] . . . suffers simplification in the successive phases of the concrescence. It starts with conditioned alternatives, and by successive decisions is reduced to coherence. The many feelings, in any incomplete phase are necessarily comparable with each other by reason of their individual conformity to the subjective end for that phase (PR, 224) . . . The subject . . . passes from a

---

17. Hampe, *Wahrnehmungen der Organismen*, 113, 131.
18. Schmaus, "Appropriationen," 774.

subjective aim in concrescence into a superject with objective immortality. At any stage it is subject-superject. (PR, 245)

It is remarkable that each process has to reach in each of its phases an unmistakable "subjective end," a point of coherence, even if it is imperfect, which at the same time means a certain self-reliance and completeness: each phase is peculiar in its own superjectivity. For God's becoming, in "conversion of processes," this has the consequence of a defined superjectivity for each phase of its process. Each of these phases, then, has its own "subjective end," and its own superjectivity, which establishes it as an unmistakable, coherent role in God's process. The everlasting roles of God form God's own superjectivity, and each role has its own unmistakable subjective end that characterizes it as permanently dissimilar to all others in the same process. If we further take into account all of this as a process of coherence, that means a reciprocal presupposition of non-deducible ultimacy, in which self-identity is realized *as* self-diversity. The way is then paved for an understanding not only of God's identity, but also of God's coherent, everlasting diversity as due to original and irreducible dissimilarity, such as would be demanded for a trinitarian theology.[19]

4. For the divine "conversion of processes," God's "phases" and roles develop neither the seriality of temporal moments, following one another, nor are they ordered successively. If all processes of becoming are forms of nontemporal, nonserial concrescence, this holds, in a very real sense, for God's becoming, which is to be as a nontemporal actuality and, at the same time, as a nonderivative actuality *(PR, 32)*. This nonseriality of God is also a certain form of nonsuccessivity, insofar as it is based on God's unfolding into phases and roles as signs of God's infinite superflow of novelty, God's superplenitude. There is no reason why this could not have also the appearance of *multiple, simultaneous communication* of the roles. God's simultaneous roles, representing God's properties within God's process, become with one another in simultaneity, although they exhibit irreversible relations of origin, and with that, equal succession.

Thus, a certain kind of "becoming within phases" can remain meaningful for the roles, considering the multiple unfolding of the process of the divine subjectivity. Entirely in the sense of the ancient trinitarian theology, it is the "one essence" that "subsists" in each divine person that permits at the same time "relations of origin" within God that are irreversible. This was

---

19. See for instance, the statement of Hans Urs von Balthasar in *Theodramatik IV*, 67–68: God is intrinsically "'ewige Bewegtheit,' da die göttlichen Hervorgänge und der darauf gründende Austausch der Personen nicht zeitlich begrenzt, sondern ewig aktuell sind. Ewig heißt hier zugleich unendlich, was . . . nur durch einen ins Je-Größere offenen Komparativ ausdrückbarst."

formulated at the Fourth Lateran Council in context of the problem of analogy as follows: *Pater in Filium transtulerit suam substantiam.*[20]

A text of Latin tradition, thus, reflects a Greek conception of the Trinity that lets the godhead find its supreme, intrinsic unity within the Father, because the Father gives his essence away to the Son who receives it as given. The Father is "Father" by reason of *diversity* of the persons, and at the same time, is the reason for the *identity* of the godhead. In the Father, the one godhead gets the "head of God." This irreversible, logical "pre" of the Father in God, this form of "successivity" that expresses at the same time also a permanent, eternal simultaneity of the persons, can be in a process mode interpreted through an everlasting communication of God's roles that proceed within irreversible phases of everlasting origination.

5. In the diversity of the roles in God's process, there is an interesting terminological and material congeniality with the ancient term *person*. The original Greek-Latin meaning of *persona/prosopon* goes back to the Persian conception of a mask carried by an actor in the tragedy, embodying a role. Throughout the drama, the role "sounds" the identity of the character it embodies ("*per-sona*" etymologically means "sound-through"). Even Whitehead was guided by this original connection between role and character in his specific concept of person, because he defines a social nexus with serial order:

> It might have been termed a "person," in the legal sense of that term. But unfortunately "person" suggests a notion of consciousness, so that its use would lead to misunderstanding. The nexus "sustains a character" and this is one of the meanings of the Latin word "persona." (PR, 35)

6. The question concerning seriality, which was explicitly excluded from the structure of processes by Whitehead, leads us to a last aspect illumining the roles in God's process. If, as discussed, God's process proceeds conversely to that of the world, then we are explicitly to pay attention to the new relationship between subjectivity and objectivity, or differently: to the meaning of primordial superjectivity. Since God is everlastingly "given away" in the wealth of self-identity *as* self-diversity, we must redefine the difference between seriality and successivity, or between actuality and nexus. For the objective efficiency of worldly actualities it means: "Thus 'perishing' is the assumption of a role in a transcendent future. The not-being of occasions is their objective immortality (AI, 237).

---

20. HD, 805.

Contrarily, for God this means: The roles that God entertains in everlasting concrescence are already God's superjective roles through which God transitionally determines the world. In this manner, the transitional character of seriality turns into an intrinsically divine realization of concrescent successivity within the simultaneity of God's everlasting self-diversity of roles, allowing us to speak of persons in God.

Conclusion

I have attempted to show the meaningful possibility of fruitfully connecting different traditions, of different ages and distinct origins. There are elements in the classical tradition of the doctrine of Trinity, and within recent trinitarian theology, that we can interpret in reference to an internal relation between God and the world. Therefore, a modified theory of analogy has been shown as a veritable, process-theologically founded structure. In its mediative role, it translates both trinitarian theology and process theology into one another with consistency. Thus, I have shown in what sense a process-theological understanding of Trinity is feasible and attainable in the context of Whitehead's categories.

By being the superject of creativity out of independent dissimilarity, God's innermost being can give itself into everlastingly coherent roles within an eternally ongoing movement toward novelty, and within the overflowing of God's existence. Therefore, God can stand in real relation with the world. The divine "persons" can express this real relation without forcing God to such roles as an outcome of God's relationship to the world. The everlasting roles of God are not a sign of imperfection, but God's primordial character of plenitude.

Within a process-theological perspective, it must metaphysically remain open in which kind of roles God would become concrete, and how such roles would appear. Not every individual prehension must develop a role; on the contrary, a complex of appropriations can also represent a complex structure that can unfold itself as a single role. And not every role is per se a primordial role of God's unfathomable, ultimate plenitude, in the emphatic sense elaborated above. Here, the principles and categories allow a huge flexibility. And it is also just this flexibility that allows us to draw a plain line between philosophical and theological speech of God in the context of the process paradigm. If to elaborate a doctrine of the trinity, one wants to appeal to the roles in the process of concretization, then, philosophically, there is an explanation coherent with the process of origination of the world as it realizes itself in the *res verae*, and primordially in God. But on the other side, of course, it is only a possible explanation. Therefore, from the perspective of process theology, there is no unavoidable requirement to understand the structures of the world in a trinitarian way. Finally, this is a question of concreteness and, therefore, of the Principle of Concretion that is embodied by God. It is a question of history and experience, or theologically speaking, of God's self-revelation in history with the world.

CHAPTER ELEVEN

The Process of Revelation

TIME AND AGAIN, PROCESS theology has been accused of reducing theology to metaphysics, thereby eliminating the genuine source of theology, i.e., the experience of God's revealing reality. In this regard, one recalls Langdon Gilkey who deplored this collapse of all problems to metaphysical problems.[1] According to Gilkey, the problem with "metaphysics" occurs when it loses its flowing, critical structure and begins to solidify into a constructional, systematic theory. Then, process theology seems to mutate into a guardian of a *true*, if not the *only* true, metaphysical theory. Consequently, the traditions of revelation devolve to mere variables of the solidified metaphysical constant. Moreover, the unique events relevant to theology, the genuine intuition of religious experience, and revelation-theological reflection cannot reach into the metaphysical core anymore and at all.[2] David Pailin appropriately summarizes this process-theological confession for the dissolution of revealed theology into general metaphysics in saying:

> God is active in all events, however difficult it may be in practice to identify his particular influence on and purpose in them. From this it follows that the distinction between natural and revealed theology is alien to a Whiteheadian understanding, whether the natural theology is empirical derived (cf. Paley and Tennet) or more metaphysically oriented (cf. Aquinas' five "ways," especially the first four). A "process theology" that is true to Whiteheadian (and Hartshornean) insight does not provide a case for affirming certain limited affirmations about the reality of God which are then to be augmented by a distinct kind of

1. Gilkey, "Process Theology," 5–29.

2. This was the criticism brilliantly addressed by Gilkey. On the part of process theology, rarely has anyone really offered an answer, with an exception perhaps in Bernard Loomer, who understood himself as a theologian, to whom metaphysics interprets, but not constitutes "revelation."

"revealed theology." Rather it derives its theological understanding from the character and processes of reality in all its aspects.[3]

Nevertheless, in order to understand the *genuine* sources from which
theology legitimizes its irreplaceable intuition, and in order to preserve the
revelation-theological relevance of process-theological theory, we may contrast the main position of process theology by identifying the counter question: Can there be found any genuine place for a revealed theology within
Whitehead's work so that theology does not have to be *subordinated* to general metaphysics but, rather, find its connection to metaphysics in *mutual*
influence?[4] Affirming this question, the thesis will be presented that, *first*,
Whitehead knows of, or at least implicitly enables us to understand, a *genuine*
claim of revelation which cannot be justified *metaphysically* (without being
metaphysically irrelevant); and that, *secondly*, metaphysics becomes relativistic in the view of a genuine revealed theology. The somehow negative-theo-
logical solution desired in this twofold thesis reads as follows: God's revelation
cannot be grasped either *non-historically* by metaphysical categories alone or
non-eschatologically by historical events already passed.

I will present my thesis in two parts. First, I will reflect on the non-
metaphysical nature of revelation, its uniqueness, and some hypotheses affirming the project of a genuine revealed theology in the context of process
theology. Secondly, I will try to support the possibility of a process-theological notion of genuine revelation by pleading for a more fluid interpretation
of the relation of metaphysics and theology.

Part I: "Universality of the Singular": Three Reflections
on the Non-Metaphysical Origin of Revelation

Religious Intuition: "Special Occasions"

In Whitehead's "theory of religion," the development of religion leads
(at least in its last level that we know of) to a *rationalization* of religious

---

3. Pailin, "God as Creator," 285. Further: "A 'process theology' that is true to Whiteheadian (and Hartshornean) insights does not provide a case for affirming certain limited affirmations about the reality of God which are then to be augmented by a distinct
kind of 'revelational theology.' Rather it derives its theological understanding from the
character and processes of reality in all its aspects and taken as an inter-locking whole
throughout which God is creatively active even though [sic!] it may consider that God's
activity is more apparent in some series of events than in others."

4. Whitehead himself notes this "mutual dependence" of metaphysics and religion.
Cf. RM, 79.

experience (RM, 20–36).[5] Although, at first, religious concerns were preoccupied with rituals, partial myths, and emotional stabilization, later religious
consciousness evolved increasingly towards the recognition of universal
connectivity, leaving behind provincial rituals and social bindings (RM,
28). For Whitehead, this process of the "rationalization" of religion occurs
within reciprocal movements towards *solitariness* and *solidarity*. Together,
these opposite features reveal the meaning of "religious intuition," namely,
to be the *universal mediation of uniquely experienced events*.

In Whitehead's words: The contrast of *singularity* and *universality*,
solitariness and *solidarity*, illuminates "the origin of rational religion" (RM,
58). "Religion is what the individual does with his own solitariness" (RM,
16) *and* "religion is world-loyalty" (RM, 59). In this contrast, the religious
experience of uniqueness is both the experience of "solitariness" *and* that
of the "loyalty" to the world (RM, 86). It is this two-faced structure that
expresses Whitehead's theory of "religious intuition":

> Rational religion appeals to the direct intuition of special occa-
> sions, and to the elucidatory power of its concepts for all occa-
> sions. It arises from that which is special, but it extends to what
> is general. The doctrines of rational religion aim at being that
> metaphysics which can be derived from the super-normal ex-
> perience of mankind in its moments of finest insight. (RM, 31)

"Religious intuition," as analyzed, has two aspects, or directions of
motion: (1) *Singularity*: religious intuition is a "*direct* intuition" which
cannot be resolved by general terms (rationality, metaphysics), but may
only be *experienced*. Hence, religious intuition cannot be conceptualized
completely, but is bound to the *uniqueness* of the experienced over against
all conceptual generality (RM, 65).[6] And in this *unpronounceable* uniqueness, religious intuition constitutes "the ultimate religious evidence,
beyond which there is no appeal" (RM, 65). (2) *Rationality*: although
"intuitions" occur as events under *unique* conditions, they must, due to
their accessibility for others, be subject to a process of communicability by
theoretical transformation, i.e., the process of their "*rationalization*" (RM,
63).[7] "Intuitions," as it were, introduce the uniquely "new" into the world.

5. Lowe, *Alfred North Whitehead*, 116, and Wilmot, *Whitehead and God*, 19–29. For
Whitehead's theory of the four steps of the development of religion cf. Welker, "A. N.
Whitehead," 287–91.

6. Whitehead in fact compares this experience of the unpronounceable that is, nevertheless, known, with the knowledge of mothers, who "can ponder many things in
their hearts which their lips cannot express" (RM, 65).

7. "But reason is the safeguard of the objectivity of religion: it secures for it the
general coherence denied to hysteria" (RM, 63).

However, at the same time, they must be generalized to be accessible *for* others experience.[8] Or, as Whitehead says, the relevance of its concepts can only be distinctly discerned in moments of insight, and then, for many of us, only after suggestion from without.

It is important to realize that, in Whitehead's thought, "religious intuition" has *irreplaceable* meaning for any general "theory of the world." On the one hand, it allows for a unique base of experience, or "one select field of interest" (RM, 86).[9] On the other hand, it maintains that concepts of religion, "though derived primarily from special experiences, are yet of universal validity" (RM, 31). For a general theory of the world, the *irreplaceable* contribution of *religious* experience consists in the fact that it proceeds from the "supernormal experience of mankind in its moment of finest insight" (ibid.).

Revelation, Part I: "Feelings Feel Particular Existents"

As Johann Baptist Metz and John Cobb have seen in correspondence, it is the *memoria* of the Christ-event that plays a crucial role in the theological notion of revelation.[10] In this view, a certain historical tradition of narration and reflection recalls the experience of a unique revealing event by memory. Nevertheless, *universality* comes to this historical revelation only if it *remains* itself "in experience" for different generations (although modified and under different conditions). This is the function of *memoria or anamnesis*. Hence, theological reflection on the revelation of God is founded historically, by *the universal relevance of unique events*. Or in turn: *only singular events have universal meaning*.[11]

In order to interpret this core-principle of revelation, we must understand its essential presupposition; namely, that events are *present* "in" other events—present not just abstractly (through "eternal objects"), i.e., mediated by the "general," but *as* singular events that effect their further

---

8. This applies in particular to the religious experience, in which "novelty" cannot be expressed by any "formula." Nevertheless, religious experience becomes (and remains) accessible by its rational generalization (RM, 129ff.). See a quite similar description of "intuition" in Lachmann, *Ethik und Identität*, 84–88.

9. See the formulas of RM, 31: "a small selection from the common experience," or "one among other specialized interests of mankind whose truths are of limited validity."

10. John Cobb takes account of this central moment of Metz's theology, namely, the *memoria*, while generalizing it at the same time. Cf. Cobb, *Process Theology as Political Theology*, 51–53.

11. In Christian theology, Jesus Christ is understood as revealing-event, as *universale concretum*.

history by their *unique* concreteness (PR, 338).[12] Whitehead recognizes precisely this constellation when he says: "[T]he truism that we can only conceive in terms of universals has been stretched to mean that we can only feel in terms of universals. This is untrue. Our perceptual feelings feel particular existents . . . " (PR, 230).

A first step to obtaining an understanding of the presence of unique revelational events in others can be made by applying Whitehead's theory of hybrid prehension. In short, and already centered on the our problem, we can say: in a "completely living nexus," mental prehensions, whereby novelty enters into events, have a *particular form.* They can be passed from occasion to occasion in a *certain completeness* (PR, 161) because, in each case, the occasions following their predecessors are not objectified in their physicality, but in their mentality (PR, 245–247). Whitehead speaks both of a direct, *non*-mediated immanence of occasions (PR, 226) and of direct, *non*-physically *mediated* contact of mental prehensions of occasions lying far apart physically (PR, 307–308).[13] The universality of unique revealing events, thus, lives by "an element of immediacy in the relations of the mental side" (AI, 248) of occasions that constitute a historical route. We may even think of a kind of "transmutational" character of this mentally connected thread of occasions (according to Whitehead's Category of Obligation VI: PR, 27) in which we recognize the historical route of revelational occasions as *one* "revelational event."[14]

Now, we can further investigate the *character* of this "immanence" of the singularities by introducing Gilles Deleuze's theory of the "universality of the singular." In his main work, *Difference and Repetition* (1968), he has shown why the conception of *concrete immediacy* in and between occasions

12. Generally, process thought holds that occasions can be present in other occasions only by simultaneous abstraction of their uniqueness. Whitehead agrees. In his early work, he had offered an analysis of "events" as unique and of "objects" as that which, can ingrediate as the repeatable within several events (CN, 169).

13. Griffin, "Hartshorne, God, and Relativity Physics," 88–95. PR, 226 stresses that, although between event A and D still are events B and C, D does not only mediate by B and C, but appears to be directly connected as a *physical* cause of A. PR, 308 speaks of "hybrid physical prehensions." Mental prehensions are subject to "immediate objectification" in contrast to the "mediate objectification" of physical prehensions. Thus, "universal, but concrete effectiveness" can take place by means of "hybrid prehensions" of passed events regarding their identity-forming novelty ("mentality") in an immediacy of actualization, which cannot sufficiently be attained by any physical causality. Cf. in addition Hamilton, *The Living God*, 82–86.

14. See Whitehead's definition of "event" in PR, 73, in which he forged "the difference between actual occasions comprised in some determined event." For the objective character of the transmutation in the defining characteristic of the nexus of occasions itself cf. AI, 213.

must not be considered *naive* in a post-Hegelian sense, but post-*Hegelian* altogether.[15] In order to achieve this aim, Deleuze replaces the categorization of the world into *the general* and *the individual* in favor of the distinction of *the universal* and *the singular*.[16] On the level of abstraction, "mediation" describes the analysis of that which is subjected to a "law." The "singular," on the other hand, is *not* mediated by "laws," but is *directly* effective in *universality*.[17] Under the paradigm of the "general," there is no "uniqueness." The "general," i.e., a "law," permits only "something similar" or "the same," yet the character of the similar is that it is *exchangeable* under a general law. Contrary to the "general," it is the essence of the "unique" *not* to be "exchangeable." Paradoxically, the "singular" can only be *repeated*. Therein, however, it is *universally* effective:

> The exchange . . . of particulars defines our conduct in relation to generality. By contrast, we can see that repetition is a necessary . . . conduct only in relation to that which cannot be replaced. Repetition as a conduct . . . concerns non-exchangeable and non-substitutable singularities . . . Generality, as generality of the particular, thus stands opposed to repetition as universality of the singular.[18]

Deleuze's idea of the "repetition" as "universality of the singular" may interpret Whitehead's idea of "repetition," i.e., the apparent paradox that only the *unrepeatable* become present in other occasions by a "conformal transference of subjective form."[19] Like Deleuze, Whitehead's "repetition" does not

15. This is the reproach against Whitehead's thesis of "immediacy" which in PR 25, Cat. Expl., XXIII, constitutes the "subjectivity" of events, i.e., their privateness that cannot be objectified. Hegel's notion of "concept," which is a process of dialectic mediation, leaves us with the impression of abstractness; cf. Kline, "Begriff und Konkreszenz," 150–51. As Deleuze, writes, the "objection to Hegel is that he does not go beyond false movement—in other words, the abstract logical movement of 'mediation'" (Deleuze, *Difference and Repetition*, 8).

16. Deleuze, *Difference and Repetition*, 70–128.

17. Ibid., 10: "This is what we are told: this movement, the essence, and the inferiority of movement, is *not opposition, not mediation,* but repetition. Hegel is the one who is denounced as the one who proposes an abstract movement of concepts instead of the Physis and the Psyche. Hegel substitutes the abstract relation of the particular to the concept in general for the true relation of the singular and the universal in the Idea . . . We must see how Hegel betrays and distorts the immediate in order to ground his dialectic in that incomprehension, and to introduce mediation in a movement which is no more than that of his own thought and its generalities."

18. Ibid., 1.

19. Nobo, *Whitehead's Metaphysics*, 18–19, 61–106, builds his understanding of "causality" on this notion. See Deleuze, *Difference and Repetition*, 1–2. For elucidation of the difference of the repetition of the singular to the forming of laws, Deleuze points

mean the "repetition of the being," i.e., that which *was*, and it does not indicate any *new* realization of what is "similar." Such process would create merely an exchangeable similarity under the paradigm of the general. Instead, "repetition" states and confirms the *un*repeatable. Again, Deleuze:

> [Repetitions] do not add a second and a third time to the first, but carry the first time to the "nth" power. With respect to this power, repetition interiorizes and thereby reverses itself: as Peguy says, it is not federation Day which commemorates or represents the fall of the Bastille, but the fall of the Bastille, which celebrates and repeats in advance all the Federation days.[20]

What can we gain by this notion of "universality?" Since "universality" no longer justifies itself by "exemplary instantiations" of laws and rules, but proceeds as the *universal effectiveness of the unique*, this structure enables us to understand how *singular events* can become reasons of *universal revealing*.

Revelation, Part II: "Transcendence is Self-Revelation"

I have tried to prepare the ground for a process-theological speech of "revelation." *First*, a unique revealing event cannot be conceptually exhausted or completely resolved into any system; it cannot be completely contained by any generality or, in its specific singularity, removed by any general experience. In its *singularity*, the revealing event is *transcendent*, i.e., irreplaceable with "generality."[21] *Second*, the revealing event, nevertheless, is universal. It repeats itself in its singularity in other events that memorize and re-activate it. In its *universality*, the revealing event is *immanent*, i.e., immediately effective in other events.[22]

---

to Kant's paradigm of the "Categorical Imperative" which states an individual standard as general law of the same or similar actions, and opposes it to Nietzsche's anti-legalistic postulate of the "eternal return": It's the repetition of the singular which cannot be understood by any law. In Deleuze's interpretation, Nietzsche's "will to power" represents precisely the will of the singular in its universal potensation; see Deleuze, *Difference and Repetition*, 5–11.

20. Deleuze, *Difference and Repetition*, 1. Theologically, this is of crucial importance for the presence of a unique event through its history, for instance for the memory of the death of Christ in the Eucharist.

21. Here, we apply the "ontological principle" which, in this context, means that history must not only be interpreted either by reason or by communication, but in the light of the "diachronic transcendence" of past and future events.

22. Note that a new event does not decide to "repeat" the revealing event, rather the revealing event repeats itself in certain way with its own power. The new event is always already a reaction to this revelation.

"Universalization" of singular revealing events names the "repetition of the unrepeatable." And this process must be recognized as a "transference" of the internal essence of one occasion to others by which the transferred event sacrifices its internality, uniqueness, and immediacy. The self-transcendence of any event, which makes it immanent for others, does not, however, only signify a process of "objectification," loss, and what Whitehead called "objective immortality," but it highlights the "repetition" of the singular *as* singular. Finally, *this* is the process of what Whitehead calls "self-revelation."

> Each actual entity is a cell with atomic unity. But in analyses it can only be understood as a process; it can only be felt as a process, that is to say, as in passage. The actual entity is divisible, but is in fact undivided. The divisibility can thus only refer to its objectification in which it transcends itself. But such transcendence is self-revelation. (PR, 227)

In its self-transcendence, each and every occasion is the *self-revelation of its singularity* for and in other events. At least three elementary consequences may follow for a theological understanding of "revelation" in process theology:

(1) *God's nature is God's self-revelation.* God reveals God's nature *as* relational, *as* all-relating, *as* essentially "pro-existent."[23] More precisely: God's *nature* is God's self-*transcendence* which is God's self-*revelation*. Such divine self-revelation covers the infinite abundance of God's graceful affection for the world, but also God's self-sacrificing and kenotic emptying.[24]

(2) *"Repetition" is the universal effectiveness of the singular revealing events within their concrete history.* Objections notwithstanding, in terms of its universality, God's self-revelation is related to a concrete history of unique

23. Both the "primordially nature" and "consequent nature" are defined as "objectively immortal" (PR, 32), i.e., they are *relatively related* to the world; see the "relativity principle." Here, we do not want to hold that God must reveal Godself *ad extra*, but that the internal reference of God to everything that is not God is of a *relational* type, i.e., essential for world events and their nexic connections beyond the difference of God's "nature" and "will."

24. It is not presupposed, however, that God's nature already is kenotic "from eternity." That opinion would be based on a gnostic misinterpretation for which the highest form of love is painful renouncing and suffering love. Against this misinterpretation, cf. Faber, *Selbsteinsatz*, 405–20. Here, rather, I understand God's nature as always already receptic and pathic; cf. Ford, "Whitehead's Transformation of Pure Act," 382. In this sense, God's nature is always already empty. See also the Buddhist interpretation of Whitehead's notion of God in Inada, "Metaphysics of Buddhist Experience," 465–88, and Odin, "Metaphysics of Cumulative Penetration," 65ff. See also Whitehead's note that the essence of a thing is to be *prehensive*, receptive, and relational (PR, 41).

events. Revealing events, as it were, constitute a history of the *anamnesis of their singularity.*[25] Their uniqueness cannot be extracted theoretically from the history of revealing events. Instead, it is the coming history in which the revealing event "repeats" itself. It has its own power to "re-enact" itself.[26]

(3) *It is the function of theology to universalize its "own contribution of the immediate experience"* (RM, 77). Consequently, the immediacy of the singular revealing event, which becomes universally "repeated" within the feelings of other events, preserves an irreplaceable element that cannot be reduced to metaphysical conceptuality—namely religious intuition's "super-normal experience of mankind in its moments of finest insight" (RM, 31).[27]

Part II: "No Triumphs of Finality": Three Reflections on Metaphysics and Revelational Theology

Revelation within Metaphysics: "Extension to What is General"

It is questionable whether Whitehead would have ever introduced "God" to his metaphysics if he had not been convinced of the *religious,* i.e., non-metaphysical, meaning of the notion of God.[28] Whitehead consciously developed his cosmology in the context of an "immediate comparison with the deliverances of religious experience" (RM, 87). He knew that "whatever suggests a cosmology, suggests a religion" (RM, 136). Indeed, as some interpreters have noticed, Whitehead's cosmological vocabulary is "itself of an elementary theological meaning."[29] But no earlier than in Whitehead's *Adventures*

25. It is justified to distinguish a "final revelation" from a "complete revelation," as Cobb already knew in his dissertation. The uniqueness of the Christ event justifies its universality *and* an open-endedness at the same time. Cf. Cobb, "Independence of Christian Faith," 155.

26. One can say that Whitehead knows of the distinction between a general and a special history of revelation. Whereas the general history of revelation relates to the "subjective aims" of all events (and God's presence in them), the special history of revelation is connected with the universality of certain events. Cf. Hosinski, *Stubborn Fact,* 231.

27. Then, the "singular" would lose its "universality" thereby gaining "generality." But "generality" would make it "exchangeable."

28. Hosinski, *Stubborn Fact,* 178 n. 2: "Clearly, Whitehead would not have introduced the concept of God into his philosophy if he judged that there was no presence of God which supported his concept."

29. The original text is written in German: ". . . *selbst eine elementare theologische Bedeutung,"* in Koch, "Schöpferischer Lockruf," 146. Whitehead's stream of thought, however, is not, by any means, "dictating to him a specific view of God," as A. H. Johnson has said. Cf. Johnson, *Whitehead's Philosophy of Civilisation,* 82. One can differentiate between a metaphysical and a religious function of Whitehead's notion of "God."

of Ideas does the philosophical relevance of revelation-theological content assume reflexive shape.[30]

Especially in his sketch of the general development of European metaphysics within "three steps" (AI, 166–167), Whitehead realizes two transitions: first, from the primordial "intellectual discovery" of Plato to the "exemplification" of its contents in Jesus' life; then, secondly, from the Christ event to its "metaphysical interpretation" within the generalizations of the Alexandrian theology (AI, 166). In Jesus' life of "non-violence," Whitehead finds *in actu* what Plato constructed *in menter*, *the* true "Icon" of the divine nature as the Eros of self-transcendence and as self-revealed power of persuasion (AI, 167; RM, 19).[31] The Alexandrian theology again rationalized the unique power of the Christ-event, thereby generalizing what has been the novelty of the revealing event over against Plato's metaphysical suggestions; namely, the modes of "mutual immanence" of singular actualities.

Although one can expect, to a certain extent, such an influence of revealed theology on the developments of metaphysics, especially in the

---

Cf. for example Cobb, "Independence of Christian Faith," 150–51, who discerns the "secular function" of God concerning "eternal objects" from God's "religious function." Cf. also Lederer, "The Term 'God' in Whitehead's Philosophy," 35ff., who speaks of a "God of the religion" within Whitehead, apart from a metaphysical notion of "God." The soteriological dimension, however, cannot be exhausted by metaphysics. With poetic weight, Whitehead formulates that events—by themselves and without God—are a "flash of occasional enjoyments lightening up a mass of pain and misery, a bagatelle of transient experience" (SMW, 192); cf. Lowe, *Alfred North Whitehead*, 188. The world "process" contains motions of adventure and tragedy: "The Adventure of the Universe starts with the dream and reaps tragic Beauty" (AI, 296). Hence, the world-process and human beings are "haunted by a vague insistence of another order, where there is no unrest, no travel, no shipwreck: 'There shall be no more sea'" (PR, 340).

30. It was the "Galilean vision" that Jesus had of a God of love that influenced Whitehead's cosmology in its basic constellations (PR, 343). In defending such a genuine Christian vision of God working in the world by means of "persuasion," weakness, and love, he was disappointed by the penetration of the later Christian theology of anthropomorphic ideas of "God" (ruler, moralist, first mover). Cf. Price, *Dialogues*, 174: "I consider Christian theology to be one of the great disasters of the human race." Later, Whitehead explains the division of the understanding of God into the vision of Jesus of a loving God and God as a ruler, on the other hand, from which Whitehead felt deeply repelled (175–76). Later theology for Whitehead, hence, distorted Jesus' vision of "gentleness and mercy" by an "old ferocious God . . . the Oriental depot, the Pharaoh, the Hitler; with everything to enforce obedience, from infant damnation and eternal punishment" (176).

31. Also AI, 167: ". . . the life of Christ as a revelation of the nature of God and of his agency the world . . . The Mother, the Child, and the bare manger: the lowly man, homeless and self-forgetful, with his message of peace, love, and sympathy: the suffering, the agony, the tender words as life ebbed, the final despair: and the whole with the authority of supreme victory."

context of Whitehead's theory of "religious intuition," Whitehead appreciates the Alexandrian theology not for its specific content and "highly special form" (AI, 167), but to the extent that it suggests "the solution of a fundamental metaphysical problem" (AI, 167). Hence, Whitehead notes: "I am not making any judgment about the details of their theology, for example, about the Trinitarian doctrine" (AI, 169).

When Whitehead protests, however, that Alexandrian theology has "made no effort to conceive God in terms of the metaphysical categories which they applied to the World" (AI, 169), his claim does not conform to the implications of his own theory of "religious intuitions." The Alexandrines developed their Trinitarian theology, universalizing the Christ-event, so that the metaphysical categories arose *in the light* of the uniqueness of a revealing event. Whereas the general analysis of the structure of experience is philosophy's concern, theology, instead, interprets the general structures of experience *through* the uniqueness of the historical Christ-event. This "universalization" is the genuine contribution of revelational theology to the "generalizations" of metaphysics.

Metaphysics within Revelational Theology: "The Way in which the Human Spirit Cultivates its Deeper Intuitions"

Laurence Wilmot has proposed the reasonable thesis that Whitehead's metaphysical vision and the advancement of his metaphysical categories permit a correction *in the light* of the salvational reality of Christianity:

> ... Whitehead published *Adventures of Ideas*, in which he reports the data upon the basis of which he was able to revise his assessment of the relative values of the Platonic and the Christian conceptions of God and the World and in the light of which his metaphysical scheme may be revised and its inadequacies removed.[32]

Since generality permits only exchangeable relations, metaphysical systems of principles and categories represent a *general* order that cannot grasp the *singularity* of the events theology draws upon. As Deleuze writes, the "universality of the singular" is "by nature ... always revealing a singularity opposed to the particulars subsumed under laws, a universal opposed to the generalities which gave rise to law."[33]

32. Cf. Wilmot, *Whitehead and God*, 72.
33. Deleuze, *Difference and Repetition*, 5.

In the light of such a *critical* function of theology in relation to the generalizations of metaphysics, metaphysical "principles," "laws," and "categories" do not appear as (transcendental) conditions of *any possible* experience, but as that of *real* experience.[34] In a certain sense, Whitehead found a way to initialize a theological project without developing it; and he grounded it in the *imperfection* of all metaphysical systems in relation to actual events that have the power to reconstruct categories in the passage of the events. And, as Deleuze adds, the *actual imperfection* of the "list of empirico-ideal notions that we find in Whitehead . . . makes *Process and Reality* one of the greatest books of modern philosophy."[35]

From the theological reconstruction of metaphysics, we have gained a new principle concerning the relativity of metaphysical requirements. This principle reads: No a-historical matrix can ever deliver a "form" for *all possible* actualizations of *all possible future events*—hence, for singular events of revelation, too."[36] Since no "form" exists beyond its future actualizations, there is no "rule" or "law" that can determine future activity in such a way that the "rule" could not be changed by the future process of becoming.[37]

A crucial, but rarely examined paragraph in Whitehead's *Adventure of Ideas*, formulates the correction of metaphysics and allows its integration within revelational theology:

34. James Bradley undertook an attempt of such an interpretation in Bradley, "Transcendentalism," 155ff. Bruce Baugh defines this connection of the conviction to have an access to the process of *real* experience (and not the bare projection of it) and, at the same time, the specification of the conditions of the possibilities of this experience as "transcendental empiricism." Deleuze does not look for *necessary* conditions as Kant did, however, he finds *transcendental* conditions of actual experience; in Baugh, "Deleuze und der Empirismus," 34,

35. Deleuze, *Difference and Repetition*, 284–85.

36. Richard Rorty underlines that "the fundamental insight of a post-Heglian philosophy" is "the abandonment of a claim to a transhistoncal frame of orientation beyond linguistic differentiation," in Rorty, "Dewey," 3.

37. Jean-Francois Lyotard shows significant similarity to our reinterpretation of Whitehead's "ontological principle," when he notes: "*Ein postmoderner Künstler oder Schriftsteller ist in derselben Situation aie ein Philosoph: Der Text, den er scbreibt, das Werk, das er schafft, sind grundsätzlich nicht durch bereits feststehende Regeln geleitet und können nicht nach Maßgabe eines bestimmenden Urteils beurteilt werden, indem auf einen Text oder ein Werk nur bekannte Kategorien angewandt uerden. Diese Regeln und Kategorien sind vielmebr das, was der Text oder das Werk suchen. Künstler und Schrilftsteller arbeiten also ohne Regeln; sie arbeiten, um die Regeln dessen zu erstellen, was gemacht worden sein wird. Daber rührt, daß Werk und Text den Charakter eines Ereignisses haben. Daber rührt auch, daß sie fürihren Autor immer zu spät kommen oder, was auf dasselbe hinausläuft, daß die Arbeit an ihnen immer zu früh beginnt.* Postmodern *wäre also das Paradoxon der Vorzukunft* (post-modo) *denken*" (Lyotard "Beantwortung der Frage," 202–3).

> [P]hilosophic systems . . . are the way in which the human
> spirit cultivates its deeper intuitions . . . Even the discordance
> of comprehensive philosophical systems is a factor essential for
> progress . . . It is a step by step process, achieving no triumphs
> of finality. We cannot produce that final adjustment of well-de-
> fined generalities which constitute a complete metaphysics. But
> we can produce a variety of partial systems of limited generality
> . . . Also the discordance of system with system, and success of
> each system as a partial mode of illumination, warns us of the
> limitations within which our intuitions are hedged. These un-
> discovered limitations are the topics for philosophical research.
> (AI, 144–145)

This passage emphasizes the following main points: (1) no philosophical system can construct a perfect "system of eternal truths" for all possible
worlds, taken off from the run of things; (2) the relation of "system," "intuition," and "reality" is a *historical* process that does not contain a promise of
finality, i.e., of achieving final clarity and security of how things really are; (3)
despite Whitehead's consideration elsewhere, one cannot attain any coherent
metaphysics of *all possible worlds*. Even regarding a reasonable "cosmology"
as a theory of *this current* world, security is impossible; (4) in actual processes,
"rules" have the status of structural facts of already realized actualities rather
than that of any transcendental apriority. They do not indicate how a process
"functions," or *must* function, due to some underlying "law," but how it "will
have functioned" when it has already happened.[38]

This relativity of metaphysical systems enables us to keep our thought
open for a *non-metaphysical dimension of rationality*. Since the events of
self-revelation are *pre-regular*, they are a gift of novelty and of grace, rather
than a mere exemplification of faceless rules. The conception of the self-
revelation of God as radical novelty over against any world, highlights God's
radical *eschatological* breaking-through of all automatic self-containing
loops of rules.[39]

---

38. In this sense, the "ontological principle" may be interpreted not only as principle
of *history*, but as principle of *eschatology*. The past is justified in the present, which creatively follows no rule. The present, therefore, grounds in the future, which will create
its own rule for its appearance. "Continuity" implements itself in the self-revealing of
God as the promise of reconciliation *beyond* the repetition of the past. In a reversal of
the time-index of the "ontological principle," we do not know what rules the future will
set up for becoming.

39. While in metaphysics discontinuity is neutralized by a *general* pattern of things,
theology detects the *surprising salvation* of the old in the new. The Biblical passage,
found in Romans 3:21-25, exemplifies beautifully this structure. Discontinuity—the
act of salvation in Christi—creates "continuity" because it justifies the old as saved.

Christian Theology: The "Empirical Basis" of Soteriology

In summary of the argument so far, we may say that theology reflects the radical novelty and universality of singular events, which no concept can seize, but only the *events of anamnesis* can demonstrate.[40] In his "general principle of empiricism," Whitehead appropriately realizes this "anamnetic structure" of theology, when he writes: "[T]he general principle of empiricism depends upon the doctrine that there is a principle of concretion which is not discoverable by abstract reason. What further can be known about God must be rest on an empirical basis (SMW, 178).

That is to say at least the following: God does *not* enter into metaphysics as a system seeking to interpret the most general structures of experience in the world (PR, 3). Prior to the general structures explored by "abstract reason," *concrete actuality* happens, i.e., a concrete *history* of the self-revelation of God that is not replaceable by any philosophical rationality (MT, 89; RM, 79).[41]

Since metaphysics investigates general structures *beyond* any specific basis of any special experience, it is understandable that it abandons the religious base of general structures of experience. The philosophical "God" is understood, if not independently of religious intuition, then definitely beyond its singular appearance (RM, 88).[42] Over against the philosophical approach, Christianity developed the double strategy which we have analyzed as "religious intuition" contributing finally to the formation of

40. Here, the importance of the structure of *anamnesis* can function for a process theological interpretation of the presence of Christ in the Christian liturgy.

41. Whitehead underlines the indispensability of the uniqueness of religious experience for the "generalizations" of metaphysics, saying that the "rational religion must have recourse to metaphysics . . . At the same time it contributes its own independent evidence, which metaphysics must take account of in framing its description" (RM, 79).

42. Whitehead can thus speak of the "secularization" the notion of "God" in making it independent of any special religious intuition: "[T]he concept of religious feeling is not an essential element in the concept of God's function in the universe" (PR, 207). Whitehead does not want to negate religious experience, but, in defining a *philosophic* meaning of "God" within a general "theory of the world," he excludes it. As Hosinski, *Stubborn Fact*, 23, proposed, Whitehead interprets "religious intuition" and "God-experience" in reciprocal connection. God is not only subject to religious experience, but also of "secular experiences." There exists a difference between both, but not in the difference of the object (the religion, the cosmology); rather, in the "subjective form" of the experience, i.e., the way in which the "object" is assumed. In "secular experience," God appears to be one of those general "factors which are either non-actual or non-temporal, disclosed in the analysis of what is both actual and temporal" (RM, 87). For the analysis of the items "non actual," "non temporal," "actual," and "temporal," which represent the Aristotelian side Whitehead's notion of "God," cf. Dalferth, "Die theoretische Theologie," 163–75.

revelational theology:[43] (1) Christianity proceeded not *from* any metaphysics, but it "has always been a religion seeking a metaphysics" (RM, 50).[44] Christianity strove for theological *rationalization*;[45] (2) Christianity, however, did not follow any *certain* metaphysics (PR, 66–68), but "has been true to its genius for keeping its metaphysics subordinate to the religious fact to which it appeals" (RM, 69). Christianity understands itself in its linkage to the unique Christ-event and its *anamnesis* (RM, 55).[46] Only in the process of a permanent critical revision of theological terms, the events, upon which theology reflects, can be "re-presented" (come into presence again) and—in *anamnesis*—may be "re-activated."

The notion of "*Christian* theology," then, means that a singular revealing event, i.e., the Christ-event, dwells as the focal point of Christian religious intuition. This theology, however, does not deal with its revealing event in order to transform it into a sample of a general patterns of how things are; rather, theology tries to understand its very singularity. It is the

43. Every religion stands within the uniqueness of religious intuition (whereby intuitions also can contradict or have a volatile character, without losing the character of intuitions: cf. FR, 38; PR 13; MT, 50) *and* general theory about "the nature of things" (RM, 49). Not every religion, however, creates a "theology." For Whitehead, the specific feature of Christianity exists in the essential relation it maintains to its unique revelatory event—the Christ event (RM, 55).

44. See RM, 50: "Buddhism is the most colossal example in history of applied metaphysics."

45. *Rationalization:* Theology is the movement of *uniqueness*, which it justifies, into *generalization*. This "uniqueness" does not just mean a unique "*intuitive experience*" of God, but the "*historical event*" by which the intuition appears within the world. Thus, rationalization does not begin with purely subjective experience of immediacy, as may apply for religion in general (RM, 16), but with one "inspired moment of *history*," i.e., "the life of Christ" (RM, 55). See RM, 16: "Religion is the art and theory of the internal live of man." Although uniqueness is irreplaceable, the "completely novel intuition" (RM, 130) must be generalized to become understandable. As Wilmot underlines, Whitehead is convinced of an "objective truth" of the experiences of faith—similar to the *Proslogion* of Anselm and, earlier, Augustine. See Wilmont, *Whitehead and God*, 22.

46. *Anamnesis:* See Lachmann, *Ethik und Identität*, 85, and Reikerstorfer, "Zur Ursprünglichkeit der Religion," 108, who speaks of "anamnetic reason" which does not fade out the "aporetic of unreconsilable existence." In the memory of the singular revealing event and in contrast to the movement of "rationalization," it happens as an "actualization" of the *uniqueness* of the original event. In the context of rationalization, the *critical* function of the *anamnesis* of the uniqueness of the original revealing event results from the *correction* of each theoretical "distortion" of concrete experience. The *memoria* of the event establishing revelation happens as actualization of the immediacy of this event. In order to present it as active, *anamnesis* actualizes its original freshness. This has a critical consequence for revealed theology: Theological terms that interpret singular revelational events exist not just for generalization, but also for their *new actualization*. In order to gain this aim, the theological vocabulary must be robbed of its "substantiality."

concern of Christian theology, then, to relativize all general terms, categories, and principles, thereby initializing the universalization of this singular
event. This "empirical basis" of theology produces an irremovable contrast
to the "general set of rules" that a metaphysics of general structures of experience is designing.[47] In light of the "general principle of empiricism," and
in order to remain loyal to the universality of its singular revealing events,
Christian theology performs a three-way movement of a *historical*, an *eschatological*, and a *soteriological* type:

1. *Historical movement*. Any general matrix of experience and, hence, the
   character of the general as such, has a *historical* structure.[48] Certain
   historical events, however, will be re-presented *directly* in the memory
   of the revelational events.[49]

2. *Eschatological movement*. God's transcendence radically breaks with
   all "repetition."[50] Since a world, in which God reveals Godself as an
   eschatological event, is of almost *apocalyptic* nature, no one can claim
   to know any given rule or any world-law that God has to follow. Instead, God is the eschatological limit of any world-immanent *logos*.[51]

3. *Soteriological movement*. God who, for Whitehead, is the beginning
   of each event (PR, 244) and the original power of novelty (PR, 67),
   is also the *release from the repetition of the past*; i.e., the repetition

47. In theology, this is represented by the connection of *general* experience of not
being reconciled, e.g., in "the moral evil . . . the pain and the suffering" (RM, 49) and
the *special* experience of salvation by Christ, carrying the evil *"solitary . . . on the Cross"*
(RM, 19).

48. The connection of "immediacy" and "historicity" is essential for the reconciliation of the classical dissonances between the two doctrines of *De Deo uno* and *De Deo
trino*, and, hence, of natural and revealed recognition; refer to Faber, *Selbsteinsatz*,
38–77, 176–92.

49. Whitehead, indeed, has seen the dialectic of "immediacy" and "history" regarding "religious intuition" in saying that the inspiration of religion lies in its *history*, i.e.,
the primary expressions of its *intuitions*. RM, 144.

50. Any theology which argues with the help of the intermittent structure of unique
events and their connection, seems to be preoccupied with infinite continuity. Process-
theological models stand generally under the cosmological assumption of an infinite
process of the production of always new events without end and aim—an assumption, to
which Whitehead gave the name of the "remorseless working of things in Greek and Buddhist thought" (PR, 244). Nevertheless, this presumption is not conclusive by any means.

51. The singularity of the self-revelation of God is not "regular," but rather "pre-
regular." As Deleuze formulates: "If exchange is the criterion of generality, theft and
gift are these of repetition" (Deleuze, *Difference and Repetition*, 1). Therefore, the self-
revealing of God is the gift of novelty, of renewal, of grace, and of reconciliation. See
that "which cannot be and nevertheless 'is'" in PR, 350.

of evil, guilt, and death.[52] On this basis, theology can follow its soteriological function; namely, "to show how the World is founded
on something beyond mere transient fact, and how it issues into
something beyond the perishing of occasions" (AI, 172). Finally we
may say: Seen under the scope of the possibility of process theology,
we *can*, indeed, construct a revelational theology which is not the
performance of a metaphysical investigation. Rather, such theology
generates a "rational" and "anamnetical" interpretation of the universal meaning of unique revealing events in historical, eschatological,
and soteriological dimensions.

52. For Deleuze, there are only these two possibilities: "memory" or "repetition."
Deleuze, *Difference and Repetition*, 14–15: "When the consciousness of knowledge or
the working thought of memory is missing, the knowledge in itself is only the repetition
of the object: it is played, that is to say repeated, enacted instead of being known . . . the
less one remembers, the less one is conscious of remembering one's past, the more one
repeats it." See the similarity to the process-theological interpretation of original sin in
Suchocki, *Fall to Violence*, 14–27, which follows Whitehead's theory of causality, as a
repetition of the (evil) past, as the inheritance from occasion to occasion, from society
to society, from person to person, as a curse of the continuity with the old.

Chapter Twelve

God in the Making

IN THE PREVIOUS CHAPTER I argued for the uniqueness of revelational experiences in the context of Whitehead's metaphysics, despite Whitehead's equally strong assertion that cosmology offers a rational scheme of all relations in the universe in which every (religious) experience is subsumed as an instance of the metaphysical system. My interest was to establish the non-metaphysical character of religious experience and revelation in the context of Whitehead's metaphysics, especially regarding his attempt in *Religion and the Making* to protect the uniqueness of religious experiences from any subsumption under a general metaphysical law (RM, 31).

Here, I will draw on this distinction of the pre-metaphysical singularity of religious experience from the general character of all possible instances of a metaphysical system, by further developing their relation. My thesis shall be that the interplay of *empirical* religious experience and *rational* cosmology not only reveals a basic and non-contingent, dual structure in Whitehead's metaphysics, but that it defines a problematic contrast, which initiates a *creative dynamics of the mutual immanence of the experience of God and God's experience of the world.*

My interest is a theological one, namely to explore this problematic duality of religious experience and cosmology within the context of an ongoing discussion in Christian theology: the problem of religious pluralism, its implications and consequences. While investigating the framework of *Religion in the Making*, I will look for mutual inspiration.

The Theological Problematic of the Experience of God

When theology analyzes religious experience and acknowledges its essence to be an experience of *God*, it distinguishes two elements: the *empirical* side, that is, the subjective, immediate perception of, and emotional

249

reaction to, the manifestation of an ultimate reality, and the *rational* side, that is, the horizon of interpretation of the religious encounter. With Ian T. Ramsey, we may define "religious experience" as "disclosure," a sudden encounter of upmost intensity, of an ultimate reality that—in Schleiermacher and Tillich's understanding—*unconditionally* concerns us by changing our existence and direction in life, and "God," on the other hand, as a "key word" that interprets this experience.[1]

For Christian theology, these two elements of religious experience hide a deep and worrisome paradox, namely that the "disclosure" must not *necessarily* be articulated as an experience of "God" or *a* "god." In other words: phenomenologically and logically, religious experience discloses only a *contingent* relation to the notion of God. In order to understand religious *experience* as experience of *God*, a process of interpretation has already happened, *inferring* rather than *intuiting* the notion of God. Surprisingly, God appears to be a moment of the rationalization of religious experience rather than its immediate emanation. Consequently, theology's knowledge of God must come from *somewhere else*—*besides* the experience that we *interpret* as experience of God.[2]

In Christian theology, this paradox is known, although rarely used constructively. Exceptions apply. Karl Rahner's whole theology is based on the "transcendental experience" of an ultimate mystery for which he invokes the notion of God.[3] "God" conceptualizes the transcendental horizon of the world as a whole, presupposed in any religious experience. Rahner's cosmological background also is known: the cosmo-theology of Teilhard de Chardin and his evolutionary panentheism for which "God" names the dynamic unity of the universe.[4] Another theologian, Wolfhart Pannenberg, has also based his theology on the difference of the particularity of religious experiences in a world of becoming, with the true sphere of the notion of God indicating the eschatological wholeness of the world. In a remarkable statement, he has sharply phrased their togetherness as an internally *problematic* paradox:

> The notion of God functions as interpreting term of such [religious] experience [. . .]. A religious experience can only be understood as an "encounter" with *God* (or with *a god*) in an interpretation that, for its part, uses the notion of God.[5]

1. Ramsey, *Religious Language*, 48–51.
2. Schleiermacher, *Glaubenslehre* (1821), §4,4.
3. Rahner, *Grundkurs*.
4. Teilhard de Chardin, "Mein Universum," 64–122.
5. Pannenberg, *Systematische Theologie*, 1:76; my translation.

This is the pivotal point: The notion of God does not originate in religious experience. In order to function as an interpreting term for religious experience, the notion of God must be *applied* to religious experience. "God" *reflects* the immediate encounter rather than emanating from the experience itself.

This paradoxical relation of religious experience and metaphysical interpretation seems to be inevitable for theology. On its constructive side, it allows for addressing the question of the *truth* of the experience of God. Ingolf Dalferth, for example, has pointed to the fact that only an interpretation of the particular experience of YHWH in the context of a universal concept of God, El or Elohim, facilitates the discernment of the true God from the false gods.[6] On the problematic side, however—and this is what we are concerned with here—it confronts us with the fact that religious experience implies a moment of intellectuality, rationality, and conceptuality that is not revealed, but metaphysically presupposed. John Hick has proposed that this dual character of religious experience shares its structure with human experience in general: Every experience includes a moment of reflection in light of a universal horizon of interpretation, without which perception would remain scattered and meaningless.[7] Every (religious) experience includes a metaphysical presupposition and, therefore, implies a cosmology.

What irritates Christian theology here is that the concept of "God" and, hence, of God's "revelation" is an *interpretation*. In the first edition of Schleiennacher's "Über die Religion" (1799), "God," indeed, appears as just one of many possible interpretations of the "universe."[8]

Theoretically, we could envision the same religious experience allowing for a variety of interpretations based on the cosmological framework of the religion within which the experience is conceptualized. We may, for exmaple, suppose that the same kind of experience that led the great Old Testament prophets to interpret their existential visions to be of YHWH's tremendous and healing holiness, may have suggested to the Buddha an understanding of his enlightenment as being of the nameless *nirvana*. We are confronted with a kind of relativism—deep as the Pacific: Not just *which* God is the true one, but *whether* there might be a God at all as true source of the religious experience, is brought into question.

Furthermore, when we accept the notion that a cosmological framework deeply *determines* the contents of the religious experience, we are

6. Dalferth, *Religiöse Rede von Gott*, 576.
7. Hick, "Religious Faith," 20–35.
8. Pannenberg, *Systematische Theologie*, 1:76 n. 10.

immediately dragged into the problem of religious pluralism.[9] In order to avoid both radical pluralistic approaches which defy the problem of truth altogether, and also fundamentalist's approaches, which irrationally favor one religion over all others, theology is forced to seek a common field of discourse.[10] Some have found it in the rational discourse of *philosophical* cosmology. But in that case, we take the discussion of religious experience to a level beyond the particular religion and, in a certain sense, beyond religion in general.[11] This again is unacceptable for Christianity, which grounds itself in *revelation*. As defined at the *First Vatican Counsel* (1870), revelation is the primary source of Christian knowledge of God, and it is beyond the *lumen naturale* of philosophical thought.[12] Above all, Christian theology seeks for the harmonization of the truth-claims of religions *only* in the context of the longstanding concept of Christianity as "absolute religion" and, hence, of Christianity's singularity.[13]

Therefore, on the most profound level, the paradox Christian theology faces is the difficulty of how to understand the togetherness of two elements of the same event which, from their own points of view, regard themselves as most important and, thereby, impose themselves as determining the whole process. While religious experience seems to resist any generalization under a law of a cosmological framework (thereby forming the identity of this particular religion, e.g., Christianity), the cosmological framework, on the other hand, tends to reductively integrate these singular experiences as mere instances of its unifying interpretation, without which experience has no meaning. This dilemma, again, is the impulse of several theological discourses: on the valuation of interreligious processes, on the danger of religious pluralism, on the interplay of revelation and reason, on the possibility of interreligious comparisons of religious experiences and dogmatic systems, and on what basis.[14] Regarding these theological quarrels, Whitehead's discussion of this problem in *Religion and the Making* may offer suggestions and even surprising solutions.

9. See Knitter, "Can Christian Theology Be Only Christian?," 83–102.
10. D'Sa, *Gott der Dreieine*, 16–18.
11. Neville, "On Comparing Religious Ideas," 187–211.
12. Hünermann, *Enchiridion symbolorum*, numbers 818–819 (= HD, 3015–3019).
13. Kasper, *Absolutheit des Christentums*.
14. Faber, "Transkulturation."

The Interplay of Religious Experience and Cosmology

In a very profound sense, Whitehead was aware of the duality of religious experience and cosmology as a particular instance of the general discussion regarding the dual structure of acts of experience. It is one of the most basic insights of Whitehead's philosophy throughout his opus: from the early distinction between event and object in *Concept of Nature* (CN, 143–170) and the interrelation of the empirical and rational side of metaphysics in *Science and the World* on, to the ontological duality of actualities in their physical/mental polarity in *Process and Reality* (PR, 22–26) and the division of the Universe into the two Worlds of Creation and Values in one of his final articles, "Immortality," from 1941 (Imm., 682).[15] But it really is the discussion of religion and cosmology in *Religion and the Making* by means of which Whitehead developed the basic framework to cope with this duality.

Since there is no time to follow Whitehead's philosophy on this matter in depth, I point directly to one of Whitehead's statements that resonates perfectly with the theological exposition given in part one. In *Science of the Modern World*, Whitehead urges us to understand the theological duality of particular experience and general cosmology as the expression of a universal law that evokes the notion of God. He proposes that

> [. . .] nothing within any limited type of experience can give intelligence to shape our ideas of any entity at the base of all actual things, unless the general character of things requires that there be such an entity. (SMW, 250)

More neutrally, we could rephrase Whitehead's law of duality by replacing "entity" with "unity," meaning that the "general character of things" is the *universal abstraction* by which every particular experience is *interpreted* as united within *one* cosmological framework. But in Whitehead's nuance—using "entity" instead of "unity"—we discover the *theological* concern: The notion of God (the "entity") is a *metaphysical* presupposition required by the general character of the universe as a whole, by which every particular religious experience is already determined. Similar to what we have analyzed in part one, God appears to be a moment of the *cosmological context* of every religious experience that understands itself as experience of God.

In *Religion in the Making*—which Whitehead considered to be the "second part" of *Science and the Modern World* (RM, preface)—this universal law reappears as the *key* to unravel Whitehead's reflection on religion precisely as analyzing the interplay of religious experience and cosmology. I

15. Faber, "Infinite Movement," 171–99.

will further discuss their polarity within this conceptual triangle of religious experience, cosmology, and their togetherness in religion.

Regarding *religious experience*, Whitehead obviously does not give any formal definition. Nevertheless, we can clarify its understanding by Whitehead's own surprising reference to—cosmology. When he states that "religious experience . . . consists of a certain widespread, direct appreciation of a character exemplified in the actual universe" (RM, 86), Whitehead obviously considers the general character of the universe as a whole to be the *contents* of religious experience. However, he not only refers to this "metaphysical presupposition" of any "religious intuition" (RM, 86) as metaphysical *abstraction* to which religious experience is subjected, he also interprets the perception of this metaphysical universality, exhibited by the universe as a whole, as "direct" and "immediate," and hence, as *unique*. What makes this cosmological experience *religious* becomes obvious when Whitehead determines it to consist in "a character of permanent Rightness" inherent "in the nature of things" (RM, 61). Religious experience is about order, value, and harmony at the ground of the world.[16]

Regarding *cosmology*, we are directed to this general character inherent in the world as a whole. Whitehead describes the metaphysical character of the universe with the now famous three "formative elements": creativity, ideal entities, and a non-temporal entity that "men call God" (RM, 90). While creativity represents "infinite freedom" and the ideal entities embody "infinite possibility," God—in further development of the "principle of determination/empiricism" in *Science and the Modern World (SMW, 178)*—manifests the actuality at the ground of the universe that determines freedom and possibility in order to allow for an actual universe to happen, and to happen as process of valuation.[17] Cosmology's relation to religious experiences becomes obvious in Whitehead's inclusion of God as "formative character" (RM, 89) of the universe. In immediate intuition, this "general character" appears as *religious* precisely by being an instance of *divine decisions* that create values.[18]

Regarding *religion*, Whitehead develops a generic conception of evolving phases of religion formed by ritual, emotion, belief, and finally, rationalization (RM, 20–36). Modern religion, in Whitehead's eyes, is *rational* religion, that is, religion seeking freedom from the particularity of ritual, the subjectivity of emotions, and the regionalism of beliefs, by bifurcating into the "solitariness" of existence and "solidarity" with the

---

16. Jung, "Zur Entwicklung von Whiteheads Gottesbegriff," 607–9.

17. Hosinski, *Stubborn Fact*, 230.

18. Faber, *Gott als Poet der Welt*, 204–11.

universe as a whole. In this sense, rational religion integrates both the existentiality of religious experience and the universality of cosmological interpretation into a coherent unity of its own—the dogma. Hence, it does not come as a surprise when Whitehead states that "whatever suggests a cosmology, suggests a religion" (RM, 141).

We can take the following quote as a summary of this interrelation of religious experience and cosmology in the context of rational religion in Whitehead's *Religion in the Making*:

> The religious insight is the grasp of this truth: That the order of the world, the depth of reality of the world, the value of the world, in its whole and in its parts, the beauty of the world, the zest of life, the peace of life, and the mastery of evil, are all bound together not accidentally, but by reason of this truth that the universe exhibits a creativity with infinite freedom, and a realm of forms with infinite possibilities; but that this creativity and these forms are together impotent to achieve actuality apart from the completed ideal harmony, which is God. (RM, 126–127)

Even if this general description of the interplay of religious experience and cosmology has not yet brought into light its own paradoxical side, this does not mean that Whitehead was unaware of it. On the contrary, while the "harmony" which God creates between two infinities at first disguises rather than reveals the inherent process of the contrasting opposites of the singularity of religious experience (on which the particularity of a given religion is based), on the one hand, and the generality of cosmological interpretations of these experiences (a scheme), on the other, their dynamic duality is certainly a major aspect of Whitehead's thought on religion in *Religion in the Making*.[19]

The Paradox of Religious Experience and Cosmology

On the most general level, the paradox of religious experience and cosmology can be restated as the problem of the relation between the *singularity* of experiences (for which rationalization is an abstraction) and the *unity* of the general character inherent in their interpretation (for which singularity is the mere instantiation of a general scheme).

In the conceptuality of *Process and Reality*, the paradox can be sketched this way: On the one hand, Whitehead constructs metaphysics as a "coherent, logical, necessary system of general ideas in terms of which every element

19. Suchocki, *End of Evil*, 104.

of our experience can be interpreted" (PR, 3). On the other hand, however, he grounds his cosmology on the fundamental law that there is "no way" in which a "concrete particular can be build up out of universals" (ibid., 20). The singular experience is a unique actuality that cannot be reconstructed by any abstraction. Paradoxically, while every experience must be interpreted by a general scheme in order to be recognizable as *this* particular instance; at the same time, the particular experience *cannot* be reconstructed within any general scheme because of its unique singularity. These two sides of Whitehead's metaphysics interact in the constant struggle and seem to constitute the inner dynamics of Whitehead's metaphysics in total.[20]

In *Religion in the Making*, Whitehead develops this paradox within the structure of rational religion with its paradoxical dynamics of both unique existentiality and universal (uniting) rationality. In an important statement, Whitehead directly describes this paradox by saying that

> Rational religion appeals to the direct intuition of special occasions, and to the elucidatory power of its concepts for all occasions. It arises from that which is special, but it extends to what is general. The doctrines of rational religion aim at being that metaphysics which can be derived from the supernormal experience of mankind in its moments of finest insight. (ibid., 32)

On the one hand, rational religion appeals to the general level of cosmology in order to interpret its unique religious experiences; on the other hand, the power of universal elucidation is not drawn from the rational scheme of metaphysics, but from the very unique occasions that form the historic character of a singular religion, which in turn cannot be reconstructed by any general scheme. Therefore, cosmology as derived from rational religion is based on unique "supernormal experiences of mankind in its moments of finest insight" (ibid.).

Again, we can elucidate this mutually antagonistic constellation within the three conceptual spheres of religious experience, religion, and cosmology:

Religious experience is unique in that it cannot be reconstructed by any cosmology: it may only be rationalized by the religion it belongs to in order to build a general cosmological horizon of interpretation. But religious experience constitutes "the ultimate religious evidence, beyond which there is no appeal" (ibid., 67). In other words: Religious experience has a *non-metaphysical origin*; and religions are founded on such unique experiences—e.g., the Christ-event or Buddha's enlightenment (ibid., 56). Religious experiences are unique in that they cannot be abstractly constructed, or properly restated,

20. Faber, "Whitehead at Infinite Speed," 39–72.

within any religious doctrine or cosmology. They can only be memorized and universalized: "Christ gave us his life. It is for Christians to discern the doctrine" (ibid.). This is the function of religion.

Religion, in developing a rational doctrine—the dogma—is the rationalization of these unique experiences in order to not let them be degraded into any rationally unjustifiable, psychological subjectivity (ibid., 63–64). Therefore, "reason is the safeguard of the objectivity of religion: it secures for it the general coherence denied in hysteria" (ibid.). Rationalization hinders the fundamentalist's appeal to "direct" revelation without interpretation. But still, religion remains only true to itself as long as it knows its "genius" by "keeping its metaphysics subordinate to the religious fact to which it appeals" (ibid., 72). In this sense, "religion claims that its concepts, though derived primarily from specific experiences, are yet of universal validity, to be applied by faith to the ordering of all experiences" (ibid., 32). Hence, the "relevance of its concepts can only be distinctly discerned in moments of insight, and then, for many of us, only after suggestion from without" (ibid.). No general metaphysics reaches down to the origin of religion, which is only found in the history of the *anamnesis* or *memoria* of its unique experiences. Nevertheless, in doing so, religion "requires a metaphysical backing" (ibid., 83), that is, a general framework of interpretation, or a cosmology.

The function of *cosmology,* therefore, is to ensure a critical valuation of the generality of the dogmatic doctrines of particular religions insofar as they always develop in contradiction with one another. In seeking objective rationality, cosmology refers to the "world-consciousness" (ibid., 41) already present in the rationalizations of the religions. Directly and critically, it addresses their contradictions by comparing their implicit cosmologies (ibid., 87; cf. AI, 144). Precisely here, the paradox reappears: While cosmology arranges its categories regarding the *most general* structures of the world *independently* from any religion, it really arises from the same kind of dual experience of solitariness and world-consciousness that forms rational religion (ibid., 39). When cosmology analyses the general character inherent in nature, it is not just "set out for immediate comparison with the deliverances of religious experience" (ibid., 89); it is itself already *based* on religious experience in as much as religious experiences is based on the direct intuition of the general character inherent in the temporal world (RM, 86)—as we have seen in part two. Hence, all cosmology is a *relative* enterprise, based on singular sets of experiences and their religious rationalizations.

The claim that even Whitehead's cosmology must be understood to be based on *religious* rationalizations can be substantiated by further analyzing the basic structure of the general character of the world, which for Whitehead crystallizes in the three "formative elements." Indeed, already the layout of the formative elements in *Religion and the Making* expresses Whitehead's urge toward an integration of religious experience and cosmology. Not only does "God" appear as one of the three formative elements, but their whole setting—in further development—led to a *panentheistic* theory of unification.[21] From Whitehead's suggestion in *Science in the Modern World* that this "unity" might be understood as an "entity" that we name "God" (SMW, 250), the dynamics were set free by which the three formative elements in *Religion in the Making* increasingly facilitated the integration of the spheres of "infinite possibilities" and "infinite freedom" into God. In *Process and Reality*, the sphere of possibilities finally reappears as God's primordial nature.[22] And it does not surprise us that, for the same reasons, some process theologians of following generations tended to also integrate the sphere of creativity into God—e.g., John Cobb, Lewis Ford, and Joseph Bracken.[23]

"God" really became the integrating element of the cosmological triad of principles Whitehead developed in *Religion in the Making*. In the 1960s, Walter Jung acknowledged that this is due to the fact that, in *Religion in the Making*, over against *Science and the Modern World*, Whitehead for the first time realized that, if a principle really has to *decide* amidst activity and possibility in order to create temporal concreteness, it *must* be understood as an "entity."[24] Hence, this cosmological structure tended to integrate all other principles as abstractions of this one non-temporal actuality, named "God." This integration again allows for the thesis that for Whitehead, on *cosmological* grounds, religious experience *is*, in fact, an experience of *God*, and that this concept of "God" is the product of theological rationalizations of unique religious experiences (see PR, 342–344; AI, 166–169; RM, 71–72).

And precisely at this point of consideration, we are led to a final, more complex, and even more puzzling, form in which the theological paradox appears in Whitehead: Religious experiences, on the one hand, are not only instances of general cosmological principles; in Whitehead's interpretation, they appear as *unique* events, but caused by *creative acts* of God (who, then, is not a mere interpretation anymore), namely by *decisions* of God, that is, by revelation (SMW, 178–179). Cosmology, on the other hand, is not a mere abstraction that, in its generality, integrates religious experiences; it already *rests* on particular religious experiences and is relative to them. Hence, in its

---

21. Faber, *Gott als Poet der Welt*, 25, 131–37, 161–70.

22. Welker, "Whiteheads Vergottung der Welt," 196–97.

23. Bracken, *Divine Matrix*; Cobb, *Beyond Dialogue*; Ford, *Transforming Process Theism*.

24. Jung, "Zur Entwicklung von Whiteheads Gottesbegriff," 610–20.

interpretation of the singular experiences of particular religions, cosmology, indeed, does not necessarily aim at an experience of "God." Cosmological interpretations, therefore, are not just expressions of a *perception* of an ultimate reality—be it named "God" or otherwise; they are really processes of the *creation* of interpretive pictures of the world with regard to this ultimate reality; they are *creative projections*. How then, taking into account this *dual creative relation* between religious experience and cosmology, can we possibly consider God as the *one* "entity" that integrates both the contradictory plurality of religious experiences of diverse religions as truly *revelatory* experiences of Godself, and the multiplicity of interpretive, cosmological systems as relative projections from singular experiences into one cosmological "unity"? In short, the paradox we are confronted with is the *problem of a plurality of revelations and a multiplicity of their (cosmological) interpretations in relation to their possible unification into "one" God.*

Mapping the Problem of the Pluralism of Revelations

The problem of religious pluralism is one of today's most important theological issues.[25] In general, its discussion is framed by the tension between religious experience and cosmology as laid out in part one, and its dynamics is based on their relation as described in part two. While Whitehead has recognized this problem in *Religion and the Making* (and, on a more general level, in all of his philosophy), he also adds to its *intensity* as analyzed in part three. In order to better understand Whitehead's contribution to the whole issue, we shall first take a glance at the three main ways of solving the problem of religious pluralism that have been developed in theology within the framework of the contrasting opposites of (singular) religious experience and (general) cosmology, and that are still in use today.

The *first solution* favors a tendency to dissolve the uniqueness of religious experience into abstract cosmology, which is held to be the *only* true dogmatic articulation of all possible experiences. The Christian concept of the *one* true religion or "absolute religion" was always the expression of such an identification. In its mode of *exclusivism*, it often furthers intolerance (crusades, the hunt for heretics, and the negation of true interreligious dialogue).[26] Although there is also an *inclusivistic* mode—as found, e.g., in Rahner's "anonymous Christian" or Teilhard de Chardin's "cosmic Christ"— it also tends to degrade the religious experiences of other religions and their cosmological rationalizations. They appear to be of minor interest because

25. Faber, "Transkulturation" and Werbick, "Heil durch Christus allein?," 11–61.
26. Rainer, *"Dominus Iesus."*

to Christianity they can only repeat what is already fully manifest in its own revelation. We can call it the *monistic* solution of our paradox: the reduction of unique experiences to mere instances of rationalization.[27]

In reacting to this monistic strain of thought, a *second solution* favors the exclusive importance of the diversification of religious experiences over against their dogmatic "unifications"—in John Hick and Perry Schmidt-Leukel for example—even to the point of losing the impulse of cosmological rationalization altogether.[28] In its more extreme forms, "religious pluralism" tends to draw on the deconstructive postmodern thought of Derrida and others in order to excommunicate "unity" as oppressive concept with regard to difference. *Différance* never unifies, but always diversifies in processes of differentiation.[29] Thereby, theology either is in danger of losing its claim to truth, which is critically kept alive by cosmology in religious discourse, or it redefines its character as referring to the quest for freedom.[30] We shall call this the *pluralistic* solution of the paradox: the dissolution of unifying cosmologies into irreducible multiplicities of pre-rational singularities.[31]

Paradoxically, this leads to the *third solution.* In some of its theological manifestations, the pluralistic trait lends itself to the dialectic move that there must be a *hidden unity of all singularities, that is, an unknown (or even unknowable) ultimate reality,* which grounds the plurality of experiences and even inspires their multiple rationalizations. Two possible instantiations come to mind: Either there is a true cosmology of the ultimate reality, but no religion is able to recognize it because of natural or sinful inability of the human intellect, or cosmology applies to the sphere of the temporal world *only,* and not to the sphere of God's life, which is totally beyond any conceptualization. Because it often draws on, and is similar to, the apophatic theology of Christian inheritance, we shall call this the *mystical* solution of the paradox: the unification of both singular experiences and abstract rationalizations within a nameless ultimate reality.[32]

Today's theology, insofar as it takes the multiplicity of revelations in diverse religions seriously, obviously prefers versions of this third solution, as can especially be seen in the emerging discipline of *comparative theology,* represented, for example, by Keith Ward, Frances Clooney, Daya Krishna, or

27. Knapp, "Dogmatik im Zeitalter des Pluralismus," 329–42.

28. Hick, *Problems of Religious Pluralism*; Schmidt-Leukel, "Das Pluralistische Modell," 353–64.

29. Welsch, *Vernunft,* 260–75.

30. Wolfinger, "Postmoderner Pluralismus," 87–96.

31. See Deleuze and Guattari, *What Is Philosophy?,* 15–60.

32. Faber, "'Gottesmeer,'" 64–95.

Raimond Panikkar.[33] While they seek to *pluralize* the *monistic* solution by suggesting that we always already do stand within more than one belief-system, they also strongly suggest that there must be some *mystical* unity manifesting itself in all of these diverse religious experiences of different religions. This is evident in the following quote from Perry Schmidt-Leukel:

> Not relativism, but perspective realism is proposed here. It is the one reality, which is perceived by different people in different contexts and in this sense differently. Transferred to revelation, respectively the experience of transcendent reality, this means that, in religious history, we encounter different experiences of the same transcendent reality.[34]

Regarding the theological problematic of how to understand the dynamic duality of (singular) religious experience, on the one hand, and of (general) cosmology by which we interpret experience as a revelation of God, on the other, the three solutions take a very different, but always one-sided stance: The *monistic* solution strengthens the rational side to the point that *one* dogma, with its implicit cosmology, represents religious truth beyond doubt. Thereby, it reabsorbs the plurality of religious experiences into *one* rational, or dogmatic, scheme by excluding a multiplicity of valuable interpretations. In its dogmatic objectivism, religious experiences only survive as instances of the dogmatic scheme. The *pluralistic* solution, on the other hand, strengthens the independence and singularity of religious experiences over against any rationalization of dogmatic schemes, even to the point that any cosmological framework must appear as oppressive dogmatism. The *mystical* solution, finally, tries to integrate elements of both the monistic and the pluralistic solutions by weakening both sides: that of *singular* experiences by interpreting this particularity as (intellectual or moral) deficit, and that of the rational, or dogmatic *reflection* on these experiences, by resolving it into a nameless and silent ultimate reality.

Especially within the matrix of *comparative theology*, the mystical solution is confronted with the same paradox, which was proposed for Whitehead in part three. With Keith Ward, we can phrase it this way: On the one hand, we must understand every religious or dogmatic framework of a given religion as based on the uniqueness of its founding unique religious experiences, and hence as expression of a *unique* revelation of God. On the

---

33. Ward, "Towards a Comparative Theology," 3–49; Clooney, "Current Theology," 521–55; Krishna, "Comparative Philosophy," 71–83; Panikkar, "What Is Comparative Philosophy Comparing?," 116–36.

34. Schmidt Leukel, "Das Problem divergierender Wahrheitsansprüche," 52–53; my translation.

other hand, none of these true revelations may be considered *the* revelation of God. Hence, every rationalization of revelations has the defect of only reductively manifesting the self-revealing God through its relative, cosmological interpretation.[35] So we are confronted with the strongest form of our paradox: How can the *one* Godhead be understood as originating *diverse* religious experiences as altogether *true revelations* of God, while, at the same time, *we* create an irreducible plurality of religious rationalizations and cosmological abstractions, which (in their deficiency) cannot be controlled by God's revelation?

Although the mystical solution was invented to comprehend this paradox, I think, it has failed to solve it because the diversity of revelations and rationalizations must be *weakened* in order to save Divine unity.[36] The singularity of the religious experiences must be weakened in order to allow for "God" to remain a rational, unifying, and interrelating concept of their interpretation. The ultimate reality, on the other hand, must be weakened in its unifying influence on interpretations of its revelatory appearance in many religions in order to allow for the multiplicity of interpretations to happen, which in turn, appear to be *deficient* realizations of the hidden Divine unity.

So, methodologically, the ultimate reality always at a certain point— disappears in mystical namelessness. In order to establish an irreducible plurality of religious experiences, revelations, and dogmatic and cosmological frameworks of diverse rational religions, God must be "grasped" as their passive, silent, hidden unity. The presupposition of the mystical solution of the paradox of religious experience and cosmology, therefore, is a *passive* relation of God to the world. And because of this passivity and secretiveness of the Godhead, the mystical solution's *identification* of the plurality of religious experience with unique experiences of *God* becomes virtually non-discernable from a mere *interpretation* in which God is an abstraction of the rational scheme that subsumes religious experiences as instances of its unifying conceptuality. We are thrown back to the paradox in its primary form as proposed in part one.

This is the point where we may take a second look at Whitehead's *Religion in the Making*, to see whether its integrating framework, relating religious experience and cosmology to one another, might offer *another* way of solving the paradox. Indeed, I think Whitehead offers a *fourth solution* that I shall call the *creative* solution because it rests on the surprising thought of God's *self-creative revelation*.

---

35. Ward, "Towards a Comparative Theology," 12–25.
36. Cf. Panikkar, "What Is Comparative Philosophy Comparing?," 126–34.

The Self-Creative Revelation of God

First, this question must be raised: How does Whitehead's thought, as developed in part two and three, fit into the theological framework of the three solutions discussed in part four?

Regarding the *monistic* way to deal with the paradox, *Religion in the Making* makes a strong case for a fundamental critique of any exclusivistic or inclusivistic claim of the lightness of one religious tradition over against all others. Such a proposal contrasts sharply with Whitehead's clear affirmation of both the singularity of religious experiences over against any cosmological unification in any religious tradition, and the relativity of cosmological conceptions among themselves (AI, 224). Whitehead's negation of the cosmological priority of the concept of God as "person" in *Religion in the Making* especially expresses his opposition to any oppressive integration of all traditions into the dogmatic scheme of *one* tradition (RM, 64). Nevertheless, Whitehead concedes the great importance for any religion of staying firm to its own religious experience, the irreplaceable uniqueness of the experience of Christ for Christianity, for example.

Regarding the *pluralistic* solution, Whitehead never embraced a mode of thought that would sacrifice the unifying rationality of cosmology. Although I have always thought that Whitehead developed quite powerful deconstructive strategies—30 years before the birth of the French philosophy of difference of Deleuze, Derrida, and others, I must admit that he always sought cosmological unification.[37] In *Religion and the Making, this* if anything is his *point*—that is, in his developing of the concept of rational religion, in comparing the cosmologies of religions, and in framing his own cosmology in relation to implicit cosmologies of religions. But even when cosmology became Whitehead's strongest interest, he developed quite a pluralistic cosmology.[38] Any of the formative elements as well as their whole arrangement exhibit pluralistic tendencies.[39] Hence, it does not come as a surprise that from *Religion in the Making* on, "creativity" became Whitehead's principle of *différance* (PR, 21).[40]

Regarding the *mystical* solution, we might be inclined to think that this was the one Whitehead was aiming at; but on deeper inspection of his thought, this proves not to be the case.[41] Evidence comes again from

37. Faber, "De-Ontologizing God," 209–34; Faber, *Gott als Poet der Welt*, 170.

38. Kasprzik, "Whiteheads metaphysische Option," 9–36.

39. Faber, *Gott als Poet der Welt*, 168–69.

40. Faber, *Gott als Poet der Welt*, 73–77; 131–34; cf. Bracken, *The One and the Many*, 49–75.

41. Faber, "'Gottesmeer,'" 83–95.

the formative elements: True, the concept of "creativity" in *Religion and the Making*, and even more in *Process and Reality* (PR, 7) deconstructs the "substantial activity" of *Science and the Modern World*—now understood as the *immanent activity* of all actualities, being a mere abstraction without its instantiations (ibid., 20).[42] Its "unifying activity," indeed, corresponds well with the mystical One of negative theology—and, hence, the mystical solution. However, although Whitehead considered creativity as protean, that is, of being beyond any character, he never conceived it as passive or hidden. On the contrary, it is a principle *of pure activity*[43] Furthermore, with God among the three formative elements, ultimate reality is also *pure actuality*— decision, determination, creation of values (RM, 127).

What distinguishes Whitehead from the mystical solution is the fact that, in facing the problem of a plurality of revelations and cosmological interpretations, he insists on *both* sides of the paradox: the singularity of religious experience and the inevitability of cosmological rationalization. His remedy against the weakness of the mystical solution's passive Godhead comes from his emerging concept of God as *self-creative actuality*.[44] This move I shall call his *fourth* solution, the *creative* solution.

In order to understand Whitehead's move, let me, one last time, re-phrase the paradox in the light of the analysis in *Religion and the Making*: If the various religious experiences are unique decisions of God, then neither is God a *mere* cosmological abstraction, nor are the experiences less than the expression of *multiple revelations* of God, even if they are not conceptualized by the notion of "God." In other words, God must have wanted a *plurality of self-revelations* to happen in unique experiences that cannot be reconstructed by any particular cosmological abstraction. If, on the other hand, cosmo-logical rationalization must be considered as a *necessary* contextualization of religious experiences in order for them to be *recognized* as revelations of God, the paradox of their diversity cannot be weakened by interpreting them as the mere deficit of human intellectuality or morality. Such rationalizations do not indicate somehow distorted perceptions of God's revelation (which is beyond understanding), but they must be determined as *indispensable projections* of unique experiences of God's revelation, even if they are not identified with the notion of "God." In other words: God must have wanted a *plurality of human rationalizations* of religious experiences, or *diverse* cos-mologies, to happen in the recognition of God's revelations.

42. Bradley "Transcendentalism," 155–91.

43. Garland, "The Ultimacy of Creativity," 212–38.

44. Faber, *Gott als Poet der Welt*, 244–51.

Now, if God wants these *two pluralities of God's self-revelations and human rationalizations* to happen, and because we are not allowed to understand this Divine act to be a mere accident of God's will, a point Whitehead consistently denies throughout the whole philosophical body of his work (RM, 66; AI, 168), they must be considered as *true self-expressions of God's nature*. In other words: Both *the plurality of Divine creative decisions*, manifested in singular, religious experiences as multiple Divine revelations, and *the plurality of human creative rationalizations* of God's revelational experiences, manifesting in diverse cosmologies, must be an expression of the working of *the creative nature of God and the world* (PR, 348). If this radical intercreative process of differentiation into pluralities of true revelations and justified cosmological rationalizations is to make any sense at all, their *intercreative unification* must be of God's "creative essence."[45]

This is Whitehead's *creative* solution of the paradox: If we cannot flee into a mystical One, which withdraws in silence beyond all manifestations (as the mystical solution suggests), the *unity* of the diverse creative decisions of God and the world regarding the indispensable multiplicity of revelational experiences and their cosmological rationalizations, must consist in a *self-creative process of unification of Godself*. In other words: When God really unites the diversity of God's self-revelations and, as part of their recognition, receives a multiplicity of human self-rationalizations as moment of God's nature, then precisely their *plurality* must constitute an *inherent moment of God's identity*. Because the religious experiences of God are *God's self-revelations*, and because their human rationalizations must become *Divine experiences* again, God, then, is *in the making*. God *becomes* God by God's revelations *and* God's experiences of their rationalizations.

Regarding the shocking consequence of the theological dilemma as outlined in part one—that God seems to be a mere *interpretation* of religious experiences—we now can say that Whitehead, in a deep and surprising move, *affirms* this thesis and *rigorously* follows its implications all the way through: In *pluralizing* God's revelation as it appears in a multiplicity of religious experiences, God *becomes* by means of God's *self-creative activity* of self-revelation; in *integrating* a multiplicity of human rationalizations, which are the world's self-creative act of creating projections of God, God *becomes* by means of God's *self-creative receptivity* of the world's reactions to God's self-revelations. In other words: God *causes* a plurality of experiences of Godself, and in order to unite them, God also *receives* the world's creative interpretations of God's revelations *as moments of God's own creative becoming*. In this sense, we can summarize: *God is in the making in and through*

---

45. Faber, *Gott als Poet der Welt*, 161–70, regarding the concept of the Divine matrix.

God's own creative revelations and from God's perception of the Creative inter-
pretations of the perception of Godself by the world.

Although I have *inferred* this creative solution by means of my analysis of the relation of religious experience and cosmology in *Religion in the Making*, some closing arguments may substantiate my claim.

In taking the formative elements to be the most basic principles of Whitehead's cosmology in *Religion and the Making*, we can argue that, by their very structure, they exhibit the *self-creativeness* of God and the world. If, indeed, creativity is the most *basic* principle of cosmology, *becoming* is the corresponding fundamental law of any actual world. Hence, if God appears to be its most basic instantiation, God must be the primordial self-creative instance of creativity—in its active and receptive modes.[46]

It is really in *Religion in the Making* that Whitehead begins to articulate this difference in God's self-creativeness, namely by introducing "the association of God with the Kingdom of Heaven" (RM, 72). On the one hand, the Kingdom appears to be related to the Divine entertainment of the "realm of ideal forms" (ibid., 154) which will become the primordial nature of God (PR, 31–32). On the other hand, it really became the proper name for God's receptive side, the later so called consequent nature of God (PR, 346–347). The Kingdom of Heaven names the two-fold Divine process of the *creation* of a multiplicity of revelations and the *integration* of their mundane interpretations within God's own nature. Hence, the "kingdom of Heaven *is* God" (RM, 154) insofar as God both encompasses God's own creative diversification of all possible revelations *and*, indeed, in Divine receptivity, "transmutes what has been lost into a living fact within his own nature" (ibid., 155). The Kingdom of Heaven is both God's self-creative process of God's "ideal harmony" (ibid., 127) *and* the perception and valuation of the world's projective reaction to God's revelations in God's own becoming this harmony (AI, 256).

In *Process and Reality*, when Whitehead has finally forged the language to express this thought properly, he articulates this difference within Divine self-creativity as a polarity of the primordial and the consequent natures of God (PR, 46). This self-creative difference corresponds to our paradox: While the primordial nature suggests the multiplicity of revelations to the a moment of God's *self-creative activity* that permanently diversifies itself as a realm of infinite possibility, of which God is the unending process of actualization in multifarious religious experiences, the consequent nature allows for the multiplicity of human rationalizations of these revelational experiences to be understood as moment of God's *self-creative receptivity*

---

46. Ibid., 131–37.

by which God experiences any reaction to God's revelations as moment of God's own nature (ibid., 345–346; 73–77; 191–204).

This self-creative process gains its final, clear, and unequivocal formulation in one of the famous six antitheses—and as their most provocative one:

> It is as true to say that God creates the World, as the World creates God. God and the World are the contrasted opposites in terms of which Creativity achieves its supreme task . . . (ibid., 348; cf. 148–161)

The whole dynamics of *this fourth* solution of the paradox of religious experience and cosmology by Whitehead's God-in-the-Making is, I think, one of Whitehead's most important and creative contributions to theology and the doctrine of God. If we follow Whitehead in his analysis of the *mutual creative relation* of God and the world—the world-creating God and the God-creating world—the theological issue at stake here is tremendous. With Whitehead's God-in-the-Making, we must accept nothing less than both the definitive importance of the diversity of experiences of God in a multiplicity of religions *as God's own process* of self-creative revelation *and* their mutually exclusive interpretations *as God's own process* of self-creative reception of the world's diverse creative interpretations of the perception of God's revelations (AI, 168–169). A theology that affirms this God-in-the-Making might be *the* challenge of the future, and for the future of theology.[47]

---

47. See Faber, "'Transkulturation.'"

EPILOGUE

(Nothing but) Mystery

PROCESS THEOLOGY IS OCCASIONALLY charged with failing to acknowledge or allow for the "mystery of God."[1] The specifically *rationalistic* version of process theology, along with all those process theologies that view Whitehead in proximity to Hegel's "conceptual process"[2] may have given this impression.[3] But a consideration of the other predominant version of process theology, namely, *empirical* theology, fundamentally relativizes this impression. In contradistinction to Hegel's understanding of the goal of the processes of God and world, namely, the sublation of the process itself in God's "absolute (self-)concept," Whitehead nowhere presents this sort of rationalistic resolution of the mystery of the world and God (or of the world *in* God).[4] Whitehead, empirical theology, naturalism, speculative theology, and deconstructive postmodern process theology consistently give priority to life before thought, event happenings (actualities) before structure (eternal objects), *différance* before presence, creativity before rationality,[5] process before reality (PR, 7), open wholeness before crystalline facticity, a feeling for the singular before (conceptual) thought (universals).[6]

The *mysterium* is deeply etched both into Whitehead's own cosmology and into process theology itself, namely, as the mystery of life, the event, creativity, and process as the "mysticism" of the unspoken (MT, 174). The theological expression is the *principle of concretion*, which a priori renders God's own concretion inaccessible to any structural elucidation, rational

1. Scheffczyk, "Prozesstheismus," 104.

2. Kline, "Begriff und Konkreszenz," 145–61.

3. Faber, *God as Poet*, §4.

4. Wiehl, "Whitehead's Kosmologie der Gefühle," 141–68.

5. Wiehl, "Whitehead's Kosmologie der Gefühle"; cf. Rohmer, *Whiteheads Synthese von Kreativität und Rationalität*.

6. Keller, "The Process of Difference."

comprehension, or theoretical articulation,[7] since concretion, being per-petually *creative*, remains inaccessible to formal explication or understand-ing. This theological expression also includes the *principle of empiricism*, by virtue of which God's temporal, historical, and creative self-revelation is not preformed by any rational disclosure or predetermination.[8] From the *theo-poetic* perspective on God, God's mystery emerges in three aspects, namely, God's *life, nondifference,* and *insistence*.

The Mystery of God's Life

Within the complex interpenetration of the processes of God and world,[9] God's life is manifested as *world-oriented relationality*. But can one speak about God's life such that it is *not* exhausted by self-transcendence toward the world process? That is, does God have a life "for Godself"? And if so, what can process theology say about *God's inner life* without in its own turn being "comprehended" as a kind of "theosophy" (*alleged* knowledge of God's being in and of itself)? The following fundamental contours emerge regarding the indissoluble intertwining of divine life within world-orienta-tion or world-anteriority.

(1) *The mystery of originless life.* That God's life "(in and) for itself" is by no means exhausted through God's self-transcendence "for us" is evident from the conversion of processes in its multiple form, namely as a creative (vs. the creaturely) process of creation,[10] as God's eschatological release of time,[11] and as inner conversion (inversion) of the divine process.[12] God's process is perpetually characterized by an inner abundance that is never wholly emptied or resolved into the world process[13] based on God's primor-dial superjectivity, which is *without* origin but from which every process nonetheless derives its origin. This primordial superjectivity refers us to the *pre-* of God's life prior to any "grounding" of world.

(2) *The mystery of revealed life.* God's life "for us" discloses God's life "for itself,"[14] since God's self-revelation bequeaths itself not arbitrarily, but rather in an *essentially relational* fashion. Hence, God's *inner* life is indeed

---

7. Faber, *God as Poet*, §29.

8. Faber, *Prozeßtheologie*; Faber, *God as Poet*, §36.

9. Faber, *God as Poet*, part IV.

10. Faber, *God as Poet*, §35.

11. Faber, *God as Poet*, §39: Figure 6.

12. Faber, *God as Poet*, §30.

13. Faber, *God as Poet*, §31.

14. Faber, *Selbsteinsatz Gottes*.

revealed in God's self-revelation precisely in its *alterity* and as *revealed mystery*,[15] which, rather than being exhausted by that revealed status, instead is revealed precisely in its *mysteriousness*.

(3) *The mystery of intercreative life.* God's life "in itself" is revealed "for us" in its *alterity*, insofar as it appears as the *essential element of life* at the "ground" of the world. The ultimate expression of that element of life and vitality in the world is the *entirely living nexus*, in which the unity of the world[16] and of personal being[17] is disclosed in transparency with respect to the mystery of God's life. Within the *divine matrix*, the living element of the chaotic nexus and of personal being is both the *possibility* (in the case of the chaotic nexus) and *reality* (in the case of personal being) of the highest, nonformally graspable intensity of life.[18]

(4) *The mystery of nonformal life.* A *Trinitarian* consideration of God's life[19] reveals the extent to which this *life*, in its unfathomable nature, bears witness to God's mystery. It is with *Sophia/Logos* that a glimpse is provided into the abyss of potentials in all their primordiality, in all their *primordial chaos*. And with the *Pneuma*, a glimpse is provided into God's eschatological vitality as the wholly delimited living nexus of all actualities within *eschatological chaos*, the delimited Peace *beyond* all order. In this sense, *Sophia/Logos* and *Pneuma* demonstrate the unfathomable quality of their life as *khora* and *hypodoche*.[20]

(5) *The mystery of the indifference of life.* The *alterity* of God's life "in itself" refers to something that is *not* immediately world-oriented, obtaining instead "for itself" prior to any world.[21] This is God's "primordiality" (God's "primordial nature"),[22] the creative beginning of God's concrescence, in which God is a *nonsocial nexus* (PR, 72) that, in its *primordiality* ("for itself"), seeks "intensity and not preservation" (PR, 105).[23] Because this intensity is primordial, there is nothing to preserve, neither anything old nor anything new in God: instead, everything "is" solely with regard to the depth of God's life:

15. Faber, *God as Poet*, §29.

16. Faber, *God as Poet*, §24.

17. Faber, *God as Poet*, §22.

18. Faber, *God as Poet*, §32: Figure 4.

19. Faber, *God as Poet*, §38.

20. Faber, *God as Poet*, §39.

21. Faber, *Prozeßtheologie*.

22. Faber, *God as Poet*, §28.

23. Faber, God as Poet, §38.

[God], in [God's] primordial nature, is unmoved by love for this
particular, or that particular; for in this foundational process of
creativity, there are no preconstituted particulars. In the foundations of [God's] being, God is indifferent alike to preservation
and to novelty. [God] cares not whether an immediate occasion
be old or new, so far as concerns derivation from its ancestry.
[God's] aim for it is depth of satisfaction as an intermediate step
towards the fulfilment of [God's] own being. [God's] tenderness
is directed towards each actual occasion, as it arises. (PR, 105)

As Gregg Lambert has shown, God's love and tenderness appear in
God's primordiality only as an interim stage on the way to the intensity and
depth of God's inner life.[24] In the process of God's *inner self-creativity*, that
is, in God's primordial superjectivity, that is, God's *process of creativity* providing the *foundation* for God's being,[25] God *peers through* every form and
every event at Godself, and this creativity *arises prior* to any world and *independent* of it. Notwithstanding that God moves toward the world as novelty
and future within this "nonsocial" creativity, God's intensity and depth are
not determined by novelty for, or origin of, the world—that is, by or from
the perspective of *any* world, whatever the nature of that world might be.
Nevertheless, in the world-oriented conversion of the divine process, God
does indeed yearn for the physical fulfillment of God's primordial creative
vision. Although divine "appetition" does strive for "enjoyment" (PR, 348),
the life of God "for itself" is nonetheless positioned beyond old and new
as *pure intensity*, indifferent to the world and yet living the satisfaction of
the life of the world "for itself." The *mystery of God's indifference* provides a
glimpse into the life of God beyond love "for us."

The Mystery of God's In/difference

God's indifference *simultaneously* manifests itself in love "for us,"[26] that is,
as God's superjective self-transcendence, as self-revelation, as God's essential relationality, as intercreative communication. Hence the mystery
of God's "indifference" is ultimately that of the *nondifference* of God "for
Godself" and "for us"[27]—something I call God's *"in/difference."*[28] Three
steps lead from the mystery of "indifference" to the mystery of God's "in/

24. Lambert, "On Whitehead's Proposition," 92–103.
25. Faber, *God as Poet*, §28.
26. Faber, "'Über Gott und die Welt.'"
27. Beierwaltes, *Identität and Differenz*.
28. Faber, "De-Ontologizing God."

difference," steps constituting a genuine expression of the tradition of mystical theology—a tradition reaching far back into the Neoplatonic articulation of "negative theology" among the Cappadocian fathers and Dionysius the Areopagite, and reaching its preeminent expression in the theology of Meister Eckhart and Nicholas of Cusa.[29]

(1) *God's essential relationality* is grounded in the *mystery of nondifference* between God and world, disclosed in what, for process theology, constitutes the fundamental *theopoetic difference* between "God" and "creativity,"[30] and finding its integrative expression in the *indistinctiveness* (undifferentiated status) of God and world,[31] as expressed in the *divine matrix*.[32] Although intercreativity does imply a "pantheistic nimbus" within process theology,[33] it does genuinely express the indistinctiveness of God and world. It is not without good reason that Bracken found the theopoetic difference between "God" and "creativity" prefigured in Meister Eckhart's distinction between "God" and "Godhead."[34] Whereas in Meister Eckhart (as in Whitehead), "God" stands for the *difference* between God and world—for God as creator and the world as creation—he understands the "Godhead" (as does Whitehead with "creativity") as a sphere of *nondifference* between God and world. In Meister Eckhart's German sermon *Beati paupers spiritu*, it stands "over all being and beyond all difference."[35] Hence in the "Godhead," there is no distinction between God and creature—albeit *not* because God and creation are *identical*, but because the "Godhead" *precedes* and *grounds* the difference between God and world.[36]

God's nondifference in this sense is part of *theopoetic difference*. Initially one can (with Rahner) understand the "pantheistic sphere" with respect to "intercreativity" or the "divine matrix" (similar to Meister Eckhart's reference to the "Godhead") as an expression of God's *self*-differentiation.[37] In this sense, there is no "difference" *between* God and world in which God might be distinguished *from the perspective of the world*, since every difference between God and world is a *self*-difference of God (from the world) that precedes all

29. Haubst, *Streifzüge in die cusanische Theologie*; Faber, "'Gottesmeer.'"

30. Faber, *God as Poet*, §28.

31. Beierwaltes, *Identität and Differenz*.

32. Faber, *God as Poet*, §32.

33. Faber, *God as Poet*, §35.

34. Bracken, *Divine Matrix*.

35. Quint, *Meister Eckhart*, 308.

36. Faber, "'Gottesmeer.'"

37. Faber, *God as Poet*, §35.

capacity for distinguishing on the part of the creaturely world itself.[38] God differentiates Godself from the world *in precisely such a way that* God is neither positioned "over against" the world (in some ultimate dualism) nor identical with it (in some ultimate pantheism). Instead, God does *not distinguish* Godself from it. God's transcendence is God's self-difference from the world, which ultimately *comes forth* from God's radical nondifference from the world. *This is why* God's *alterity* (God's "own" life in "indifference" toward the world) consists in *radical relationality* and *loving proximity* to the world.[39] Nicholas of Cusa referred to this radical alterity of God with what for him was one of the highest divine names, namely, God as the "non-other" (*non aliud*). In God's nondifference, God is *so* "different" that no other contrast or opposite to God can be adduced.[40] This *non aliud* comes to expression in the *intercreativity* of the divine matrix insofar as God's self-creativity bequeaths itself to the world as the world's *own*, innermost self-creativity. Within the *nondifference of the divine matrix*, God comes forth (paradoxically) precisely *as* God, and the world *as* world.[41]

(2) The "indifference" (of God's "inner life") discloses itself within the Trinitarian mystery of the *nondifference of the "threefold character*,"[42] and in God's Trinitarian love "for us."[43] In light of the *non aliud*, *Sophia/ Logos* in herself, is God's primordial concrescence because she represents the primordial nondifference of form and act and thereby carries through "for us" the primordial difference of form and act that renders the world possible as creation—precisely in the nondifference between God and world, and as the *source* of the difference between God and creature in the initial aim.[44] In light of the *non aliud*, the *Pneuma* "in itself" is the primordial delimited condition in which everything in God is "God," and thereby simultaneously—"for us"—the *reconciled nondifference* of creature and God in eschatological Peace.[45] In light of the *non aliud*, God's *superject* is the primordiality in which God grounds the nondifference of nature and person, act and actuality "for Godself" and carries through the primordial difference of nature and person "for us."[46]

---

38. Rahner, *Grundkurs*.
39. Faber, *Prozeßtheologie*.
40. Faber, "Gottesmeer.'"
41. Faber, *God as Poet*, §32.
42. Faber, *God as Poet*, §34.
43. Faber, *God as Poet*, §38.
44. Faber, "Zeitumkehr."
45. Faber, *Prozeßtheologie*.
46. Faber, *Prozeßtheologie*.

This "inner" divine life (God's "indifference") is nothing other than the *Trinitarian nondifference of love.* Nicholas of Cusa, we remember, described this connex in *De venatione sapientiae* with the succinct Trinitarian formulation deriving from the notion of *non aliud,* namely, that the "non-other *(non aliud)* is nothing other *(non aliud)* than the non-other *(non aliud)*."[47] Reference to this subtle Trinitarian formula of the *non aliud* is simultaneously reference to God's indifferent life "for Godself" *and* the radical, nondifferent intimacy of God's love for us. This paradoxical distance (God's "inner" life) and intimacy (God's love for creation) attaching to God's nondifference, comes to expression in the fact that everything *in God* is Trinitarian nondifference, and *in the world,* exhibits the Trinitarian character of God's life *(vestigium Trinitatis).*[48] Nicholas of Cusa speaks about this movement of nondifference in which everything in God is "God" and in the world is "itself" as a "complication" *(complicatio)* of God through which God has *enfolded* everything in Godself, and as an "explication" *(explicatio)* through which God is *unfolded* in everything in the world.[49] This Trinitarian "complication" and "explication" (exchange of life and love) that *is* the divine matrix, is the mystery of continuity between God and world that is inter-creativity.[50]

(3) God's "in/difference" refers to the *mystery of the nondifference between difference and nondifference* in God. "In/difference" is the loving origin of all difference, the real expression and operation of the "foundational process of creativity" in God, that is, of God's superjectivity.[51] The event of God's superjectivity *is* the event of "in/difference," and the latter the "source" of all difference—even that between difference and nondifference. In his final essay, "Immortality" (1941), and largely unnoticed by process theology, Whitehead discloses the theopoetic difference between God and creativity in precisely this fashion, namely, as the in/difference between the *personal difference* of God and world and the *transpersonal nondifference* of creativity in God and world.[52] "God" appears as the ground of the valuation process—of the "World of Value," which provides both aesthetic and ethical relevance, intensity and harmony in difference (Imm., 696). By contrast, "creativity" appears as the ground of the creative process—of the "World of Creativity," of the self and intercreativity within which both world and God "live" their spontaneity nondifferently (Imm., 694). Whitehead views both "worlds" and

---

47. Gabriel, *Nikolaus von Kues,* 65.

48. Faber, *God as Poet,* §33.

49. Flasch, *Nikolaus von Kues.*

50. Faber, "Creation as Differentiation."

51. Faber, *God as Poet,* §28.

52. Faber, *God as Poet,* §28.

their "grounds" "for themselves" as an *abstraction* from the *one* universe, from the *one wholeness of the process itself* (Imm., 696).[53]

Theopoetic difference is grounded ultimately in *theopoetic in/difference.* That is, God not only is *the* nondifference beyond all differences as such ("Godhead," creativity, *non aliud*); God also has *no* juxtaposed or opposite "counterpart"—not even that of a theopoetic difference between difference ("God") and nondifference ("creativity").[54] Here Whitehead's "one totality of the process" takes its place within the tradition of mystical theology.[55] Nicholas of Cusa "defines God not only as *non alind* (nondifference), but "prior to all differences . . . even prior to the difference of indifference and difference."[56] This is what I refer to as God's "in/difference," which is *beyond* the difference of "God" and "creativity," "God" and "Godhead," "value" and "creativity," "difference" and "nondifference."[57] It is here, in *theopoetic in/difference*, that the circle is completed between the "indifference" (of God's life "for itself") and the divine intimacy of "nondifference" (as love "for us"), both ultimately *expressing* the same in/difference.

The Mystery of God's Insistence

Theopoetic in/difference *happens* as differentiation *and* nondifferentiation and refers to the *primordial act of God's superjectivity*, that is, the *creative in/difference of self-creativity and self-transcendence* generating (*explicatio*) and simultaneously gathering within itself (*complicatio*) all difference and non-difference.[58] I borrow a term from Gilles Deleuze in referring to this *movement of God's superjective in/differentiation* as the mystery of God's *insistence* (as opposed to *ex-sistere*, existence).[59] God, precisely in God's alterity, being all-relational and acting *creatively* within the primordial process of "in/differentiation," can thus be referred to as the primordial act of *différance*, an act no longer comprehensible in the categories of "essence"/"existence"; at this point, even reference to "God" as such thus becomes in/different.

(1) For the "negative theology" of the mystics, God is the "One" beyond all categories (of being). In its emphasis on God's alterity, however, and on the basis of God's in/difference, this negative assertion paradoxically

---

53. Faber, *God as Poet*, §12.
54. Faber, "De-Ontologizing God."
55. Beierwaltes, *Identität and Differenz.*
56. Flasch, *Nikolaus von Kues*, 608.
57. Faber, "'Gottesmeer.'"
58. Faber, "Creation as Differentiation."
59. Faber, "Insistenz."

requires that because God is indeed *nothing* beyond all differences, God thus appears only *in* difference. The negative "One" is paradoxically *simultaneously* already the *world-oriented* "All-One."[60] The "All-One" is *all-relational*. This mystical paradox of the "coincidence of opposites" (*coincidencia oppositorum*) brings the theopoetic in/difference to genuine expression by describing the element of God's self-relatedness simultaneously as *essential relationality*. This is God's "insistence," namely, superjective in/difference as pure *agape*, God's self-creativity as pure self-transcendence.

(2) This superjective in/difference, as the primordial *process* of in/differentiation (*complicatio* and *explicatio*), is the primordial creative act that God "is."[61] For the superjective in/difference is already the creative *origin* of the difference between difference ("God," "value," "person") and nondifference ("Godhead," "creativity," "nature") and thus the *source of all* difference. The essential relationality of God's essence, which effusively moves beyond itself in the communication of the divine matrix, is grounded in the paradoxical countermovement of the creative "in/differentiation" of *complicatio* and *explicatio*. Because theopoetic in/difference has no intention of being something "for itself" without at the same time being such "for others" as well (principle of relativity), that is, has no intention of being some dark mystery "behind all differences," it is always already living *as* self-transcendent, creative love; that is, God's creative in/difference *in-sists*.[62]

(3) Theopoetic in/difference is the origin of, that is, the insistence on, *différance*. Like the latter, it too—as Derrida puts it—is "older" than ontological difference; because it does *not* refer back to any sort of "foundation," it is not comprehensible in categories of "ground," "presence," "being," or "existence." Although Whitehead is well aware of the cosmological, teleological, and ontological proofs for God's existence, he rejects them as being incapable of reaching God (PR, 93; MT, 113).[63] Although rationalistic process theology was tempted to adduce Anselm of Canterbury's ontological argument,[64] a consideration of the mystery of superjective in/difference shows this to be impossible. Because God's primordiality is what differentiates the categories of form and act, person and nature, being and nothingness in the first place, it cannot be comprehended with their aid. As in the mystical theology of Nicholas of Cusa, the *coincidencia*

---

60. Faber, "'Gottesmeer.'"

61. Faber, "Creation as Differentiation."

62. Faber, "De-Ontologizing God."

63. Connelly, "The Existence and Nature of God"; Phillipson, *A Metaphysics for Theology*; Faber, *Prozeßtheologie*.

64. Hartshorne, *Logic of Perfection*; Faber, *God as Poet*, §4.

oppositorum and the *non aliud* are *antecedent* to the difference between being and nothingness.[65] That is why one can speak about them in the form
neither of "existence" nor of "essence." Contra references to God's "ex-
sistence," the mystery of in/difference is better served by understanding
God as a *superjective event that insists by loving*, as that which in the primal
act of primordial differentiation (primordial envisagement)—which one
can understand with Ford as corresponding to originless origin in God
(the Father)[66]—first creates the difference between being and nothingness
through which it is itself thus *not* comprehensible.[67] And yet it is still "present" insofar as it *insistently loves*, freely giving of itself as *agape*.[68] Contra
references to God's "hyperessence,"[69] which ultimately understands God
(in Derrida's sense) as fulfilled presence,[70] God is now understood as that
particular *eschatological event that insists insofar as it remains the "supreme
Adventure."*[71] It delimits everything into God (*complicatio*) by simultaneously opening up *différance* and insisting *within* it.[72]

(4) In this theopoetic in/difference, language reaches the boundaries
at which negative and positive theology begin to flow into each other.[73]
Nicholas of Cusa encountered this final consequence of mystical theology
in his last great work, *De apice theoriae* (1464), by considering the most
extreme alterity (negativity) of the *non aliud*, and in its radical world-
orientation (positivity) by trying to articulate these beyond the difference
between negation and position. Here he "de-fines" (de-limits) God in pure
positivity as "can itself" (*posse ipsum*).[74] This is the crowning step beyond
all difference within in/difference insofar as it manifests itself wholly *in
differences*. Here, God is interpreted as *can (potency)*, as the *in/difference of
possibility and power*. Such is attained in theopoetic in/difference insofar as
God is understood as *creative insistence* in the form of a primordial creation
of the difference between idea and creativity. Insistence comes to express
theopoetics itself, since God's *poiesis* is in fact God's threefold *posse*, the
superjective in/difference of the *creative power of primordial possibility* (of

65. Faber, "'Gottesmeer.'"
66. Faber, *God as Poet*, §34: Model II.
67. Ford, "Creativity as a Future Key," 179–97.
68. Faber, "De-Ontologizing God."
69. Almond, "How Not to Deconstruct a Dominican."
70. Faber, *God as Poet*, §18.
71. Ibid., §39.
72. Faber, "Creation as Differentiation."
73. Faber, "'Gottesmeer.'"
74. Flasch, *Nikolaus von Kues*; Faber, "Creation as Differentiation."

that which provides space for that which is real) within the primordial nature and the *delimitation of all power into its eschatological possibility* (that
which redemptively enfolds everything toward its highest possibility) in
the consequent nature.

Here, divine *poiesis* is the pure affirmation of the *posse*; but, I would
add, now, that this posse must be deprived of its complicity with "power,"
thereby becoming erased into *pure polyphilia without any power* and *pure
theoplicity without leering at the wrinkleless "One."* To remind us a last time
of Whitehead's line on the "poet of the world," the *posse* of the divine *poiesis* must *completely subtract itself from the complicity of "creation"*—God as
being "someone" creating, a "self" being subject of self-creativity, a "force-
field" of creativity, a "divine matrix"—and *affirm nothing but the salvation
of the manifold, that is, in-sist only in/as/on infinite manifoldness.* Yet it is
a "transpantheist" manifold, a "theoplicity," a divine folding in all foldings
that is not identical with any of them, or with the whole of foldedness, but
not different from them either: complete subtraction as the divine in/differ-
ence in/from the world (all worlds) as creative in/finity.

Bibliography

Abe, Masao. *Zen and Western Thought*. Honolulu: University of Hawaii Press, 1985.

Alighieri, Dante. *The Divine Comedy (The Inferno, The Purgatorio, and The Paradiso)*. New York: NAL Trade, 2003.

Almond, Ian. "How *Not* to Deconstruct a Dominican: Derrida on God and 'Hypertruth.'" *Journal of the American Academy of Religion* 68/2 (2000) 329–44.

Aquinas, Thomas. *Summa Contra Gentiles. Book One: God*. Notre Dame: University of Notre Dame Press, 1992.

Badiou, Alain. *Being and Event*. New York: Continuum, 2005.

———. *Infinite Thought: Truth and the Return to Philosophy*. New York: Continuum, 2003.

Baker, Robert. *The Extravagant Crossings Of Modern Poetry and Modern Philosophy*. Notre Dame: University of Notre Dame Press, 2005.

Barstow, Anne L. *Witchcraze: A New History of European Witch Hunts*. London: Pandora, 1995.

Bataille, George. *Inner Experience*. Albany: SUNY Press, 1988.

———. *Theory of Religion*. New York: Zone, 1992.

Baugh, Bruce. "Deleuze und der Empirismus." In *Gilles Deleuze—Fluchtlinien der Philosophie*, edited by Friedrich Balke and Joseph Vogl, 34–54. München: William Fink, 1996.

Beelitz, Thomas. *Die dynamische Beziehung zwischen Erfahrung und Metaphysik. Eine Untersuchung der Spekulativen Philosophie von Alfred North Whitehead im Interesse der Theologie*. Frankfurt: Peter Lang, 1991.

Beierwaltes, Werner. *Identität und Differenz*. Frankfurt: Klostermann, 1980.

Bell, Jeffrey A. *Philosophy at the Edge of Chaos: Gilles Deleuze and the Philosophy of Difference*. Toronto: University of Toronto Press, 2006.

Balthasar, Hans Urs von. *Theodramatik*. Vol. 4. Einsiedeln: Johannes, 1983.

Boethius. *The Consolation of Philosophy*. Oxford: Oxford University Press, 2002.

Bond, H. Lawrence. *Nicholas of Cusa: Selected Spiritual Writings*. Mahwah, NJ: Paulist, 1997.

Bracken, Joseph A. *The Divine Matrix: Creativity as Link between East and West*. Maryknoll, NY: Orbis, 1995.

———. "Energy-events and Fields." *Process Studies* 18/3 (1989) 153–65.

———. *The One and the Many: A Contemporary Reconstruction of the God-World Relationship*. Grand Rapids: Eerdmans, 2001.

———. "Process Philosophy and Trinitarian Theology." *Process Studies* 8/4 (1978) 217–30.

———. "Process Philosophy and Trinitarian Theology-II." *Process Studies* 11/2 (1981) 83–96.

———. *Society and Spirit: A Trinitarian Cosmology.* Selinsgrove, PA: Susquehanna University Press, 1991.

———. "Whitehead and the Critique of Logocentrism." In *Process and Difference: Between Cosmological and Poststructuralist Postmodernism*, edited by Catherine Keller and Ann Daniels, 91–110. New York: SUNY Press, 2002.

Bradley, James. "Transcendentalism and Speculative Realism in Whitehead." *Process Studies* 23 (1994) 155–91.

Butler, Judith. *Bodies That Matter: On the Discursive Limits of "Sex."* New York: Routledge, 1993.

———. *Gender Trouble: Feminism and the Subversion of Identity.* New York: Routledge, 1999.

———. *Giving Account of Oneself.* New York: Fordham University Press, 2005.

Caputo, John D. *Deconstruction in a Nutshell: A Conversation with Jacques Derrida.* New York: Fordham University Press, 2005.

———. *Heidegger and Aquinas: An Essay on Overcoming Metaphysics.* New York: Fordham University Press, 1982.

———. *The Prayers and Tears of Jacques Derrida: Religion without Religion.* Bloomington: Indiana University Press, 1997.

———. *The Weakness of God: A Theology of the Event.* Bloomington: Indiana University Press, 2006.

Carlson, Thomas. "Postmodernity's Finitude and Apophatic Unknowing of Dionysian Traditions." In *AAR/SLB-Abstracts*, 1996.

Case-Winters, Anna. *God's Power: Traditional Understandings and Contemporary Challenges.* Louisville: Westminster John Knox, 1990.

Casey, Edward. *The Fate of Place: A Philosophical History.* Berkeley: University of California Press, 2003.

Catechism of the Catholic Church. 2nd ed. New York: Doubleday, 2003.

Celenza, Christopher S. "The Revival of Platonic Philosophy." In *The Cambridge Companion to Renaissance Philosophy*, edited by James Hankins, 72–96. Cambridge: Cambridge University Press, 2007.

Clayton, Philip, and Arthur Peacocke, eds. *In Whom We Live and Move and Have Our Being: Panentheistic Reflections On God's Presence In A Scientific World.* Grand Rapids: Eerdmans, 2004.

Clearly, Thomas. *The Original Face: An Anthology of Rinzai Zen.* 1st ed. New York: Grove, 1978.

Clooney, Francis X. "Current Theology: Comparative Theology: A Review of Recent." *Theological Studies* 56 (1995) 521–55.

Cobb, John B., Jr. *Beyond Dialogue: Toward a Mutual Transformation of Christianity and Buddhism.* Philadelphia: Fortress, 1982.

———. *A Christian Natural Theology.* Philadelphia: Westminster, 1965.

———. "Freedom in Whitehead's Philosophy." In *Explorations in Whitehead's Philosophy*, edited by Lewis S. Ford and George L. Kline, 45–52. New York: Fordham University Press, 1983.

———. "The Independence of Christian Faith from Speculative Reliefs." PhD diss., Chicago Divinity School, 1952.

———. *Process Theology as Political Theology*. Manchester: Manchester University Press, 1982.

Cobb, John B., Jr., and David Ray Griffin. *Process Theology: An Introductory Exposition*. Louisville: Westminster John Knox, 1976.

Cobb, John B., Jr., and Christopher Ives, eds. *The Emptying God: A Buddhist Jewish-Christian Conversation*. Maryknoll, NY: Orbis, 1990.

Connelly, George E. "The Existence and Nature of God in the Philosophy of Alfred North Whitehead." PhD diss., St. Louis University, 1962.

Cooper, Ron L. *Heidegger and Whitehead: A Phenomenological Examination into the Intelligibility of Experience*. Athens: Ohio University Press, 1993.

Corbin, Henry. *Alone with the Alone: Creative Imagination in the Sufism of Ibn Arabi*. Princeton: Princeton University Press, 1997.

———. *Face de Dieu, Face de l'homme: Herméneutique et soufisme*. Paris: Entrelacs, 2008.

Dalferth, Ingolf U. "Die theoretische Theologie der Prozeßphilosophie Whiteheads." In *Religion im Denken unserer Zeit*, edited by W. Harle and E. Wölfel, 163–75. Marburg: 1986.

———. *Religiöse Rede von Gott*. München: Kaiser, 1981.

Deleuze, Gilles. *Bergsonism*. Brooklyn: Zone, 1988.

———. *Desert Islands and Other Texts, 1953–1974*. Paris: semiotext(e), 2004.

———. *Difference and Repetition*. New York: Columbia University Press, 1994.

———. *Essays: Critical and Clinical*. Translated by Daniel W. Smith and Michael A. Greco. Minneapolis: University of Minnesota Press, 1997.

———. *Expressionism in Philosophy: Spinoza*. New York: Zone, 1992.

———. *The Fold: Leibniz and the Baroque*. Minneapolis: University of Minnesota Press, 1992.

———. "Immanence: A Life." In *Pure Immanence: Essays on a Life*. Translated by Anne Boyman. New York: Zone, 2005.

———. *Lecture on Spinoza in Vincennes of December 16, 1980*. https://www.webdeleuze.com/textes/10.

———. *The Logic of Sense*. New York: Columbia University Press, 1990.

———. *Negotiations: 1972–1990*. New York: Columbia University Press, 1995.

———. *Nietzsche and Philosophy*. New York: Columbia University Press, 2006.

———. *Two Regimes of Madness: Texts and Interviews, 1975–1995*. New York: semiotext(e), 2006.

Deleuze, Gilles, and Félix Guattari. *Anti-Oedipus: Capitalism and Schizophrenia*. Translated by Robert Hurley, Mark Seem, and Helen R. Lane. Minneapolis: University of Minnesota Press, 1996.

———. *A Thousand Plateaus*. Minneapolis: University of Minnesota Press, 1987.

———. *What Is Philosophy?* New York: Columbia University Press, 1994.

Deleuze, Gilles, and Claire Parnet. *Dialogues*. Translated by Hugh Tomlinson and Barbara Habberjam. New York: Columbia University Press, 1997.

Denzinger, Heinrich. *Kompendium der Glauhensbekenntnisse und kirchlichen Lehrentscheidungen*. Edited by Peter Hünermann. Freiburg: Herder, 1991.

Derrida, Jacques. "Back from Moscow, in the USSR." In *Politics, Theory, and Contemporary Culture*, edited by Mark Poster, 197–235. New York: Columbia University Press, 1993.

———. "Chora." In *Chora L Works: A Collaboration Between Peter Eisenman and Jacques Derrida*, edited by J. Kipins. New York: Monacelli, 1993.

———. "Geschlecht: Sexual Difference, Ontological Difference." *Research in Phenomenology* 13 (1983) 65–83.

———. "Khora." In *On the Name*, edited by Thomas Dutoit, David Wood, and John P. Leavey Jr., 89–127. Translated by Ian McLeod. Stanford: Stanford University Press, 1995.

———. "*Ousia* and *Gramme*: Note on a Note from Being and Time." In *Margins of Philosophy*, 26–68. Chicago: University of Chicago Press, 1985.

———. "Violence and Metaphysics." In *Writing and Difference*, 79–153. Chicago: University of Chicago Press, 1978.

———. "White Mythology: Metaphor in the Text of Philosophy." In *Margins of Philosophy*, 207–71. Chicago: University of Chicago Press, 1985.

Douglass, James W. *The Non-Violent Cross: A Theology of Revolution and Peace*. Eugene: Wipf & Stock, 2006.

D'Sa, Francis X. *Gott der Dreieine und der All-Ganze. Vorwort zur Begegnung zwischen Christentum und Hinduismus*. Düsseldorf: Patmos, 1987.

Duns Scotus, Johannes. *God and Creatures: The Quodlibetal Questions*. Edited by Felix Alluntis and Allan B. Wolter. Princeton: Princeton University Press, 1975.

Eckhart, Meister. *Deutsche Predigten und Traktate*. 3rd ed. Edited by Josef Quint. München, 1969.

Eissfeldt, Otto. "Gott und das Meer in der Bibel." In *Kleine Schriften*, 3:256–64. Tubingen: Mohr, 1966.

Emmet, Dorothy. *The Nature of Metaphysical Thinking*. New York: St. Martin's, 1966.

Faber, Roland. "'Amid a Democracy of Fellow Creatures'—Onto/Politics and the Problem of Slavery in Whitehead and Deleuze (with an Intervention of Badiou)." In *Event and Decision: Ontology and Politics in Badiou, Deleuze, and Whitehead*, edited by Roland Faber et al., 192–237. Cambridge: Cambridge Scholars, 2010.

———. "Apocalypse in God: On the Power of God in Process Eschatology." *Process Studies* 31/2 (2002) 64–96.

———. *The Becoming of God: Process Theology, Philosophy and Multireligious Engagement*. Eugene, OR: Cascade, 2017.

———. "Ecotheology, Ecoprocess, and Ecotheosis: A Theopoetical Intervention." *Salzburger Zeitschrift für Theologie* 12 (2008) 75–115.

———. "Creation as Differentiation: Toward a Third Space-Concept of Creation as 'Self-Differentiating In/Difference' in Dialogue with Mystical and Process Theology." Conference paper presented at Drew University, New Jersey, September 2001.

———. "Cultural Symbolization of a Sustainable Future." In *New Directions in Sustainable Design*, edited by Adrian Parr and Michael Zaretsky, 242–55. London: Routledge, 2011.

———. "De-Ontologizing God: Levinas, Deleuze and Whitehead." In *Process and Difference: Between Cosmological and Poststructuralist Postmodernism*, edited by C. Keller and A. Daniels, 209–34. New York: SUNY Press, 2002.

————. *Der Selbsteinsatz Gottes. Grundlegung einer Theologie des Leidens und der Veränderlichkeit Gottes. Studien zur systematischen und spirituellen Theologie.* Würzburg: Echter, 1995.

————. *Die neue Zukunft Gottes. Eine biblische und systematische Untersuchung der Frage nach dem 'Neu-Werden' des trinitarischen Gottes und seines 'neuen Zu-Kommens' im Eschaton als Aspekte christlichen Gottesverständnisses.* Vienna: University of Vienna Press, 1985.

————. *The Divine Manifold.* Lanham, MD: Lexington, 2014.

————. *Freiheit, Theologie und Lehramt: Trinitätstheologische Grundlegung und wissenschaftstheoretischer Ausblick.* Innsbruck: Tyrolia, 1992.

————. "Forgotten Among the Lillies: Mother Teresa's Experience of Eternal Abandonment." Lecture and panelist on "The Absence and Presence of God—Four Commentaries on Mother Teresa's Dark Night of the Soul." Claremont Graduate University, October 2007.

————. *The Garden of Reality: Transreligious Relativity in a World of Becoming.* Lanham, MD: Lexington, 2018.

————. *God as Poet of the World: Exploring Process Theologies.* Louisville: Westminster John Knox, 2008.

————. "God's Advent/ure: The End of Evil and the Origin of Time." In *World Without End: Christian Eschatology from Process Perspective*, edited by Joseph Bracken, 91–112. Grand Rapids: Eerdmans, 2005.

————. "God's Love without God? The Non-Difference of God as Mystical Solution of Feuerbach's Antinomy of Love." American Academy of Religion Annual Meeting, Denver, CO, November 2001.

————. *Gott als Poet der Welt: Anliegen und Perspektiven der Prozesstheologie.* 2nd ed. Darmstadt: Wissenschaftliche Buchgesellschaft Darmstadt, 2004.

————. "'Gottesmeer'—Versuch über die Ununterschiedenheit Gottes." In *"Leben in Fülle." Skizzen zur christlichen Spiritualität*, edited by Th. Dienberg and M. Plattig, 64–95. Münster: LIT, 2001.

————. "Immanence and Incompleteness: Whitehead's Late Metaphysics." In *Beyond Metaphysics? Conversations on A. N. Whitehead's Late Thought*, edited by Roland Faber et al., 91–110. Contemporary Whitehead 1. Amsterdam: rodopi, 2010.

————. "In the Wake of False Unifications Whitehead's Creative Resistance against Imperialist Theologies." Claremont School of Theology, March 2005.

————. "'The Infinite Movement of Evanescence'—The Pythagorean Puzzle in Plato, Deleuze, and Whitehead." *American Journal of Theology and Philosophy* 21/1 (2000) 171–99.

————. "Insistenz—Zum, 'Nicht-Sein' Gottes bei Levinas, Deleuze und Whitehead." In *Das integrale und das gebrochene Ganze*, edited by Yvanka Raynova and Susanne Moser, 131–55. Frankfurt: Peter Lang, 2005.

————. "Introduction: Negotiating Becoming." In *Secrets of Becoming: Negotiating Whitehead, Deleuze, and Butler*, edited by Roland Faber and Andrea Stephenson, 1–50. New York: Fordham University Press, 2010.

————. "Khora and Violence: Revisiting Butler with Whitehead." In *Butler on Whitehead: On the Occasion*, edited by Roland Faber et al., 105–26. Lanham, MD: Lexington, 2012.

————. "The Manifestation of God in the View of Process Theology." *Lights of Irfán* 20 (2019) 7–54.

———. "My Faith in Baha'u'llah: A Declaration." *Bahá'í Studies Review* 20 (2014) 149–74.

———. *The Ocean of God: On the Transreligious Future of Religions*. London: Anthem, 2019.

———. "'O bitches of impossibility!'—Programmatic Dysfunction in the Chaosmos of Deleuze and Whitehead." In *Deleuze, Whitehead, Bergson: Rhizomatic Connections*, edited by Keith Robinson, 200–219. New York: Palgrave Macmillan, 2009.

———. "Personsein am Ort der Leere." *Neue Zeitschrift für Systematische Theologie* 44 (2002) 189–98.

———. "Prozesstheologie." In *Theologien der Gegenwart. Eine Einführung*, edited by C. Barwasser, R. Bioschki, G. Collet, R. Faber, 179–97. Darmstadt: Wissenschaftliche Buchgesellschaft Darmstadt, 2006.

———. *Prozeßtheologie. Zu ihrer Würdigung und kritischen Erneuerung*. Mainz: Gruenewald, 2000.

———. "'Sounding the Depth of Things?'—The Love of Multiplicity in Catholic, Process, and Poststructuralist God-Talk." Chicago Divinity School, January, 2007.

———. "Surrationality and Chaosmos: A More Deleuzian Whitehead (and a Butlerian Inter-vention)." In *Secrets of Becoming: Negotiating Whitehead, Deleuze, and Butler*, edited by Roland Faber and Andrea Stephenson, 157–77. New York: Fordham University Press, 2010.

———. "Tears of God—In the Rain with D. Z. Philips and J. Keller, Waiting for Wittgenstein and Whitehead." In *Metaphysics, Analysis, and the Grammar of God*, edited by Randy Ramal, 57–103. Tübingen: Mohr Siebeck, 2010.

———. "'Über Gott und die Welt . . . ' Struktur analoger Gottesrede und prozeßtheologische Perspektive," In *Variationen über die Schöpfung der Welt*, edited by E. Schmetterer, R. Faber, and N. Mantler, 118–42. Innsbruck: Tyrolia, 1995.

———. "Wahrheit und Maschine: Wider das transsylvanische Argument von der Gewalt im Diskurs der Erkenntnis." *Labyrinth: International Journal for Philosophy, Feminist Theory and Cultural Hermeneutics* 3 (2001).

———. "Whitehead." In *The Deleuze Dictionary*, edited by Adrian Parr, 302–4. Edinburgh: Edinburgh University Press, 2010.

———. "Whitehead at Infinite Speed: Deconstructing System as Event." In *Schleiermacher and Whitehead: Open Systems in Dialogue*, edited by Christine Helmer, Marjorie Suchocki, John Quiring, and Katie Goetz, 39–72. Berlin: Walter de Gruyter, 2004.

———. "Zeitumkehr. Versuch über einen eschatologischen Schöpfungsbegriff." *Theologie und Philosophie* 75/2 (2000) 180–205

Faber, Roland, and Jeremy Fackenthal, eds. *Theopoetic Folds: Philosophizing Multifariousness*. New York: Fordham University Press, 2013.

Faber, Roland, and Catherine Keller. "A Taste for Multiplicity: The Skillful Means of Religious Pluralism." In *Religions in the Making: Whitehead and the Wisdom Traditions of the World*, edited by John Cobb, 180–207. Eugene, OR: Cascade, 2012.

———. "Polyphilic Pluralism: Becoming Religious Multiplicities." In *Divine Multiplicity: Trinities, Diversities, and the Nature of Relation*, edited by Chris Boesel and Wesley Ariarajah, 58–81. New York: Fordham University Press, 2014.

Faber, Roland, Henry Krips, and Daniel Peltus, eds. *Event and Decision: Ontology and Politics in Badiou, Deleuze, and Whitehead.* Cambridge: Cambridge Scholars, 2010.

Faber, Roland, and Andrea M. Stephenson, eds. *Secrets of Becoming: Negotiating Whitehead, Deleuze, and Butler.* New York: Fordham University Press, 2010.

Feuerbach, Ludwig. *The Essence of Christianity.* Amherst, MA: Prometheus, 1989.

Fiddes, Paul S. *The Creative Suffering of God.* Oxford: Oxford University Press, 1988.

Flasch, Kurt. *Nikolaus von Kues: Geschichte und Entwicklung.* Frankfurt: Klostermann, 1998.

Ford, Leighton. *The Attentive Life: Discerning God's Presence in All Things.* Downers Grove, IL: InterVarsity, 2008.

Ford, Lewis. "An Alternative to Creatio ex Nihilo." *Religious Studies* 19/2 (1983) 205–13.

———. "Creativity as a Future Key." In *New Essays in Metaphysics*, edited by Robert C. Neville, 179–97. Albany: SUNY Press, 1986.

———. "Divine Persuasion and Coercion." *Encounter* 47/3 (1986) 267–73.

———. *The Lure of God: A Biblical Background for Process Theism.* Philadelphia: Fortress, 1978.

———. "Neville on the One and the Many." *Southern Journal of Philosophy* 10 (1972) 79–84.

———. *Transforming Process Theism.* Albany: SUNY Press, 2000.

———. "The Viability of Whitehead's God on Time and Eternity." *Proceedings of the American Catholic Philosophical Association* 44 (1970) 141–51.

———. "Whitehead and the Ontological Difference." *Philosophy Today* 29 (1985) 148–55.

———. "Whitehead's Transformation of Pure Act." *The Thomist* 41/3 (1977) 381–99.

Ford, Lewis, and George L. Kline, eds. *Explorations in Whitehead's Metaphysics.* New York: Fordham University Press, 1983.

Foucault, Michel. *Power/Knowledge: Selected Interviews and Other Writings, 1972–1977.* New York: Pantheon, 1980.

———. *Überwachen und Strafen.* Frankfurt: Suhrkamp, 1977.

Frank, Richard. *Al-Ghazali and the Asharite School.* Durham, NC: Duke University Press, 1994.

Frankenberry, Nancy. "The Power of the Past." *Process Studies* 13/2 (1983) 132–42.

Franklin, Stephen. "God and Creativity: A Revisionist Proposal within a Whiteheadian Context." *Process Studies* 29/2 (2000) 237–307.

Franklin, Stuart. *Speaking from the Depth: Alfred North Whitehead's Hermeneutical Metaphysics of Propositions, Experience, Symbolism, Language, and Religion.* Grand Rapids: Eerdmans, 1990.

Gabriel, Leo, ed. *Nikolaus von Kues: Philosophisch Theologische Schriften I.* Vienna: Herder, 1989.

Garland, William. "The Ultimacy of Creativity." In *Explorations in Whitehead's Philosophy*, edited by Lewis S. Ford and George Kline, 212–38. New York: Fordham University Press, 1983.

Garland-Hill, Marlene L. *Slavery and Christianity: The Untold Story.* Ramona, CA: Vision, 2009.

Gilkey, Langdon, "Process Theology." *Vox Theologica* 43 (1973) 5–29.

Girard, Rene. *Violence and the Sacred.* Baltimore: The Johns Hopkins University Press, 1979.

Griffin, David Ray, ed. *Deep Religious Pluralism*. Louisville: Westminster/John Knox, 2005.

———. *God, Power, and Evil: A Process Theodicy*. Philadelphia: Westminster, 1976.

———. "Hartshorne, God and Relativity Physics." *Process Studies* 21/2 (1992) 85–112.

———. "John Cobb's Whiteheadian Complementary Pluralism." In *Deep Religious Pluralism*, edited by David Ray Griffin, 39–66. Louisville: Westminster/John Knox, 2005.

———. "Process Theology as Empirical, Rational, and Speculative: Some Reflections on Method." *Process Studies* 19/2 (1990) 116–35.

———. *Reenchantment without Supernaturalism: A Process Philosophy of Religion*. Ithaca, NY: Cornell University Press, 2001.

———. "Religious Pluralism: Generic, Identist, and Deep." In *Deep Religious Pluralism*, edited by David Ray Griffin, 3–38. Louisville: Westminster/John Knox, 2005.

Grillmeier, Alois. "Jesus von Nazareth—im Schatten des Gottessohnes?" In *Diskussion über Hans Küngs "Christ Sein"*, edited by Hans Urs von Balthasar. Mainz: Matthias-Grünewald, 1976.

Grosz, Elizabeth E. *Space, Time, and Perversion: Essays on the Politics of Bodies*. New York: Routledge, 1995.

Gutting, Gary. *French Philosophy in the Twentieth Century*. Cambridge: Cambridge University Press, 2001.

Haines, Simon. *Poetry and Philosophy from Homer to Rousseau: Romantic Souls, Realist Lives*. New York: Palgrave Macmillan, 2005.

Hamilton, Peter. *The Living God and the Modern World*. London: Hodder and Stoughton, 1967.

Hampe, Michael. *Die Wahrnehmungen der Organismen: Über die Voraussetzungen einer naturalistischen Metaphysik Whiteheads*. Göttingen: Vandenhoeck & Ruprecht, 1990.

Hardt, Michael. *Gilles Deleuze: An Apprenticeship in Philosophy*. Minneapolis: University of Minnesota, 1995.

Harman, Graham. "On Vicarious Causation." In *Collapse: Philosophical Research and Development*, edited by Robin MacKay, 2:187–221. Oxford: Urbanomic, 2007.

———. *Prince of Networks: Bruno Latour and Metaphysics*. Manchester: Re-press 2009.

———. *Tool-Being: Heidegger and the Metaphysics of Objects*. Chicago: Open Court, 2002.

———. *Towards Speculative Realism: Essays and Lectures*. Winchester, UK: Zero, 2010.

Hart, Kevin. "The Experience of Nonexperience." In *Mystics: Presence and Aporia*, edited by Michael Kessler and Christian Sheppard, 188–206. Chicago: Chicago University Press, 2003.

Hartshorne, Charles. *Anselm's Discovery: A Re-Examination of the Ontological Argument for God's Existence*. Chicago: Open Court, 1965.

———. *Divine Relativity: A Social Conception of God*. New Haven: Yale University Press, 1982.

———. *The Logic of Perfection*. La Salle, IL: Open Court, 1962.

———. "Whitehead's Idea of God." In *The Philosophy of Alfred North Whitehead*, edited by Paul Arthur Schilpp, 513–60. La Salle, IL: Open Court, 1991.

Haubst, Rudolf. *Streifzüge in die cusanische Theologie*. Münster: Aschendorff, 1991.

Haught, John F. *God and the New Atheism: A Critical Response to Dawkins, Harris, and Hitchens*. Louisville: Westminster John Knox, 2007.

———. *What Is God? How to Think about the Divine*. New York: Paulist, 1986.

Heidegger, Martin. "The Anaximander Fragment." In *Early Greek thinking*, translated by David Farrell Krell and Frank A. Capuzzi, 41–42. New York: Harper & Row, 1975.

———. *Being and Time*. New York: Harper & Row, 1962.

———. "Building Dwelling Thinking." In *Basic Writings*, edited by David Farrell Krell, 343–91. San Francisco: Harper, 1993.

———. "The Essence of Truth." In *Basic Writings*, 111–38. San Francisco: Harper, 1993.

———. *An Introduction to Metaphysics*. Garden City, NJ: Doubleday Anchor, 1961.

———. *Kant and the Problem of Metaphysics*. Bloomington: Indiana University Press, 1962.

———. *The Metaphysical Foundations of Logic*. Translated by Michael Heim. Bloomington: Indiana University Press, 1984.

Heim, S. Mark. *Salvations: Truth and Difference in Religion*. Maryknoll, NY: Orbis, 1995.

Hick, John. *An Interpretation of Religion: Human Responses to the Transcendent*. New Haven: Yale University Press, 2005.

———. *Problems of Religious Pluralism*. New York: St. Martin's, 1994.

———. "Religious Faith as Experiencing—As." In *Talk of God*, edited by G. N. A. Vesey, 20–35 Royal Institute of Philosophy Lectures 2. London: MacMillan, 1969.

Higgis, Paul, director. *Crash*. September 10, 2004. Santa Monica: Lionsgate Films, 2004.

Hilkert, Mary Catherine. "Experience and Tradition." In *Freeing Theology: The Essentials of Theology in Feminist Perspective*, edited by Catherine M. Lacugna, 59–82. San Francisco: HarperSanFrancisco, 1993.

Hosinki, Thomas E. *Stubborn Fact and Creative Advance: An Introduction to the Metaphysics of Alfred North Whitehead*. Lanham, MD: Rowman & Littlefield, 1993.

Howe, J. Thomas. *Faithful to the Earth: Nietzsche and Whitehead on God and the Meaning of Human Life*. Lanham, MD: Rowman & Littlefield, 2002.

Hufeaker, Lucinda A. "Feminist Theology in Process Perspective." In *Handbook of Process Theology*, edited by Jay McDaniel and Donna Bowman, 177–87. Atlanta: Chalice, 2006.

Hünermann, Peter, ed. *Enchiridion symbolorum definitorum et declaratum de rebus fidei et morum*. 37th ed. Freiburg: Herder, 1991.

Huxley, Aldous. *The Perennial Philosophy*. New York: HarperPerennial, 2009.

Inada, Kenneth. "The Metaphysics of Buddhist Experience and the Whiteheadian Encounter." *Philosophy East and West* 25 (1975) 465–88.

Irigaray, Luce. "Equal to Whom?" In *The Postmodern God: A Theological Reader*, edited by Graham Ward, 198–214. Oxford: Blackwell, 1998.

Izutsu, Toshihiko. *Sufism and Taosim: A Comparative Study of Key Philosophical Concepts*. Berkeley: University of California Press, 1983.

Johnson, A. H. *Whitehead's Philosophy of Civilization*. Boston: Beacon Hill, 1958.

Joy, Morny. *Divine Love: Luce Irigaray, Women, Gender, and Religion*. Manchester Studies in Religion, Culture and Gender. Manchester: Manchester University Press, 2007.

Jung, Walter. "Zur Entwicklung von Whiteheads Gottesbegriff." *Zeitschrift für Philosophische Forschung* 19/4 (1965) 601–36.

Kaiser, Otto. *Die mythische Bedeutung des Meeres in Ägypten, Ugarit und Israel*. Berlin: Alfred Töpelmann, 1962.

Kann, Christoph. *Fußnoten zu Platon. Philosophiegeschichte bei A. N. Whitehead.* Hamburg: Felix Meiner, 2001.

Kasper, W., ed. *Absolutheit des Christentums.* Freiburg: Herder, 1977.

Kasprzik, B. "Whiteheads metaphysische Option." *Allgemeine Zeitschrft für Philosophie* 13 (1988) 19–36.

Kasser, Rodolphe, et al., eds. *The Gospel of Judas from Codex Tchacos.* Washington, DC: National Geographic, 2006.

Kato, Bunno, and Yoshiro Tamara, trans. *The Threefold Lotus Sutra.* Tokyo: Kosei, 2005.

Kaufman, Gordan. *In the Beginning . . . Creativity.* Minneapolis: Fortress, 2004.

Keller, Catherine. *Apocalypse Now and Then: A Feminist Guide to the End of the World.* Boston: Beacon, 1997.

————. *Face of the Deep: A Theology of Becoming.* New York: Routledge, 2003.

————. "No More Sea: The Lost Chaos of Creation." In *Christianity and Ecology: Seeking the Well-Being of Earth and Humans,* edited by Dieter T. Hessel and Anne Daniell, 55–72. Albany: SUNY Press, 2000.

Kessler, Michael, and Christian Sheppeard, eds. *Mystics: Presence and Aporia.* Chicago: University of Chicago Press, 2003.

Kline, George. "Begriff und Konkreszenz: Über einige Gemeinsamkeiten in den Ontologien Hegels und Whiteheads." In *Whitehead und der Deutsche Idealismus,* edited by George R. Lucas Jr. and Antoon Braeckman, 150–51. Bern: Peter Lang, 1990.

Knapp, M. "Dogmatik im Zeitalter des Pluralismus." In *Erfahrung–Geschichte–Identität. Zum Schnittpunkt von Philosophie und Theologie,* edited by Matthias Laarmann and Tobias Trappe, 329–42. Freiburg: Herder, 1997.

Knitter, Paul. "Can Christian Theology Be Only Christian? A Dialogical Theology for the Third Millennium." In *Theology Towards the Third Millennium: Theological Issues for the Twenty-First Century,* edited by David G. Schultenover, 83–102. Lewiston, NY: Edwin Mellen, 1991.

Kraus, Elizabeth M. *The Metaphysics of Experience: A Companion to Whitehead's "Process and Reality."* New York: Fordham University Press, 1998.

Krishna, Daya. "Comparative Philosophy: What It Is and What It Ought to Be." In *Interpreting Across Boundaries: New Essays in Comparative Philosophy,* edited by Gerald Larson and Eliot Deutsch, 71–83. Princeton: Princeton University Press, 1988.

Kristeva, Julia. *Revolution in Poetic Language.* New York: Columbia University Press, 1984.

Koch, Kurt. "Schöpferischer Lockruf im Prozess der Welt. Perspektiven der Gottesfrage in der amerikanischen Prozesstheologie." *Theologische Berichte* 12 (1983) 129–71.

Küng, Hans. *Does God Exist? An Answer for Today.* Garden City, NJ: Doubleday, 1980.

————. *A Global Ethic for Global Politics and Economics.* New York: Oxford University Press, 1997.

Lachmann, Rolf. *Ethik und Identität: Der ethische Ansatz in der Prozessphilosophie A.N. Whiteheads und seine Bedeutung für die gegenwärtige Ethik.* Freiburg i.Br.: Alber, 1990.

Lambert, Gregg. "On Whitehead's Proposition 'Life is robbery.'" In *Secular Theology: American Radical Theological Thought,* edited by Clayton Crockett, 92–103. London: Routledge, 2001.

Laquer, Thomas Walter, and Catherine Gallagher. *The Making of the Modern Body: Sexuality and Society in the 19th Century.* Berkeley: University of California Press, 1987.

Leclerc, Ivor. *Whitehead's Metaphysics: An Introductory Exposition.* London: Allen and Unwin, 1958.

Lederer, Mary Ann. "The Term 'God' in Whitehead's Philosophy." PhD diss., Temple University, 1974.

Leue, William Hendrichs. *Metaphysical Foundations for a Theory of Value in the Philosophy of Alfred North Whitehead.* Ashfield, MA: Down-to-Earth, 2003.

Leukel, Perry Schmidt. "Das Problem divergierender Wahrheitsansprüche im Rahmen einer pluralistischen Religionstheologie. Voraussetzungen zu seiner Lösung." In *Pluralistische Theologie der Religionen. Eine kritische Sichtung,* edited by H. G. Wand. Frankfurt: Lembeck, 1998.

Levin, Susan B. *The Ancient Quarrel between Philosophy and Poetry Revisited: Plato and the Greek Literary Tradition.* Oxford: Oxford University Press, 2007.

Lewis, David. "Possible Worlds." In *Contemporary Readings in the Foundations of Metaphyiscs,* edited by Stephen Laurence and Cynthia Macdonald, 96–102. Oxford: Blackwell, 1998.

Loomer, Bernard. "The Conceptions of Power." *Process Studies* 6/1 (1976) 5–32.

Lorraine, Tamsin. *Irigaray and Deleuze: Experiments in Visceral Philosophy.* Ithaca, NY: Cornell University Press, 1999.

Lowe, Victor. *Alfred North Whitehead: The Man and His Work.* Vol. 2, *1910–1947.* Edited by J. B. Schneewind. Baltimore: The Johns Hopkins University, 1990.

Lucas, George, Jr. *The Rehabilitation of Whitehead: An Analytic and Historical Assessment of Process Philosophy.* Albany: SUNY Press, 1989.

Lundeen, L. *Risk and Rhetoric in Religion: Whitehead's Theory of Language and the Discourse of Faith.* Philadelphia: Fortress, 1972.

Lycan, William. "Possible Worlds and Possibilia." In *Contemporary Readings in the Foundations of Metaphyiscs,* edited by Stephen Laurence and Cynthia Macdonald, 83–95. Oxford: Blackwell, 1998.

Lyotard, Jean-Francois. "Beantwortung der Frage: Was ist postmodern?" In *Wege aus der Moderne. Schlüsseltexte der Postmoderne-Diskussion,* edited by Wolfgang Welsch, 193–203. 2nd ed. Berlin: Acta humaniora, 1994.

Maassen, Helmut. *Gott, das Gute und das Böse in der Philosophie A. N. Whiteheads.* Frankfurt: Peter Lang, 1988.

———. "Offenbarung, Mythos und Metaphysik." In *Die Gifford-Lectures. Materialien zu Whiteheads 'Prozess und Realität',* edited by Michael Hampe and H. Maassen, 2:217–33. Frankfurt: Suhrkamp, 1991.

Malpas, Jeff. *Heidegger's Topology: Being, Place, World.* Cambridge, MA: MIT, 2007.

Marks, John. *Gilles Deleuze: Vitalism and Multiplicity.* London: Pluto, 1998.

May, Gerhard. *Creatio ex Nihilo: The Doctrine of "Creation out of Nothing" in Early Christian Thought.* Edinburgh: T. & T. Clark, 1994.

Mazis, Glen. *Emotion and Embodiment: Fragile Ontology.* New York: Peter Lang, 1993.

McDaniel, Jay. *Gandhi's Hope: Learning from Other Religions as a Path to Peace.* Maryknoll, NY: Orbis, 2005.

McGinn, Bernard. *The Mystical Thought of Meister Eckhart: The Man from Whom God Hid Nothing.* New York: Herder & Herder, 2003.

McTernan, Oliver. *Violence in God's Name: Religion in an Age of Conflict*. Maryknoll, NY: Orbis, 2003.

Merleau-Ponty, Maurice. *The Visible and the Invisible*. Edited by Claude Lefort. Translated by Alphonso Lingis. Evanston, IL: Northwestern University Press, 1968.

Mesle, Robert C. *Process Theology: A Basic Introduction*. St. Louis: Christian Board of Publication, 1993.

Moltmann, Jürgen. *God in Creation: A New Theology of Creation and the Spirit of God*. Minneapolis: Fortress, 1993.

———. *Trinität und Reich Gottes*. Munich: Christian Kaiser, 1980.

Momen, Moojan. *The Phenomenon of Religion: A Thematic Approach*. Oxford: Oneworld, 1999.

Morgan, John H. *In the Absence of God: Religious Humanism as Spiritual Journey with Special Reference to Julian Huxley*. South Bend, IN: Cloverdale, 2006.

Morrow Lindbergh, Anne. *War Within and Without*. New York: Harcourt Brace Jovanovich, 1980.

Naddaff, Ramona. *Exiling the Poets: The Production of Censorship in Plato's Republic*. Berkeley, CA: Zone, 2003.

Neville, Robert. *God and Creativity: A Challenge to Process Theology*. Albany: SUNY Press, 1995.

———. "On Comparing Religious Ideas." In *Ultimate Realities: A Volume in the Comparative Religious Ideas Project*, edited by Robert Neville, 187–211. Albany: SUNY Press, 2001.

Nobo, Jorge Luis. *Whitehead's Metaphysics of Extension and Solidarity*. Albany: SUNY Press, 1986.

Notomi, Noburu. *The Unity of Plato's Sophist: Between the Sophist and the Philosopher*. Cambridge: Cambridge University Press, 2001.

Odin, Steve. "A Metaphysics of Cumulative Penetration: Process Theory and Hua-yen Buddhism." *Process Studies* 11/2 (1982) 65–82.

———. *Process Metaphysics and Hua-Yen Buddhism: A Critical Study of Cumulative Penetration vs. Interpenetration*. Albany: SUNY Press, 1982.

Otto, Rudolf. *The Idea of the Holy*. Oxford: Oxford University Press, 1958.

Pailin, David. "God as Creator in a Whiteheadian Understanding." In *Whitehead und der Prozessbegriff. Beiträge zur Philosophie Alfred North Whitehead's auf dem Ersten Internationalen Whitehead-Symposion 1981*, edited by H. Holz and E. Wolf-Gazo, 273–99. Freiburg: Suhrkamp, 1984.

Panikkar, Raimond. *The Intrareligious Dialogue*. New York: Paulist, 1999.

———. "What Is Comparative Philosophy Comparing?" In *Interpreting Across Boundaries: New Essays in Comparative Philosophy*, edited by Gerald Larson and Eliot Deutsch, 116–36. Princeton: Princeton University Press, 1988.

Pannenberg, Wolfhart. "Atom, Dauer, Gestalt. Schwierigkeiten mit der Prozeßphilosophie." In *Whiteheads Metaphysik der Kreativitat. Internationales Whitehead-Symposium Bad Homburg 1983*, edited by Friedrich Rapp and Reiner Wiehl, 185–96. Freiburge: Karl Alber, 1986.

———. *Systematic Theology*. Vol. 1. Grand Rapids: Eerdmans, 1988.

———. *Systematische Theologie*. Vol. 1. Göttingen: Vandenhoeck & Ruprecht, 1988.

Pawson, David. *The Road to Hell: Everlasting Torment or Annihilation?* London: Hodder & Stoughton, 1996.

Philips, D. Z. *The Problem of Evil and the Problem of God*. Minneapolis: Fortress, 2005.

Phillipson, Sten. *A Metaphysics for Theology: A Study of Some Problems in the Later Philosophy of Alfred North Whitehead and Its Application to Issues in Contemporary Theology*. Atlantic Highlands, NJ: Humanities, 1982.

Phipps, Ron. "The Background and Historical Significance of Alfred North Whitehead's Letter to His Personal Assistant Henry S. Leonard: The Relation between Science and Philosophy." *Process Studies Supplement* 17 (2011) 1–83.

Pickstock, Catherine. *After Writing: On the Liturgical Consummation of Philosophy*. Oxford: Blackwell, 2000.

Plantinga, Alvin, ed. *The Ontological Argument: From St. Anselm to Contemporary Philosophers*. New York: Doubleday Anchor, 1965.

Price, Lucien. *Dialogues of Alfred North Whitehead*. Jaffrey, NH: Godine, 1954.

Quint, Josef. *Meister Eckhart: Deutsche Predigten und Traktate*. Munich: Goldmann, 1969.

Rahman, Fazlur. *Islam*. Chicago: Chicago University Press, 1966.

Rahner, Karl. *Foundations of Christian Faith: An Introduction to the Idea of Christianity*. New York: Crossroad, 2005.

———. *Grundkurs des Glaubens. Einführung in den Begriff des Christentums*. Freiburg: Herder, 1976.

———. "Trinitatstheologie." In *Herder Theologisches Taschenlexikon*, 7:352–60. Freiburg: Herder, 1972.

Rainer, Michael J., ed. *"Dominus Iesus." Anstößige Wahrheit oder anstößige Kirche? Dokumente, Hintergründe. Standpunkte und Folgerungen*. 2nd ed. Münster: LIT, 2001.

Ramsey, Ian T. *Religious Language: An Empirical Placing of Theological Phrases*. London: Macmillan, 1958.

Reikerstorfer, Johann. "Zur Ursprünglichkeit der Religion." In *Fides quaerens intellectum. Beiträge Zur Fundamentaltheologie*, edited by M. Kessler, W. Pannenberg and H. J. Pottmeyer, 3–16. Tübingen: Francke, 1992.

Rescher, Nicholas. *Pluralism: Against the Demand for Consensus*. Oxford: Oxford University Press, 1995.

Rivera, Mayra. *The Touch of Transcendence: A Postcolonial Theology of God*. Louisville: Westminster John Knox, 2007.

Robinson, Keith, ed. *Deleuze, Whitehead, Bergson: Rhizomatic Connections*. New York: Palgrave Macmillan, 2009.

Rockmore, Tom. *Heidegger and French Philosophy: Humanism, Antihumanism and Being*. New York: Routledge, 1995.

Rohmer, Stascha. *Whiteheads Synthese von Kreativität und Rationalittät. Reflexion und Transformation in Alfred North Whiteheads Philosophie der Natur*. Freiburg: Alber, 2000.

Rorty, Richard. "Dewey Between Hegel and Darwin." In *Rorty and Pragmatism: The Philosopher Responds to His Critics*, edited by H. J. Saatkamp, 1–15. Nashville: Vanderbilt University Press, 1995.

Rose, Philip. *On Whitehead*. Belmont, CA: Wadsworth/Thomson Learning, 2002.

Ruether, Rosemary Radford. *Sexism and God-Talk: Toward a Feminist Theology*. Boston: Beacon, 1983.

Russell, Robert John. *Cosmology: From Alpha to Omega: Theology and the Sciences*. Minneapolis: Fortress, 2008.

Rust, Alois. *Die organismische Kosmologie von Alfred N. Whitehead: Zur Revision des Selbstverständnisses neuzeitlicher Philosophie und Wissenschaft durch eine neue Philosophie der Natur.* Frankfurt: Athenäum, 1987.

Sainsbury, R. M. *Paradoxes.* 2nd ed. Cambridge: Cambridge University Press, 1995.

Sayer, Rowanne. *Wert und Wirklichkeit: Zum Verständnis des Metaphysischen Wertbegriffes im Spätdenken Alfred North Whiteheads und dessen Bedeutung für den Menschen in seiner kulturellen Kreativität.* Würzburg: Ergon, 1999.

Sayre, Kenneth M. *Plato's Late Ontology: A Riddle Resolved.* Princeton: Princeton University Press, 1983.

Scheffczyk, Leo. "Prozesstheismus und christlicher Glaube." *Münchner Theologische Zeitschrift* 35 (1984) 81–104.

Schmaus, Michael "Appropriationen." In *Lexikon für Theologie und Kirche,* 1:773–75. Frankfurt: Herder, 1957.

Schmidt-Leukel, Perry. "Das Pluralistische Modell in der Theologie der Religionen. Ein Literaturbericht." *Theologische Revue* 89 (1993) 353–64.

———. "Das Problem divergierender Wahrheitsansprüche im Rahmen einer pluralistischen Religionstheologie. Voraussetzungen zu seiner Lösung." In *Pluralistische Theologie der Religionen: Eine kritische Sichtung,* edited by Hans-Gerd Schwand, 39–58. Frankfurt: Lembeck, 1998.

Schneider, Laurel. *Beyond Monotheism: A Theology of Multiplicity.* New York: Routledge, 2008.

Scholem, Gershom. *Die jüdische Mystik in ihren Hauptströmungen.* Frankfurt: Suhrkamp, 1980.

Scholes, Robert. *Polydoxy of Modernism.* New Haven: Yale University Press, 2006.

Schulte, Raphael. "Die Vorbereitung der Trinitätsoffenbarung." In *Mysterium Salutis. Grundriss heilsgeschichtlicher Dogmatik,* edited by Johannes Feiner and Magnus Löhrer, 2:49–84. 3rd ed. Einsiedeln: Benziger, 1970.

Shaviro, Steven. "The Actual Volcano: Whitehead, Harman and the Problem of Relations." In *The Speculative Turn: Continental Materialism and Realism,* edited by Levi Bryant, Nick Srniceck, and Graham Harman, 279–90. Melbourne: Re-press, 2011.

———. *Without Criteria: Kant Whitehead, Deleuze, and Aesthetics.* Cambridge: MIT, 2009.

Sosnoski, James J., et al. "Deconstruction in America: An Interview with Jacques Derrida." *Critical Exchange* 17 (1985) 30–31.

Staeheli, Lynn, ed. *Mapping Women, Making Politics: Feminism and Political Geography.* New York: Routledge, 2004.

Stagoll, C. "Becoming." In *The Deleuze Dictionary,* edited by Adrian Parr. Edinburgh: Edinburgh University Press, 2005.

Stambaugh, Joan. *The Formless Self.* Albany: SUNY Press, 1999.

Stengers, Isabelle. "Beyond Conversation: The Risks of Peace." In *Process and Difference: Between Cosmological and Poststructuralist Postmodernism,* edited by C. Keller and A. Daniels, 235–55. New York: SUNY Press, 2002.

———. *Thinking with Whitehead.* Cambridge, MA: Harvard University Press, 2011.

Strindberg, August. *A Dream Play.* Austin, TX: Bard, 1901.

Suchocki, Marjorie. "The Anatman and the Consequent Nature." Center for Process Studies, Papers of the Buddhism Conference of the CPS. Claremont: CPS-files, 1978.

———. *The End of Evil: Process Eschatology in Historical Context*. Albany: SUNY Press, 1988.

———. *The Fall to Violence: Original Sin in Relational Theology*. New York: Continuum, 1995.

———. *God, Christ, Church: A Practical Guide to Process Theology*. New York: Crossroad, 1995.

———. "The Metaphysical Ground of the Whiteheadian God." *Process Studies* 5 (1975) 237–46.

Teasdale, Wayne. *The Mystic Heart: Discovering a Universal Spirituality in the World's Religions*. Novato, CA: New World Library, 2001.

Teilhard de Chardin, Pierre. *Christianity and Evolution: Reflections on Science and Religion*. San Diego: Harvest, 1969.

———. *Letters from My Friend, Teilhard De Chardin, 1948–1955: Including Letters Written during His Final Years in America*. Mahwah, NJ: Paulist, 1980.

———. *Lettres Intimes à Auguste Valensin*. Paris: Aubier Montaigne, 1993.

———. "Mein Universum." In *Christus und Wissenchaft*, 64–122. Olten: Walter, 1970.

———. *Science and Christ*. New York: Harper & Row, 1968.

Wainwright, Geoffrey. *Doxology: The Praise of God in Worship, Doctrine and Life: A Systematic Theology*. New York: Oxford University Press, 1980.

Ward, Keith. *Religion and Revelation*. Oxford: Clarendon, 1994.

Ware, Bruce A. *God's Lesser Glory: The Diminished God of Open Theism*. Wheaton, IL: Crossway, 2000.

Weber, Michel. *Whitehead's Pancreativism: The Basics*. Frankfurt: Ontos, 2006.

Welker, Michael. "A. N. Whitehead: Relativistische Kosmologie." In *Grundprobleme der großen Philosophen. Philosophie der Gegenwart I*, edited by J. Speck, 287–91. Göttingen: Vandenhoeck & Ruprecht, 1995.

———. "Whitehead's Vergottung der Welt." In *Whitehead and the Idea of Process: Proceedings of The First International Whitehead-Symposium*, edited by H. Holz and E. Wolf-Gazo. Freiburg: Karl Alber, 1984.

Welsch, Wolfgang. *Vernunft: Die zeitgenössische Vernunftkritik und das Konzept der transversalen Vernunft*. Suhrkamp taschenbuch wissenschaft 1238. Frankfurt: Suhrkamp. 1996.

Werbick, J. "Heil durch Christus allein? Die Pluralistische Theologie und ihr Plädoyer für einen Pluralismus der Heilswege." In *Der Einzige Weg zum Heil?: Die Herausforderung des christlichen Absolutheitsanspruchs durch pluralistische Religionstheologien*, edited by M. v. Brück and J. Werbick, 11–61. Questiones disputatae 143. Freiburg: Herder, 1993.

Whitehead, Alfred North. *Adventures of Ideas*. New York: Free Press, 1967.

———. "Autobiographical Notes." In *The Philosophy of Alfred North Whitehead*, edited by P. A. Schilpp, 3:3–14. 2nd ed. Library of Living Philosophers. La Salle, IL.: Open Court, 1951.

———. *The Concept of Nature*. Cambridge: Cambridge University Press, 1993.

———. *An Enquiry Concerning the Principles of Natural Knowledge*. New York: Dover, 1982.

———. "Immortality." In *The Philosophy of Alfred North Whitehead*, edited by P. A. Schilpp, 3:682–700. 2nd ed. Library of Living Philosophers. La Salle, IL: Open Court, 1951.

———. "Mathematics and the Good." In *Essays in Science and Philosophy*, 97–113. New York: Greenwood, 1968.

———. *Modes of Thought*. New York: Free Press, 1968.

———. *Process and Reality*. Corrected ed. Edited by Donald S. Sherburne and D. R. Griffin. New York: Free Press, 1978.

———. "Process and Reality." In *Science and Philosophy*. Paterson, NJ: Littlefield, Adams, 1964.

———. *Prozeß und Realität*. Translated by Hans Günter Holl. Frankfurt: Suhrkamp, 1987.

———. *Religion in the Making*. New York: Fordham University Press, 1996.

———. *Science and Philosophy*. Paterson, NJ: Littlefield, Adams, 1964.

———. *Science and the Modern World*. New York: Free Press, 1967.

———. *Symbolism: Its Meaning and Effect*. New York: Fordham University Press, 1985.

Wiehl, Reiner. "Aktualität und Extensivität in Whiteheads Kosmo-Psychologie." In *Materialien zu Whiteheads 'Prozess und Realität,' Die Gifford-Lectures*, edited by Michael Hampe and Helmut Maassen, 313–68. Frankfurt: Suhrkamp, 1990.

———. "Whitehead's Kosmologie der Gefühle zwischen Ontologie und Anthropologie." In *Whiteheads Metaphysik der Kreativität. Internationales Whitehead-Symposium Bad Homburg 1983*, edited by Friedrich Rapp and Reiner Wiehl, 141–68. Freiburg: K. Alber, 1986.

Wieman, Henry Nelson. *The Wrestle of Religion with Truth*. New York: Macmillan, 1927.

Williams, James. "Deleuze and Whitehead: The Concept of Reciprocal Determination." In *Deleuze, Whitehead and the Transformations of Metaphysics*, edited by André Cloots and Keith A. Robinson, 89–106. Brussels: Koninklijke Vlaamse Academie van België voor Wetenschappen en Kunsten, 2005.

———. *Encounters and Influences: The Transversal Thought of Gilles Deleuze*. Manchester: Clinamen, 2005.

Wilmot, Laurence. *Whitehead and God: Prolegomena to a Theological Reconstruction*. Waterloo, ON: Wilfrid Laurier University Press, 1978.

Wolfinger, F. "Postmoderner Pluralismus und die Pluralität der Theologie." In *Wege der Theologie: An der Schwelle zum dritten Jahrtausend*, edited by Günter Riße, Heino Sonnemans, and Burkhard Theß, 87–96. Paderborn: Bonifatius, 1996.

Yannaras, Christos. *On the Absence and Unknowability of God: Heidegger and the Areopagite*. New York: T. & T. Clark, 2007.

Young, Julian. *Heidegger's Later Philosophy*. Cambridge: Cambridge University Press, 2001.

Index